Here's Looking at You

David A. Schultz, *General Editor*

Vol. 3

PETER LANG
New York • Washington, D.C./Baltimore • Boston • Bern
Frankfurt am Main • Berlin • Brussels • Vienna • Canterbury

Here's Looking at You

Hollywood, Film, and Politics

PETER LANG
New York • Washington, D.C./Baltimore • Boston • Bern
Frankfurt am Main • Berlin • Brussels • Vienna • Canterbury

Library of Congress Cataloging-in-Publication Data

Giglio, Ernest.
Here's looking at you: Hollywood, film, and politics / Ernest Giglio.
p. cm. — (Politics, media, and popular culture; vol. 3)
Includes bibliographical references and index.
1. Motion pictures—Political aspects. 2. Politics
in motion pictures. I. Title. II. Series.
PN1995.9.P6G56 791.43'658—dc21 98-45271
ISBN 0-8204-4421-9
ISSN 1094-6225

Die Deutsche Bibliothek-CIP-Einheitsaufnahme

Giglio, Ernest:
Here's looking at you: Hollywood, film, and politics / Ernest Giglio.
–New York; Washington, D.C./Baltimore; Boston; Bern;
Frankfurt am Main; Berlin; Brussels; Vienna; Canterbury: Lang.
(Politics, media, and popular culture; Vol. 3)
ISBN 0-8204-4421-9

Cover design by Lisa Dillon

The paper in this book meets the guidelines for permanence and durability
of the Committee on Production Guidelines for Book Longevity
of the Council of Library Resources.

Printed in the United States of America

To my wife Karin, and to
Christopher, David, and Elisabeth,
who had to endure many bad movies in
order to catch the occasional gem

Contents

Illustrations

Preface

This book began a long time ago in the fertile imagination of a small boy whose childhood was entwined with the movies. In the early stages of childhood the boy and his sister would be taken by their mother after school each Friday afternoon to the local movie theater while their father worked the night shift at the Brooklyn Navy Yard. The world of work and the travails of war were remote events to youngsters compared to the fun and games in the schoolyard.

The trip to the movies became a weekly ritual—a double feature at the theater followed by a stop at Fisher's Jewish bakery on the way home to pick up danish pastries and a loaf of rye. Of course, I must confess that often I failed to understand much of what I saw on the big screen, but I still found it fascinating, often funny, occasionally sad, and sometimes boring. The westerns were exciting, and I laughed heartily at the cartoons and the slapstick comedies. Sometimes my mother had to nudge me when I dozed off during the love scenes. But at my age, what did I know of such things!

When I reached twelve I was permitted to go to the movies with my friends. Now the weekly picture show involved Saturdays rather than Friday afternoons. I have no sense of what Saturday matinees were like elsewhere, but a kid in New York City during World War II could spend six hours in a dark movie theater and never see the same film twice. I remember the routine well: all the boys (girls were not part of the gang) would pack a lunch, hide it inside our knickers, enter the theater around 9:00 in the morning, and emerge sometime after 3:00 in the afternoon with eyes that had to adjust to the light. Once several of us were caught with our lunch and had to eat it standing up in the theater lobby shortly after having had breakfast. But that was a small price to pay for more than six hours of entertainment.

During those hours in the theater we would get to see a double feature (the first film was usually a major Hollywood production and the second, a shorter feature known as the B-film), the weekly serial and newsreel, cartoons, several short subjects, and even play one or two give-away contests. Going to the movies was a social experience in those days. I even saw Babe Ruth once when the local theater was showing

Pride of the Yankees. But mostly those Saturday matinees featured war movies in which actors like John Wayne, Humphrey Bogart, and Errol Flynn single-handedly took on the Nazis and the Japanese. For a youngster, they were larger-than-life heroes; reel characters who invaded our dreams and assured us that we would be victorious against the forces of fascism. For a change of pace, the theater would show an animated film from Walt Disney, a Lassie adventure story, a musical, or a Bing Crosby/Bob Hope road movie as those at home waited out the war.

But as a typical teenager, going to the movies was a way to escape from homework for a few hours or a diversion from a game of stickball in the schoolyard. Movies were not to be taken seriously, an attitude, I later learned, that I shared with the Justices on the United States Supreme Court, who considered movies to be purely entertainment, much like us kids. It was not until the 1950s that the Court would reverse itself and bring movies under the protection of the First Amendment to the United States Constitution.

Similarly, I did not come to appreciate film as an art form or as a politicizing agent until, as an undergraduate student at Queens College (CUNY), I religiously took the subway into Manhattan every Wednesday afternoon to attend the newly opened Museum of Modern Art's film series. Now the weekly ritual took on substance as I became familiar with the great directors of the silent screen—D. W. Griffith, Fritz Lang, Erich von Stroheim—and with the films of Charlie Chaplin, Lillian Gish, John Barrymore, John Gilbert, and Rudolph Valentino. These weekly visits provided an opportunity to see some of the truly great film classics of the silent cinema, such as *Birth of a Nation, Intolerance,* and *Modern Times*, and to develop an interest in film as an expression of the political culture. Going to the movies was no longer a social diversion; it became serious business.

I was so smitten by the movies that as a graduate student at Syracuse University in the 1960s, I found it possible to combine my interest in constitutional law with my love affair with the movies. After completion of the academic coursework, I had to decide on a topic for my doctoral dissertation. Hence, my interest in law and my fascination with film provided a perfect opportunity for a marriage of convenience. Doing the dissertation proved to be more exciting than any film script. Imagine the excitement when your research discovers that in the second half of the twentieth-century, movies were subject to censorship by state agencies and local censor boards in addition to the internal rules and regulations of the industry's Production Code Administration. The history of film censorship also proved to be indicative of the revolution in social mores that had occurred during the century. For example, the earliest known instance of film censorship occurred in 1896 on the boardwalk in Atlantic City where the peep show, *Dolorita's Passion Dance*, was apparently too risque for the local police, who proceeded to shut it down. If Dolorita's shaking and shimmering was too provocative for a Victorian public that covered itself in head-to-toe swimwear, it would strike contemporary audiences, comprised of individuals whose swimwear is just enough to cover the essential "private parts," to be downright silly. With virtually two-thirds of contemporary Hollywood films R-rated, it is a rare film indeed where the major characters keep their clothes on. At the beginning of the twenty-first century, motion pictures serve to document the changes that have occurred in social mores, gender and racial attitudes, and sexual values and practices.

As a college professor, the young boy who watched the movies grow up with him now had an opportunity to fuse his love for movies with his professional interests in an undergraduate course on *The Political Film*. To provide material for the course, I put together a custom made in-house reader, which subsequently provided the impetus for this book. It has proven to be a long, but rewarding journey.

Acknowledgments

This book has been a labor of love, but even efforts of affection are enriched by external stimulation and assistance. Without a doubt, this project has benefited greatly from numerous contributors, many of whom remain unaware of the extent of their support and encouragement. However, there are colleagues, libraries, and organizations that have provided the kind of valuable assistance that demands recognition.

I am particularly indebted to Lycoming College for providing part of the research funding for this project and for allowing me to take a sabbatical leave at an opportune time in order to complete the manuscript. I also want to thank the librarians and staff at the University of Wisconsin Film & Television Archives, the Wisconsin State Historical Society, the British Film Institute in London, and especially the reference librarians at Lycoming College—Janet Hurlbert, Tasha Cooper, Margaret Murray, and Lisette Ormsbee—who provided the kind of services that researchers desperately require at a moment's notice. Additional support came from several colleagues: Alan and Meryl Aldridge at the University of Nottingham (UK) offered valuable suggestions during the early stages of the manuscript, Professor Christa Slaton of Auburn University made several helpful suggestions regarding the first two chapters, and Professor John Williams of Principia College read a good deal of the first draft and tested the manuscript in his political film course. His students' comments were immensely valuable during the subsequent rewrite. Also of importance was the information collected during the documentary film program at the 1998 Robert Flaherty Film Seminar, particularly in writing chapter three. I would be remiss if I failed to mention the importance of the feedback received from the students in my Political Film course as well as the comments obtained from several Elderhostel groups. A number of student assistants helped with the library research, but Emily Hautala and Stephanie Wilkie deserve mention for putting the filmography together. Special recognition has to be given to Elisabeth Giglio whose editorial skills and insightful comments improved the quality of the writing and provided the text with structure and clarity. Without her invaluable suggestions, this book might have remained on computer disk rather than the printed page. Finally, Heidi Burns, senior editor at Peter Lang, read through the entire first draft with a keen eye for detail and a razor-sharp pencil to detect the mistakes. Hollywood, of course, has been a silent collaborator, providing the films that serve as the primary textual material. While many film studios were helpful, a few were uncooperative, refusing permission to use photo stills from their films.

Naturally I accept responsibility for any errors or omissions in the manuscript. As is usually the case in writing a book, the buck always stops at the author's desk.

Williamsport, Pa.
April 1999

One

Hollywood and Washington: The Marriage of Film and Politics

"If you want to send a message, use Western Union!"
—Producer Samuel Goldwyn

Imagine the following scene taking place in a Hollywood studio where two writers are brainstorming a script involving the American president:

First Screenwriter: "Let's see. We'll start with a popular president who is also a notorious womanizer. One day he gets caught, sort of with his pants down and the media have a field day publicizing the discovery. Unfortunately for the president, the timing is lousy since election day is imminent. Not to worry, though. The White House staff recruits a noted spin doctor to do damage control."

Second Screenwriter: "Mm, continue."

First Screenwriter: "After these initial scenes, the film shifts to salvaging the president's political career. The consultant decides to wage a phony war to divert attention away from the president's indiscretions. He hires an egotistical Hollywood producer to stage this fake war against Albania in a TV studio. The TV war achieves the desired effect of rallying the country round the flag. The scheme works and the president is reelected. How does that sound to you? I don't believe this storyline has been done before. Do you?"

Second Screenwriter: "Pretty far-fetched plot. Who's going to believe it? Besides, will it sell?"

First Screenwriter: "Well, the plot has everything for a successful film—sex, political intrigue, war, a happy ending, and it even takes a swipe at television."

Second Screenwriter: "I have a better idea. We change the central character from an incumbent president to a married wannabe Southern governor, 'a good old boy-type' who has a weakness for donuts and a fondness for women. Despite his paunch and his womanizing, the governor plunges into the presidential race. He puts together a loyal and competent campaign staff to gain the Democratic Party nomination. But to discredit his rival and force him out of the race, the governor confronts his opponent with harmful personal information compiled by his staff, justifying his action as being in the public interest because the governor's social and economic policies will be better for the country. How does that grab you?"

First Screenwriter: "It has possibilities. Let's see, we retain the sex but we add some serious moral and political decisions faced by politicians seeking public office. So, the film appeals to the intellect as well as the libido. I like it. Let's sketch out the scenario and take it to the studio."

How likely is it that the above scene unfolded as described? Farfetched? Maybe. But the idea of an American president besieged by charges of improper sexual behavior appears in two recent Hollywood films, *Wag the Dog* (1997) and *Primary Colors* (1998). Both movies were in release during the time when President Clinton faced charges of sexual misbehavior with Paula Jones and Monica Lewinsky. The reel president in *Wag the Dog* wages a phony war against Albania as a diversion while President Clinton initiated a campaign of saber-rattling against Saddam Hussein which moved the Jones and Lewinsky accusations temporarily off the front page. Four days after Clinton admitted to the American people that he had an "inappropriate relationship" with Lewinsky, he ordered cruise missile strikes against terrorist camps in Sudan and Afghanistan.

And then several months later, during the congressional impeachment hearings, the president ordered more air strikes against Iraq. Coincidence? Fortuitous timing? Or another effort by the president's spin doctors to divert attention away from the impeachment hearings at home? Meanwhile, John Travolta's portrayal of the Southern governor in *Primary Colors*, who is mounting a campaign for the presidency, is an undisguised imitation of the real Bill Clinton, right down to the Krispy Kreme donuts. Accidental? Hardly. The film was a fictionalized account of Clinton's 1992 presidential campaign by political writer Joe Klein.

These two films provide contemporary evidence that seriously questions the accuracy of Goldwyn's quotation. Hollywood is in the entertainment business all right, but the industry also delivers political messages in selected films. For example, the cynical message of *Wag the Dog* seems to be that the American people are easily manipulated by political spin doctors and readily fooled by second-rate media talent. The film wants the audience to believe that the American public is so gullible that its decisions rest on emotion rather than reasoning; a concept usually associated with fascism rather than democratic government. Moreover, the wicked satire in *Wag the Dog* distorts the line between truth and virtual reality when it enables an egotistical Hollywood director to successfully create a studio war to save the president's political career, an act that ultimately costs the filmmaker his life.

Primary Colors, meanwhile, plays like an apology for sleazy and ruthless politicians, asking audiences to accept human imperfections as a trade-off for popular public policies. In essence, the movie asks audiences to forgive the flaws of the Clintonesque character because, if elected, he will make a good president. These may not be the kind of civics lessons American parents want their children to learn, but *Wag the Dog* and *Primary Colors* serve to remind us that Goldwyn's remark reflected neither the Hollywood of the past nor the Hollywood of the present. Instead his statement serves to perpetuate the myth that all Hollywood provides is entertainment without acknowledgment that it is a powerful and influential industry. Of course Hollywood is a business operated for profit. It is undisputed that the vast majority of Hollywood films are designed to capture audiences through appeal to our senses rather than our intellect. Yet recognition of the profit motive in Hollywood does not alter the history of the American film industry, which includes the deliverance of political messages, some intentional, others inadvertent, since the beginning of the century.

As early as D. W. Griffith's *Birth of a Nation* (1915), a biased presentation of slavery, Reconstruction policies, and the Ku Klux Klan, selected filmmakers have viewed the medium as an instrument to communicate stories that express their personal opinions and beliefs about love, life, and politics. Had the film industry produced commercial entertainment exclusively, the history of Hollywood (and America too) would have to be rewritten. Given that task, revisionists writing today would have no choice but to ignore the historical record, excluding from their accounts all of the following: efforts by governments to censor and regulate motion pictures; the film industry's anti-union hostility, which erupted occasionally into violent conflict between workers and the studios; the government's utilization of the film industry for propaganda purposes during both World Wars; and the sanctioned compliance by the film industry with the questionable aims and methods of the House UnAmerican Activities Committee (HUAC) and their imposition of the dreaded blacklist. This revisionist task would challenge even the best efforts of Orwell's Big Brother.

The Relationship Between Film and Politics

Despite Hollywood's protestations and disavowals, the film-politics association is traceable through an examination of their relationship in two distinct, but related contexts. The most obvious setting occurs on the movie screen where Hollywood releases some 400 films annually. While the vast majority are purely commercial ventures, there exists a small minority of films, five to ten percent, that present explicit, and often latent, political messages.

The other context is set in the arena of practical politics, which requires that its practitioners raise substantial sums of money. Candidates for public office seek financial support for their increasingly expensive political campaigns. Without financial resources, a campaign will be stillborn. Only those candidates with money or with the ability to attract sufficient funding have an opportunity to compete for political power. This is where the Hollywood-Washington connection plays an important role; first in providing the funding for outsiders to run and second, in encouraging those within the entertainment industry to seek public office. There is nothing intrinsically evil about Hollywood fulfilling these functions because it is not a crime for film personalities to run for elective office. Nor is it illegal for Hollywood to protect its economic self-interest by recruiting its leadership elite from the White House staff. Neither is there a law against Hollywood soliciting political assistance from its Washington friends. But what is truly alarming, however, is that Hollywood money gains the industry an unequal amount of access and an inordinate amount of influence while it blurs the line between public office and celebrity status. The development and acceptance of a "culture of celebrity" has led one critic to observe that popular entertainment has replaced ideology in American politics, that political candidates emulate movie stars, that primary campaigns resemble casting calls, that political campaigns are closer to auditions than to the articulation of substantive policy agendas, and finally, that the electorate today behaves as if it were a film audience passively surveying the political performance.[1]

The Hollywood-Washington Connection

The relationship between film and politics dates back at least to the pre-World War I period when Hollywood was dominated by movie moguls like Sam Goldwyn, Louis Mayer, and Jack and Harry Warner;

studio executives who produced films while mixing in national politics. Even in the early days of the film industry it was evident that the men who invented Hollywood were gamblers willing to take a chance on a high-risk business. But when the country needed their services in 1917 and 1941, they responded as patriots and community leaders.[2]

The Hollywood-Washington connection is best understood in terms of access and influence.[3] Access gains entrance to the power brokers and political wheeler-dealers. Financial contributions and fund-raising events can surpass mere access to political figures; these activities bestow on celebrities the status of (unofficial) political advisor. Warren Beatty, for instance, exerted considerable influence over Senator Gary Hart. Louis B. Mayer of Metro-Goldwyn-Mayer (MGM) cultivated a close friendship with Herbert Hoover, first when Hoover served as secretary of commerce and later, as president. To gain support for Hoover's run for the presidency in 1928, Mayer intervened to persuade newspaper magnate William Randolph Hearst to lay aside his personal aspiration for the White House to back Hoover's candidacy. This was the first of numerous personal Hollywood-Washington associations that developed into political support. Conversely, when the studio moguls felt threatened by a political candidate, such as Upton Sinclair's 1934 gubernatorial bid, they joined to defeat his aspiration to become governor of California. Intervention by the film moguls essentially sought to protect economic interests, but these men also craved national respect equal to that accorded public officials at the time. Power and influence were their goal, money the means to achieve it.

World War I presented the industry with an opportunity to enlarge its relationship and enhance its favor with the government. When America finally entered the war in 1917 the government asked the film industry to volunteer its most important stars to aid in the war effort. The studios responded by sending Douglas Fairbanks, Charlie Chaplin, and America's sweetheart, Mary Pickford, on tour to sell Liberty war bonds. This scene was repeated during the Second World War when Washington again called on Hollywood to aid the war effort and the industry responded anew. In one 1942 bond drive, for instance, 337 stars participated in selling a staggering $850 million in war bonds. Singer Kate Smith reportedly sold $39 million in war bonds during a single radio marathon. Later in the war, news of the Nazi atrocities against the Jews led the studio heads to make financial contributions to support the creation of a Jewish Palestine.[4]

Exploiting the reputation and popularity of film stars, whether by government or special interest groups, forged national political alliances and led to more intimate and extensive intervention by the film industry into domestic and international politics. Hollywood kept its eye on state policies that impacted the industry, but its primary attention focused on Washington as the acceptance of its films extended worldwide. The popularity of Hollywood films abroad, shown in venues as diverse as makeshift theaters inside Chinese factories to glamorous movie palaces installed with stereophonic sound, reinforced the industry's concern with its global image. Back in the thirties the studios worried about the response to its films in countries like Nazi Germany and Fascist Italy. Today, it frets over China's response to two 1997 films on the life of the Dalai Lama, *Seven Years in Tibet* and *Kundun*. Due to its sympathetic portrayal of the Dalai Lama and the Tibetan people, neither film has been shown in China. Moreover, the Chinese government denied permission for location shooting and threatened economic reprisals against the studios that produced the films. The Disney Company, which made *Kundun*, became so alarmed at the damage the film might do to its other financial investments in China (Disney stores and merchandise) that it hired Henry Kissinger, former secretary of state in the Nixon Administration, to run interference for them.

Occasionally the impetus for political intervention emanates from the American side. In 1997 news reports that President Clinton had asked MGM to delay the release of its movie, *Red Corner* (1997) starring Richard Gere, until after the official visit of Chinese President Jiang Zemen. Instead this film about an American lawyer falsely accused of murder, originally scheduled to open in November, was moved up to coincide with Jiang's October visit. It is unclear whether the change in the theatrical release date was politically motivated, given Richard Gere's support for the Dalai Lama, or a marketing ploy by MGM to capitalize on the additional publicity surrounding Jiang's visit. In either event, this incident supports the financial importance of global interests to the film industry. Just fifty years ago, the film studios worried how their pictures would "play in Peoria"; today the industry's concern is how their films will be received in Beijing.

Domestically, Hollywood has been actively involved in political campaigns since the days of the studio moguls. What is different today is the magnitude of its involvement and its largess. Since the 1960s, political candidates have beaten a steady path to Hollywood; some seeking to raise funds to launch a campaign, others to add to the coffers of their political war chests. If Dorothy in *The Wizard of Oz* (1939) followed the "yellow-brick road" to reach her destination, American politicians continue to walk the well-traveled path to the riches of the film capital as Hollywood stars, producers, agents, and studio heads become major sources of campaign funding.

Is it profitable for a politician to have friends in Hollywood? Undoubtedly. Actor Warren Beatty, for example, reportedly raised one million dollars for the 1972 McGovern presidential campaign; while singer Barbra Streisand raised $1.5 million for the Democratic Party in 1986 by hosting a $5000 a plate dinner.[5] A decade later, Streisand exceeded even that amount by raising an estimated $3.5 million for the Democratic Party with a posh affair for President Clinton at her Beverly Hills estate. Ticket prices ranged from $2500 to $12,500, the latter sum entitled the donor to a preferred seat close to the president.[6] President Clinton's friendship with the married acting team of Kim Basinger and Alec Baldwin has helped him raise money for Democratic candidates. Hollywood stars like Tom Hanks even contributed money to the president's legal defense fund to settle the Paula Jones lawsuit. The entertainment industry raised more than $2 million for the defense fund.[7] In return, the president allows Hanks and his wife to stay at the White House and Basinger and Baldwin to share photo opportunities with him. Occasionally, the president can do a favor or two for the stars as when Clinton sent his national security adviser to explain the Administration's position on Scientology to an interest group headed by actor John Travolta.[8] These activities only serve to reinforce the culture of celebrity and to cloud the line between entertainment and politics.

During election campaigns Hollywood becomes a bustle of political activity, especially with fund-raising events. At such times it is not uncommon for a celebrity to be invited to a brunch, a late afternoon cocktail party, and an evening black-tie dinner—all in the same day—in order to raise money for political candidates. As it turns out, the people who comprise the film industry raise money for both major political parties. According to the public interest group, Common Cause, the film industry contributed almost $2 million dollars to the Democratic and Republican national committees during the 1993–94 congressional election campaigns.[9] This kind of money provides the type of access unavailable to ordinary citizens.

Fund-raising events also are utilized by politicians to determine the level of support for their potential campaigns. Such was the case in 1992 when Senator Bill Bradley sought to "test the waters" for a possible presidential run. When the senator raised only $600,000 at a $1000 a-plate dinner sponsored by a collection of Hollywood entertainment figures and local business executives,[10] he decided against waging a presidential campaign. Other film stars like Jodie Foster and Cybill Shepherd sponsor peace and women candidates, and the money raised is often crucial in determining which candidates run for political office.

Money is not the only form of political involvement by members of the film industry. Movie stars often campaign for their favorite candidates while other celebrities become actively involved in anti-nuclear, anti-pesticide, anti-war, and various pro-environment issues.[11] As individuals, movie stars are free to lobby for one cause or another, knowing that they are likely to draw media attention. Actor Richard Gere, for example, delivered a public plea to free Tibet during the Academy Award ceremonies. Sometimes, Hollywood's participation raises moral and ethical questions as when Frank Sinatra introduced President Kennedy to Judith Exner while she was the mistress to gangster Salvatore (Sam) Giancana. Sometime later, Kennedy asked Sinatra to dump blacklisted screenwriter Albert Maltz from the singer's film project on World War II deserter Eddie Slovak. Actor John Wayne secured government assistance that made it possible for him to make his pro-Vietnam war film, *The Green Berets*. But Warren Beatty's close friendship with Gary Hart cost the Senator politically as he fell under the spell of a Hollywood lifestyle that was at odds with public morals. As a consequence, Hart's promising political career came to a dramatic end.[12] Whether Senator Hart would have won the 1988 presidential race is conjecture, but at the time he was considered to be one of the brightest young candidates on the national political scene before he succumbed to the glamorous life of the Hollywood bachelor.

Although political activists and campaign contributors represent a minority of the Hollywood community, they have the capacity to overwhelm the political efforts of the average American. Unlike ordinary citizens, Hollywood stars have two special qualities attractive to politicians: money and celebrity status. Hollywood is not hesitant to exploit these advantages, even while it actively engages in the fantasy world of its own films.

Whereas in the past individuals usually entered political life through the practice of law, public service, or business, it is acceptable today for candidates in the entertainment field to test their popularity in the political arena. Californians Ronald Reagan (president) and George Murphy (U.S. senator) come naturally to mind while actor Alec Baldwin muses about the possibility of a political race. Even widows continue the political career of their dead husbands; the wife of deceased entertainer-turned congressman, Sonny Bono (of Sonny & Cher fame) was elected to her husband's congressional seat in her first venture into politics.

Additionally, Hollywood celebrities may come to realize that active participation in high-profile organizations present opportunities for national leadership. Heading a special interest group also may provide an occasion for a recognizable Hollywood figure to capitalize on his/her mythic screen persona as a springboard to elective office. The election of actor Charlton Heston, long associated on the national scene with conservative causes, to head the National Rifle Association (NRA) potentially offers him a platform from which to comment on other social and political issues. The Constitution assures Mr. Heston of that right. Even though lobbying the government is a protected activity under the First Amendment, its exercise can assume a conspiratorial hue as occurred after the Republicans captured the Congress in 1994. After the Republican victory, former House Speaker Newt Gingrich, freshman representative Sonny Bono, and Jack Valenti, president of the Motion Picture Association of America (MPAA), met in Washington to develop a plan to promote support for the film industry on Capitol Hill. Why would the film industry lobby Washington? The answer lies in its current global economic power, a far cry from its humble beginnings in penny arcades and urban nickelodeons. Hollywood films have become the second largest American export after military hardware and receipts from foreign distribution contribute more than half of a film's revenue.[13] Often, foreign receipts mean the difference between a profit or a loss.

It is an economic fact of life within the industry that a strong showing in foreign markets usually determines the fiscal fate of a film. Take the case of the Academy Award-winning film, *Titanic* (1997). While the film did not have to rely on foreign distribution to make a profit, its universal popularity enabled it to become a box office blockbuster. After being in release for six months, *Titanic* already had earned a hefty $585 million at home, with an additional two billion abroad.[14] Financial receipts of this magnitude explain why the film industry turned to Washington to recruit Jack Valenti, former aide to President Lyndon Johnson (LBJ), as its leader. It also helps to explain why the MPAA has offices in New York and Washington while its film production and auxiliary services operate out of Los Angeles. This arrangement allows Valenti to oversee the interests of the film industry close to the seat of government in the nation's capital. The universal appeal of Hollywood movies also reveals why Valenti's voice is heard in the halls of government. Like Coke and McDonald's, Hollywood is symbolic of the economic rewards under corporate capitalism. For better or worse, Hollywood movies have dominated the world market since the 1920s, overpowering the production capacity and the film budgets of other countries. By the middle of the nineties, American films accounted for 80 percent of the European box office. While American films glutted global markets, European films failed to receive worldwide distribution. The situation reached a crisis during the GATT negotiations when Hollywood lobbied the Clinton administration to include its films under the terms of the agreement so that the industry could trade freely throughout the world. On the other hand, the European Union (EU) demanded quotas be placed on American films to protect their respective film industries. The stalemate was broken by Clinton's intervention after the president consulted with Lew Wasserman, chairman of MCA-Universal, the mega-entertainment corporation.[15]

Film Content

The place where the film-politics association is most obviously displayed is in the movies themselves; stories and visual images that make audiences laugh or cry, feel anger or compassion, and occasionally, even deliver powerful messages. Hollywood seldom takes advantage of that prerogative, however, but knowing that the industry has this residual power should be cause enough for concern. Why does Hollywood avoid the dogmatic political film, the critical political biography, or the straight political drama? The reason is quite simple: political movies are box office poison.[16] To admit that 90 percent of Hollywood films are purely commercial ventures ignores the remaining ten percent that deliver messages that can be ideological, propagandistic, historically deceptive, and politically motivated.

Film as Ideology

For all their global popularity and financial prosperity, there remains a reluctance within the industry to acknowledge a symbiotic relationship between the world of film and the world of politics. The denial is periodically reinforced by the industry's leadership. Will Hays, former postmaster-general, recruited by the film industry to be its chief censor and production czar in the 1930s, echoed Goldwyn's sentiments when he said that "American motion pictures continue to be free from any but the highest possible entertainment purpose."[17] It is not surprising, therefore, that as a mainstream industry Hollywood steers clear of any ideology that challenges the existing order in films that promote or advocate alternative political systems. But that admission is a far cry from perpetuating the myth of political neutrality. According to Hays, Hollywood was in the business of providing entertainment—period. Although this opinion expresses the majority sentiment within the industry, notable exceptions can be found in the films of contemporary "auteurs": directors like Costas-Gavras, Oliver Stone, and Spike Lee who exercise a greater degree of total control over their productions than normally permitted under the old studio system. Actor-turned-director John Cassavetes's films of the sixties and seventies were highly original examinations of American society; they encompass personal statements the studios were reluctant to support. Cassavetes made his films anyway, using his own resources and borrowing from his friends. This kind of artistic freedom enables directors to select their subject matter and present events to suit their personal interpretations, whether that agenda includes government cover-up in Latin America (*Missing*), a challenge to the historical record on the assassination of President Kennedy (*JFK*), the depiction of contemporary race relations (*Do the Right Thing* and *Jungle Fever*), and early skirmishes in the gender *wars (A Woman under the Influence)*. What differentiates these directors from their peers is their control over the creative process, from initial script idea to final editing, stamping the film with their imprint in a way that cannot be duplicated by another filmmaker.

Traditional Hollywood, on the other hand, hedges its bets by producing films that promote a conservative political agenda (*Green Berets, Death Wish*, and the *Dirty Harry* series), as well as those that advance a liberal policy perspective or examine flaws in the existing system (*Modern Times*, *The Grapes of Wrath*, *The China Syndrome*, and *Norma Rae*). But while mainstream Hollywood avoids controversial subjects and ideological treatment, the few auteurs are willing to risk box office failure by exploiting the medium for political purposes. For instance, Oliver Stone's films (*Platoon*, *Salvador*, *JFK*, and *Nixon*) certainly put the neutrality-entertainment myth to the test. If Stone's films are pure fantasy creations, why did the Justice Department declassify the Kennedy assassination files after the release of *JFK* (1991)?[18] Mere coincidence or reaction by the government to defuse the controversy caused by the film? Also why did Stone's portrayal of Nixon raise such criticism and cries of inaccuracies from the former president's family and members of his administration[19] when the film was advertised and marketed as commercial entertainment and not as a political documentary? Why should Nixon supporters worry about the screen representation if *Nixon* is intended strictly for entertainment? Furthermore, in the Reagan-era of the 1980s, Stone took a risk in distributing *Salvador* (1985); a stinging indictment of American policy in Central America that was advertised to suggest that the film represented political reality in El Salvador, a marketing strategy also utilized by Stone to maximum effect with JFK. Filmmakers like Stone, however, are the exception, not the rule in Hollywood.

Contemporary auteurs have no monopoly on sending messages to American audiences. Charlie Chaplin's *The Great Dictator* (1940), for instance, was a devastating satire on Hitler and Mussolini that also served as a warning to the world of the dangers of fascism. Because Chaplin's film was released at a time when the United States officially declared a neutral policy towards the European war, its ideological stance against fascism was financially risky and politically controversial. More recently, Kevin Costner presented a revisionist view of Native Americans in his *Dances with Wolves* (1990) while Oliver Stone's *JFK* promoted his version of the conspiracy behind the Kennedy assassination. Stone's *Nixon* provided the director with an opportunity to portray the former president in psychological terms as a tormented individual. These films qualify as ideological because they represent deliberate, conscious attempts to create a piece of work with a definite political perspective, narrated within a particular historical setting, and featuring characters who are readily recognizable or representational.[20]

Film as Propaganda

In 1936, the German-Jewish literary critic Walter Benjamin wrote that the film medium had emerged as a significant propaganda tool because of its ability to lend support to, and provide a rationale for, mass movements.[21] Benjamin, naturally, had Nazi Germany and Fascist Italy in mind. He warned that even the weekly newsreel, with its ability to engage the individual in the presentation of big parades and political rallies, has the potential to become an unwitting ally of fascism. Benjamin's essay was published the year after the completion of *Triumph of the Will* (1936), Leni Riefenstahl's homage to Hitler and the Nazi Party. Riefenstahl admitted that the filming of the *1934 Nuremberg Party Convention* was more than a straightforward recreation of a historical event but denied that it was politically motivated. Commissioned by Hitler himself and approved by Goebbels, the film employed deft camera work, sound, lighting, and editing, to create a testimonial to the glory of Nazism.

Similarly, during World War II, the American government asked Frank Capra, the director of *Mr. Smith Goes to Washington* (1939), to produce a series of films on *Why We Fight* (1942–45) scheduled for showing to military personnel. These films were produced under the auspices of the Army Signal Corps, and like *Triumph of the Will*, gave a distorted image of American society in the early forties because, intended by the government to serve as morale boosters for the American G.I., no references to segregation, discrimination, poverty, labor strife, or class antagonism were depicted. The *Why We Fight* series portrayed a nation so unspoiled and uncorrupted that it led actor-director John Cassavetes to comment that America might have been the invention of Frank Capra rather than a real place.[22] Cassavetes's quip referred to Hollywood's perpetuation of the cherished myths of an unblemished America. But whether genuine or fake, Capra's representation of America was an idealization of a place that a majority of the public either believed or wished to believe, was real. Certainly the series portrayed a country where the people regarded government as decent and honest, where right would triumph over force, where the average American's faith and wisdom would overcome adversity, and where capitalism delivers the American dream to all people.

Not all political propaganda is overt and government sponsored, however. Besides the kind of overt propaganda distributed by governments, Dan Nimmo's typology also includes examples of covert propaganda in commercial films.[23] One example is the western, *High Noon* (1952), released during the Red Scare. On the surface, the film is a standard western with a plot that pits the good sheriff (Gary Cooper), standing alone, against a gang of outlaws he once sent to prison. However, Nimmo insists that a viewer knowledgeable about the HUAC hearings and the subsequent blacklisting could interpret the film as an answer to those friendly witnesses who abandoned their colleagues before the committee. Such an interpretation would stamp covert political propaganda on a film that many viewed at the time as a lean and tough western rather than an attack on the HUAC inquisition. Naturally, it could be interpreted on both levels, but its true intention remains in the hearts of those involved in the film.

Nimmo treats commercial films that are covered with a slight indoctrination veneer as "thinly veiled propaganda."[24] Within this category, Nimmo places such films about American politicians as *Mr. Smith Goes to Washington* and *The Seduction of Joe Tynan* (1979), which are produced primarily for entertainment purposes but also deliver some propaganda in the process. For example, Mr. Smith preaches the message that grassroots democracy can work; hence the ordinary citizen has the ability to overcome evil. Joe Tynan, on the other hand, portrays Washington politics in romantic terms as a game of legislative trade-offs between lobbyists and politicians, especially when Meryl Streep plays the lobbyist. Senator Joe Tynan's (Alan Alda) personal ambition to occupy the White House someday may be attainable, but the film hints that if he becomes president, his soul will not be intact.

Film as Political History

After seeing *Birth of a Nation*, President Wilson reportedly described the movies as "history written in lightening."[25] The President could just as readily have characterized the medium in class terms too since historians remind us that movies had humble roots, serving as entertainment for the masses in the inner cities of industrial America. Is there a better way for future generations to experience the misery and poverty of the Great Depression than through a systematic viewing of 1930s Hollywood fare? Workers crowded into movie theaters during the Depression years to escape from their economic misery and allow themselves to be transported temporarily into the fantasy world of the Busby Berkeley musical and the wholesome comedies and dramas distributed under the film industry's production code. Occasionally, however, Hollywood deviated from its usual assembly-line films with movies that reminded the working class of their disadvantaged socioeconomic status. Warner Brothers, in particular, exposed the evils of slum living, delinquency, and urban crime in a series of thirties' films like *Crime School* (1938), *Angels with Dirty Faces* (1938), and *Hell's Kitchen* (1939); the last featured a young midwestern actor named Ronald Reagan. These films served as determinist indictments of the economic condition of the American underclass in the political context of Depression America.

On other occasions, studios produced films on a specific political figure, usually biographies of presidents before and after their tenure in the White House. Such was the case in *Abe Lincoln in Illinois* (1940), *Wilson* (1944), *Sunrise at Campobello* (Franklin Roosevelt) (1960), and *Nixon* (1995). But whether these films accurately portrayed reality or respected the historical record remains a matter of debate.[26] In the films cited above, only Stone's *Nixon* comes off as a flawed personality; all the others are romantic dramas that distort history.

Nonetheless, historians have come to extol the virtues of studying film because the camera is capable of recording an event for posterity at a particular time and place, subject to the caveat of reconstructing the past from a contemporary viewpoint. Hollywood often takes liberties with the historical record, justifying its necessity on dramatic grounds. Such was the case with two films on the civil rights movement, *Mississippi Burning* (1988) and Spike Lee's *Malcolm X* (1993), as well as Steven Spielberg's film on the slave trade, *Amistad* (1997), about an African mutiny aboard a slave ship and its subsequent trial, where the legal issue eclipses the morality of slavery. The educational value of these films diminishes proportionally to the dramatic liberties taken with the historical record. Good intentions may prove deceptive when filmmakers tamper with history, converting historical events into film propaganda. Educators who show these films will have to provide explanations and guidance lest their students learn the wrong lessons.

Film as Socializing Agent

Describing film as an agent of political and social change is problematic since the empirical evidence that would prove a causal relationship between film and political action has yet to be firmly established. To demonstrate that significant exposure to film affects attitudes and values sufficiently as to alter behavior is scientifically less convincing due to the number of variables involved in determining human causality. In those situations where social scientists are able to establish a relationship between two variables, the empirical evidence is usually insufficient to establish causality. Still, Stephen Vaughn,[27] in his book on Reagan's Hollywood tenure, presents a convincing argument for adopting a "preponderance of the evidence" approach when the methodology is applied to political figures. Vaughn's analysis of the former president's film career furnishes clues towards understanding his shifting position on social and political issues while occupying the White House. Vaughn's work is crucial to understanding Reagan's transformation from a liberal New Deal Democrat to a conservative Cold War warrior.

But speculating on the factors that motivate the politics of political leaders is quite different from documenting the influence of films on social and political behavior. This issue arose as early as the beginning of the century when lynching of blacks increased after showings of *Birth of a Nation*. Did the film's release incite mob violence? Did the film help to recruit members for the Ku Klux Klan? The findings suggest a relationship but not enough to prove causality. This issue of cause-effect persisted into the thirties when publication of the Payne Fund Studies, which linked delinquent behavior to the Hollywood crime and gangster films of that era, served as a catalyst for establishing tougher regulations over motion pictures. Although methodologically flawed, the film industry and the government interpreted the results as proof of a causal connection between film content and criminal and delinquent behavior. These studies lent "scientific respectability" to the industry's establishment of the production code, a content-based guideline for the production of movies; this code served as the basis for the industry's regulation over film content for more than thirty years.[28]

In the nineties, politicians revived the cause-effect issue when in seeking votes, they blamed Hollywood and the entertainment industry for criminal behavior, particularly that of juveniles and teenagers, and for the loss of moral values. The subject became a campaign issue during the 1996 presidential race when the Republican candidate, Senator Bob Dole, condemned the entertainment industry for depicting "mindless violence and loveless sex," which he cited as the cause for the erosion of the nation's standards of morality and civility.[29]

Hollywood was unfazed by the criticism. Gratuitous violence continues to appear in many Hollywood action films. Take the case of *Money Train* (1995). When a New York City token clerk died as a result of the firebombing of his subway booth, police and politicians blamed the film because it contained a similar scene and because it had opened in theaters four days earlier. But whether the young men responsible for the crime saw the film and were stimulated to copycat the crime is virtually impossible to answer empirically.[30] The incident, however, raised anew the fundamental behavioral question: does life imitate art or does art merely mirror life?

Failure by social science to document the nexus between film representations and anti-social behavior does not negate the possibility that specific films play a limited, but influential, role in the formation of individual beliefs and values. Current research on the subject continues to bring forth new evidence. Two attitudinal studies sought to measure the influence of a specific film on attitudes rather than exposure to a particular group of films identified as a genre. One study focused on the impact of the Watergate scandal by collecting data from the viewing of *All the President's Men* (1976).[31] The study found that a substantial attitudinal change had occurred, with the students who had viewed the film exhibiting a marked increase in political alienation while simultaneously displaying a more positive attitude towards the press. While the result could be expected, the authors, nonetheless, concluded that exposure to a clearly delivered political message in a well-crafted film can have a short-term influence on a particular attitude, in this case, judgments on politicians and the press.

In the other study, which involved Michael Moore's film, *Roger and Me* (1989),[32] the researchers discovered similar findings in both an American sample and a Japanese comparison group. *Roger and Me* concerns the unsuccessful attempt by filmmaker Moore to locate and interview Roger Smith, the CEO of General Motors (GM), to explain on camera why GM was closing plants in Moore's native city of Flint, Michigan. But despite some controversy over whether the film was a documentary or a comedic fable, the study results suggest that the American sample who viewed the film had substantially more negative feelings towards American corporations than the control group, who had not seen the film. Similarly, the Japanese sample group of university students duplicated the American findings except that, in addition to the negative attitudes displayed towards business, the Japanese also expressed more positive feelings towards their home companies.

While these studies are unlikely to end the debate over the power of the film industry to shape public opinion, their findings add to the body of existing evidence that suggests that films that contain political messages are capable of providing audiences with more than harmless diversions.

This chapter details the Hollywood-Washington connection, both on and off the screen. The next step is to make the case for the inclusion of "political film" as a distinct genre within the film lexicon. But before reaching that conclusion, the political film has to be identified.

Two

Defining the Political Film: From Riefenstahl to the *Three Stooges*

There is a scene in the film *Casablanca* between Claude Rains, who plays the corrupt Vichy French police chief, Captain Renault, and Humphrey Bogart as the cynical American owner of *Rick's Cafe*, where Rains warns Bogart:

> Renault: "We're going to make an arrest in your cafe."
> Rick: "Again."
> Renault: "This is no ordinary arrest, a murderer no less. If you're thinking of warning him, don't put yourself out. He cannot possibly escape."
> Rick: "I stick my neck out for nobody."
> Renault: "A wise foreign policy."

What Makes a Film "Political"?

Does this scene at the beginning of *Casablanca* set up the audience to expect an anti-Nazi, pro-Allies political film? In production before the Japanese bombing of Pearl Harbor, but released to theaters in 1942, this classic film has earned high praise from screen critics and film buffs. Yet no consensus exists on the question of whether *Casablanca* is essentially a romantic drama or a political film. Or both.

Defining a "political film" is the subject of this chapter. After confirming the existence in Hollywood of a modest political film genre in chapter one, our efforts turn to identifying those characteristics that determine whether a film such as *Casablanca* qualifies for inclusion into this very select group. But first a working definition of the political film is necessary. The effort to define a political film genre is so fraught with traps and tricks that scholars and practitioners ought to heed the warning by anthropologist Clifford Geertz,[1] who reminded his colleagues of their scholarly obligation to more precisely identify the object of their studies by recounting this Javanese folktale of a legendary figure, "Stupid Boy," who having been counseled by his mother to seek a quiet wife, returns to his village with a corpse.

Similarly, political scientists and film scholars searching for the political film have to provide satisfactory answers to the following questions. What distinguishes a political film from other genres? How does the viewer know when a film contains a political agenda or seeks to promote a particular political ideology? These questions are vital to the classification process, but unfortunately they are easier to raise than to resolve.

To simplify the task, the film scholars and practitioners have been assigned to three distinct groups. The first group includes those who consider all films to contain some level of meaning, however silly or simple-minded; possibly including political messages which express the ideas and values that reflect the spirit of the government in power, mirror the national mood at the time, and provide support and reinforcement for the status quo.[2] For example, the films of the 1980s reflected both the new populism and the renascent nationalism of the Reagan administration. Movies such as *Country* (1984), which portrayed ordinary farmers struggling to retain their property despite the policies of the federal bureaucracy, and films that rewrote American foreign policy, such as *Rambo: First Blood Part II* (1985), *Red Dawn* (1984), and *Uncommon Valor* (1983): jingoistic fables that led audiences to believe that America remained a potent military power after the defeat in Vietnam.[3]

All films contain messages, so the argument goes, even if conveyed unintentionally by Hollywood because their creators express the underlying values of the larger society. A Hollywood film that displays and even flaunts the material goods of American society to the Third World conveys the message, however unintended, that capitalism produces the affluent society. In this sense, foreign nations receive a mostly positive image of the United States through a steady diet of commercial films which reinforce the achievements of capitalist ideology, even when the objective is to provide mass entertainment.

At the other extreme of the spectrum, the second group includes those who consider the mere suggestion of a political film genre to be an oxymoron. To these purists, the only true political film is a piece of propaganda. This group argues that filmmaking is essentially a collaborative process, from the banks that provide the studios with the finances to support film projects to the editing process that completes the film's final form. With so many participants involved in the financing, distribution, and production, it is hardly likely that the creative process encourages ideological films. In fact, the film industry is more likely to promote traditional plots and recycled formulas than fresh ideas and innovative filmmaking.

The film industry is generally sensitive to audience response. Hollywood avoids ideological films for the same reason it abstains from making pornography—fear of public reaction as measured at the box office. If Hollywood films were intended as political tracts, why do the studios bother with research on alternative film endings?[4] These audience reaction surveys ("sneak previews") are designed to elicit viewer feedback to permit producers to alter their films before national distribution. But whenever Hollywood tackles an obvious political subject, such as election campaigning, the industry dilutes the political message with comedy, romance, or action. Warren Beatty's *Bulworth* (1998) is a recent example of diffusing a political message—the need for campaign finance reform—within the parameters of farce.

Besides, the second group maintains that past Hollywood ventures into the political arena have resulted in disappointing box office profits. The old adage that political films are "box office poison" is supported by the financial returns of three nineties' Hollywood films that present clear political issues. While *Wag the Dog* and *Primary Colors* had respectable domestic grosses, the results were less than expected. Similarly, after five weeks in distribution, *Bulworth*, about a depressed U.S. senator who falls in love and discovers new reasons for remaining in politics, earned just $24 million. Contrast these receipts with blockbuster films during their first five week run: *Titanic* (1997) earned over $235 million and *Godzilla* (1998) over $126 million. Some blockbusters earned more in their first five days than all the political films cited above. Consider these figures: *Independence Day* (1996) took in $85 million, *Men in Black* (1997) earned $79 million, and *Armageddon* (1998) grossed $54 million.[5] The feeble box office showing for political films reinforces the view that Hollywood cannot make a commercially successful political film because

> … the issues are complex and, to some extent, abstract, and have to be embodied in human antagonists to make them come alive. But then in order to make the characters both dramatic and human in a 90 or 100 minute context, the issues usually have to be foreshortened and oversimplified. In effect, the filmmaker is caught between the scylla of depersonalization and the charybdis of oversimplification.…[6]

Finally, these second group skeptics insist that whenever Hollywood undertakes to produce a film with a political theme, the industry reduces the subject to easily recognizable cliches and stereotypes, reminding us once again that filmmaking is a commercial venture that seeks a mass audience. In Hollywood, that means appealing to non-discriminating mainstream viewers with a plot that arouses emotions rather than provoke logical reasoning. Thus Hollywood reduces the complexities of political life to personal stories that are most likely to attract the masses. This tendency to dilute political ideas led film critic John Simon, relying on classical music as a reference point, to remind us that "Beethoven will not sound like Beethoven if played on a kazoo."[7]

Neither position is defensible. The first group is too inclusive; if every Hollywood film delivers a political message the film studios would have had to file for bankruptcy given their usual weak showing at the box office. On the other hand, to maintain that all films contain messages of social, economic, or political import relieves studies of the task of classifying thousands of Hollywood-made films, thereby ending the discussion. This absolutist posture is neither useful to the film scholar nor the student who seeks to narrow the frame of reference.

Meanwhile, the second group's argument that the film medium is an inadequate venue to deliver political messages and that filmmakers cannot produce films that are ideological ignores the historical record. For instance, how would this group explain such commercial propaganda pieces as *Birth of a Nation* and *The Great Dictator?* Both films were produced before World War II when the major studios dominated film output and controlled their distribution. Subsequent legal decisions and the success of independent producers has eroded the studios' monopoly over quality productions. To cite but one example. Four of the five films nominated for best picture in 1996 came from independents. It is much easier today for young filmmakers like Quentin Tarantino (*Reservoir Dogs*, *Pulp Fiction*) and Steven Soderbergh (*Sex, Lies, and Videotape*) to secure financial backing for their projects. These independents are more likely to tackle controversial subjects and assume more risk than the major film studios. Once these filmmakers acquire an audience, the prospects for exploring subjects once held to be taboo from a business or socially acceptable viewpoint is likely to expand over time.

To argue that Hollywood is a business "pure and simple" overlooks a small group of films, possibly five to ten percent of the annual Hollywood production, that probe serious public policy issues. The argument that film cannot serve as a useful medium for the dissemination of ideas expresses an elitist attitude, almost a rejection of popular culture as a contributor to social life. To disregard a political film because it is imperfect reflects the viewpoint of the aesthete rather than the film scholar. The fundamental question is not whether political films are good or bad, which is the venue of the film critic, but whether they exist, in what context, and with what effect.

Identifying the Political Film

Fortunately, a third group has emerged as an alternative to these absolutist positions. The members of this group accept the realities of film as an essentially commercial enterprise but maintain, nonetheless, that there exists a select but limited category of films with political overtones.[8] Even though the political ideas contained in these films may be presented in a simplistic manner or hidden within the subtext, their presence is sufficient to warrant inclusion in a separate and distinct genre described as the political film.

This, at least, is the position adopted by the Cineaste circle, a group of film writers and critics, who define the political film through an analysis of the body of work of such European filmmakers as Bernardo Bertolucci, Costa-Gavras, Bertrand Tavernier, Andrzej Wajda, and Lina Wertmuller.[9] The Cineaste circle represents a middle ground between the two viewpoints of inclusivity and exclusivity; defining political films through their directors instead of their content. American political scientist Michael Genovese, however, made an effort to place parameters around a political film genre and to set criteria for inclusion into the category. For a film to qualify in Genovese's political taxonomy, it has to satisfy at least *one* criterion from among the following requirements:

- the film serves as a vehicle for international propaganda;
- the film's major intention is to bring about political change;
- the film is designed to support the existing economic, political, and social system.[10]

The value of Genovese's taxonomy lies in the acceptance of a limited category with specific conditions for inclusion in the genre, aspects not addressed by the first two groups. But however noble his intention, Genovese's effort to categorize political film falls somewhat short. Admittedly, all definitions are inherently incomplete and subjective, but Genovese's criteria raise the following concerns. First, films produced by or at the request of those in power undoubtedly serve propaganda objectives. But is it absolutely necessary that films advocate political change as required in the second criterion? Why would an expose of the political system without an explicit mandate for change disqualify a film from the political category? Suppose a film scrutinizes the government of the day or the fundamental principles supporting the political system, the unequal distribution of justice within the legal system, the social class structure, or the prevailing power relationships without offering a prescription for change? Why should such a film be excluded from the political genre because it merely discloses wrongs without advocating a political solution? For example, the 1979 film, *The China Syndrome*, does not preach against the use of nuclear power per se but it nevertheless demonstrates the capability for disaster should a nuclear accident occur while it also alerts the audience to expect a possible government cover-up should such a catastrophe befall the country. In light of the Three Mile Island nuclear accident outside of Harrisburg, Pa., which coincidentally happened a few weeks after the film's release, why is it not legitimate to state that the film served a political function by informing the public about the negative side of utilizing nuclear power as an energy source, a viewpoint unlikely to be publicized by the nuclear power industry or the U.S. government?

Genovese's third criterion includes films that support the status quo. His contention is that any film that justifies the government in power, or supports the existing legal/justice system or the socioeconomic class structure is inherently political because it works against institutional reform and social change. But it is naive to think that Hollywood will attack an economic system that has made entertainment a profitable business. In Nazi Germany or the old Soviet Union, filmmakers had no choice but to support the totalitarian regime. In a democracy, however, supporting the existing political structure is a natural consequence of First Amendment freedom for the creative process and a byproduct of traditional middle-to-upper class support. Why would Genovese expect Hollywood to attack corporate capitalism? We do not expect the Ford Motor Company to manufacture automobiles, like the failed Edsel, which the public refused to buy. Then why would the film industry produce films that the public refuses to spend their entertainment dollars to see? Since the film industry seeks to attract a mass audience, its product usually follows consumer tastes. Again, should Genovese not have expected a film like *The Man in the Gray Flannel Suit* (1956) to support business conformity during the 1950s while touting the virtues of corporate capitalism? Is the expected support of the status quo sufficient to warrant inclusion in the political film genre? It would have been preferable for Genovese instead to have qualified the status quo criterion to include only films which support the existing political and socioeconomic systems at *the expense of disadvantaged and deprived groups*. This simple alteration would exclude *The Man in the Gray Flannel Suit* from consideration in the political genre but would include films like *The Grapes of Wrath* (1940), *Salt of the Earth* (1953) and *Alamo Bay* (1985); films that attack the uneven distribution of goods and rewards while addressing issues of sectional poverty, labor exploitation, and racial and ethnic discrimination. In this way, inclusion of the status quo qualification would have narrowed Genovese's definition without doing harm to its intent.

Redefining the Political Film

To build on Genovese's pioneer efforts to identify the political film, an alternate proposal is advanced that takes two factors into account—intention and effect. Taking a page from constitutional law scholar Cass Sunstein, who defined political speech as speech that is "both intended and received as a contribution to public deliberation about some issue,"[11] this alternative definition of a political film requires that *both* criteria be satisfied for inclusion. That, at least, is the abstract definition which still must pass the application test if it is to be of practical value.

Intent

At the production level, the definition requires that those involved in the filmmaking process—producer, director, film studio—either intend to deliver a political statement or such intention is reasonably implied from media interviews, commercial advertisements, or the consensus of film scholars and reviewers. An unmistakable example of an intended political film is the propaganda film typified by Leni Riefenstahl's *Triumph of the Will* or Frank Capra's *Why We Fight* series. These nonfictional films were made with the support of their respective governments to further state interests. Similarly, commercial features under the creative direction of auteurs occasionally are utilized to critique government actions taken at home or abroad. For instance, Oliver Stone disputed the "lone gunman" theory of the Warren Report in his film, *JFK*, while another of his films, *Salvador*, was critical of American support to Latin American dictators. Both films express the director's personal opinion, which differs from the official explanation.

Many directors, however, have to fulfill contractual obligations under which the studios exercise final judgment over their films. Under such conditions, filmmakers first must satisfy the demands of the studio before personalizing the film with any political messages. One relevant example from the 1950s was Carl Foreman's script for the western *High Noon*. Was the film a tribute to rugged individualism and personal courage or an intended attack on the friendly witnesses, which included the major studio heads, who testified before HUAC during the post-World War II Hollywood hearings into communism?[12] Foreman's script had to receive studio approval before filming began. If it was intended as an attack on the HUAC hearings, would the studio have approved?

On other occasions, the initial intention behind a film may change during the course of production. This is what happened to *Force of Evil* (1949),[13] a film about two Jewish brothers coming to terms with crime and greed in a New York City ethnic ghetto. Director Abraham Polonsky, whose name would subsequently be placed on the blacklist, wanted to make a traditional gangster film, but was asked to deliver a popular movie that had liberal overtones. During the shooting, the content became more radical as the film reached its conclusion, resulting in a film that challenged the acquisitive and materialistic values under capitalism. Films like *High Noon* and *Force of Evil* are capable of delivering multiple messages to an audience. But which message the audience receives remains problematic.

To complicate matters further in determining a film's intent is the nature of the film business as a collective enterprise, particularly when a film is made under contract for a major studio. Peter Biskind explains the problem inherent in the making of any political film:

> A conservative director may work with a liberal writer, or vice versa, and both, even if they are trying to impose their politics on their films ... may be overruled by the producer who is only trying to make a buck and thus expresses ideology in a different way, not as a personal preference or artistic vision, but as mediated by mainstream institutions like banks and studios, which transmit ideology in the guise of market decisions....[14]

Under these conditions only established auteurs and independent filmmakers have an opportunity to make a political film with few, if any, strings attached. Another necessary consideration is the required capital to finance film projects. The studios borrow millions from banks to finance their projects, and banks are notoriously conservative institutions that minimize risks and maximize profits. Even the independents require national distribution if their films are to compete with the studios at the box office. Hence, it remains highly unlikely that a political film, even one that supports the government in power and the socioeconomic system, will materialize without the necessary financial support.

Effect

If a film's intent is not always discernable to the casual viewer, its impact on a viewing audience is even more problematic. How to gauge the reception of a film's political text raises additional obstacles to defining the genre. An appropriate measuring instrument would measure an audience's understanding of the film's political text, that is, whether the primary story depicts some aspect of political history, promotes a particular ideology, serves as propaganda, supports capitalism in situations where others are exploited or disadvantaged by the socioeconomic class system, and advocates political change or reform. Audiences that saw Neil Jordan's film, *Michael Collins* (1996), or Richard Attenborough's *Gandhi* (1982), to cite but two examples, are unlikely to mistake these films for something other than political biographies. Nor will audiences misconstrue the intent of a film like *Welcome to Sarajevo* (1997). Shot in Bosnia, the film depicts the plight of two reporters, one American, the other British, caught up in wartime perils. The political nature of the film *Sarajevo* is reinforced by news reports from Kosovo province on the fighting and the killings.

The history of Hollywood is marked by films that examined American institutions and found them deficient. Audiences in the thirties empathized with the plight of the Okies during the Great Depression as depicted in John Ford's *The Grapes of Wrath* (1940), a sympathetic story of poor farmers struggling to hold on to their land despite adverse weather conditions, callous banks, and an indifferent federal bureaucracy. Reform of the prison system was the message of *I Am a Fugitive from a Chain Gang* (1932) while prejudice against outsiders and minorities depicted in films like *Fury* (1936) and *They Won't Forget* (1937) cautioned against the injustices of mob violence. Meanwhile, in the post-World War II era, films like *Crossfire* (1947) and *Gentleman's Agreement* (1947), spoke out against anti-Semitism while a cycle of 1949-50 movies dealt with the issue of racial prejudice and discrimination: *Home of the Brave*, *Lost Boundaries*, *Pinky*, *Intruder in the Dust*, and *No Way Out*. The message these films conveyed could hardly be misinterpreted by audiences living in America when segregation was the law of the land.

Audiences experienced little difficulty in deciphering the message of these films as pleas for religious and racial tolerance. But not every political message, however intended, is accepted by a film audience. The political content of a film may be dismissed altogether by filmgoers for a variety of reasons, including the desire of viewers to be entertained. Other film messages are subject to audience interpretation and categorical assignment by critics and reviewers. Take the case of *Forrest Gump* (1994). Audiences who saw this sentimental film could root for its dim-witted hero as he overcame adversity or viewers might have been offended by its celebration of ignorance over intellectualism.

Forrest Gump is the kind of film Hollywood loves to make because its ambiguous message is encased within a slick entertainment production. Another film with an enigmatic message was liberal director Stanley Kramer's *Guess Who's Coming to Dinner?* (1967). The plot revolves around the romance and intended marriage of black actor Sidney Poitier to the daughter of two white liberals, a judge (Spencer

Tracy) and his wife (Katharine Hepburn). Audiences could view the film at two levels; at face value, *Guess Who's Coming to Dinner?* is accepted as another romantic comedy by the popular Hepburn-Tracy team. However, viewers who came to the theater with relevant background information, discovered that the film also was a plea for racial harmony and integration. But in order to reach that level of understanding, viewers in 1967 had to be aware that interracial cohabitation and marriage were illegal in sixteen American states at the time of the film's theatrical release. Armed with that knowledge, viewers could interpret the Kramer film as a political statement against these state anti-miscegenation laws, albeit packaged in a highly entertaining movie.[15]

The same could be said about the film classic, *Casablanca.* Viewed by millions worldwide during its fifty plus years in circulation, *Casablanca* is another film subject to different interpretations depending on the knowledge of the audience. For many viewers, the Rick-Ilsa (Humphrey Bogart-Ingrid Bergman) romance remains the quintessential love story. But there are individual scenes and dialogue that would lead viewers, cognizant of the pre-World War II political climate, to accept the film's anti-isolationist, pro-democracy message. In this scenario, Rick's neutrality is transformed by his love for Ilsa, a passion so strong it overcomes his worldly cynicism and persuades him to help Ilsa and her husband, Victor Laszlo, a leader of the Free French forces, escape Nazi-occupied Morocco. However, if *Casablanca* is really about world politics, why is it that the Victor Laszlo anti-Nazi character is secondary to the Bogart-Bergman love story? Furthermore, if Warner Brothers intended the film to deliver a pro-interventionist message, why was it not made and released a few years earlier, before Pearl Harbor? The timing of the film's national distribution in the late thirties, together with Warner Brothers' anti-fascist stand, would have lent credibility to the film's pro-intervention message. But minus the presence of these factors, *Casablanca* remains an enigma.

Audiences that went to see the film, *Destination Tokyo* (1944), during World War II could view it as one of many action/adventure war movies. But because the film also was shown by the U.S. Navy to military personnel for training purposes, it took on another dimension for viewers with the additional knowledge. For audiences to understand the film as wartime propaganda requires filmgoers to be more than passive viewers. Such an audience would have to be well-read about movies and filmmakers; this, though, is likely to be considered a burden for American filmgoers who patronize movies to be entertained. Not to overstate the case but Chaplin's *The Great Dictator* and his later film, *A King in New York* (1957), both provide good illustrations about the duality of film content. As mentioned previously, viewers can appreciate *The Great Dictator* as vintage comedy or as an anti-fascist statement. Similarly, *A King in New York* also can be viewed at face value as one of Chaplin's lesser comedies or as political drama, a satiric attack on HUAC and McCarthyism. A viewer seeing the film without the relevant background information is likely to consider it comedy. But the viewer who brings factual knowledge to the film surely will view it differently. English-born, Chaplin never became an American citizen. When his loyalty was questioned during the 1950s, Chaplin left the country for his native England. But when he wanted to return to the States, he discovered that he was *persona non grata* and refused re-entry by the Immigration and Naturalization Service. *A King in New York*, therefore, was produced in London but not exhibited in the U.S. for two decades.[16] As scriptwriter, director, and star of *A King in New York*, Chaplin exercised complete control over the film, lending support to the view that Chaplin sought to critique America when it had questioned his loyalty while it embraced mindless conformity and vacuous cultural values. Or was *A King in New York* second-rate Chaplin at best?

The duality of meaning in film content took an unexpected turn with the publication by film scholar Don Morlan arguing that the popular shorts of the *Three Stooges* were more than exercises in mindless slapstick; rather they were films of social criticism and pro-World War II interventionism.[17] It is Morlan's contention that during the period from 1934 to 1958, the Stooges made a total of 190 shorts for Columbia Pictures, in which thirty-four films portrayed conflicts between the upper and lower classes, including their signature pie-in-the-face routine. The recipients of these pies were the wealthy and snobbish upper classes who were victimized by the Stooges in their film capacity as domestic servants or manual workers. Supposedly, these shorts helped to uplift the morale of working Americans during hard economic times. Morlan also insists that the Stooges contributed to pro-World War II propaganda in several shorts released between 1935 and 1941, before the advent of Pearl Harbor. One short in particular, *You Nazty Spy* (1940), was released to theaters nine months before Chaplin's *The Great Dictator*, leading Morlan to conclude that the Stooges were turning out shorts that, in their own slapstick style, warned Americans of the evils of nazism and fascism before the Chaplin film. But for Morlan's thesis to be more than mere speculation it requires tangible evidence of intent and viewer perception. Even if we concede that Jules White, the head of Columbia Pictures Short Subjects division, was an admitted interventionist and even if Curly, Larry, and Moe were Popular Front activists (no evidence exists to support the truth of this assertion) who abhorred fascism and deliberately poked fun at Hitler and Mussolini in their films, these assumptions would merely satisfy the first requirement of intent. However, in the proposed two-tier definition, political intention alone is not enough. The affective requirement must also be met and this is where the Morlan thesis breaks down, namely: what did the audience at the time think of the Three Stooges and what did the masses make of their films? Were Curly, Larry, and Moe recognizable political activists? Did they appear at public pro-war rallies? Were they outspoken members of the Popular Front movement? The basic question here, which neither Morlan nor the author can answer with authority, is whether audiences who viewed the Stooges in the thirties and early forties accepted their films as social criticism and pro-war interventionism. Or to state the question differently, did a consensus exist among critics, film scholars, and the moviegoing public that their short films preached revolution, the overthrow of the government, or political and socioeconomic reform? Unless such a consensus existed at the time, it remains problematic what messages, if any, the Three Stooges were communicating in their slapstick routines.[18] Unlike *The Great Dictator*, which made a statement against anti-Semitism and fascism that angered Hitler and Mussolini, the shorts made by the *Three Stooges* were generally conceived to be mindless slapstick routines from beginning to end, recycling the same plot in different contexts. If dictators were the patsies in one film, the victims in others were employers, the rich, and the military. In sum, the Stooges' shorts were no more than mass produced "fillers" to accompany the main feature or to round out a double bill at a Saturday matinee.

In theory, the two-tier requirement to determine whether a film's content qualifies for inclusion as a political film postulates the kind of empirical proof that would satisfy academic scholars. But as the above discussion demonstrates, the two-tier definition represents the ideal solution; serious practical problems arise in its application. In those instances when the intent requirement is met, documentation of the second criterion involving audience perception is even more difficult to achieve. Naturally it is easier to identify intentions in films like *Wag the Dog*, *Primary Colors*, and *Bulworth* because these movies feature a political subject, place the action in Washington, and include representational political characters. When these factors are joined in one narrative text, the likelihood is that an audience will perceive the film as political.

However, even proof of a single political factor is insufficient evidence on which to make a valid judgment. For example, take the Geena Davis-Michael Keeton film, *Speechless* (1994), about two speechwriters for opposition candidates in a U.S. senatorial race in New

Mexico. The political subject is electioneering, with the story's inspiration coming from the real-life romance of two speechwriters in the 1992 Clinton-Bush presidential campaign. But that is where the similarities end because if the actual speechwriters acted as the two stars do in the film, both would have quickly been unemployed. While politics provides the background in *Speechless*, the film's focus is on romance. Except for a few brief scenes of campaigning, *Speechless* could have been about two sportswriters who meet, fall in love, have a misunderstanding, but end happily in a romantic embrace. The Davis and Keeton characters struggle to imitate the romantic comedy team of Tracy and Hepburn in a 1990s film that has love, not politics, on its mind. The audience, meanwhile, learns no more about running a U.S. senatorial campaign than if it had stayed at home.

Placing the action in a governmental location, such as the nation's Capital, may add local color to the narrative, but the locale alone does not guarantee that a film will be political. Although the Kevin Costner film *No Way Out* (1987) is set in the Washington area, particularly in and around the Pentagon, and has the secretary of defense as a major character, its narrative focus is on romance and suspenseful action. Similarly, four other nineties' films center around sitting presidents: *Dave* (1993), *The American President* (1995), *My Fellow Americans* (1996), and *Air Force One* (1997), are played strictly for laughs or thrills. Despite the inclusion of actual politicians and background shots of the Capitol building and the White House, the real world of politics is definitely not the major preoccupation of these film presidents.

On the other hand, a successful political film takes advantage of location and integrates it into the context of the film. Contrast the above films with *City Hall* (1996), shot on location in New York City, with a plot that involves a besieged mayor (Al Pacino) actively engaged in trying to keep racial peace after a black boy is shot. Pacino's mayor is occupied by politics in virtually every frame. The audience learns little about this mayor's personal life because the focus of the narrative is on his public activities. Pacino's mayor is a political animal while Kevin Kline's stand-in president, *Dave,* and Michael Douglas's widower president (*The American President*) are cardboard political characters that audiences are unlikely to take seriously.

Finally, the question remains: how to measure audience reaction? While it is theoretically feasible to measure audience feedback, it is also impractical. To gauge a film's affective impact requires exit polling strategies to survey viewers immediately upon leaving the theater after a film's showing. Such a methodology, however, would not guarantee a representative sample. On the other hand, cluster sampling of viewers in selected locations throughout the county would be more representational, but its application would be even more uncertain. There also is the question of the expense involved and whether the benefits would be worth the cost. Besides, what government agency or private organization would be willing to commit the time and resources to collect the data? Hollywood could do it in conjunction with its "sneak previews" by inclusion of directed questions on the film's message. But while Hollywood and the government have the resources, neither has the motivation or the interest.

Even assuming that funding is available and sampling problems satisfied, the results of an audience feedback survey still could prove ambiguous. To illustrate this point, take the case of the film, *Romero* (1989), about the Catholic Archbishop of El Salvador who was assassinated in 1980 by members of the military government. On its face, *Romero* can be understood in terms of rights and liberties; a repressive government denies human rights to its citizens and seeks to silence those clergy who support political and economic reform. But since a good deal of the financial resources to make the film came from the Catholic Church and since the film adheres closely to actual events in the life of the Catholic Archbishop, the Church might have produced the film for alternative motives. Therefore, was the intention behind the film to portray a human interest story about an ordinary religious man thrust by history into becoming a spokesperson against injustice in Central America? Or was its real motive to show the schism in the Catholic Church between the adherents of liberal theology and those who support ruthless governments in Third World countries as long as these governments do not interfere with Church practices? It is highly unlikely that even a methodology sound survey will provide a definitive answer.

The truth of the matter is that to require both production intention and audience effect as essential characteristics of the political film is no more likely to be empirically possible than past definitions. For the overwhelming majority of Hollywood films, delivering entertainment is the message, profit is the goal. But for that small minority of films, mostly made by auteurs, the political message is paramount and takes precedent over commercial success. For every acknowledged political film, there exist hundreds more for which the search for consensus remains elusive.

Can it be that the task of defining the political film is similar to the law's efforts to define obscenity? In the final analysis both the obscene and the political character of a film may lie in the eye of the beholder rather than any textbook definition. Certainly, however, the intention of the nonfiction film is less ambiguous than the entertainment purpose of many commercial features, even if their effect on audiences remains in doubt.

Three

Nonfiction Film: Investigating the Real

"Sometimes you have to lie. One often has to distort a thing to catch its true spirit."
—Robert Flaherty

"The objective-subjective argument is from my point of view, at least in film terms, a lot of nonsense."
—Frederick Wiseman

The opening scene in Leni Riefenstahl's documentary, *Triumph of the Will*, about the 1934 Nuremberg Party conference, pans the sky as the camera tracks the landing of a small twin-engine plane. When the plane is on the ground, the door opens and Adolph Hitler emerges triumphant, greeting the crowd of worshiping faces, waving flags and offering party salutes. It is a dramatic introduction to one of the greatest propaganda films on record; a film in which Hitler comes across as the benevolent leader, *der Führer*, who has descended, God-like from Heaven, to restore the German people to their rightful place in history.

The film is wonderful theater, but also a blatant piece of Nazi propaganda. Propaganda is one film type under the more comprehensive genre known as the "nonfiction" film; a category that includes newsreels, documentaries, and propaganda tracts. Thus, this chapter examines the effort by filmmakers to investigate the real and to transfer that reality to film. However noble the intention, the evidence indicates that few nonfiction films depict actuality.

Nonfiction Film

It would simplify matters if a consensus existed on an accepted definition of the nonfiction film. But like most attempts at classification, the nonfiction film defies simplistic explanation. This is not surprising

Leni Riefenstahl's classic propaganda film of the 1934 Nazi Party rally, *Triumph of the Will*, was commissioned by Hitler. (Courtesy: Riefenstahl Produktion, c. 1935).

since the genre encompasses visual images from newsreels and travelogues to rock concerts and Nazi Party rallies. One effort to distinguish the nonfiction film from the commercial feature describes the former as "discourses of sobriety";[1] films that depict an unedited truth. Critics insist, however, that such films straddle fact and fiction, information and entertainment. Consequently, as a film category, works of nonfiction are tainted because the term implies that the events depicted must be true.[2]

If an acceptable definition of nonfiction film cannot marshal a consensus, at least Richard Barsam has identified half-a-dozen characteristics essential for inclusion in the genre.[3] These include the following:

- a focus on a particular event, person, group, or social problem
- the film is shot on location with the actual participants and without costumes, stage sets, or sound effects
- the film has a structured narrative with a beginning and an ending
- the film is usually photographed in black and white, although color is becoming more popular
- the work typically is filmed without spoken narration, relying on the words of the actual participants
- the film is customarily not intended for commercial distribution. However, there are exceptions to the last characteristic, notably in the films of Michael Moore, *Roger and Me* and *The Big One* (1998), which produced respectable box office returns.

The Development of Nonfiction Film

Although film historians are likely to associate the development of the documentary with Robert Flaherty's 1922 recording of the life of Inuit Eskimos, *Nanook of the North*, or with the work of John Grierson in England, the cinematic effort to capture reality began decades earlier when European colonial companies engaged photographers to take pictures of their economic holdings to impress their home governments. By the first decade of the twentieth century, all the great European colonial powers employed cameramen to record activities in their African colonies and to show these films to private investors and the general public in commercial theaters.[4] Meanwhile, in the U.S., some sixty-eight films of the Spanish-American war and the subsequent Philippine Insurrection, 1898 to 1901, were produced for national distribution, making it the first war in American history to employ the camera as recorder.[5]

World War I Era

In the years before the First World War, when labor unions were struggling to organize and gain public acceptance, the American labor movement decided to use the new medium to educate and politicize the working class and to counter the negative images presented in the silent films distributed by Hollywood. For example, the American Federation of Labor (AFL) made *A Martyr to His Cause* (1911), a film about the trial of the McNamara brothers, accused of bombing the *Los Angeles Times*. Two years later the labor movement produced *From Dusk to Dawn* (1913), using professional actors to depict a story about labor strife that eventually ends in a socialist party election victory.[6] These silent films were important recruiting tools as the labor movement sought to organize unskilled immigrant workers, many unable to understand English. For these workers, a picture was worth a thousand words.

The nonfiction film came of age during the First World War because, for the first time, film became an instrument of modern warfare, providing valuable information to the warring nations and a propaganda tool to use against their enemies. The British government, for instance, screened its 1915 film, *Britain Prepared*, to President Wilson and the Congress in an attempt to persuade the U.S. to enter the war. Germany, meanwhile, put its film industry under state control to counter the Allied propaganda.[7] Both Germany and Britain were in competition for American support, but before 1917 few Hollywood films about the war treated the conflict in a way that would offend either side. However, once the U.S. officially entered the war, all films that dealt with the war came under the control of the government's Committee on Public Information (CPI). Furthermore, World War I marked the first official effort by the U.S. to produce its own films when the government created a film section inside the Signal Corps with responsibility for turning out films that would aid the war effort.

Between the Wars

When the First World War ended, the factual film returned to recording other subjects. Filmmakers like Pare Lorentz, founder and head of the U.S. Film Service, made documentaries about the resettlement of the Dust Bowl dispossessed in the *Plow That Broke the Plains* (1936) and the benefits of the Tennessee Valley Authority in *The River* (1937), both underwritten by the government. Actually, the Department of Agriculture had been making films since the beginning of the century as part of its educational mission. By the thirties, the government had built its own sound stage in the nation's capital to facilitate film production.[8] Documentary film flourished at this time and led to efforts to improve production and national distribution. To consolidate filmmaking during this period, the labor movement advocated east and west coast production and distribution facilities. Subsequently, the Labor Film Services was based in New York while the Federated Film Corporation was set in Seattle. However, the federal government considered labor's efforts suspicious; the FBI monitored their activities and attended their films while the postal service denied mailing permits to labor film groups that sought to advertise films in their own magazines. Additionally, both liberal and leftist films were made of the Spanish Civil War and the tragic effects of the economic depression. One leftist group, Frontier Films, included among its members such directors and screenwriters as Elia Kazan, John Howard Lawson, and Albert Maltz, all of whom joined the Communist Party and were called to appear before HUAC in the 1950s. To combat labor's efforts, the corporate sector countered with a stream of its own films designed to portray labor organizers as Bolsheviks and un-American radicals. This anti-labor viewpoint is found in *Courage of the Commonplace* (1917), *Bolshevism on Trial* (1919), and *Dangerous Hours* (1920). These films depicted union leaders as corrupt, Bolshevik agents intent on generating discontent and subverting American industry.[9] During the twenties and thirties documentaries and feature films were used as propaganda weapons in the struggle between employers and the working classes.

World War II Era

Nonfiction films were never intended as popular entertainment. Initially, these travelogues, newsreels, and short documentaries were used by theater owners to supplement the main feature. But in the 1930s, the studios forced theater distributors to rent a "film package" for commercial showing, which generally included a major feature, a shorter, minor film that usually ran about an hour, cartoons, and short subjects. As a consequence, the market for documentaries plummeted.

The German invasion of Poland in 1939 revived interest in documentary film. The U.S. government, although proclaiming neutrality, gave military and economic support to the Allies. The government also was not above propagandizing the war to the American people. For example, Louis de Rochemont's documentary, *The Ramparts We Watch* (1940), conveyed the message that the democratic ideals of freedom and justice were not confined to the European conflict alone but affected Americans as well. Once America entered the war, the government encouraged the making of films that explicitly served the war effort. Subsequently, a wide range of government films was produced, covering subjects as varied as military training pictures and venereal disease educational films for service personnel to propaganda pieces like Frank Capra's *Why We Fight* series. But unlike the First World War, the government was better prepared to initiate the propaganda war the second time around. The Office of War Information (OWI) modeled itself on its World War I predecessor. After the war, the duties of the OWI were assigned to the Division of International Information, which became the U.S. Information Agency (USIA), housed within the State Department.[10]

Post World War II Developments

Nonfiction films flourished in the post-World War II period as enthusiastic young filmmakers turned their cameras on home and country with a fresh, and often critical, eye. Their subjects were as diverse as their personalties. Some, like Frederick Wiseman, remain prolific creators continuously at work on film projects. Others like Barbara Kopple produced a handful of films over two decades but two, *Harlan County, USA* (1976) and *American Dream* (1989), won Academy Awards for Best Documentary Feature.[11] A third group of nonfiction filmmakers, including John Sayles and Michael Moore, have become commercially successful contrary to the general rule in the industry. Sayles has been a respected director and screenwriter in Hollywood for fifteen years and his work has been nominated for several Academy Awards. While it is difficult to resist the tempting rewards of money and fame, Sayles has been able to maneuver his career from independent filmmaker, *Matewan* (1987), to mainstream commercial drama, *Lone Star* (1996), without sacrificing his integrity. Moore, on the other hand, moved from the documentary-style of *Roger and Me* to his second film, *Canadian Bacon* (1995), a commercial feature about a war with Canada. He returned to the documentary form in his recent endeavor, *The Big One* (1998), skewering corporate downsizing while companies contract work overseas. Several documentarians have found steady work in television; others find an outlet for their talent in state-funded assignments and in projects for educational institutions. Few retain box office power; many produce one or two films and fade out of sight.

The Documentary Film

The origins of the documentary film are generally acknowledged to be closely related to the development of filmmaking in Europe a hundred years ago. The documentary film style arose in response to the oversimplified and romantic representation of reality in fiction films, even though both forms could include a narrative and a dramatic structure. The documentary differs from fiction in several ways. First, it seeks to present the world the way it actually is rather than through an imaginary representation. Second, if the subject is historical, the documentary tries to recreate an era or a specific factual event without embellishment. Third, the emphasis in the documentary is on fashioning an argument or a point of view through the presentation of visible images or through the testimony of experts or witnesses. Finally, because the documentary represents people directly rather than through an intermediary actor, the film engages the viewer more than even the most explicit fiction film since the viewer knows the event is real rather than simulated.

In the U.S., documentary film dates from the nineteenth century with the early recordings of the Spanish-American War and extends to the *cinema vérité* style of contemporary filmmaker, Frederick Wiseman. Wiseman deserves credit for popularizing the form as his documentaries appear regularly on public television and are made available to educational institutions. Of the contemporary documentarians, it is Wiseman who has the best track record and has sustained the most interest. Educated in law at Yale, Wiseman's prolific filmmaking career spans three decades and thirty films.[12] His documentaries often engage viewers in the emotional plight of their subjects even when the films lack the necessary historical context to make sense of their feelings. But there is no denying the power of his films, characterized as social tracts where the emphasis is on powerful institutions rather than the individuals entrapped within.[13] Wiseman's films often remind audiences of the early twentieth century muckrakers. For instance, Wiseman's film, *Meat* (1976), exposes the details of the slaughtering process and is favorably compared to Upton Sinclair's novel, *The Jungle*. In films like *Titicut Follies* (1967), *High School* (1968), *Hospital* (1970), and *Juvenile Court* (1973), Wiseman's camera often captures public institutions in ways that encourage viewers to reflect on a society that tolerates such establishments. In his latest documentary, *Public Housing* (1997), Wiseman depicts the despair of the Chicago projects and the failure of public housing policy in the U.S. The film does not require commentary because the camera substitutes for the spoken word.

A proponent of direct cinema, Wiseman has filmed subjects as varied as the slaughtering business (*Meat*), mental institutions (*Titicut Follies*), and department stores (*The Store*). His films bear the stamp of his personality and his cinematic technique, identifying Wiseman as the American filmmaker who comes closest to being an "auteur" among contemporary documentarians. Wiseman's films should be viewed as empty canvases on which the filmmaker records images, leaving it to the imagination of the audience to complete the painting. For instance, in *The Store* (1983), Wiseman brought his camera into the very exclusive Nieman-Marcus department store in downtown Dallas. His camera recorded fashion shows where champaign is served, marketing sessions where the employees are almost as well-dressed as the customers, and sales transactions involving $37,000 for a sable jacket and $45,000 for a diamond bracelet. Wiseman then takes his camera outside, showing scenes of ordinary people walking the streets and riding the buses downtown and commentary is unnecessary to illustrate the contrast between the elites, who can afford to spend lavishly on luxuries at Nieman-Marcus, and the people outside who look like they barely have enough money to make ends meet.

Wiseman's work is characterized by most of the attributes of *cinema vérité*: use of the lightweight, portable camera and sound equipment, hand-held filming, working without a script or narration, recording events as they develop and focusing the camera on hand gestures and body language that accompanies the dialogue.[14] While Wiseman's films are never staged or rehearsed, the filmmaker's stamp is put on the film during the editing process when he imposes a structure on the film footage.

Wiseman is the rare documentarian who is willing to admit the subjectivity of his work, namely, that it expresses a point of view. The notion of objectivity in capturing the real is often lost in the editing process. Many documentarians maintain that their work is factual—that the camera never lies despite evidence to the contrary. Omitted from mention is a history of documentaries that contain staged scenes, misidentified footage, arranged events to misrepresent chronology, and stock film incorporated with authentic footage. Even the father of American documentary, Robert Flaherty, manipulated the actual for dramatic effect. As early as the silent newsreels, sound effects were added during the editing process. The *March of Time* newsreels, for example, contained staged events and studio reconstructions if genuine footage was unobtainable. Perhaps the worst case of reconstruction occurred in the pre-World War II era when the newsreel made a film that depicted life inside Nazi Germany but shot it in the New Jersey farmlands.[15] Frank Capra's *Why We Fight* series also included staged footage and scenes inserted from commercial features.

A recent flap over the authenticity of the documentary form occurred with Michael Moore's film, *Roger and Me*. The young filmmaker's first project became a popular success when it was released in 1989. Advertised as a documentary about the woes of Moore's home town, Flint, Michigan, the film became something of a *cause celebre*. When General Motors (GM) shut down its auto plant in Flint, thousands of workers lost their jobs. At the heart of Moore's film is his unsuccessful attempt to track down GM's Chief Executive Officer (CEO), Roger Smith, in the company's Detroit headquarters and query him about plant closings. But the interview never takes place because Smith is able to avoid the confrontation. The real star of *Roger and Me* is the absent Smith, similar to another documentary at the time, *Who Killed Vincent Chin* (1988), where the titled character is dead and the film is really about his killer, an unemployed Detroit auto worker.

Roger and Me cost $260,000, a sum befitting a struggling documentarian. However, it was later learned that Warner Brothers gave Moore $3,000,000 for the rights to distribute the film, an amount that expressed confidence in its commercial value. But when the Motion Picture Academy listed its Oscar nominees for best documentary, Moore's film was omitted because its commercial distribution qualified it for the feature film category. However, when the film was later released on video, it was reclassified as a documentary. In some ways, this story of *Roger and Me* is more interesting than the film itself because it questions the social construction of categories. Who decides whether Moore's film is a documentary or a commercial venture? The film studio? The Motion Picture Academy? The film critics? Moore himself? What *Roger and Me* demonstrates is the arbitrary classification of documentary films as authentic depictions of reality.

Ironically, it was the commercial success of *Roger and Me* that led movie critics and film scholars to more closely examine Moore's film. Moore considered his film a documentary,[16] but eventually it was revealed that he had taken liberties even beyond editing and the rearranging of scenes. For example, Moore charged that the plant closings resulted in 30,000 workers being laid off but the actual figure for the Flint plant was a more modest 5,000. The 30,000 figure actually referred to jobs lost in plant closings in four states over a twelve-year period. Furthermore, Moore had insinuated that while GM was closing its plant, the city spent millions on projects that eventually failed. In fact, the three city projects that failed were underway *before*, rather than after, the 1986 shutdowns. There were other minor discrepancies as well. One scene showed President Reagan touring the city, leaving the viewer with the impression that all the hoopla surrounding the president's visit contrasted sharply with the image of a dying city. In actuality, Reagan visited Flint in 1980 as a presidential candidate rather than as president six years later.[17] These discrepancies led one film critic to comment that the problem with the film was not that it expressed a personal viewpoint, but rather that it was unfair.[18] While the film left the audience with a negative impression of corporate capitalism, Moore resorted to misrepresentation and dramatic reconstruction to demonstrate it.

Moore's film can be profitably contrasted with Barbara Koppel's documentary, *American Dream* (1989), which was released in the same year as *Roger and Me*. *American Dream* concerned the 1985 strike by the meatpackers' union at the Hormel plant in Austin, Minnesota. Whereas Koppel's film is a traditional documentary, complete with exposition, detailed observation, and support for the strikers' cause, Moore's film, while sympathetic to the plight of his home town, uses humor and sarcasm as social commentary. What these films share in common is that neither filmmaker was successful in gaining access to the power brokers—the corporate leaders—demonstrating the powerlessness of ordinary workers who challenge the authority of the modern corporation.[19] Unlike Koppel, however, Moore was criticized for the misrepresentation of his subject.

If Moore's ego was bruised by the criticism his film received, he could take small comfort in knowing that there are other, more serious, consequences to filming documentaries. For instance, while filming *Harlan County, USA*, Koppel was harassed and even shot at.[20] Another filmmaker, Hugh O'Connor, was shot dead while working on a documentary about Appalachia in the 1960s. There are repercussions for the participants as well. The Loud family agreed to be filmed for a twelve-part television series on the American family in the seventies. The TV series required that a camera crew invade their home and film their daily movements and activities. Shortly after the series was aired on television, the Louds divorced. The family charged that the filmmakers selected for inclusion all the negative portrayals, shouting matches, and bad times that had happened during the filming schedule and ignored all the positive details and the good times. Wiseman ran into a different problem with *Titicut Follies*, where his film was shot inside Bridgewater (Massachusetts) State Prison for the Criminally Insane. Although Wiseman received legal consent from the patients before filming, his critics questioned whether mental patients could give informed consent. He ran into privacy problems because the male inmates were presented in the nude and while no names were used, they nonetheless could be identified by relatives and friends. The most depressing fact about the above events is that, with one or two exceptions, there is a lack of evidence that the documentaries actually led to penal reform or promoted family solidarity. Of course, the documentarian might contend that the filmmaker is an artist first rather than a political activist. However, public exposure does not necessarily produce social action. But for the propagandist, ideology requires that film manipulate an audience to accept and comply with the message depicted on screen.

The Propaganda Film

Propaganda films come in several configurations. One is the documentary, a supposedly objective recording of an actual event, a political movement such as Nazi Socialism, or the depiction of a culture portrayed through its inhabitants. The propaganda in these films often is deceptive because their creators claim neutrality, as if their films were unedited newsreels. Riefenstahl's *Triumph of the Will* is an example of a propaganda message delivered in a documentary context. Another form of propaganda occurs in commercial films where the message frequently is muted or surreptitiously hidden in the subtext, evident only to the scholar or trained viewer.

But what exactly is propaganda and why does the term invoke such disdain? *Propaganda* is a term that virtually defies classification since one person's truth is another's falsehood. While no one definition is universally accepted, there is general agreement that the term has come to include the twin elements of premeditation and manipulation. Hence, David Culbert says that propaganda is "the controlled dissemination of deliberately distorted notions in an effort to induce action favorable to predetermined ends of special interest groups."[21] His definition is broad enough to encompass the output from state-controlled film industries to political campaign television broadcasts in the United States.

Propaganda differs from both fact and opinion in that its goal is to present information in such a manner as to influence or persuade an intended audience in a particular way. On the other hand, facts are statements whose authenticity is observable by the senses or verifiable by research. In the world of film, for example, the title credits, listing the film's players, writers, technicians, and director represent factual information about the movie. In *Casablanca*, for instance, the names of Humphrey Bogart and Ingrid Bergman in the title credits provide us with the major players while Michael Curtiz's name indicates that he served as its director. All these "facts" are subject to corroboration from other, external sources. But to insist that *Casablanca* is a political film is to render an opinion about it, that is, to express a personal feeling or intuition concerning the film which may actually make good sense and which could prove to be correct, but which still requires factual evidence for verification. Sometimes fact and opinion are blended into one statement, and it is necessary to extract and distinguish one from the other. Staying with the film *Casablanca*, suppose a film critic were to describe the film in the following manner:

> *Casablanca* takes place in Nazi-occupied Morocco where Humphrey Bogart, as the American owner of Rick's Place, helps two European refugees, including Ingrid Bergman, his former lover, escape to freedom. Bogart's character represents the American position favoring intervention in the European war before the Japanese attack on Pearl Harbor.

In this hypothetical review, the first sentence includes information which can be confirmed from the film itself. But the last sentence states an opinion rather than historical fact since prior to December 7, 1941, there was considerable sentiment in regions of the country with substantial German populations for the U.S. to remain neutral and stay out of the European conflict.

The term propaganda began as a neutral label but acquired a pejorative meaning in the nineteenth century. Its origin is found in Pope Gregory XV's establishment of the Congregation for the Propagation of the Faith in 1622 to counter the Protestant Reformation that was spreading through Europe.[22] Thus in the seventeenth century propaganda meant the spreading of theological dogma or religious doctrine. By the nineteenth century, however, the technique came to be identified with the efforts of governments to manipulate public opinion.

In the twentieth century, the term became associated with Nazi Germany. While it is true that Hitler came to power in 1930 by democratic means, he resorted to force and mass manipulation to consolidate that power. The Nazis systemically eliminated their opponents via assassinations, cold-blooded murders, and terrorist threats so that when Hitler became chancellor, the Nazis had already eliminated or frightened most of the political opposition. Once in command, the Nazis sought to mobilize the German people via a campaign of emotional and patriotic appeals. These were coupled with the manipulation of public opinion through the selection of "ethnic and racial scapegoats" that had to be eliminated before Germany could fulfill its historical destiny. This campaign to capture the hearts and minds of the German people was entrusted to the propagandists. Hitler understood the value of film as a tactical weapon in his goal to "purify" Germany and resurrect the Third Reich to its former glory. While documentarians acknowledge that film is an ideal method for portraying reality, it also can distort reality by strategic editing and cutting. In that sense, it is the perfect propaganda weapon by which to rearrange ideas and phenomena in such a way as to make them appear to be true. To cite but one example, Hitler ordered a "film hour for the young" as part of the official school curriculum. By 1934, every German school was required to show Nazi-produced films during this one-hour period. Hitler had discovered in the film medium the ideal methodology by which to indoctrinate the young, excite the street bullies, convert the apathetic, and persuade the indecisive. Historians usually mark the 1933 book burning or "kristallnacht" as symbolic of the Nazis rise to power. But the underlying explanation for their rise and their ability to retain control rested on their utilization of propaganda to forge a mass psychology that supported their physical show of power.

Nazi propaganda had two national objectives. One was to enlist internal support for Hitler's global plans for a Third Reich that "would last a thousand years" and the other goal sought to weaken the morale and the resistance of the enemy. The first goal is shown in the film, *Baptism of Fire* (1940), which trumpeted the superiority of German air power; the second goal is best illustrated by another 1940 film, *The External/Wandering Jew*, which portrayed the Nazi ideal of a master race.[23] As Minister of Propaganda, Goebbels' efforts were directed at solidifying support at home. Contrary to much of the popular mythology found in American World War II movies, Goebbels disdained the overtly propaganda film replete with swastikas, SS uniforms, and "Heil Hitler" salutes—characteristics more common to American-made movies during this period than anything found in German films. Of the 1,097 feature films produced under Goebbels' orders between 1933 and 1945, only 183 or one-sixth, were overtly propagandistic;[24] this figure confirms that the Nazis produced fewer wartime propaganda films than the Americans or the British.

Instead, Goebbels preferred historical dramas that contained mythic heroes rather than the blatantly propagandist *Triumph of the Will*. Despite Riefenstahl's plea that the film was merely a recording of a historic event by an artist rather than a piece of Nazi propaganda, she failed to satisfactorily explain why her film contained restaged scenes, some reshot without Hitler present.[25] Other scenes were arranged so as to give coherence to the series of events, thus "dramatizing" the film footage. *Triumph* took months of planning, shooting, and editing in order for Riefenstahl to present a view of a united Nazi Party when, in truth, Hitler had ordered the assassination of a rival faction the night before the Nuremberg Party Congress scene depicted in the film. Furthermore,

Riefenstahl insisted that she was an artist and not a political figure. She had never joined the Party nor was she anti-Semitic. But she liked Hitler and so one would assume that she supported the cause as well. Given the hierarchical structure of the Nazi Party with its emphasis on loyalty and submission, an intelligent woman like Riefenstahl, who had access to the top echelon of party leadership, presumably did not have to become an official party member to know what was happening. Riefenstahl could hardly claim independence as a filmmaker since under Goebbels' command all film producers and artists had to register with the propaganda ministry and all scripts were subject to review and party clearance. Working within this hierarchical structure, Riefenstahl was as much a civil servant as Lorentz was in depression-era America.

World War II Propaganda

The Nazis were not alone in manufacturing propaganda during the Second World War. The U.S. had cranked up its own propaganda machine under the auspices of the OWI, to coordinate film activities with Hollywood. Actually, however, there was an existing propaganda campaign at work in Hollywood long before Pearl Harbor. Morlan notes that in the five years leading up to America's entrance into World War II, the industry was busy producing both anti-Nazi and war preparedness films.[26] The anti-Nazi films included *Blockade* (1938), *Confessions of a Nazi Spy* (1939), *The Mortal Storm* (1940) and *Man Hunt* (1941). Four films released between 1940 and 1941, *Flight Command*, *Dive Bomber*, *A Yank in the RAF* and *Sergeant York*, promoted the advantages of military readiness. If the U.S. was going to enter the war, these films suggested that it would not be on the German side. Morlan also insists that a number of the early Three Stooges' comedy shorts, such as *You Nazty Spy*, were really directed at the fascists.

Whether the Three Stooges shorts were intended to help the Allied war effort is problematic, but there is no doubt that the film studios were anxious to cooperate with the government once the U.S. officially entered the war. Animated studios like Walt Disney especially welcomed government business since the war had cut off part of the foreign market. Hence, the studios recruited cartoon makers to produce training films for U.S. soldiers in addition to churning out propaganda shorts. Warner Brothers proved to be the busiest studio, using the Bugs Bunny cartoon character to sell war bonds and introducing a new character, Private Snafu, to star in a series of military training films. Warners produced twenty-five Private Snafu films between 1942 and 1945 in which the hapless private would be lectured on subjects ranging from malaria to venereal disease. Also a number of Bugs Bunny cartoons made fun of the

Japanese in a manner that would be considered racist slander today; Daffy Duck cartoons sent a similar message to Hitler and the Nazis. Walt Disney studios, meanwhile, lent its Donald Duck character to the war effort by placing him in patriotic cartoons. One Donald Duck episode, *Der Fuehrer's Face* (1942), had the duck waking up in a world conquered by the Nazis to illustrate what life would be like living under fascism.[27]

Movies became a popular form of entertainment during the war. Like cartoons and short subjects, feature films also had to make a wartime adjustment. Hollywood no longer could portray the Axis Powers in a positive light. The most significant attitude conversion, however, was reserved for the Russians. Before the signing of the Nazi-Soviet non-aggression pact in June 1941, Hollywood either ignored or poked gentle fun at the Russians in films like *Ninotchka* (1940) and *Comrade X* (1940). But after the Nazi invasion, Hollywood supported the Allies' newest member in the most praiseworthy terms. At least four features released in 1943 and 1944 glorified Stalin, the military, and the courage of the Russian people. Two war films, *The North Star* (1943) and *Days of Glory* (1944), paid tribute to the heroism of partisans and guerrillas in their fight against overwhelming German forces. Reportedly, the Russians loved *The North Star*, a big hit in Siberia where it played to 50,000 people.[28] Meanwhile, MGM's *Song of Russia* primarily portrayed a love affair between an American conductor (Robert Taylor) and a Russian concert pianist (Susan Peters), two unlikely combatants. But when the Germans invade Russia, the lovers exchange their musical talents for military weapons and join the partisans in their fight against the invading Nazis. Although a love story set against a war background, *Song of Russia* abounds with praise for collectivism, comparing, for example, the Soviet collective farms with those in midwestern America. Its pro-Soviet ideology put the film on HUAC's subversive list, even though Taylor's patriotism was never questioned during his appearance before the committee.

The resonant complaints, however, were saved for the film, *Mission to Moscow* (1943), a box office fiasco released after the Battle of Stalingrad to drum up American support for the Russians. *Mission to Moscow* purported to be a factual record of Ambassador Joseph Davies's three years of service (1936-38) in the Soviet Union, but proved to be such an exaggerated glorification of Stalinist Russia that its credibility was seriously damaged.[29] For example, condensing the four purge trials into one for dramatic purposes may be forgiven, but not at the expense of historical accuracy. For the film, however, to present the Moscow trials as justification for Stalin to remove traitors plotting against him is pure fiction and content manipulation to serve political ends. Historians now accept the fact that during the party purges of 1933 and 1938, Stalin removed an estimated 850,000 members from the party, ordered one million put to death, and another twelve million political enemies (real or imagined) shipped to Siberian labor camps. For *Mission to Moscow* to portray Stalin as a friendly, smiling "Uncle Joe" character to the American people is equivalent to Riefenstahl showing Hitler in *Triumph of the Will* as a kindly grandfather figure rather than a monster directly responsible for eleven million deaths. After the war, these four pro-Soviet films were considered "un-American" by HUAC. But during its hearings, HUAC never questioned the loyalty of Warner Brothers, which produced and distributed *Mission to Moscow*, even though final approval for the film rested with the studio. In Cold War America, the issue of individual loyalty proved to be highly selective.

Post World War II Propaganda

After 1945, only a select few films dealt frankly with pressing social issues such as intolerance, racial injustice, anti-Semitism, and discrimination. But these had to contend for audience attention with a slew of anti-communism films; these movies warned against communist infiltration and subversion and recruitment of disillusioned Americans as spies, traitors, and dupes for the Soviet Union. Since these films featured respected Hollywood stars like John Wayne, Robert Taylor, Helen Hayes, and Elizabeth Taylor, their appearance lent credibility to the anti-communist message. But the most blatant piece of anti-communist propaganda was a low-budget B-film called *The Red Menace* (1949), intended as a warning to dissatisfied Americans considering membership in a communist cell. The amateurish plot relates the story of a war veteran duped by the communists. The irony is that the communists in the film are portrayed as much smarter than the decent, but weak and naive, American followers. *Red Menace* remains the classic, although sophomoric, propaganda film of the postwar era. Fourteen years later, Warner Brothers (perhaps as penance for producing *Mission to Moscow*) produced a film entitled *Red Nightmare* following the Cuban missile crisis. Told in flashback as in a dream, the plot has communists taking over an entire community, thereby depicting what life would be like under Soviet domination. The audience is saved from this dreadful fate when the major character wakes up from his dream. Despite the anti-communist theme, the film was an embarrassment and never was released to theaters. Thus, the reputation of *The Red Menace* as the most overt piece of Cold War propaganda remained intact.

Another propaganda film from that era, but from an entirely different perspective, is *Salt of the Earth*. This fictional recreation of a successful strike in the zinc mines of the American Southwest of the early 1950s was denied commercial distribution in the U.S.[30] Dismissed as a piece of "communist propaganda" by film critic Pauline Kael and blacklisted nationally, the film remained a source of controversy for many years. While it is true that the movie starred Hollywood actors and was produced, written, and directed by blacklisted filmmakers, and that the real union organizer actually was a member of the Communist Party, the film nonetheless depicted, in gritty black and white, corporate violence and a disregard for the health and safety of the mostly Chicano mine workers. When the mine owners succeed in securing an injunction to stop the workers from picketing, their places on the picket line are taken by wives and mothers. Indeed, the film underrepresents the real amount of violence that occurred during the actual strike when sixty-two women were arrested and several shot by company guards and local police. Besides the threat to life, the cast of professional actors and local citizens and members of the crew were subjected to physical abuse and death threats in the wake of the Red Scare hysteria. In addition, the filmmakers were denied technical facilities and the lead actress was deported, requiring that the film be finished in Mexico. Looking back, the movie could be perceived as a piece of anti-capitalist propaganda, but it also can be viewed as a piece of social muckraking and as an early feminist tract since the strongest characters in the film are women. *Salt of the Earth* is a good illustration of a film that is multilayered: it can be viewed as a piece of "communist propaganda," a promotional for the trade union movement, an argument against laissez-faire capitalism, or a consciousness-raising tract as a precursor to the women's movement.

Salt of the Earth is hardly the traditional Hollywood film fare. While the vast majority of Hollywood films provide straight entertainment, a small fraction every year are intended by their creators to deliver a political message.[31] Some are more subtle, containing political messages in the subtext which must be ferreted out. For instance, Oliver Stone's films *JFK* and *Nixon* are good examples of historical fiction, although promoted by the filmmaker as though his interpretation was grounded in indisputable facts. In *JFK*, Stone interpreted past events, not as straightforward historical facts such as "Oswald shot Kennedy" but as a series of conditional theories such as "Oswald might have been part of a conspiracy to assassinate Kennedy." In this sense, Stone's film lends cinematic support to the fascist conspiracy theory surrounding the president's death.[32]

Categories of Propaganda

Nimmo contends that there are four distinct forms of film propaganda. He identifies the first category as the overtly propagandistic movie such as Frank Capra's *Why We Fight* series and *Triumph of the Will*. A second category includes commercial films loosely based on actual political figures and real events such as *Mission to Moscow* and *Salt of the Earth*, which are transparent propaganda efforts. A third category includes covert propaganda films that require audiences to possess relevant factual knowledge before viewing the film. Such would be the case for the 1950s western, *High Noon*. The last category, Nimmo reserves for films that contain what he identifies as "potential propaganda"; in other words, these are selected films with nonpolitical subjects that are produced for entertainment purposes, yet have the potential to carry propaganda messages. To illustrate his point, Nimmo maintains that the 1948 John Wayne western, *Red River*, which deals with a cattle drive over the Chisholm Trail, also can be viewed as a vindication for empire building (accumulation of territory) and capitalism (the search for a cattle market in the old West).[33]

Few would differ with Nimmo about the overt propaganda films within his classification scheme because these are films of political advocacy promoted by the state. But both second and third categories require the viewer to integrate previous knowledge with the action on screen. Without this prior information, both *Mission to Moscow* and *High Noon* can be accepted at face value. In the case of *Mission to Moscow*, much of the negative material on Stalin is excluded; hence the film became an apologia for the party purges, a strictly Stalinist view of historic events. Also important to note is the film's timing; the factual material on Stalin was not available to the American people when the film was released in 1943.

More questions arise when a film like *Birth of a Nation* has to be categorized. The film was not sponsored by the government although President Wilson did contribute some scholarly footnotes to the text. Based on the novel, *The Clansman*, and written by a Southern evangelist, the film is a particularly nasty portrayal of blacks, even for the beginning of the century. Not only are blacks presented as undisciplined beasts, lusting after white women, but the rise of the Ku Klux Klan is justified as a necessary measure to protect white society and keep blacks in a subservient place within the social structure. The film enjoyed a successful showing around the world and it is difficult to gauge just how much damage it caused to black Americans in its reinforcement of racial stereotypes since the film added the characteristics of meanness and violence to the cliché of the shuffling, befuddled, and easy-going Afro-

Lynching by the Ku Klux Klan in the post-Civil War South as depicted in D. W. Griffith's epic film, *Birth of a Nation.*

American. To add insult to injury, all the major parts were played by white actors, including the principal black characters. Griffith restricted the participation of blacks to the crowd scenes.[34] Contrary to Nimmo, *Birth of a Nation* should be understood as a piece of overt propaganda thinly disguised as Reconstruction history.

The fourth category, "potential propaganda," deserves little serious consideration. To cite just one example, Nimmo would have us believe that *Red River* is really an endorsement of American capitalism rather than a critically acclaimed Howard Hawks western. However, several different interpretations have been offered about the film, including a story about male bonding (cowboys on the trail), intergenerational strife, (father Wayne versus foster son Montgomery Clift), and a remake of *Mutiny on the Bounty* (1935) (with Wayne as the tyrannical Captain Bligh). Which interpretation should an audience accept as authentic? This is one example of why latent political messages, such as those Nimmo attributes to *Red River*, require documentation, rather than personal opinion.

There is enough overt political propaganda around that it is unnecessary to deconstruct the texts to further personal hidden agendas. Recent documentaries on political campaigns present another arena for propagandists to portray both negative and positive images of politics. Take the contrasting portrayals depicted in the documentaries, *The War Room* (1993) and *A Perfect Candidate* (1996). The first is an optimistic presentation of the successful 1992 Clinton campaign for the presidency; the other paints a dark picture of the electoral process as depicted in Oliver North's 1994 unsuccessful campaign for a seat in the U.S. senate. Which film more accurately depicts American politics may ultimately rest, not in any personal analysis or textual deconstruction, but in the eye of the beholder.

Four

Flesh and Blood: Regulating Sex and Violence on Screen

"My constituents can't read but they can understand pictures."
—Boss Tweed

"Censorship made me." —Mae West

The Politics of Culture

Hollywood came under public attack in the 1990s, particularly from political conservatives, religious fundamentalists, and parent groups, for producing films that feature excessive violence and explicit sex. The moral outcry against the film industry reached its peak in the 1996 presidential campaign between liberals, who advocate screen freedom and conservatives, who demand that Hollywood films return to traditional family values. The Republican candidate, Bob Dole, went so far as to admonish industry leaders when he reminded them of their public responsibility:

> Take your influence seriously. You have a lot of it. Respect your talent and power. Stop the commercialization of drug abuse. Stop the glorification of slow suicide. Not because you are frightened of public outrage, but because you are responsible adults, with duties and standards.[1]

Ever since *Dolorita's Passion Dance* (1896) was considered unacceptable for public viewing on the Atlantic City boardwalk, Hollywood films have come under the scrutiny of religious leaders, politicians, and pressure groups. For what reasons? These censors, or advocates of content control, accept as fact the assertion that movies exercise a negative influence, especially on young and impressionable minds. Protecting the young, however, is only one reason for Hollywood to tone down its portrayal of sex and violence on screen. Another argument for restriction comes from parents and grandparents, as surveys indicate that even adults are weary of the level of crime, sex, violence, and profanities on screen.[2] On the other hand, the film industry takes the position that parents are responsible for their children's socialization, including selection of their movie fare. Hollywood also defends itself by maintaining that in a free market economy any business that wants to survive responds to public demand; in the case of movies—box office receipts. Hollywood contends, therefore, that in a democracy, the people get what they deserve.

The Film Industry: From Censorship to Regulation

Virtually every new form of popular entertainment has been a target of public criticism; movies were no exception.[3] Efforts to control film content evolved through three stages in cinema history; in its early years, federal, state, and local governments censored movies, permissible until the 1952 U.S. Supreme Court decision in *Burstyn v. Wilson*[4] brought movies under the protection of the First Amendment and led to the end of government film censorship. The next stage saw the industry create self-regulating mechanisms, such as the Production Code and the ratings system, to exercise internal control over film content and avoid government regulation. In the final stage, pressure groups based on religious, racial, ethnic, gender, or sexual preference grounds have resorted to the strategy of economic boycotts and sanctions against the showing of specific films, a tactic utilized increasingly during the past two decades.[5] But these groups also were successful during the industry's early years as their efforts led to the passage of city censorship ordinances, state censorship statutes, and the creation of state and local censor boards. By the 1920s, at least seven states and more than a dozen cities had put motion pictures under government regulation, requiring a permit or license from the censors prior to public exhibition.

To discourage government censorship and to quiet public criticism, the film studios hired former Postmaster General Will Hays to become their new head. Hays saw his job as twofold: clean up film content and polish the industry's tarnished image. To achieve these goals, Hays sought to screen out undesirables from the film industry, discourage migration of young people to Hollywood to pursue a film career, and persuade producers to make the kind of movies acceptable to civic and religious leaders. He also took a step towards self-regulation by encouraging the studios to permit his staff to review scripts for objectionable material. He then sought to control screen content by convincing producers to accept his list of "Don'ts" and "Be Carefuls," in the making of their films; first, through avoidance of certain subjects altogether and second, by treating particular topics with special care. For example, Hays' content rules prevented even married screen couples from sharing the same bed. Profanity, nudity, white slavery, miscegenation, and ridicule of the clergy were to be avoided at all cost. Traditional social institutions like marriage and family were to be properly presented while religion and symbols of authority, such as the police, were to be respected. Hays soon learned that verbal acceptance of the guidelines by studio executives did not guarantee implementation on the screen. By 1930, Hays had become disenchanted with efforts to improve screen morality.

Discouraged by the ineffectiveness of his office to control film content, Hays's next step was to convince the industry of the need for a code of moral principles that would serve as a guide during the production stage. These guidelines, developed by a Catholic priest and a trade paper journalist and strongly supported by the Catholic Church, became the internal regulating mechanism for the film industry for more than three decades.

The Production Code

Making movies under the code was a game of barter and exchange between the studios and the Production Code Administration (PCA) office headed by Joseph Breen. The studios sought to stretch the limits of permissibility under the code's regulations, often trading one suggested film cut in order to retain another. Not only did the code contain a list of prohibited subjects, but it also defined basic moral principles and applied these to specific plots involving crime and sex. Strict application of the code, however, made the honest treatment of adult material on the screen virtually impossible.

When box office receipts were good, the studios were more likely to faithfully abide by the code. But when the depression hit and receipts declined, the studios were more interested in filling theater seats than promoting public virtue. For example, after gangster films drew patrons into the theaters, similar violent screen fare followed. The success of *Little Caesar* (1930) encouraged other gangster films like *The Public Enemy* (1931) and *Scarface* (1932). Between 1934 and 1968, when the major studios operated under the code guidelines, few movies were rejected solely because they depicted gangsters and violent crime. Instead, the code expressed a tougher stand on sex than violence.[6] But when Mae West's films, with their suggestive dialogue and their immoral plots, proved popular at the box office, the industry churned out imitations rather than censure.

Mae proved a real challenge to local censors and to the code administrator because even her most innocent line of dialogue could be interpreted as sexual innuendo. Born in Brooklyn to immigrant parents, Mae's stage career began at age seven. For two decades she performed in vaudeville, burlesque, and legitimate theater before reaching stardom in 1930s Hollywood. Mae was no dummy; she wrote most of her material and learned to use her sexuality to further her career. Her first two starring films, *She Done Him Wrong* and *I'm No Angel*, both released in 1933 before implementation of the code, tested the resolve of the Hays Office. For instance, in *She Done Him Wrong*, Mae plays Lady Lou, a barroom entertainer who tries to seduce Cary Grant, the leader of the Salvation Army. Not only does Mae invite Grant to "come up sometime and see me," but she flaunts her sexuality in a song about liking "A Guy What Takes His Time." Then in this scene from *I'm No Angel*, Mae, dressed in a low-cut form-fitting sequin gown, rubs up against co-star Grant, who praises her good behavior, and replies: "When I'm good, I'm very good, but when I'm bad, I'm better."[7] Everyone in the audience howled while the censors fumed.

Film historian Gregory Black argues,[8] with some justification, that the production code served as the instrument by which a conservative political agenda was promoted in Hollywood since the code demanded that movies show respect for government and all authority figures, present only acceptable social behavior, and adhere to Judaic-Christian morality. But whether Hollywood adopted the code because it believed in its moral precepts or because it proved a useful instrument to fend off government regulation is a moot point. There is little evidence to suggest that the major studios had acquired a social conscience rather than follow sound business practice. Determining motivation in the entertainment industry is not a science.

During its early years, the code was accepted more often in theory then in practice. The code might have survived a brief tenure had it not been for the Legion of Decency. Created by the Catholic hierarchy and armed with its concomitant threat of a boycott, the Legion supported the code's moral principles with an economic hammer. The power of the Legion lay in the pledge that Catholics took to boycott films condemned by the Church. Black contends, however, that the Church was more bluff than performance because it failed to deliver the boycotts in any consistent and systematic way. While the Church exercised clout in cities like Cincinnati, Philadelphia, St. Louis, and San Francisco, Black maintains that it was largely ineffective in communities without a strong

Catholic presence.[9] However, there are two logical explanations for the inconsistency. The first reason is found in the population demographics. Where the Church had a large and faithful following, its pulpit commands naturally would have more clout. For instance, when Elia Kazan's *Baby Doll* opened in Albany, New York, the bishop condemned the film and warned Catholics to avoid both the film and the theater that had booked it. When the Albany newspapers refused to advertise the film, that action combined with the bishop's condemnation, virtually guaranteed that *Baby Doll* would have a limited playing engagement.

But even when the Church could not deliver an effective boycott on every film it condemned, the Legion still could exert pressure on the industry to make cuts and alter scenes. Moreover, the Church had an ally in Joseph Breen, a Catholic, who headed the PCA. Most contemporary interest groups would consider what the Legion achieved as a model in effective lobbying. However, contrary to popular opinion, the Catholic Church is not a monolithic institution in practice, save for a handful of Papal infallibility rulings. Divisions exist among the clergy as well as the laity. Catholic bishops occasionally disagreed with the Legion over the ratings assigned to specific films and over the action that should be taken against condemned films. Still, a combination of economic forces and Catholic pressure led Hollywood to produce more musical comedies, children's pictures, and family movies in the decade prior to World War II.

The major problem with the code, as with any content-restrictive system, rested with its implementation by Breen and the PCA staff; their narrow construction of the guidelines made film production a series of obstacles to overcome, usually by circumvention. For example, Breen applied the code strictly to prohibit the filming of certain subjects whether written by established authors such as Leo Tolstoy, William Faulkner, and Sinclair Lewis, or by commercial hacks. Lewis's novel, *It Can't Happen Here*, was prevented from reaching the screen because of PCA objection. Breen also had the authority to demand cuts, eliminate or edit dialogue, and even exclude a proposed film project. Possibly the silliest example of code application occurred during the filming of *Gone With the Wind* (1939) when Breen's staff wanted to rewrite the following dialogue between Scarlett O'Hara and Rhett Butler:

> Scarlett: "Oh, my darling, if you go, what shall I do?"
> Rhett: "Frankly, my dear, I don't give a damn."[10]

The code administrators had penciled in the line "My dear, I don't care" as Rhett's response and only the persuasion of the producer, David O. Selznick, preserved one of the great lines in screen history along with Bogart's "Here's Looking at You, Kid" from *Casablanca*. The original intention of the code to place sensible restraints on screen material may have been laudable, but its implementation was often arbitrary and unreasonable.

The petty squabbling over words, coupled with the growth of independent producers and the recognition by the Supreme Court of the importance of film as a means of communication in the 1952 *Burstyn v. Wilson* decision, led eventually to the code's demise. The catalyst for the downfall of the code came in 1966 with the selection of Jack Valenti, former aide to President Lyndon Johnson, to head the Motion Picture Association of America (MPAA). After a few weeks on the job, Valenti faced two challenges involving the code that would ultimately seal its fate.[11] The first dispute involved the film version of Edward Albee's play, *Who's Afraid of Virginia Woolf* (1966), where the words "screw" and "hump the hostess" were included in the original dialogue. Both raised problems under the code and the resolution, worked out after hours of negotiation, resulted in the exclusion of the word "screw" but with retention of the phrase, "hump the hostess," even though both phrases refer to identical sexual practices. The second incident proved more serious. Director Michael Antonioni's British-Italian production, *Blow-Up* (1966), contained scenes of nudity, prohibited under the code. It therefore was denied an exhibition certificate. But the film's distribution by MGM, albeit through a subsidiary company, marked the first time a major studio planned to exhibit a film without a PCA certificate. Encouraged by MGM's defiance, other independent producers followed suit and within two years, Valenti replaced the code with a film rating system that classifies films according to audience suitability. As the decade of the sixties came to a close in Hollywood, the code was dead; long live the ratings.

The Hollywood Movie Rating System

The rating system that Valenti persuaded the Hollywood moguls to adopt in 1968 was a stroke of administrative genius. The old production code clearly was nonfunctional, yet the prospect of government censorship was unacceptable. Hence Valenti was able to sell the new rating system to the studios as a reasonable compromise. The film classification system designed by Valenti is age-based and intended for parents; its sole purpose is in "giving advance cautionary warnings to parents so that parents could make the decision about the moviegoing of their young children."[12] In application, the rating system is intended for film patrons seventeen and younger.

The Hollywood classification system has undergone several versions since 1968. New categories have been added and one category has been substituted for another so that by the millennium, the rating system requires films to be placed in one of five categories based upon audience suitability:

G: General Audiences
PG: Parental Guidance Suggested; some material may not be suitable for children
PG-13: Parents Strongly Cautioned; some material may be inappropriate for children under 13
R: Restricted; under 17 requires accompanying parent or adult guardian
NC-17: No one 17 and under admitted

The ratings applied to Hollywood films are the result of the deliberations of a Los Angeles-based group of reviewers who work in the Code and Rating Administration (CARA), under the supervision of a chairman appointed by the MPAA president. The film rating process works like this. A producer/distributor who wants his/her film to be rated prior to national exhibition submits it, along with a fee, to CARA. Why would a producer/distributor voluntarily submit to the rating process? The answer is quite simple. Unrated films, and sometimes even NC-17 rated films, are not booked to play in the large theater chains like United Artists, Cineplex Odeon, Sony, AMC, and National Amusements. Thus, to receive a satisfactory rating (PG-13 and above preferred, R accepted) from CARA is simply a sound business decision by the studios and distributors.

After CARA reviews a film, each staff member assigns an appropriate rating accompanied by a justification. The staff then meets to discuss the initial ratings. The final rating is the result of a majority vote. There are options for the producer/distributor who is unhappy with the assigned rating, namely, to edit the film and resubmit it to receive a less severe classification or appeal the decision to the Rating Appeals Board. This group of reviewers comes from within the film industry. After listening to arguments to overturn the initial rating, the appeals group decides by a two-thirds vote either to uphold the assigned rating or overturn it. Their decision is final and not subject to further appeal. In order to render some semblance of objectivity, Valenti's office is not involved in the rating process at any stage of the proceedings. While fairness is an important attribute for any classification system, the real test is whether the Hollywood rating system actually achieves its stated objective and performs a vital service to parents. Since government also is concerned with the public interest and since Hollywood provides entertainment for the general population, the rating system should be judged on its contribution to the civic culture as well.

Putting Hollywood to the Test: The Rating System Assessed

In theory, Hollywood's voluntary classification system neither acts as a censorship agent nor as a review guide to recommended films. Its stated purpose is to assist parents in selecting appropriate movies for their children's viewing. The question for assessment, therefore, is this: does the rating system achieve its stated objective?

The classification system represents an agreement within the film industry (studios, distributors, and theater owners) to abide by the assigned ratings. CARA has the authority to suggest changes in film content, which the filmmakers and the studios may reject. But the rating process favors CARA because there are economic consequences attached to an assigned rating; the most restrictive NC-17 rated film as compared to a less restricted R-rated classification may significantly affect the number of theater bookings and, consequently, box office receipts. That is why the studios often make it a contractual obligation for a filmmaker to deliver a movie with a specific rating. For instance, director Paul Verhoeven was required by Tri-Star to secure at least an R-rating for his sex-violence thriller, *Basic Instinct* (1992).[13] Verhoeven was upset with the required cuts but, in the end, the studio and CARA exercised the necessary leverage.

While CARA has the power to tone down film violence, bad language, and explicit sex, statistics reveal that the R-rating has become the most popular classification. Between 1968 and 1996, CARA assigned ratings to more than 13,000 films; 54 percent received the R-rating.[14] But what is more significant is that the number of R-rated films, which requires those under seventeen to be accompanied by a parent or guardian, has steadily increased over each previous decade. Thus, in the seventies, 42 percent of the films distributed by the MPAA were R-rated. This percentage increased to 59 percent in the eighties and to 63 percent in the nineties. In 1995, for instance, two-thirds of the almost 700 films released for distribution were R and NC-17 rated. Thus, by the mid-nineties, Hollywood already had surpassed the number of R-rated films for the entire decade of the eighties.

What sense can we make of this trend? While no empirical answer is procurable, two reasonable inferences can be drawn from the statistical data. One explanation is internal; CARA's ratings emulate public opinion and conform to public tastes. While older adults may shudder at what is being shown on the screen, teenagers and young adults seem to accept the excessive depiction of sex and violence in films as normal. Hence, the official MPAA line is that in a free economy, market forces determine production; sex and violence is good box office. If the moviegoing public disapproves of such films, Hollywood reasons, it has the option of staying away, or in cases where opposition to a film is particularly robust, to picket the theaters. Ultimately, the film industry maintains, the choice rests with the American public.

Theoretically, the public has the capability to exert tremendous economic clout by boycotting such films at the box office. But Hollywood recognizes that the moviegoing audience is unorganized, and that individual and small group protests have little, if any, financial impact at the box office. In his recent research on censorship groups, Charles Lyons confirms that most films targeted by protesters have survived at the box office.[15] For example, the protests of gays and lesbians failed to effect the box office receipts of *Basic Instinct* (1992), nor is it clear that Asian-American protests against *Year of the Dragon* (1985) hurt the film financially. The exception seems to be religious films, particularly if they are perceived to be an attack upon a major religion such as Christianity. Catholics and other Christian groups, for example, vehemently protested Martin Scorsese's *The Last Temptation of Christ* (1988) because the clergy considered it "blasphemous."[16] As a result of the protests, three major theater chains decided against booking the film and the film's scheduled engagements were canceled in several cities.

The fact that Hollywood is a capital-dependent industry that needs to borrow heavily from banks to finance its film projects requires that it be mindful of prevailing public tastes and sensitive to audience reaction during "sneak previews" as well as the total number of tickets sold at the box office. But Hollywood also knows that the industry is capable of generating demand for certain films through emotional manipulation and creative advertising. Common sense dictates that Hollywood observes audience demands as expressed at the box office, but the industry has the ability to create the desires underlying the wish fulfillment. Writing in the late 1940s, anthropologist Hortense Powdermaker characterized Hollywood as the "dream factory";[17] a place like Oz where dreams inevitably come true. Over the years, audiences have been conditioned to accept Hollywood's world as reality. Recently, however, that fantasy world has been inhabited by drug dealers, sadistic criminals, rapists, and sexually uninhabited young people.

Another plausible explanation for the above trend can be found in the changing American mores and morals of the last three decades. Generally speaking, the assumption is that Americans no longer find sex and violence offensive. As evidence, take the two recent sexual accusations against President Clinton. At no time during the discovery and publication of these charges did pollsters report that a majority of Americans wanted the president to resign or be impeached by the Congress. Moreover, when the American Film Institute (AFI) published its "100 Best American Movies" list in 1998, the 1500 survey voters selected more recent popular movies, including at least half that deal with violent subjects such as crime (*The Godfather* 1972), assassinations (*Taxi Driver* 1976), urban dysfunction (*Pulp Fiction* 1994), and the Vietnam War (*Platoon* 1986).[18]

While neither explanation is empirically verifiable, both suggest that the increase in the R-restricted category denotes a trend in the industry to include more adult material in films. But does this increase in R-rated movies mean that screen violence and explicit sex have reached such alarming proportions as to warrant more stringent internal controls, and even governmental action?

First, it contradicts the historical record to state that earlier Hollywood films, dating back to the silent era, were devoid of the kind of emotional appeals that would attract customers into theaters today. Even silent films contained nudity while violence and sexual suggestiveness is found in the films of the twenties and thirties. To explain this phenomenon, film critic Peter Keough argues that whenever the U.S. finds itself in the midst of an economic downturn, rapid social change, or political crisis, the public and the media scapegoat the entertainment industry rather than place blame on real villains, such as arms manufacturers, industrial polluters, and the tobacco industry.[19] Furthermore, Keough insists that there is little hard evidence that film violence and explicit sexuality encourage or cause criminal behavior and moral decline. Keough maintains, instead, that Hollywood is primarily a reactive business, rather than an innovative industry. Hence its films reflect contemporary values already accepted in the larger society. He insists that Hollywood serves to disguise the country's real culprits by suggesting in its films that America's real enemies are external; communism after World War II and, since the breakup of the old Soviet empire, aliens and creatures from outer space.

Keough's defense of Hollywood, while not original, still deserves analysis. Naturally, Hollywood should not be blamed for all of the country's social ills. And Keough is correct when he suggests that the causal connection between screen sex and violence and real life crime and immorality are largely anecdotal rather than demonstrated. Nonetheless, he avoids entirely the issue of Hollywood films as a contributory agent to social problems, possibly because no empirical data are available because of the complexity of variables at work in determining human behavior. But because no definitive causation theory exists does not necessarily rule out a correlation between film depictions and social behavior and moral values.

Some facts are inescapable. It would be difficult to refute the general observation that films of the past decade have shown a tendency towards excessive and graphic violence (*Reservoir Dogs* 1992), (*Natural Born Killers* 1994), (*Pulp Fiction* 1994), to treat nudity and sex in more explicit and mean-spirited ways (*Showgirls* 1995), and to interface the sexual material with physical brutality (*Basic Instinct* 1992). Children and impressionable youngsters who come from homes that lack positive parental or guardian role models fail to develop a strong personal moral code to offset the temptations of a bad neighborhood environment and a deprived childhood and are likely to become the most susceptible audience for imitating screen sex and violence. In this conditional sense, the above Hollywood films do influence antisocial behavior. Therefore, should the film industry not have a civic obligation to avoid gratuitous screen sex and violence and to provide positive role modeling for children and youngsters?

MPAA president Jack Valenti claims that the audience suitability ratings are not meant for adults *per se* but only to help parents select appropriate films for their children. Therefore, for Hollywood to pass the assessment test, it must satisfy two criteria. First, parents should expect that the ratings have internal integrity and second, that they are systematically enforced at the theater.

Internal Integrity

No film classification system devised could be flawless and guarantee universal satisfaction because a certain amount of subjectivity is inherent in any evaluation process. Even if we concede that the CARA reviewers are sincere and that concerned parents have their children's best interests at heart, differences of opinion are still likely to occur. The issue is not simply the quantity of the film violence or the explicitness of sexuality on the screen but rather the context in which such material is presented. At what point do scenes of graphic violence become excessive? In one sense, the serious portrayal of the holocaust on screen makes violence, as well as evil, banal. There is a qualitative difference, however, between gratuitous violence in a film without serious purpose and the bloody violence that erupts throughout *Michael Collins*, a film depicting the IRA's guerrilla warfare against the British presence in Ireland. Similarly, when does the showing of sexuality on screen succumb to pandering and exploitation? The explicit sexuality expressed in Louis Malle's *Damage* (1992) is quite different in intent from the vulgar display of sexuality in *Showgirls*. How do the CARA reviewers distinguish one from the other? What factors were compelling in arriving at the assigned rating? Unfortunately, the industry provides minimal information because the deliberation process is secret and generally not made public.

However, the increasing popularity of the R-rating in Hollywood means that a majority of films being released are restricted to viewers seventeen and over unless accompanied by a parent or guardian. The problem is not simply with the rating *per se* but the criteria utilized for the category. CARA claims not to employ a litmus-paper test for the R-category; that is, so many shootings, knife stabbings, drug abuse scenes, explicit sexuality, and bad language automatically earn the restricted rating. All CARA literature states is that an R-rated film may include "hard language, or tough violence, or nudity within sensual scenes, or drug abuse or other elements, or a combination of some of the above."[20]

While the application of a litmus test would be overly rigid and restrictive, the sex and violence content of a film should be considered within the context of the narrative. Quantifying the appropriate amount of sex and violence is unrealistic and would be harmful to the creative process. But there is an alternative. Rather than restrict film content, Hollywood should follow the example of the British Board of Film Classification (BBFC) and place films with adult content in an 18 and over category. Adoption of the British 18 classification would enable Hollywood to eliminate both the R and NC-17 categories, substituting instead an age classification grouping that would allow filmmakers to treat serious subject matter in an adult way. The preference for age eighteen as the benchmark for an adult film category can be justified on the ground that eighteen is almost universally recognized in the U.S. as the legal demarcation point between being treated as a minor rather than an adult. While all age distinctions are arbitrary, eighteen, rather than seventeen, is a more appropriate division line between adolescence and adulthood. At age eighteen, most American youngsters will have graduated from high school, joined the workforce, entered the military, or began their college careers. Also, except in a few states, eighteen is the minimum age for voting, marrying without parental consent, making a valid will, serving on a jury, and buying tobacco products. Under this proposed reorganization of the rating system, former NC-17 rated films like *Bad Lieutenant* (1992), *Henry and June* (1990), and *Showgirls* would qualify for the 18 rating while films like Louis Malle's *Damage* and Oliver Stone's *Natural Born Killers*, which required cuts to receive the R-rating, also would be assigned the 18 rating—but without subjecting the films to deletions. When the 18 category is supplemented by content information provided by the industry and film reviewers and critics, adults are in a better position to make an informed decision about their screen fare.

But how about the children? To protect youngsters from seeing restricted, adult movie fare, Hollywood should follow the British system and apply the film rating to every patron who enters the theater. The logic of the British system is quite simple. Violent films along the lines of *Reservoir Dogs* and *Natural Born Killers* and films with explicit sexual content like *Showgirls* and *Basic Instinct* are not suitable for children, with or without adult accompaniment. It defies logic to have a rating system that permits youngsters under seventeen to see an adult film simply because a parent or adult purchases the tickets. The content of an adult film does not magically change and become acceptable for viewing by youngsters simply because they are accompanied by a parent or guardian. Rather, the current Hollywood rating system encourages circumvention. To discourage youngsters from viewing an adult (18 rated) film, theaters should require a valid photo-ID (such as a school ID card) or driver's license in cases where the age of the viewer is in doubt. Whatever initial delays this procedure brings to the box office eventually will be minimized as youngsters discover that they cannot beat the system.

It is imperative today that the rating system apply to videos as well. This requirement should include theatrical films released on video, films released directly to video, and versions of theatrical films that differ from the print shown in theaters. In a technical sense, CARA does rate videos. But there are loopholes that need to be plugged. For example, a theatrical film that has been reedited for the video version is considered to be a different film from the original. Such "director's cuts" or "unrated" versions often include material omitted from the initial theatrical release. Yet this material, usually sexual or violent in nature, that CARA considered too strong for movie audiences, miraculously becomes acceptable for home viewing on videotape. Stone's R-rated theatrical film, *Natural Born Killers*, required the director to make 150 cuts which were restored when a "director's version" was released on video. Also, R-rated films such as Stone's *JFK* and the lesbian thriller *Bound* (1996) are reissued on video as "unrated" versions with additional footage cut from the original. Afterwards, these videos become available for rental to teenagers. In addition, a small percentage of films are produced for video distribution only. These do not pass through CARA's rating system but wind up on the video shelf without a classification label. These loopholes make a mockery of the entire rating process since they permit youngsters to view adult material on video that they were prohibited from seeing on the theater screen.

Box Office Enforcement

In addition to adoption of an 18 category and the application of the film's rating to every theater patron, parents must have confidence that the age classification ratings are being enforced at the box office. Unfortunately, no systematic study pertaining to the level of enforcement of film ratings at the box office has been undertaken. But Hollywood, citing as its source the National Association of Theater Owners (NATO), claims that 85 percent of the theater owners in the nation voluntarily subscribe to the rating system, which obligates the box office to make certain that children under seventeen are not admitted to an R-rated film without accompanying parent or adult guardian, or that children seventeen and under are barred from viewing an NC-17 rated film.[21] NATO insists that if underage viewers are gaining entrance to R and NC-17 rated films it is because parents and guardians are purchasing the tickets. But no hard evidence exists to support the assertion. Similarly, no solid evidence exists to refute Hollywood's contention. Most moviegoers, however, probably have seen R-rated and NC-17 rated films with an audience, including underage youngsters, some accompanied by adults and others alone or in groups. The enforcement problem is exacerbated at the suburban multiplex/cineplex theaters with their dozen or more screens. One metro New York reporter observed teenagers buying tickets to R-rated violent films, *12 Monkeys* (1995) and *Sudden Death* (1995), at a suburban multiplex where a fourteen-year old boy bought three tickets to an R-rated film for his younger siblings, ages twelve, eleven, and eight.[22] Unlike their parents, whose movie experience involved supervision at the theater if unaccompanied by an adult, today's teenagers have learned how to outwit the ticket-sellers and the theater management. Besides, what their parents saw as youngsters was much less graphic and explicit than material found in contemporary films. Parents are not without fault either, since some have failed to exercise good judgment in taking their under seventeen children to R-rated films that feature drugs (Spike Lee's *Clockers* 1995), extreme violence (Martin Scorsese's *Casino* 1995) and sexual violence (Verhoeven's *Basic Instinct* 1992). The essential question is this: If the film ratings are not honored at the theater, how can parents have confidence in the integrity of the classification system?

Censorship vs. Classification

What options exist in a democratic society like the U.S. to regulate screen sex and violence? Democratic theory provides governments with three choices. They may take a *laissez-faire* attitude towards popular entertainment, leaving the choice entirely up to market forces and public demand. Under a "hands-off" policy, films like *Natural Born Killers* and *Basic Instinct* would be free to contain any content and be shown to any audience. Government would abstain from playing any regulatory role. Although the Supreme Court's decision in *Burstyn v. Wilson* brought movies under the protection of the First Amendment, the justices have yet to endorse an absolute view of free speech. Furthermore, many politicians and parents would consider such a policy irresponsible.

On the other hand, government censorship, where the state either owns or controls the production and distribution of films, is anathema to First Amendment theory and unacceptable to a free society. Censorship, in the Blackstonian sense of "prior restraint," controls both the production and distribution of information. In a series of decisions dating back to the twenties, the U. S. Supreme Court consistently has held government efforts at censorship, except for national security reasons and the prohibition of obscene material, to be unconstitutional violations of First Amendment law.[23] Hollywood could not impose such content restrictions even if it had the desire.

But not every censorship attempt qualifies as unconstitutional prior restraint. The decision to prevent the distribution of information must be imposed by government or a related state-sponsored agency. For example, director/producer Stanley Kubrick's decision to ban his 1971 film, *A Clockwork Orange*, from distribution in the United Kingdom is not censorship in the Blackstonian sense. Similarly, if Adrian Lyne's version of *Lolita* (1998),[24] which features a romance between a twelve-year old girl and an older man, has trouble finding an American distributor even with its R-rating, this also is not censorship in the legal sense.

Common sense repudiates the *laissez-faire* position while democratic theory rejects government censorship. Whenever feasible, the U.S. prefers self-regulation over government control and this is the route taken by the film industry with the creation of the rating system. By internal policing, Hollywood has avoided government intervention. In its present form, however, the Hollywood-based age classification system fails to either shield children from adult material or reassure parents that their children are viewing films appropriate for their respective age group.

While film classification is preferable to censorship, both seek to control the visual images an audience sees on screen. The intent of censorship, however, is to dictate content and to restrict distribution. Kubrick's decision means people in the United Kingdom, adults as well as children, do not have access to *A Clockwork Orange*. On the other hand, a classification system that places films according to age suitability governs the composition of the audience. Unlike censorship, a classification system temporarily denies access to a certain age group; youngsters, therefore, are not permanently banned from the film in question but must wait to view it at a later date.

Faced with government censorship or absolute freedom, Hollywood chose self-regulation. Although the present system is flawed, the industry is right to reject Michael Medved's call for stricter guidelines and a return to the old production code.[25] Medved's characterization of most Hollywood films as being against the nuclear family, opposed to the institution of marriage, and against traditional moral values, even if accurate, implies that all movies under the code were wholesome and sanitized representations. Instead the studios continued to make gangster and sexual suggestive films, although kept within limits by code guidelines. But it also is evident that trying to make honest movies under the numerous code restrictions made filming serious subjects a course in jumping hurdles. To further refute Medved's charge, some of the most violent films being made today (*Natural Born Killers*, *Pulp Fiction*, and *Reservoir Dogs*) are being produced by independents rather than the major studios.

However, Medved has cause to be concerned about the pervasive amount of screen sex and violence in current Hollywood films, but if such content was missing from the films of the thirties and forties, its absence was due more to cultural mores than Hollywood ethics. Valenti was correct in 1968 to abolish the code and replace it with a classification system based upon audience suitability. Americans prefer self-regulation to government interference anyway, and the rating system is a way to satisfy two desires simultaneously—the absence of content control (censorship) over screen fare with the preference for viewer freedom of choice. The fault with the rating system lies not in the idea but in its implementation. Instead of abolishing the rating system or continuing it in its present form, Hollywood should adopt three British reforms: an 18 classification for adult material to replace the current R and NC-17 categories, application of the film rating to each theater patron, and more effective enforcement at the box office.

The British accept the fact that science may never provide the kind of proof necessary to establish a causal link between film viewing and bad conduct, but common sense dictates that the nation not wait until the linkage is demonstrated and the damage is done. Films and videos need to be regulated as to sexual and violent content and the classification system is the least intrusive remedy available. Whenever the BBFC is in doubt about a particular film, it exercises caution. For instance, the release of Stone's *Natural Born Killers* in the UK was delayed until an investigation was made into allegations that the film caused imitation killings in both France and the U.S. When the allegations were not substantiated, the film was given an 18 rating and released for distribution. Also, when *Money Train* came before the BBFC, the Board asked the London Transport police to review the incendiary scene which caused such controversy in the U.S. The film was certified for theatrical showing after the Transport police decided that a similar incident was unlikely to occur in the London underground.[26]

Adoption of these changes, taken together with external film reviews available in daily newspapers, magazines, religious literature, and on the Internet, would assist parents in selecting appropriate films for their children's viewing as well as provide some assurance that their choice is verified at the box office. Adults also might profit since the studios and filmmakers would enjoy greater creative freedom to make serious films in the 18 category without the threat of deletions. It is time for Hollywood to look across the Atlantic for guidance from its British cousins.

Five

HUAC and the Blacklist: The Red Scare Comes to Hollywood

"Come back, Robert Rich, wherever you are,... You screen-writing,... son-of-a-bitch!"
—Dalton Trumbo

"I could answer that [question] but if I did I would hate myself in the morning."
—Ring Lardner, Jr.

"I wouldn't know a communist if I saw one."
—Jack Warner

In a scene at the end of Irwin Winkler's 1991 film, *Guilty by Suspicion*, actor Robert DeNiro, playing a prominent film director falsely accused of being a communist, rises from his chair and shouts at the members of the congressional committee interrogating him: "Shame on you! Shame on you!" Television viewers old enough to remember the Army-McCarthy hearings might recall a similar scene where special counsel for the army, Joseph Welch, turns to the senator from Wisconsin and says: "Have you no sense of decency, sir, at long last? Have you left no sense of decency?"

Unfortunately, that final scene in *Suspicion* is the highlight of a rather lackluster film about life in post-World War II Hollywood where the real drama being played out was far more exciting and tumultuous than anything portrayed on screen. Is it mere coincidence or an industry conspiracy that *Guilty by Suspicion* is only the second major feature that Hollywood has ever made about that dark period in film history when friends turned against friends, colleagues accused other colleagues, and the studios, succumbing to the political pressure of the day, instituted an industry blacklist in an effort to prove their loyalty.[1] The one significant resistance to the HUAC hearings was the failure of the Screen Directors Guild to impose a loyalty oath on all filmmakers; a proposal that would have barred a director with communist membership or affiliation from making any more films in Hollywood.[2] *Guilty by Suspicion* touches on the effect the blacklist had on people in the industry but it cannot compare with its predecessor, *The Front* (1976), the first feature film that compelled Hollywood to confront its past. In the film, Woody Allen plays a small-time bookie who lends his name to the writings of his blacklisted friend, a tactic used by several of the Hollywood Ten. Possibly to protect itself, the film concerned blacklisting in the television industry rather than the movies; surprising since the screen credits listed half-a-dozen Hollywood artists who had suffered through the blacklist.

Forty years later, Hollywood still could not deal honestly with its past and *Suspicion* cops out and settles for a tepid melodrama instead. In the original screenplay by blacklisted writer Abraham Polonsky, the DeNiro character was supposed to be a former party member called before HUAC, a factual situation closer to the real events played out in 1947. When director Irwin Winkler changed the status of the DeNiro character from party member to non-communist, Polonsky had his name removed from the film credits.[3] Polonsky's stand may have been a victory for the integrity of the creative process, but it also was an admission that communists had worked in the film industry.

The truth of the matter is that the Hollywood film industry voluntarily resorted to blacklisting as an industrial weapon, first against the trade unions and later, against employees named during the HUAC investigations. To put the Hollywood blacklist in perspective, a summary of the post-World War II period is in order.

Cold War America, 1945–55

In retrospect, the decade following the end of World War II might best be described as another watershed in American history as the U.S. emerged as the economic and political leader of the democratic West but in a bipolarized world fraught with danger, where a wrong decision or misunderstood movement could trigger nuclear war.

That fear of total destruction hung like Damocles' Sword over the decade, leading schools to prepare children for a possible atomic attack and for people to build bomb shelters in their backyards.

Culturally, the more interesting projects of the decade were being created for the new medium of television while Hollywood retreated into producing predictable dramas, inane comedies, and musicals as the studios sought to meet the challenge of TV with gimmicks (3-D movies) and new technology (cinemascope projection). A few "social message" films were made at this time but in the wake of the prison sentences handed out to the Hollywood Ten and the blacklisting of unfriendly witnesses, the studios played it safe. However, Hollywood was not reluctant to produce a number of clearly anti-communist films. Even the fledgling medium of television aired a successful series, *I Lived Three Lives*, about a real FBI agent working undercover as a communist spy.

As 1955 approached, few heroes or villains emerged out of the predominantly verbal hostilities of the Cold War. Americans settled down in their suburban homes, content to enjoy their new consumer goods without much concern for world affairs. However, the break with the Soviet Union over numerous postwar issues provided the catalyst for the anti-communism campaign that erupted in the country. This campaign of fear was manipulated by a political opportunist named Joseph McCarthy, the U.S. senator from Wisconsin, whose wild assertions and unsubstantiated charges created an atmosphere of such terror that the term, "McCarthyism," came to define the decade.

McCarthyism and the Red Scare

The Red Scare

Actually, there were two "red scares" in American history. The first occurred after the first world war when Attorney General Palmer in the Wilson administration conducted a series of "roundup raids," led by a young FBI agent named J. Edgar Hoover, in response to the Bolshevik victory in Russia. These raids were more like the kind of "collective sweeps" common in totalitarian regimes, where the government arrests political activists, suspected radicals, and "outsiders" with the wrong religion or ethnicity and places them into one generic category labelled "subversive" and "dangerous" to national security. In the 1919 twelve-city sweep against the Union of Russian Workers, the federal government made 300 arrests, resulting in the deportation of 199. The following year, raids in thirty-three cities led to 591 deportations and over 4,000 arrests; but more than half of those arrested were subsequently released.[4] This fear of subversion from within also led to the imposition of immigration quotas in the 1920s and helped to create the atmosphere of intolerance that led to the injustice done in the Sacco and Vanzetti case. There was no middle ground in this internal war: you were either for America or against it, either a patriot or a traitor.

When the anti-communist campaign emerged after World War II, the seeds of nativism and anti-radicalism hysteria already had been planted two decades earlier, waiting to resurface when the "right person at the right time" appeared. That person turned out to be the junior senator from Wisconsin.

McCarthyism

So much has been written about Joe McCarthy that his life story is familiar to most:[5] his early childhood in Appleton, Wisconsin, his rather humble beginnings, his decision to quit school and go to work, his subsequent return to education to complete law school, and finally, his determination to enter politics. What is remarkable about McCarthy's early career is its lack of any discernable characteristics; he loses some electoral races and wins others. His military service record is also undistinguished. His first significant electoral victory comes in 1946 when he defeats the popular senator Robert LaFollette for the Republican nomination and goes on to whip his Democratic opponent in the general election. Still, after three years in the U.S. senate, McCarthy is indistinguishable from many of his colleagues: in foreign affairs, he votes for NATO, the Marshall Plan, and aid to Greece and Turkey; in domestic matters he votes for high price supports for farmers and follows the advice of Republican party leaders. With his political career languishing, McCarthy seized the opportunity presented during the traditional Lincoln Day Birthday address and turned it into political capital when he discarded his prepared speech on housing in favor of one on communism, and the rest is history. McCarthy never had a list of State Department employees who were communists nor did he have any plan in mind. He was strictly an *ad hoc* politician, grabbing headlines by announcing daily charges of new communists discovered in the government, academia, and the military. George Reedy, Lyndon Johnson's press secretary, once said contemptuously of McCarthy: "Joe couldn't find a Communist in Red Square—he didn't know Karl Marx from Groucho."[6] His accusation that there were 205 communists in the State Department would be pared down to fifty-seven and eventually reduced to four names supplied by his staff. McCarthy had a knack for manipulating the media, providing newspapers and broadcasters with tomorrow's headlines. He was as much a creation of the media as any contemporary rock star, whose entourage of reporters printed accusations without checking or verifying them first. McCarthy was instant news, driving even President Eisenhower off the front page. The senator came to dominate the news during the five years of his ascendancy (1950-54) to such an extent that historians label the period as "McCarthyism," adding a new word to the American vocabulary; a word synonymous with "the practice of publicizing accusations of political disloyalty or subversion with insufficient regard to evidence."[7]

But historian Albert Fried maintains that McCarthyism was a complex political occurrence that cannot be adequately understood by a simple explanation.[8] Instead Fried offers a tripartite definition of

McCarthyism. First, unlike previous red scares that were brief, the effects of McCarthyism lasted for decades. For example, Hollywood has only recently acknowledged the wrong done to blacklisted writers and directors by restoring screen credits to their work. The pseudonyms and "fronts" were removed from forty-seven films produced during the red scare era and replaced by the names of their creators, the blacklisted writers.[9] Second, Fried holds McCarthy responsible for creating anxiety in the hearts of liberal democrats in the 1960s because they feared a political backlash against public perception during the Cold War of any sign of weakness towards communism. This fear supposedly drove the administrations of John Kennedy and Lyndon Johnson into the Bay of Pigs and Vietnam. Finally, Fried believes McCarthyism can also be viewed in terms of the abuse of power by government and its agents, encouraging errant behavior on the part of the FBI and the Justice Department.

McCarthyism, therefore, was not nurtured in a vacuum but is best understood as a mixture of fact and fiction stimulated by public fear and intolerance. The reality was that an active American Communist Party (CPUSA) did exist, but the U.S. government only could speculate on the actual number of hardcore Stalinists dedicated to overthrowing the institutions of government by force and violence. Also, it seems fruitless to guess that there were 100,000 or 10,000 members because joiners moved in and out of the party and others attended local meetings without becoming members. What is much easier to account for in the Cold War hysteria was Soviet imperialism in eastern Europe, the fall of China, the outbreak of the Korean War, the disclosure of the Amerasis spy ring that left the Foreign Service vulnerable to accusations, the passing of atomic secrets to the Soviets by the Rosenbergs, and the subsequent Soviet explosion of a nuclear device. These political realities provided substance to the communist threat; opinion polls overwhelmingly showed that the public would allow the government to outlaw the Communist Party, force communists to register, and bar them from college and university teaching.[10] Hence, current events and public opinion lent comfort and support to McCarthy and his political allies.

As a political phenomenon, McCarthyism may be interpreted in three ways. One is to see it as the articulation of working-class intolerance, a sort of lower class reaction against intellectualism. Another is to place it within a historical line of American paranoia that exhibits a deep distrust of both elites and strangers; this suspicion is ripe for exploitation by an adept demagogue. The third explication sees his downfall after the Army-McCarthy hearings as the national rejection of extremism; simply put, McCarthy had gone too far in his accusations and had exceeded

American limits of tolerance.[11] But quite possibly Shakespeare summed it up best in *Julius Caesar* when he wrote: "The fault, dear Brutus, is not in our stars but in ourselves."

Hollywood and the Blacklist

Against Labor

Hollywood has never admitted the practice of "blacklisting," an underhanded way of depriving a person of his/her livelihood without formal acknowledgment. Those blacklisted are frequently locked out of a whole industry or line of work as employers conspire against them. It is a form of punishment without trial and Hollywood has used it twice against its own employees. Years before HUAC came to Hollywood and McCarthyism became a national phenomenon, the film industry resorted to the blacklist in an attempt to discourage unionization.

The complete story of early blacklisting in the film industry has been documented in a recent book by Mike Nielsen and Gene Mailes, *Hollywood's Other Blacklist*.[12] The authors argue that Hollywood was not only anti-communist, it was also anti-union. The industry fought unionization in the courts and on the streets.[13] Labor organizing in the entertainment industry began in the 1890s when stage hands sought to protect themselves against exploitation by theater managers. The organizing process eventually would reach the motion picture industry, involving all craft workers (carpenters, electricians, and painters) employed in film production. These laborers worked long hours under poor conditions and without benefits. While the studios employed a core of regular workers, most of the laborers had to "shape-up" everyday, similar to conditions on the waterfront. Apparently, the industry had a "sweetheart" arrangement with organized crime whereby mob bosses "fronted" for the company union, keeping wages and benefits low in return for payoffs from the studios. This is not a story likely to be seen on any movie screen.

Not until 1926 did the International Alliance of Theatrical & Stage Employees (IA) and the studios sign the first labor agreement which provided for negotiations over wages, hours, working conditions, and grievances. Referred to as the Studio Basic Agreement, it became the cornerstone for labor relations within the film industry. In the thirties, discontent over labor conditions led the professional employees—the writers, actors, and directors—to create their own unions along the lines of the medieval guilds. The more active leaders in the labor movement would be called later to appear before HUAC and to discover that their names appeared on the industry blacklist.

Labor organizing in Hollywood did not come easy or peaceful. In fact, labor unrest and violence cover three decades of Hollywood history; this was a labor-management war every bit as intense as any military engagement, with reports of arbitrary firings, beatings by goon squads, mob murders, violent clashes on picket lines, and collusion of the studios with organized crime figures like Chicago gangster Frank Nitti. It is also a story of jurisdictional strikes and clashes within the labor movement for control of the film industry. Although several strikes occurred in the thirties, labor was committed to its "no strike" pledge during World War II, a pledge that the American Communist Party endorsed against the wishes of a few labor leaders. But it was during the postwar strikes from 1945 to 1947 that union-studio confrontations became quite nasty. One 1945 strike at Warner Brothers, in particular, was so vicious that it earned the label, "Bloody Friday." Some one thousand strikers set up a mass picket line around the Warner Studios and were confronted by company security, non-strikers, and local police. The ensuing two-hour melee resulted in forty casualties as the picketers were dispersed with tear gas, clubs, and fire hoses. Screenwriter Dalton Trumbo, one of the Hollywood Ten, described the day as "fascism in action."[14] The following Monday, the picket line was broken by police and non-strikers using metal chains, clubs, and battery cables, resulting in more bloodshed. Additional injuries occurred when Warner Brothers had its security cops drop heavy bolts from a five story sound stage down on unsuspecting picketers. To make sure that strikers did not return the next day, the studio hired a private "goon squad" to beat up those who were still walking the picket line. In total, almost one hundred fifty persons required hospitalization or suffered physical injuries during the course of the strike.

But even more insidious than the physical violence was the conspiracy by the major studios to "blackball" the participating strikers by placing the names of union activists on a sheet of unsigned paper which circulated among the film studios and the independents. The Hollywood blacklist indicated that the persons named should be fired if they were working or not hired if they applied for work. For example, labor organizer Irv Hentschel, who formed the IA Progressives, lost his job because of his union activities. Under union rules, Hentschel, a machinist by trade, was listed as eligible to work but he received no calls from the studios. He finally decided to call the studios directly and was told that the word around the industry was not to hire him.[15] Hentschel's name had landed on the "invisible" blacklist.

Another tactic used by the film studios and their mobster henchmen at this time was to label union organizers and activists as "communists." This strategy aimed to discredit union advocates and isolate studio dissenters as "un-American." When the union bosses who fronted for the mob and the film studios wanted to purge the IA of local troublemakers, they filed "conduct unbecoming a loyal member of the union" charges, which required a union trial. All the IA progressives were cited as "communists," even though only one of the five local leaders was a party member at the time.[16]

The Hollywood blacklist, then, was a product of the early labor wars in the industry; this strategy of labelling foes as "communists" or "un-American" was later used during the HUAC hearings to discredit both the post-World War II peace movement and the promotion of civil rights. Discrediting a foe or a movement by labelling was still in vogue in the 1980s as evidenced by President Reagan's characterization of the nuclear freeze proponents as "communists."[17] Thus when HUAC came to town in 1947, the atmosphere in Hollywood was conducive to a public trial that would expose, and then exorcise, the evil forces that plagued the industry. The hearings provided an opportunity for the studios to silence activists, individuals to pay back personal grudges, and politicians to exploit patriotism to advance their careers.

Against Communists, Radicals, and Liberals

The HUAC investigation of the film industry occurred in three stages. Initially, HUAC met informally with studio heads and individual actors, many of whom were members of the conservative Motion Picture Alliance for the Preservation of American Ideals (the Alliance), an organization which worked with the committee to cleanse Hollywood of communists and other radicals. These were the so-called "friendly" witnesses, who either provided the committee with names of communists or reinforced the suspicion already held by the committee about particular people.[18] Often their testimony was based on rumor and gossip; the kind of hearsay evidence not permitted in a court of law. For example, Walt Disney could name the League of Women Voters as a communist group without proof or fear of cross-examination. Film stars Adolphe Menjou and Gary Cooper cited persons who associated with actor-singer Paul Robeson or who had criticized the Constitution and the government in Washington. Based on this sort of testimony, HUAC created a list of seventy-nine "named communists" scheduled to be called before the committee. In October 1947, HUAC narrowed the list to nineteen Hollywood writers, directors, producers, and actors, issuing them subpoenas to appear before the committee. Of the nineteen subpoenaed, eleven appeared (Bertolt Brecht was the last to appear, said he was not a communist, and left for Europe), leaving the ten "unfriendly" witnesses (the Hollywood Ten) to be cited for contempt and sent to prison. The final act in the drama occurred during the second round of hearings between 1951 and 1953, when HUAC subpoenaed the remaining eight names on the original list in addition to others identified during the hearings. It was during this stage that witnesses broke down (actor Larry Parks begged the committee not to force him to "name names"), others recanted (director Edward Dmytryk, one of the original Hollywood Ten admitted his communist past and named twenty-six of his colleagues as communists), while still others purged themselves of their radical pasts by reciting every conceivable name that came to memory. According to one source,[19] fifty-eight informers recited 902 names before the committee, an average of twenty-nine names per witness. If you discount duplications, the informers identified roughly 200 Hollywood artists as "communists" associated with the film industry. But those who were blacklisted probably exceeded 200 since those with valid passports left the country to seek work elsewhere and those who remained were "graylisted," that is, they found work in the industry scarce because they had supported the Hollywood Ten or worked for liberal causes. The "graylisted" were victims of "guilt by association," best illustrated on screen by the DeNiro character in *Guilty by Suspicion*. The exact number of film industry people blacklisted is unlikely to be ever publicized but estimates range between 200 and 250.[20] A few like Trumbo, Lawson, and Polonsky eventually would resume their film careers, but others were less fortunate and often forced to take odd jobs to survive. It is estimated that only ten percent of those blacklisted returned to work in the film industry.[21] Possibly the saddest aspect of the HUAC hearings was that the committee already knew about the activities of many of those named, reducing the third phase of the Hollywood investigations to a public spectacle staged by members of the committee to advance their political careers.

The Hollywood Ten: Heroes or Villains?

The drama that unfolded during the hearings of the original ten "unfriendly witnesses" was not accidental or even spontaneous. HUAC singled out the most successful Hollywood radicals to interrogate; the implication being that while the 1947 hearings were about communism, some of the politicians and friendly witnesses took the opportunity to strike a blow against aggressive trade unionism and left-liberal political activism. Membership in Popular Front, Radical, and Peace organizations automatically placed an individual under HUAC's suspicion.[22] Since the majority of the Hollywood Ten were or had been members of CPUSA, their strategy was to attack the committee directly by questioning its authority and its constitutionality under the First Amendment. Moreover, if any of them had answered "no" to the question: "Are you now or have you ever been a member of the Communist Party?" he would have been subject to perjury charges. But answering "yes" to that question would subject the witness to even more intensive questioning, increasing the chances of breaking down and "naming names." To the political left, the Hollywood Ten were heroes, standing up to demagogues and fascists. They drew support from their liberal colleagues, many of whom joined the Committee for the First Amendment and travelled to Washington for the hearings, petitioned Congress to disband HUAC, and donated their time and names to fund-raising campaigns. However, most of the studio heads, the leadership of the various screen guilds, and the members of the Motion Picture Alliance believed the Ten were everything from dangerous to naive. Actor Ward Bond, a leader in the Alliance and a close friend of John Wayne, lobbied the Motion Picture Academy not to give an Oscar to actor Jose Ferrer, whom Bond considered to be a communist well *before* the actor received a subpoena to appear before the committee.[23]

On the other hand, the informers were either praised or despised. Some former party members, like director Edward Dmytryk, finally testified because they did not want to be punished for their past associations, especially since they no longer believed in the cause.[24] Others such as screenwriter Leo Townsend admitted their communist past and repented, seeking salvation through public confession. To Albert Maltz, one of the Hollywood Ten, there was no justification for informing; he considered them all rats and he hated their guts. He went so far as to pay for a two-page advertisement to correct the *Saturday Evening Post* story on Dmytryk's change of political heart. Trumbo, on the other hand, was more conciliatory, citing both "friendly" and "unfriendly" witnesses as victims of the postwar hysteria.[25]

The Unfriendly Witnesses

The Original Eleven Witnesses

Alvah Bessie: novelist and screenwriter; author of *Bread in the Stone*; wrote screenplay for two Errol Flynn World War II movies, *Northern Pursuit* and *Objective Burma* (with Lester Cole). Supported

Spanish Republic and served in the International Brigade and later in the Second World War.

Herbert Biberman: director and producer; co-produced film *New Orleans*, and directed another film, *The Master Race*; married to blacklisted actress, Gale Sondergaard. Directed *Salt of the Earth*, a film project of the Blacklist Company.

Lester Cole: writer of forty screenplays, including *None Shall Escape* and *Blood on the Sun* and co-author of *Objective Burma*; founder of Screen Writer's Guild (SWG).*

Edward Dmytryk: noted director of such films as *Hitler's Children*, *Back to Bataan*, *Tender Comrade*, and *Crossfire*. Resumed his career after becoming an informer.*

Ring Lardner, Jr.: writer, author of screenplays, *Woman of the Year* and *Forever Amber*; co-author with Albert Maltz of film, *Cloak and Dagger*; served as officer of SWG; did not write under his own name until the 1965 script for *The Cincinnati Kid*.*

John Howard Lawson: critic and writer; author of numerous screenplays, including two Humphrey Bogart World War II films, *Action in the North Atlantic* and *Sahara*; served as president of SWG.*

Albert Maltz: novelist, playwright, and screenwriter; wrote scripts for *Destination Tokyo* and *Pride of the Marines* and the award-winning documentary, *The House I Live In*. Was "ghost writer"on film scripts for *The Robe* and *Broken Arrow*, receiving no screen credits.

Samuel Ornitz: novelist and author; wrote screenplays for *The Man Who Claimed His Head* and *Three Faces West*. After prison he turned his attention to research and writing.*

Adrian Scott: screenwriter and film producer of such films as *Crossfire* and *Murder My Sweet*; wrote script for film, *Mr. Lucky*.*

Dalton Trumbo: novelist and screenwriter; author of *Johnny Got His Gun*; wrote scripts for *Thirty Seconds Over Tokyo*, *A Guy Named Joe*, and *Our Vines Have Tender Grapes*. Active in Hollywood trade union movement and Screen Writers Guild. Wrote thirty scripts under pseudonyms during the blacklist.*

Bertolt Brecht: novelist, poet, and playwright. After HUAC appearance, fled to Europe, thereby avoiding further interrogation and prosecution.

The Remaining Eight Witnesses

Richard Collins: screenwriter for *Song of Russia*; served on the executive board of the Screen Writers Guild; turned informer during second round of HUAC hearings, 1951-53.*

Gordon Kahn: author and correspondent for *The Atlantic Monthly*; managing editor of *The Screen Writer*; served on SWG executive board.*

Howard Koch: scriptwriter for *Casablanca, Sergeant York*, and *Mission to Moscow*; served on SWG executive board.*

Lewis Milestone: film director of *All Quiet on the Western Front, A Walk in the Sun, Arch of Triumph*, and *Of Mice and Men*.

Irving Pichel: actor and director; directed *The Moon Is Down*, *OSS*, and *A Medal for Benny*.

Larry Parks: actor on verge of stardom after playing the lead in *The Jolson Story*; became informer, which ruined his film career.

Robert Rossen: author and director; wrote screenplays for World War II films, *Edge of Darkness* and *A Walk in the Sun*; directed *Body and Soul* and *Johnny O'Clock*; served as officer in SWG; also became an informer.*

Waldo Salt: screenwriter for films like *Shopworn Angel* and *Mr. Winkle Goes to War.**

*Self-confessed or named as member of the Communist Party.

The Communist Threat in Hollywood

The search for communists, real and imagined, by HUAC and McCarthy's Senate committee took a wide sweep through the unions, education, the legal profession, the military, and even the clergy. Few occupations were spared during this national campaign allegedly designed to protect America's internal security from its enemies. But how strong was the CPUSA? The estimates of party membership ranged from J. Edgar Hoover's exaggerated half-million to several thousand at the other extreme. The exact number is impossible to determine since people moved freely in and out of the party. For example, writer and director Cy Endfield, named in the 1951 HUAC hearings, attended communist meetings during the thirties and forties but actually never joined the party.[26] Were people like Endfield included? The best estimate of CPUSA membership at this time ranged anywhere from 10,000 to 100,000 members, most likely fluctuating between 30,000 to 50,000.[27] In addition to the transitory nature of party membership, left-liberals joined communists in a number of Popular Front causes against fascism during this period. Take the case of Charlie Chaplin. The actor was accused of being a communist for his leftist speeches and political activities. Amidst charges of tax evasion and paternity suits, Chaplin fled to his native England, eventually establishing residency in Switzerland. He did not return to the U.S. until 1972 when Hollywood honored him for his lifetime achievement in the cinema.[28] However, Chaplin's politics were inconsistent. He flirted with communism in the 1920s, deserted the cause in the thirties, only to return when he believed that the Soviets were the singular anti-Nazi power in Europe.[29] Should people like Chaplin have been counted in the membership figures? How many other Hollywood entertainment figures besides Chaplin pursued politically erratic paths but were counted as committed communists?

While the red scare dragnet snared many in its net, the logical question remains: why focus on the entertainment industry? What possible harm could communists do in Hollywood? There are two very plausible reasons why HUAC would find Hollywood an attractive venue. First, and of paramount importance, was the obvious publicity the discovery of a communist conspiracy in Hollywood would provide to the committee and its members. The hearings had the potential to be as dramatic as anything on the silver screen as the appearance of recognized stars lent an air of show business to the entire proceedings. As it turned out, the hearings had the effect of furthering the political career of a young California representative named Richard Nixon.[30] The second reason is that Hollywood, like the rest of the popular arts, is vulnerable to public scrutiny. The arts attract creative people, free spirits who often ignore the rules of social conventions. Artists are particularly drawn to new ideas and to critical analysis of the existing order. When the vulnerability of the arts is combined with whispered allegations by the American Legion[31] and printed accusations of publications like *Red Stars and Fellow Travelers in Hollywood*,[32] which listed some 200 Hollywood stars as "reds" and partners in a fifth column aimed at overthrowing the government, HUAC's focus on Hollywood is not surprising.

How strong was the Communist Party in Hollywood? One estimate puts total party membership around 300 between 1936 and 1949.[33] Still another calculation identifies 145 screenwriters as party members, the largest number of active members during this period, with some fifty to sixty actors, fifteen to twenty producers and directors, and some sixty to ninety members working on the backlots or in studio offices.[34]

Regardless of their number, how influential were they? Their greatest effectiveness seemed to be in the trade union movement and in the screenwriters guild. HUAC focused in on the latter group since sixteen of the first nineteen witnesses were writers. This was likely due to the misguided assumption that the scripts written by these writers were tainted with communist propaganda or, at minimum, contained material dangerous to the social order.

In reality, however, the old studio system operated like the American system of checks and balances; all film scripts were subject to internal review by studio heads and producers. Screenwriters never had the last word. As Dorothy B. Jones confirmed in her study of film content, it was virtually impossible to incorporate Marxist ideology into films produced by the major studios because

> … the very nature of the film-making process which divides creative responsibility among a number of different people and which keeps ultimate control of content in the hands of top studio executives; the habitual caution of moviemakers with respect to film content; and the self-regulating practices of the motion picture industry . . . prevented such propaganda from reaching the screen in all but possibly rare instances.[35]

If HUAC considered the films themselves to be "subversive" or "dangerous," why did the committee reject Dalton Trumbo's offer to review eighteen of his film scripts, including several written for movies on the Second World War?[36] Furthermore, if the films that involved the Hollywood Ten are subject to content analysis, the review would demonstrate that the majority of films included subjects that were definitely nonpolitical. For example, between 1929 and 1949, the Hollywood Ten participated in the making of 159 feature films in the following subject categories:

> 45 were a combination of biography and historical films, romances, love stories, and comedies;
> 28 were murder, mystery, and espionage films;
> 23 were war or military service films;
> 22 were social message films;
> 17 were westerns and action/adventure films;
> 15 were gangster, crime, and prison films.[37]

Without a doubt, the bulk of the films made by the Hollywood Ten were typical Hollywood entertainment fare, free from political ideology.

History has brought the HUAC hearings into perspective. The committee was not interested in the films per se because if they had been, the studio heads would have been held accountable rather than the writers, directors, and actors. Films like *Song of Russia* and *Mission to Moscow*, for instance, were considered by friendly witnesses to be pro-Red. But even if written or directed by hardcore Stalinists, they were made with the blessing of MGM and Warner Brothers. Louis Mayer told HUAC he made *Song of Russia* because "Russia was an ally. It seemed the patriotic thing to do."[38] And Jack Warner supposedly agreed to do *Mission to Moscow* at the request of the Roosevelt administration; a film so kind to the Soviet leader that American parents might be tempted to recruit "Uncle Joe" Stalin as godfather for their children.[39] Furthermore, both these films as well as the pro-Soviet movie scripted by Lillian Hellman, *The North Star*, had to be cleared through the Office of War Information. However, neither Mayer nor Jack Warner's loyalty was questioned at the time. Was it merely ironic or deliberate that two of

HUAC's friendliest witnesses, director Sam Wood (first president of the Motion Picture Alliance) and actor Gary Cooper, both involved in *For Whom the Bell Tolls*, the pro-Republican film of the Spanish Civil War that was based on the Hemingway novel, never had their loyalty or patriotism questioned? Clearly, film content was not what most concerned HUAC.

Even had the Hollywood Ten and the other unfriendly witnesses been committed Stalinists who attended every cell meeting and followed every communist command, the content of their films under the old studio system required approval at the executive level. It is now clear that the Ten and the other blacklistees were singled out because they posed a threat to the industry due to their union and off-screen political activities rather than for the content that appeared on the screen. Possibly Ronald Reagan, head of the Screen Actors' Guild at the time, hit the nail on the head when he characterized the risk of having communists and subversives in the film industry in these terms: "The danger is not what is on the screen. It is what these people do behind the scenes to gain power in organizations to further their beliefs."[40] Thus, the 1947 HUAC hearings in Hollywood and those held from 1951 to 1953 were intended by the committee, with the collaboration of the film studios and the Motion Picture Alliance, to put an end to what they considered to be radical unionism and leftist-liberal politics.

The Impact of the Red Scare and the Blacklist

Personal Harm

The Hollywood hearings had personal and professional repercussions, both on the informers and those they named. But which group had the heaviest burden to bear? In economic terms, all the unfriendly witnesses suffered personal loss and endured economic hardship through blacklisting. The informers, on the other hand, carried the mark of Judas around with them throughout the remainder of their careers. Trumbo was right when he characterized the informers and the blacklistees as victims because both were shunned by former friends and despised by their enemies. Blacklisted actors, directors, and producers were hardest hit because they were visible to their enemies; however some writers such as Trumbo, Michael Wilson, and Ned Young could still work under pseudonyms. Even though they were paid for their scripts, these blacklisted writers worked without recognition. Furthermore, blacklisting was open-ended; there was no deadline or date when redemption began and careers resumed. Actress Lee Grant spent sixteen years on the blacklist while actress Gale Sondergaard, Herbert Biberman's wife, went seven years without a paid acting engagement. Meanwhile, turning informer did not provide actor Larry Parks with salvation; he played a supporting role in only one major Hollywood film after his HUAC appearance. His actress wife, Betty Garrett, also found work in the industry hard to come by.[41] Blacklisted director Abraham Polonsky would not direct another film for twenty years while screenwriter Samuel Ornitz deserted the film industry altogether.[42] Others, like Albert Maltz, had screen projects pulled out from underneath them. Maltz was hired by Frank Sinatra, who had purchased the film rights, to do the screenplay for *The Execution of Eddie Slovak* (1974), a story about an American deserter in World War II. Maltz claims that he did considerable research for the film script and even had a first draft ready for review when Sinatra fired him, presumably because of intense pressure from the Motion Picture Alliance and the Kennedy White House.[43]

Those writers who were unable to find work even with pseudonyms and those who were unsuccessful in locating "fronts" to submit their scripts to the studios, resorted to any kind of work just to survive. Ned Young was forced to work as a bartender, salesman, and junkman; meanwhile others left the country to pursue their film work in England (Joseph Losey, Carl Foreman, Adrian Scott), France (Jules Dassin, Paul Jarrico, John Howard Lawson), and Mexico (Maltz, Trumbo). Still others sought to continue their professional lives by forming a production firm, the Blacklist Company, to make their own films. But after losing considerable money on their first production, *Salt of the Earth*, the company abandoned the attempt.

There were personal casualties as well. Ned Young's wife, blacklisted along with her husband, committed suicide after years of depression. There is some speculation that at least a half-dozen Hollywood deaths, including actors John Garfield, J. Edward Bromberg, and Canada Lee, can be attributed directly to the hearings and the blacklist.[44] There were marriage breakups and divorces and the effect the blacklist had on the children of those on the list only recently has been recognized. In gatherings in Los Angeles and New York called for the purpose of filming a documentary on the subject,[45] the children of the blacklist, now middle-aged, offered bittersweet recollections of their parents with occasional reproaches against their accusers. Julie Garfield described the studio heads as "racists" who went after her father because he was Jewish; Joshua Mostel claimed his father, Zero, was apolitical, if anything he likely was an anarchist; Martha Randolph told how her father was allowed to work in the theater but not on radio or in film; Liz Schwartz talked about her mother's suicide; others recalled being prohibited to play with or socialize with the children of informers, still others had memories of fleeing California in the middle of the night and hiding out in desert motels. Although their evidence is largely anecdotal, these personal stories reveal a second generation scarred by the blacklist. Thus the blacklist continues to touch the lives of its victims to this day.[46]

Professional Consequences

Many of the participants in the HUAC proceedings—friendly witnesses, informers, unfriendly witnesses—not only knew each other but worked together on film projects, belonged to the same guilds, and occasionally, joined the same Popular Front organizations. Maybe their political and working association explains the depth of the bitterness held by the unfriendly witnesses towards the informers.

The personal conflict between informer and unfriendly witness ultimately moved from the congressional hearing room to the big screen and is best epitomized in the dispute between film director Elia Kazan and playwright Arthur Miller. Witnesses before HUAC were limited to three choices: talk as the friendly witnesses did or remain silent, which was the tactic of the unfriendly witnesses. The third option, a compromised position whereby the witness speaks about him/herself but not about others, is best exemplified by the testimony of Lillian Hellman. Kazan, however, was a willing witness before HUAC, talking freely about the political activities of himself and his colleagues. Miller, on the other hand, took the same position as Hellman, namely, that it was honorable to talk about oneself but not about others.[47]

Prior to the hearings, Kazan and Miller talked of collaborating on a film about longshoreman and their life on the docks. When Kazan named "names" before HUAC, Miller broke off their relationship. Kazan, meanwhile, went ahead with the project, which became the critically acclaimed film, *On the Waterfront* (1954). Kazan persuaded Marlon Brando to play the main character, the washed-up fighter, Terry Malloy, who through the efforts of the local priest (Karl Malden) and the love of a good woman (Eva Marie Saint), turns state informer against the organized crime mob that controls the waterfront. In a dramatic ending, Terry receives a vicious beating from the mob but still leads the strikers back to work against the wishes of the crime boss (Lee J. Cobb). In *On the Waterfront*, the informer is transformed into a hero by cooperating with the authorities. Kazan used the film to justify his decision to name names.[48] Meanwhile, Miller countered with a play about the Salem witch trials, *The Crucible*,[49] which was clearly intended to demonstrate the evils associated with paranoia and public hysteria. In his play, Miller argues that the informer is a villain whose action supports and encourages wrongdoing.

Because Miller's play took place in seventeenth-century New England, it could be viewed as a historical recreation. But in order to directly confront Kazan's informer as hero, Miller wrote *A View from the Bridge*; a play about the Brooklyn waterfront that subsequently became a motion picture. In the Miller version of *On the Waterfront*, Eddie Carbone, a longshoreman who lives with his wife and his sister's daughter Catherine, agrees to hide illegal immigrants (called "submarines"), from the immigration authorities. Eddie understands the law of the waterfront: act deaf, dumb, and blind. But when Eddie takes in these two illegals, all the pieces for a Greek tragedy are in place. When the younger illegal falls in love with Catherine, Eddie becomes jealous because he also harbors suppressed feelings of affection for his niece. These feelings lead Eddie to inform, to break the unwritten code of silence on the waterfront by reporting the location of the two submarines to immigration. It is this act of betrayal that the Miller play dramatizes; this treacherous deed results in Eddie's death because there is no honor in informing.

The Kazan-Miller clash was but one piece of personal drama played out as a result of the HUAC hearings and the subsequent blacklisting. Although neither Kazan nor Miller had their careers destroyed by the blacklist, each suffered from its effects. Miller felt betrayed by a friend and colleague; Kazan's career endured but not without retribution from his peers in the industry who denied him professional recognition.[50] As Dalton Trumbo might have said, both Kazan and Miller were victims of the Hollywood blacklist.

The blacklist was instituted to appease the government; a familiar strategy previously utilized by the industry in the twenties and thirties when the studio heads agreed to internal regulation in order to ward off government censorship. Then in the fifties, the industry sought to impress the government with its patriotism by refusing to hire named "communists" and by insisting that anyone named by HUAC pass a loyalty clearance before being employed.

The studios also sought to illustrate their allegiance by making over forty anti-communist films between 1949 and 1953.[51] Films like *The Red Menace* (1949), *I Married a Communist* (1950), *I Was a Communist for the FBI* (1951), *My Son John* (1952), and *Big Jim McLain* (1952) were blatant pieces of patriotic propaganda that would hardly qualify for Academy Awards in any era. In *The Red Menace*, for example, an ex-serviceman joins a local communist party cell with the assistance of a seductive woman. If all Americans were as naive as the main character, the U.S. would have voted for the communist party in 1952 instead of

Eisenhower. Similarly, the film *Big Jim McLain* has John Wayne smashing a communist cell in Hawaii, thereby preventing a takeover of the island. Actually, the film adhered to a formula plot that would have enabled the producers to have substituted the Nazis, Japanese, or cattle rustlers for the communists without too many script changes. It so happened that the communists were the "bad guys" of the day and Hollywood capitalized on the current mood in the country.

Few films dared to criticize the anti-communist message directly. Instead a scattering challenged the communist paranoia and the effects of McCarthyism allegorically, expressing their condemnation of HUAC and the blacklist in plots that dealt with subjects ranging from space aliens to westerns. *The Thing* (1951), for example, a film about a frozen creature that comes to life and threatens an Arctic expedition, was interpreted as a metaphor for the spate of communist invasion movies; one scriptwriter insisted that the evil creature, *The Thing*, represented McCarthy(ism).[52] Another film released in 1951, *The Day the Earth Stood Still*, concerned a flying saucer that lands in Washington, D.C. The two aliens aboard have come to the nation's capital on a peace mission, to warn planet Earth against a global nuclear war. Of course, no one in government pays any attention to the peace message and, subsequently, events turn ugly as the alien leader is shot due to public fear and ignorance. Eventually the aliens return to their own planet. Certainly, the pro-peace message of *The Day the Earth Stood Still* was a daring theme in an age when atom bombs and nuclear weapons were part of military strategy and when release of the film coincided with McCarthy's announcement about communists in the State Department.[53] Meanwhile, another film, *Invasion of the Body Snatchers* (1956), dealt with giant seed pods that take over the bodies of people and turn them into cold, soulless creatures similar to the Soviets. Supposedly the pods represented the three dominant forces of the fifties: conformity, paranoia, and alienation. The film was designed to confront America for exhibiting similar forces during the Cold War.[54] Even a Nicholas Ray western, *Johnny Guitar* (1953), which featured a guitar-playing drifter (actor Sterling Hayden, HUAC informer) in the middle of a town feud between two women, saloon-owner Joan Crawford, who befriends outlaws, and upright citizen and banker, Mercedes McCambridge. Was the film intended to be a western parody or a political allegory about McCarthyism? If you accept the latter interpretation, then the outlaws represent the communists, Hayden is the former communist, Crawford the fellow-traveler, and McCambridge the McCarthy-clone who manipulates the townspeople into "naming names," converting their fear and ignorance into an ugly lynch mob.[55] When the mob turns on the Crawford character, the script gives the actress an opportunity to address the crowd and deliver a speech against the making of false accusations (friendly witnesses and informers) and against the making of guilty judgments on the basis of the company she keeps (guilt by association). These films, at least, reveal that there were a few in the industry who tried to counter the propaganda of the studios' anti-communist films.

Film Content

Except for a handful of serious films that confronted American racism and prejudice, Hollywood played it safe in the fifties, concentrating on musicals, Doris Day–Rock Hudson romantic comedies, crime thrillers, and westerns. This rather bland film diet is not so surprising since some of the very best Hollywood writers were on the blacklist. Between 1938 and the 1947 HUAC hearings, the eight major Hollywood studios released over 3100 films, about 600, or one-fifth, were scripted by radicals or leftists. It is this group of writers who combined to win four Oscars and receive nineteen Academy Award nominations. No wonder the studios considered them a valuable commodity, paid them well (Dalton Trumbo received $3000 per week from MGM while Ring Lardner, Jr. received a salary of $2000 per week from Twentieth-Century Fox), and agreed to let some of them write under pseudonyms or use "fronts" to submit their work.[56]

Hollywood released more than 2500 movies during the decade of the fifties; fewer than one percent were serious dramas that confronted the important social problems of the time. The witch-hunt in Hollywood had succeeded in silencing dissent and stifling creativity. It was not until the mid-sixties that Hollywood returned to the exploration of contemporary social issues.[57] Two decades would have to pass before the film industry recovered from the wounds inflicted by the red scare hysteria.

Six

Reel Politics: American Politicians on Screen

"The sad duty of politics is to establish justice in a sinful world."
—Reinhold Niebuhr

"It could probably be shown by facts and figures that there is no distinctly native American criminal class except Congress."
—Mark Twain

"If it wasn't for graft, you'd get a very low type of people in politics."
—from *The Great McGinty*

"I haven't committed a crime. What I did was fail to comply with the law." —David Dinkins, former Mayor of New York

"Only two things can wreck a political career in this town [Washington]—being caught with a live boy or a dead girl."
—from *True Colors*

Ehrlichman: "We don't mind being called crooks, but not stupid crooks."
Nixon: "That's right. We know we'll never convince them on our morality, but do they think we're that dumb?" —The New Nixon Tapes

There is a marvelous scene at the end of Robert Redford's *The Candidate* (1972) where he is sitting in his hotel suite surrounded by staff and friends in celebration of his election to the U.S. Senate. In walks his father (Melvyn Douglas), the former Governor of California and consummate wheeler-dealer. Douglas approaches Redford, who is seated on the bed looking rather glum, and with a quizzical grin that runs from ear to ear, says: "Congratulations, son. You're a politician now." If there is one scene in all the films on American politics that would discourage, if not totally destroy, the interest of young people to run for political office, this is it! The scene's cynicism offends two vital concepts in a democratic society; first, the notion that the electorate believes politicians hold office as a public trust and second, that politics is an honorable and commendable profession. Congress ought to make it unlawful for any American youngster to view this scene on the ground that it could destroy whatever is left of the civic virtue. Does the scene represent reality or Hollywood's version of the U.S. Congress?

On second thought, Hollywood has not always been kind to the presidency either. Recent Hollywood presidents, such as Bill Pullman fighting alien invaders in *Independence Day* (1996) or Harrison Ford socking it to hijackers who have taken over his plane in *Air Force One* (1997) reinforce a macho image that defies credibility as well as historical accuracy. Americans expect their presidents to reside in Camelot, but also mingle with common folk, be compassionate but act tough against external enemies, be human but not too seriously flawed. The reel presidents—Pullman and Ford—however, are glamorous heroes, creative inventions rather than real people. Most American presidents have understood the difference between fact and fantasy, but occasionally a Nixon or a Reagan is inspired by the fictions on the screen: Nixon bombing Cambodia the day after viewing *Patton* (1970), Reagan watching *Rambo: First Blood, Part II* (1985), to reinforce his "evil empire" foreign policy against the old Soviet Union.[1]

Since Hollywood deals in illusions and fantasies, the industry should find politics an attractive partner in the entertainment business. Not true. Only a small percentage of the 150,000 films turned out by Hollywood over the past century actually feature American politics as the primary subject and politicians as the central characters. Historically, the studios decided that serious films on politics would not fill theater seats. Whenever a studio disregarded the conventional wisdom and made a film depicting American politics, either the finished product was accorded a bland treatment or the plot took liberties with the facts and the historical record. Moreover, in films that attempt to present serious domestic or foreign policy issues, the script is likely to focus on the personal foibles of the political characters, dwell on their private lives rather than the actual workings of the legislative process, and ignore the means by which the president reaches a policy decision.[2] Seldom does the industry portray evil politicians as expressions of institutional wrongdoing or virtuous politicians as defenders of constitutional principles.[3]

Hollywood's reluctance, however, does not mean that the film industry has ignored American politics completely. In fact, several silent films, e.g., *The Senator* (1915), dealt with politics but after the twenties

Hollywood's interest in the subject waned only to be revived again in the thirties and sixties. Hollywood preferred political biographics in the 1930s, including three on Lincoln. In the sixties, four feature films (*The Best Man*, *Dr. Strangelove*, *Fail Safe*, and *Seven Days in May*) released in 1964 centered on the presidency. Hollywood returned to the presidency in the 1990s with no less than six features placing the Oval Office center stage. These screen presidents are: in love, *The American President*; whiny womanizers, *Absolute Power*; macho patriots, *Air Force One*; dark figures on the verge of madness, *Nixon*; wimpy impostors, *Dave*; and political hacks, *My Fellow Americans*.

Despite these bursts of periodic interest, Hollywood has avoided the serious treatment of American politicians because ideological or partisan politics is bad box office. The film industry's primary commitment to profit mandates that political subject matter be avoided, but whenever attempted, diluted. Essentially, what happens in Hollywood is that if politics is the central story line, it serves as a framework for more familiar plots, such as assassination thrillers or as an ambiance for love and romance.

American Politics on Screen

When Hollywood enters the world of politics, it often does so through the back door. Political activities in feature films frequently express individual behavior that is motivated by self-interest; bad politicians act out of greed and ambition while good politicians act in response to the deeds of bad politicians. Few act out of a deep commitment to democratic principles. Observe the intentions of the screen politicians below and draw your own conclusion.

Political Campaigns and Conventions

Political elections provide scriptwriters with a dramatized event around which to develop a narrative that can be melodramatic, exciting, and funny. Some of Hollywood's finest political films have depicted the electoral process. Hollywood became interested in political elections as screen fare as early as the 1930s with the release of several films on campaign politics, including *Judge Priest* (1934), a star vehicle for humorist Will Rogers. This early John Ford film has Rogers playing a small town judge in 1890s Kentucky, dispensing justice and wisdom equally from his courtroom seat and his front porch. Although up for reelection, Rogers' judge seldom leaves his home or works up a sweat campaigning. The film is best viewed for contrast with contemporary elections dominated by high technology and media promotion.

Hollywood took a hiatus from the political campaign film until the post-World War II era when three features, *The Dark Horse* (1946), *The Farmer's Daughter* (1947), and *State of the Union* (1948) hit theater screens. The *Dark Horse* is a serious political drama about a veteran of the Second World War who runs for city alderman only to discover that the local political machine is exploiting his war record for personal gain. In *The Farmer's Daughter*, a young Swedish woman (Loretta Young) goes to work as a maid for a wealthy family and falls in love with the son (Joseph Cotten), a Congressman. Billed as a comedy in the advertisements, most of the screen action concerns the budding romance between the two stars. When a local congressman dies in office, Young decides to run for the vacant seat, even though her opponent is supported by Cotten's family. She is successful despite an attempted smear by the opposition. However, the script avoids most of the hard work done in a real election. The film's political campaign consumes about five minutes of screen time; a majority of the political events occur off-camera and the film's most impressive political speech is given by a supporting actor rather than the candidate herself.

Frank Capra's *State of the Union* features Spencer Tracy and Katherine Hepburn in one of their nine films together. The plot has Tracy playing Grant Matthews, a successful and idealistic industrialist, persuaded by an ambitious newspaper owner to run for the presidential nomination on the Republican ticket. His estranged wife, Mary (Hepburn), reluctantly agrees to accompany her husband on the campaign trail. Except for one or two unnecessary scenes in an airplane, the film sticks to the business of electioneering, which allows the major characters to make speeches expressing Capra's liberal philosophy and general belief in the wisdom and essential decency of the American people. When Grant discovers that he is being used by the party bosses, he withdraws from the race but not from politics. Reunited with his wife at film's end, he intends to go to the convention and influence the selection of the Republican candidate. The film is best remembered today for the one-liner, "Politics makes strange bedfellows."

During the days of the Red Scare, Hollywood was too preoccupied with the HUAC hearings and Cold War themes to concern itself with political elections. But the industry returned to the subject again in the sixties. On the surface, John Ford's *The Man Who Shot Liberty Valance* (1962) appears to be a traditional western with John Wayne playing rancher-gunman Tom Doniphon. But the story quickly shifts to the other major character, a tenderfoot Eastern lawyer named Ransom Stoddard

(James Stewart), who, in contrast to Doniphon's resort to violence, believes the West can be civilized by adherence to the rule of law rather than the gun. Of course, when Stoddard is beaten and threatened by the town bully and outlaw, Liberty Valance (Lee Marvin), it is Doniphon who comes to his rescue in the climactic shootout. The townfolks, however, believe it was Stoddard's gun that rid the community of Valance; an act that makes Stoddard the town hero and catapults him into politics, first as a representative to the territorial legislature and later as one of the state's U.S. Senators. Ford intends Stoddard's political career to parallel the development of the West from a lawless frontier into statehood and civilization. While Stoddard goes east to civilized Washington, Doniphon remains in the West. Doniphon's death signals the passing of the Old West as well; its future development delivered into the hands of businessmen, railroaders, shopkeepers, and law-abiding citizens like Ransom Stoddard. The fact that Stoddard profited from a lie should not be overlooked; his political career was built on a fabrication he benefitted from because he chose not to disclose the truth to the electorate. Released at a time when campaign managers, public relation specialists, and media experts had begun to market candidates as commodities to be sold to the public like commercial products, Ford's film is a reminder of the significant role that myth plays in American politics.

The first Hollywood entry into convention politics, *The Best Man* (1964), was based on the Gore Vidal play. The action revolves around the politics of a presidential nominating convention. The film studios, apparently, were so apprehensive about offending Democrats or Republicans that the convention depicted in *The Best Man* remains unidentified. The narrative has two candidates seeking the endorsement of the incumbent president, who is dying of cancer. William Russell (Henry Fonda), the principled Secretary of State, is seeking the nomination against rival candidate, the ambitious and unscrupulous U.S. Senator, Dan Cantwell (Cliff Robertson)—the president's endorsement will virtually guarantee the nomination. Which one will the president select? That question lies at the heart of the drama because each candidate has a flawed past—Russell's bout with depression raises questions of his competency under stress while Cantwell's homosexual affair fosters concerns about his electability. In the end, the president selects neither, throwing his support instead behind a third candidate who goes on to win the nomination. *The Best Man* is rich in backroom convention politics as it explores the characteristics that make for an "ideal" presidential candidate. It also proved prescient since during the 1972 campaign, Senator Tom Eagleton's vice presidential candidacy was derailed when the media revealed that he had suffered a nervous breakdown and received electroshock therapy.

Of the more recent films about political campaigning, Robert Redford's *The Candidate* (1972) is usually singled out for acclamation. Scripted by a former staffer for Eugene McCarthy's 1968 presidential race, the film concerns a liberal antipoverty lawyer, Bill McKay (Redford), who is the son of the former governor of California. When the Democrats ask him to run against the incumbent Republican U.S. senator, McKay is reluctant to join the race. He finally consents after receiving assurance that he can discuss the real issues and run his own campaign, even if doing so will guarantee his defeat. Since he is expected to lose, McKay enters the race discussing the issues to bored audiences. But when he outperforms his opponent in a televised debate and his election chances improve according to the polls, McKay relinquishes more and more of the control over his campaign to his managers who exploit his good looks and charisma. On the campaign trail, McKay begins to spout ready-made slogans and cliches while he accepts the support of his father's old cronies. To illustrate that he has become a media-managed candidate, the film contains a scene at a women's luncheon where McKay's speech is reduced to the apology: "I'm sorry, ladies, that I ate all the shrimp." McKay smiles, the women laugh. Removed from his own ideals, McKay has succumbed to the manipulation of his campaign managers. He wins the election and as the reinvented U.S. senator-elect in the fade-out scene, McKay asks his manager, "What do we do now?" Criticized as lacking substance,[4] *The Candidate*, on the contrary, warns the audience of the pitfalls of contemporary electioneering where superficiality is preferred over hard content, personal appeal is celebrated over intelligence and ethical principles, and thirty-second campaign sound bites are favored over detailed analysis of complex issues. Can an image-created candidate win a national election? After the two terms of Ronald Reagan, is there anyone today who would wager against a successful race by a Redford, a Harrison Ford, or an Alec Baldwin? The successful election of neophyte politician, pro-wrestler Jessie Ventura to the governorship of Minnesota in 1998 reminds us that politics is as much a celebrity game today as popular entertainment.

Actor Tim Robbins depicted a nineties version of a political campaign in his film *Bob Roberts* (1992). Whereas Redford's film was a commercial and critical success, *Bob Roberts* failed at the box office. Robbins, who wrote the script and served as director, plays the title character, a self-made, guitar-playing right-wing conservative millionaire from Pennsylvania, who runs for the U.S. Senate. Filmed in mock documentary style, *Bob Roberts* unfolds as a diary of a political campaign, from the initial announcement to election day results. Roberts' campaign slogan is PRIDE, which he displays on his motorbus as he tours the state campaigning against drugs, sexual promiscuity, and wasteful social programs. On the surface, Roberts is a sincere charmer who preaches family values and national pride but off-camera is prone to dirty campaign tricks. When a local reporter threatens to expose him as a fraud, Roberts and his staff plot a fake assassination attempt on the candidate's life. The strategy works as the reporter is killed, but Roberts supposedly is seriously wounded and confined to a wheelchair. However, in the ironic conclusion, Roberts is seen tapping his feet under the blanket that covers his legs as he celebrates his election victory with a song. The film's failure at the box office may have been due to its portrayal of a gullible electorate; an assessment too harsh for American audiences to accept.

The latest entries in the political campaigning mold include Mike Nichols' *Primary Colors* (1998) and Warren Beatty's *Bulworth* (1998). *Primary Colors*, based on the book by political reporter Joe Klein, does not hide the fact that it is a re-creation of the Clinton 1992 presidential campaign. *Bulworth*, however, is different. In this film, Beatty plays Bulworth, a despondent U.S. senator whose life changes after he falls in love with a political activist. He changes campaign strategy in his re-election bid and adopts rap music to express his ideas on campaign financing and race relations. The film has many of the attributes of *Bob Roberts*, particularly in using comedy to deliver the political message. Knowing Beatty's past involvement with the Democratic Party and his work on the McGovern, Bobby Kennedy, and Gary Hart campaigns, however, cannot compensate for the fact that the film is primarily intended as entertainment.

Probably the most realistic presentation of a political campaign remains *Tanner '88* (1988), the result of the collaboration of director Robert Altman and cartoonist Gary Trudeau. The film has never been shown in theaters but aired originally as a miniseries on cable television. *Tanner '88* runs six hours and depicts in documentary style the story of the 1988 presidential race from the New Hampshire primary to the convention in Atlanta as viewed through the eyes of one Democratic hopeful, Jack Tanner. Tanner is a divorced former congressman with a college-aged daughter and a lover whom he meets occasionally for trysts while on the campaign trail. Despite his academic credentials (he holds a Ph.D. in economics), Tanner is very much a manufactured candidate—the product of his campaign staff. Similar in style to Altman's earlier film, *Nashville* (1975), *Tanner '88* weaves a rich tapestry of American electioneering that includes attempted assassinations, dirty tricks, media-styled campaign slogans, and appearances by real presidential candidates

Bob Dole, Gary Hart, Bruce Babbitt, and Pat Robertson. Whether the series impressed viewers as the real campaign or whether some voters decided to play a prank, the fact remains that the fictitious Jack Tanner actually received write-in votes in the November election. By interweaving Tanner together with the real candidates in the New Hampshire and Tennessee primaries, Altman was able to depict the grungy work of running a major campaign along with the gaffs and disasters. For instance, when Tanner is speaking to an outdoor rally in New Hampshire he is upstaged by a group of snowmobilers. Later, when he attends a quilting party with his daughter, the women are more interested in his daughter than in his prepared remarks. As the campaign moves towards the convention and Democratic candidates begin to drop out of the race, Tanner's remaining opponents are Michael Dukakis and Jesse Jackson. In an effort to influence convention delegates, Tanner announces his Cabinet choices, which include, among others, Ralph Nader, Gloria Steinheim, Barbara Jordan, and Robert Redford. But when Jackson releases his votes to Dukakis at the convention, Tanner's chances for the nomination are squashed. At film's end, Tanner turns down a Cabinet post in the Dukakis administration while he ponders a presidential race as an independent. Taking full advantage of the expanded running time, Altman produced a commercial film on political campaigns that is eclipsed only by documentaries like *The War Room* and *A Perfect Candidate*.

Political Machines

Hollywood movies about political machines usually depict two very different attitudes about politics: either the films portray the machine as a monolithic force that controls votes and remains in power through corrupt deals made by self-serving politicians and justified on grounds of political necessity or the existing machine becomes the target of reform politicians who overthrow it only to succumb to the temptations provided by absolute power.

But what exactly is a political machine? Most political scientists would agree that any acceptable definition would have to include a political party organization, longevity, and the exchange of patronage and social services for election day votes. In the U.S. the machine was primarily associated with big cities and with the arrival of an immigrant population that required jobs, housing, and assistance with the English language. Ellis Island became the primary arrival point for immigrants from Europe, who were met at the Customs House by Tammany Hall bosses and helped with the assimilation process into their new environment. In exchange for this assistance, immigrants were asked to vote for

Democratic candidates, an arrangement which kept Tammany Hall in control of New York City for virtually eighty years. George Washington Plunkitt, ward boss for the city's Fifteenth Assembly District, revealed the secret of Tammany's power: understand human nature, familiarize yourself with the local neighborhood, and make government friendly and personal.[5]

Films that depict a cynical view of machine politics include Preston Sturges's *The Great McGinty* (1940) and *The Glass Key* (1942), which is based on the Dashiel Hammett novel. The Sturges film is a satirical look at big city politics with a moral message that honesty in politics does not pay. On the other hand, *The Glass Key* depicts both reformers and machine bosses as double-crossing, unscrupulous politicians, reducing political reform to changing personnel but not policies. Although Frank Capra's *Meet John Doe* (1941) has a happy ending, the film's message is that the masses are easily swayed by sentimentality and democratic cliches, weaknesses that leave the people vulnerable to domination by political machines.

Can there be a decent political boss? Novelist Edwin O'Connor thought so in *The Last Hurrah* (1958), which John Ford transferred to the big screen. In this paean to Irish politics, Spencer Tracy plays Frank Skeffington, a Boston political boss who resembles the charismatic Beantown Mayor Frank Curley. Skeffington is a wily old politician, ruthless yet charming, whose power base rests on personal favors and debts collected at election time. Skeffington is the consummate politician, even campaigning at the wake of Jocko, a not particularly admired constituent. Skeffington makes sure, however, that a crowd shows up at the wake to pay tribute to Jocko, who now has more friends in death than he ever had in life. But personal politics are no match for a sophisticated television crusade by his opponent in the new era of media-based campaigns. Skeffington loses his bid for a fourth term, a victim of mediated politics. While *The Last Hurrah* is a nostalgic and romantic examination of machine politics, it does serve as an indictment of contemporary media-created politicians. After viewing *The Last Hurrah*, audiences may wonder whether the replacement of the political machine by reform candidates without character or concern for individual welfare actually has improved the public good.

Two decent politicians who are corrupted by machine politics turn up in *All the King's Men* (1949) and *City Hall* (1996). The former film was based on Robert Penn Warren's Pulitzer Prize winning novel and transferred to the screen with the message that unchecked power can destroy political reformers. Warren's novel is a thinly disguised biography of the political career of Louisiana governor, Huey Long. In the film version,

Broderick Crawford plays Willie Stark, a poor backwoods Southern lawyer who gains political power through a populist attack on state corruption. But once in office, Stark becomes as ruthless and corrupt as the political machine he ousted. Although Stark sets up a fascist government complete with thugs and goons and resorts to blackmail, beatings, and even murder, he remains popular with the masses because of his building projects, which create jobs, result in school improvements, and advance social programs. Stark's popularity reaches its peak after an unsuccessful impeachment attempt by the state legislature. Like the real Huey Long, Stark has his eye on the White House but an assassin's bullet cuts his political career short. After two hundred years of American politics, Huey Long's regime in 1930s Louisiana came closest to homegrown fascism and a threat to democratic state government.[6]

In the second film, Al Pacino plays a beleaguered mayor in *City Hall* (1996), scripted by Ken Lipper, former deputy mayor in the Ed Koch administration, and filmed on location in New York City. *City Hall* relates the story of Mayor John Pappas (Pacino), a popular and liberal mayor, who has had to make deals with the political bosses, especially Frank Anselmo's (Danny Aiello) Kings County political leader, in order to rebuild the city, create jobs, and foster race relations. This richly detailed film portrays the political process as a series of compromises and tradeoffs; Pacino's Mayor plays this game until one unacceptable deal is struck that comes back to haunt him and the other politicians and judges involved. The film's location shots and finely detailed characters will prove recognizable to New Yorkers with memories of city politics in the 1980s complete with revelations of political cover-ups, shady deals, and personal corruption. *City Hall* will help New Yorkers to recall the scandal-ridden Koch Administration in the eighties that sent one political boss to prison and another to commit suicide.[7] Pacino's alter-ego and conscience is the Deputy Mayor, Kevin Calhoun (John Cusack), whose investigation uncovers murder and drug deals that ultimately destroy the political aspirations of his boss. At its center, *City Hall* questions whether any elected official, however decent, can be an effective politician without support from the power brokers. This film comes closest to challenging the simplistic textbook explanation of machine politics as evil per se and reformers as "white knight" politicians in its depiction of the realities of governing our cities where policy choices are reduced to compromises among legitimate, but competing, interests.

Capital Crimes and Misdemeanors

A number of very good dramatic films exploit the Washington, D.C. location in narratives that both praise and damn the federal government. Foremost among this group is Frank Capra's film, *Mr. Smith Goes to Washington*. Jimmy Stewart's character, Jefferson Smith, boy ranger and ingenuous idealist, is appointed to the Senate because he is expected to serve as a patsy for his state's corrupt political machine, headed by Jim Taylor (Edward Arnold). Incidentally, Arnold made a film career out of playing corrupt politicians and unscrupulous characters. Capra's movies often revolve around decent, common men, exploited by the rich and the powerful, who, nonetheless, manage to triumph over their adversaries in the final reel. In order for Smith to win his battle against the political bosses, however, he must engage in a filibuster. While Capra utilizes this political tactic for a good cause in the film, historically the filibuster has been employed to defeat and delay liberal legislation such as civil rights.

Meanwhile, in *Advise and Consent* (1962), the film version of the Allen Drury novel, the appointment of a Secretary of State provides the basis for the drama. In the American political system, the presidential appointment of a Cabinet-level post, federal judgeship, and an ambassadorship requires Senate approval. When the film president (Franchot Tone) nominates the controversial Robert Leffingwell (Henry Fonda) to be secretary of state, the Senate divides over his selection. Foes of the president take the appointment as an opportunity to settle old scores. Dixiecrats (Southern Democrats) object to Leffingwell's liberalism while conservatives are concerned that he is soft on communism. To neutralize one of Leffingwell's Senate supporters (Don Murray), the opposition threatens to expose a homosexual incident in his past, which leads the young senator to commit suicide. At the end, the president dies and the vice president decides to name his own candidate. While the film reflects America's Cold War concern of Soviet expansion and the need for policy-making officials to be committed to the containment of communism as the cornerstone of foreign policy, it also exposes Capitol Hill as a ruthlessly competitive place.

The Seduction of Joe Tynan (1979), a film scripted by and starring Alan Alda, is another film with a plot grounded in the politics of the U.S. Senate. Alda plays the title character, a young, liberal senator and contented family man. The political issue at the forefront of this film is a presidential appointment to the U.S. Supreme Court, which requires Senate confirmation. Southern senators, led by senior Senator Birney (Melvyn Douglas), favor a candidate that the NAACP characterizes as "racist" and unacceptable. Both sides lobby for Tynan's support. Should he side with the black lobby or should he do the expedient thing and promote his career by standing with the Southern coalition? Tynan's eventual decision to oppose the Southerners' candidate aborts the nomination and rewards him with the political plum of making the presidential nominating speech at the convention, a selection normally reserved for potential presidential candidates.[8] Although Tynan makes the right choice politically, he makes the wrong choice morally when he has an affair with a Southern lobbyist (Meryl Streep) that almost destroys his marriage. But true to Hollywood form, reconciliation, if not repentance, is implied at the end along with fulfillment of presidential ambitions.

Political skulduggery is at the heart of a couple of films about Washington politics that deal with the abuse of political power. *True Colors* (1991) tracks the careers of two bright law school students, Peter Burton (John Cusack) and Tim Garrity (James Spader). Burton is an ambitious manipulator with a Nixon personality, who chooses politics as a career while his law school friend, Garrity, joins the Justice Department. Burton romances and marries the daughter of a influential senator (Richard Widmark) and becomes his father-in-law's aide as part of his ambitious political scheme. Using an assortment of dirty tricks, blackmail, and his father-in-law's money and influence, Burton decides to run for Congress. Meanwhile, Garrity is content to prosecute cases for the government. Their paths cross when Burton implicates Garrity in a shady deal with a land developer, which guarantees Burton the developer's financial support. To save his job and his reputation, Garrity turns informer, becoming Burton's campaign manager in a plan to secure incriminating evidence for a Justice Department prosecution. At film's end, Burton wins his congressional seat but loses his wife and likely will go to prison for his illegal dealings with the land developer. Still the final scene implies that an unrepentant Burton is ready to resume his political career after serving his prison term, which is not an encouraging assessment of what film politicians think of the American electorate.

More serious crimes are committed in *No Way Out* (1987) where Lt. Cmdr. Tom Farrell (Kevin Costner) is a Naval intelligence officer assigned to locate a suspected mole inside the Pentagon. But the mole story is part of an elaborate cover-up to protect the secretary of defense (Gene Hackman), who accidentally has killed his mistress during a lover's quarrel. Farrell is the one person who knows the mole story is fake because the secretary's mistress was his mistress, too. Worse yet, Farrell is the last person to see her alive. Thus, the film's Washington, D.C. locale serves to authenticate this suspenseful thriller in which Farrell must expose the real killer before he is caught by the authorities. Much of the action in the film takes place inside the Pentagon, but the audience receives virtually no information about this octagon building or the workings of the Defense Department, except that the secretary is a cheat and a coward who is willing to allow someone else to be punished for a crime he committed.

Hail to the Chief and Get off My Plane

With few exceptions, the film industry has treated the American presidency with respect and dignity, if not reverence. Before the Second World War it would have been virtually impossible to find a negative portrayal of an American president on screen. Even in an early film, such as *Gabriel Over the White House* (1933), an indifferent and corrupt President Judd Hammond (Walter Huston) is transformed into a decent and caring person after a visit from the angel Gabriel. At the beginning of the film, Hammond acts like former President Hoover, expressing political platitudes but doing nothing to meet the challenge of the Depression. But when the angel Gabriel visits him after a serious automobile accident puts him at death's door, Hammond is miraculously converted into a political activist, taking steps for economic recovery, rooting out political corruption, and supporting the efforts for world peace.[9]

Recently, however, Hollywood has forsaken its respectful attitude and presented the American people with a new and different version of the presidency. One example is found in Clint Eastwood's *Absolute Power* (1997), where the president (Gene Hackman) is a boozy womanizer who enjoys rough sex. During a sexual encounter, the president goes too far and when the woman fights back, she is shot by secret service men who mistakenly believe the president is at risk. As the story unfolds, the president becomes involved in an elaborate cover-up scheme to hide the murder from the Washington police. A completely opposite portrayal is found in *Air Force One* (1997), where Harrison Ford plays the heroic, if implausible, President James Marshall. When Air Force One is taken over by Russian terrorists, President Marshall decides to stay on the plane rather than take the safety chute. As a combat veteran who refuses to negotiate with terrorists, Marshall is the right person to handle this situation, singlehandedly killing all the terrorists and recapturing the plane. He is certainly no middle-aged, soft-bellied wimp of a president. During the struggle with the leader of the terrorists, Marshall overpowers him and shoves him out the open door yelling: "Get off my plane!" Audiences clapped and cheered, demonstrating that Americans prefer their presidents to be larger-than-life heroes as in the movies. No wonder Americans loved President Reagan; he too was perceived to be the dashing hero of his films.

Hollywood has depicted the presidency in three different contexts; as characters in dramatic action films such as *Air Force One* and *Absolute*

Power, as comedic figures as in *Dave* (1993), and, after a respectful waiting period, as appropriate public figures for screen biographies. As a comedy, *Dave* proved a hit with audiences. In this satire, the president is depicted as another womanizer who suffers a stroke and later dies during a sexual encounter with an aide. His wicked chief of staff decides to cover up the death by recruiting a presidential look-alike, Dave Kovic (Kevin Kline), to impersonate the dead president as part of a devious plot to deny the executive office to the liberal vice president. Historically, presidents did not have "doubles" who served as decoys, especially for crowded events. In such situations, the secret service is more likely to use two limousines and one president to confuse would-be assassins.[10] Being a fantasy, naturally, the plan fails as the impostor Kovic becomes a more compassionate president than the one he replaced. *Dave* is a Hollywood fairy tale as Kovic returns to his real job at the end and wins the heart of the president's widow, too.

Prior to the Second World War, Hollywood's interest in the presidency was restricted largely to the format of screen biography. Three film biographies on Lincoln and one each on Wilson and Franklin Roosevelt (FDR) presented reverential and flattering views of the presidency. Usually the action unfolded chronologically and these screen biographies were intended to be mythic personal stories of human courage and sacrifice rather than political tracts. What moviegoer will forget President Wilson's stirring speeches or FDR's efforts to battle polio? Uplifting yes, but biased presentations because *Wilson* (1944) ignored the president's prejudicial views on race and gender while Roosevelt's adultery was omitted from *Sunrise at Campobello* (1960).

But a new generation of filmmakers is less reverential and more critical of the country's leaders. Oliver Stone's *Nixon* (1995), for example, reconstructs the presidency as a dark and secret place inhabited by an unstable leader. Stone's three hour plus film is a psychological study of a tortured and lonely man whose ego constantly requires social acceptance and public love. Although the Nixon family did not care for the film, George McGovern, Nixon's Democratic opponent in the 1972 presidential race, considered Stone's treatment to be balanced.[11] In any event, Nixon's story is told in flashback, culminating in the Watergate break-in and his subsequent resignation. Despite his personal fall from grace, Nixon was still an important political player in the twentieth-century, particularly in foreign affairs. Although he left office in disgrace, history may be kinder and remember Nixon as the president who brought Vietnam to closure and who opened China to the West. But if Stone's film is considered too harsh, Robert Altman's view of Nixon in *Secret Honor* (1985) is absolutely devastating. Although not a screen

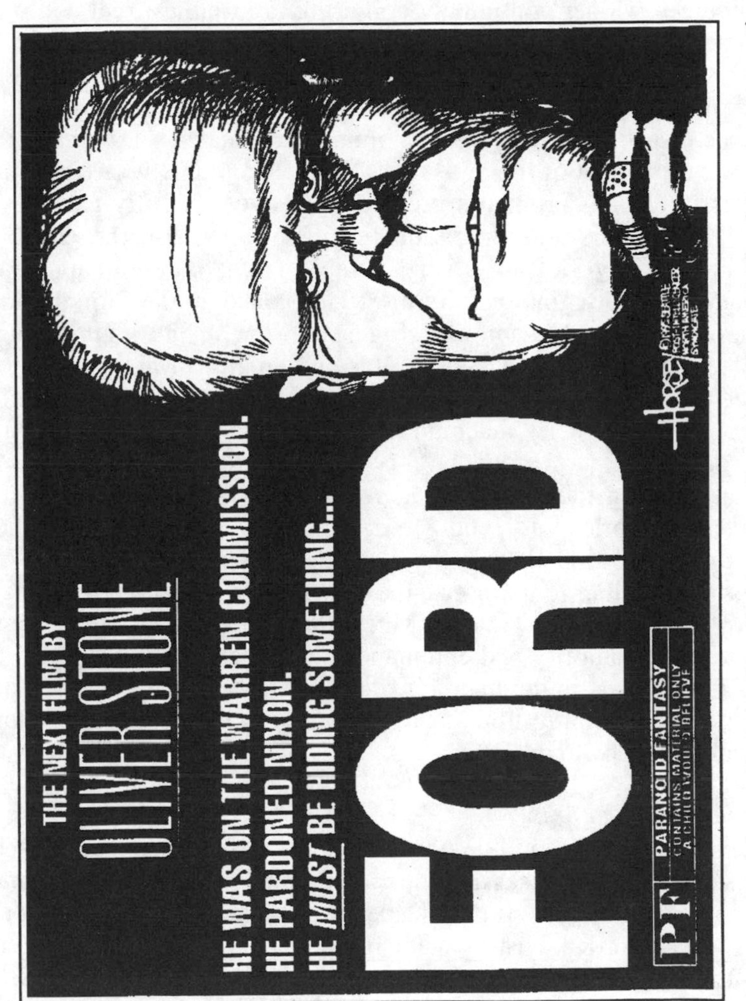

Cartoon of Oliver Stone's hypothetical film project on President Gerald Ford seen as a continuation of his conspiracy theory of American politics. (Reprinted with permission, *Seattle Post-Intelligencer*).

biography per se, *Secret Honor* is a ninety-minute monologue filmed on a set designed to represent Nixon's private White House quarters, where actor Philip Baker Hall paces, raves, and curses his fate. Altman's Nixon is a sad, lonely figure who drinks too much and blames everyone else—Kennedy, Eisenhower, his mother—for his misfortune. This Nixon is a foul-mouthed whiner continually conjuring up enemies, real and imagined, and searching for scapegoats. The only prop missing from the film is a straightjacket.

Another presidential biography—that of Harry Truman—was made for cable distribution rather than commercial theaters. *Truman* (1995) reverts to the format of the pre-World War II biography where the film's intent is to elevate Truman's presidency above the thirty-two percent approval rating his administration received in 1952 at the end of its second term. Gary Sinise is a very credible Truman, in both appearance and mannerisms. Beginning with the 1948 campaign, the film unfolds in a series of flashbacks, commencing in 1917 with the young Truman volunteering for the First World War and ending in his second term. Between these two events, Truman enters politics with the support of the Pendergast Kansas City machine and ascends to the presidency on the death of FDR. The second half concentrates on the difficult issues Truman faced in the White House: namely, whether to use the atom bomb during World War II; how to desegregate the military; if he should seize the steel mills during the Korean War; how to thwart Soviet aggression; whether to recognize the new state of Israel; and whether he should fire the popular General MacArthur during the Korean conflict over issues of authority and command. These were momentous political issues but as usual in commercial films, are treated superficially during its 135 minute running time. Still, *Truman* represents the most honest political biography to date.

Political Assassinations

Conspiracies abound in the minds of Hollywood screenwriters because films about assassinations and attempted assassinations make highly dramatic movies, full of suspense and action sequences that draw well at the box office. History and cultural factors provide another reason why political assassinations interest the film studios. The U.S. is a country with a violent past, from the war for independence to slavery, the winning of the West, the systemic extermination of Native American tribes, the exploitation of women and children as cheap labor, many of them immigrants, the birth of organized crime during Prohibition, the development of urban street gangs in the post-World War II era, and the growth in violent crime by youthful offenders. These historical benchmarks provide the background for crime in the U.S. today and help explain why the country has one of the highest murder rates in the industrial world.

Political figures have not escaped becoming victims of violence. Of the forty-two American presidents, ten had attempts made on their lives. Four presidents actually died at the hands of assassins: Lincoln, Garfield, McKinley, and Kennedy. Six unsuccessful attempts were made against Presidents Jackson, Teddy Roosevelt, Franklin Roosevelt, Truman, Ford, and Reagan. Add to this list of presidents, the assassination of such prominent political figures as Martin Luther King, Medgar Evers, Bobby Kennedy, and Malcolm X and the attack on former Governor George Wallace, which left him permanently paralyzed. Consider—almost one-fourth of American presidents have been the targets of assassins. That is a sobering statistic. But what do foreigners make of it? Do they believe violence is inherent in America's genetic makeup? Is it perhaps due to the racial and class differences which breed discontent and hate? Or might it be the increasingly gratituous violence found in Hollywood films? Whatever the reason, officials and political figures in contemporary America perform their public duties at considerable personal risk.

Virtually all of Hollywood's assassination films have focused on the presidency. The notable exception is John Frankenheimer's *The Manchurian Candidate* (1962), a film about a conspiracy to plant a communist functionary inside the White House. Although the final assassination attempt on the life of a U.S. senator is thwarted, the film's conspiracy theory preceded Oliver Stone by almost three decades. The film stars Laurence Harvey as Korean War POW Raymond Shaw, who is brainwashed by the Chinese communists into becoming an assassin. He returns to the States to be reunited with his mother, the politically ambitious wife of a right-wing, McCarthyesque senator. Her intention is to promote her husband's career as a ruse to infiltrate communists into the White House. But the assassination plan is foiled by Lt. Bennett Marco (Frank Sinatra), Harvey's former army commander. Sinatra also figures prominently in another assassination film, *Suddenly* (1954), where he plays the role of a presidential assassin. Sinatra portrays a disgruntled war veteran, John Baron, turned professional assassin, who arrives in the small town of Suddenly, California, to wait for the president to appear on his scheduled whistle-stop tour. To carry out the planned assassination, Baron and his gang take over a strategically located house, hold the family hostage, and set up headquarters in a second floor room with a good vantage point from which to shoot the president. But the motivation for the assassination attempt in this film is more personal than political: Baron believes that only by killing the president will he "become somebody." Because Baron's character slightly matched that of Lee Harvey Oswald, the film was temporarily withdrawn from television after 1963.[12]

A number of films have dealt directly with President Kennedy's assassination and its aftermath. In addition, several films used the assassination as a reference point from which to develop the narrative. For instance, the culmination of Robert Altman's metaphor on the seventies, *Nashville*, assembles all its characters together for the grand finale—an outdoor country–western songfest as a prelude to a political rally for fictitious presidential candidate, Hal Phillip Walker. However, before Walker's motorcar reaches the Nashville Partheon Theater where the rally is being held, a disturbed young man shoots the lead singer, Barbara Jean,[13] frightening off the Walker cavalcade. As the shooter is subdued, the audience is persuaded to remain calm by the master of ceremonies, Haven Hamilton, who reminds the crowd that "This isn't Dallas, this is Nashville." Although candidate Walker is never seen in the film, his name, nonetheless, ended up on several write-in ballots in 1976, just as the fictitious Jack Tanner received votes in the 1988 presidential election.

Since the Kennedy assassination, five feature films have used this tragic event as the basis for screen material involving conspiracies of one kind or another. Robert Robins and Jerrold Post maintain that the conspiracy theme is attractive to filmmakers because such plots appeal to the political paranoia by which Americans seek to explain tragedies that appear incomprehensible to them.[14] An early entry into political paranoia, *Executive Action* (1973), is pure speculation as screenwriter Dalton Trumbo reconstructs a conspiracy theory in which a group of millionaires, joined by military leaders, plot to kill Kennedy and use Oswald as the patsy. To give the appearance of being a documentary, the film is constructed around a daily log of events, leading up to the assassination day, and supported with newsreels from the Kennedy era that are interspersed with fictitious characters from the film. To further enhance its appearance of authenticity, the film's prologue contends that it is documented by the evidence when, in actuality, it is based on Mark Lane's book, *Rush to Judgment*, an attempt to prove a more plausible explanation than the "lone assassin" theory accepted by the Warren Commission Report. *Executive Action* would have the audience believe that Kennedy was targeted for death because of three fears: that he would withdraw the U.S. from Vietnam, that he would eventually end nuclear testing, and that he would encourage the civil rights revolution. However, there is not one shred of evidence to support these assertions. Furthermore, the film advances a three gunmen thesis rather than the

Barbara Harris (Albequerque) singing "It Don't Worry Me" after Barbara Jean (Ronee Blakely) has been shot during a political rally in Robert Altman's metaphor in the 1970s, *Nashville*. (Courtesy: ABC Television Network.)

conventional "lone assassin" or suspected two. In this scenario, Oswald is guilty of murderous intentions, but innocent of the deed itself.

Two subsequent films, *The Parallax View* (1974) and *Winter Kills* (1979), have scenarios that parallel the Kennedy assassination. In *The Parallax View*, Joseph Frady (Warren Beatty) is a Seattle television reporter who stumbles onto an old political assassination story. When Frady digs deeper into the mystery, he discovers parallels with the Kennedy assassination, such as the lone assassin being killed by the police and several eyewitnesses dying under mysterious circumstances. Sound familiar? Frady's investigation leads him to the monolithic Parallax Corporation; an organization that specializes in political assassinations. This discovery puts Frady's life in danger. In *Winter Kills*, Jeff Bridges is Nick Kegan, the younger brother of an assassinated president. Based on the Richard Condon novel, Kegan's investigation into his brother's death uncovers an implausible conspiracy. This time the assassination occurs in Philadelphia rather than Dallas. However, the convicted assassin is shot dead by a nightclub owner prior to trial. Why did the president have to be killed? The film script wants the audience to believe that the president had taken money from the mob but had failed to deliver favors as his part of the bargain. Kegan's family is obscenely rich and conspicuously dysfunctional—a womanizing bully of a father, an alcoholic mother, a weak older brother, and the dead president, who had a madame supply him with an endless array of women. If all this sounds too familiar, the similarities with the Kennedys are meant to be intentional.

Like *Executive Action*, Oliver Stone's conspiracy version of the Kennedy assassination depicted in *JFK* deals directly with the subject and the personalities involved. Based on several books, including one by New Orleans District Attorney Jim Garrison (played by Kevin Costner), Stone's film, however, mixes fact with fiction, interfaces historical newsreel footage with filmed events, and includes a "deep throat" informer to weave a sweeping conspiracy tale that embraces the military, the Dallas police, the intelligence community, and multinational corporations.[15] Stone's film centers around Garrison's efforts to prosecute businessman Clay Shaw (Tommy Lee Jones) for complicity in Kennedy's assassination. But the actual legal record indicates that the trial was a fraud, an attempt by Garrison to blame Kennedy's death on a small group of homosexuals, including Shaw, together with an unidentified military-industrial complex. Shaw's jury took just forty-five minutes to acquit him while Stone took over three hours on screen to convict him. Stone's supposedly "documented evidence" neglected to include Shaw's trial record.[16] The film's distributor, Warner Brothers, contributed to the deception with advertisements that promoted the film as if the contents were the truth rather than Stone's version of it.[17] Stone's film deceptively intertwines the two worlds of illusion—Washington and Hollywood—to propagandize an unsubstantiated theory.

Conspiracy theories appear to be the most recent fad in American popular culture as evidenced by Stone's *JFK*, Mel Gibson's *Conspiracy Theory* (1997), and the popular television series, *The X-Files*. Why this fascination with conspiracy theories today? Political scientist Michael Barkun believes that there are two reasons for this attraction.[18] First, Barkun points to the human need to make sense of the world and conspiracy theories greatly simplify reality when the world appears inordinately complex. The end of the Cold War and the dissolution of the old Soviet Union, for instance, removed an identifiable enemy that could be blamed for world problems. Even Hollywood has been at a loss to locate new screen enemies for audiences to hate, vacillating between aliens and creatures from outer space on the one hand and rogue terrorists who want to reinstate the hostility of the Cold War on the other. Second, Barkun speculates that the approach of the millennium is often associated with a literal or metaphysical Armageddon—a New World Order—ranging from religious fundamentalists preaching against the Antichrist to UFO enthusiasts who believe the government deliberately denies the truth about extraterrestrial life. Hollywood conspiracy films, therefore, provide us with convenient scapegoats to blame for the ills of the world rather than struggle with the complex problems that confront humanity in the twenty-first century.

Reel Politicians: From Saints to Sinners?

What generalization can be derived from this overview of American politics and politicians as portrayed in Hollywood feature films? To an oldtime movie fan, one answer is that Hollywood has done an 180 degree turnabout in its attitude toward American politics. While there is a kernel of truth to that observation, particularly as applied to political biographies, it is seriously flawed because it wrongly suggests that historically Hollywood treated politicians with more respect and depicted political institutions in the past with greater deference than the present.

The truth is more complicated. American politicians have been depicted as less than honorable figures as early as the silent movies. For instance, *The Racket* (1928) portrayed politicians as being cohorts with Prohibition bootleggers; the president was depicted as a crook in *Gabriel Over the White House*, and the Congress in Capra's *Mr. Smith Goes to*

Washington is characterized as a trading market where corrupt deals are struck for power and profit. As an alternative, this analysis suggests that the film industry always has been willing to take a critical look at its political leaders and institutions. However, whenever the portrayals were negative, they usually were balanced and mitigated by the more positive attributes of the film's political characters. Recall that in *Gabriel Over the White House*, Walter Huston's crooked president is redeemed and transformed into a man of the people after a visit from the angel Gabriel. Meanwhile, Jefferson Smith's idealistic freshman senator triumphs in the end over the weak and flawed Senator Paine and the ruthless political boss, Jim Taylor. Capra was willing to criticize the political system and point a disapproving finger at some of the people in it, but he never attributed their flaws and failures to representative government.[19] And Loretta Young's resourceful farmer's daughter wins her novice congressional race despite the opposition's attempt to smear her reputation. In 1940s' Hollywood, the prevailing imagery of decency triumphed over evil, reflecting the heroic and mythic culture of an era where even politicians could become screen heroes.

But there have been few Jefferson Smith "white knight" type heroes on the silver screen since the sixties. For several decades, the political characters on screen have all been flawed, open to political opportunities regardless of the cost, willing to cheat on their spouses, and not above abusing their friends and colleagues—sometimes without having to pay the price of disgrace and rejection. As a scheming and ambitious political animal in *True Colors*, the John Cusack character shows little remorse for his criminal behavior. Instead of displaying shame and disgrace for his misdeeds, he defiantly intends to remain in politics. Less than a decade later, President Clinton lied about his affair with Monica Lewinsky and even when the lie was disclosed, he refused to admit it or to consider resignation as a honorable solution. Although Alan Alda's philandering Joe Tynan reconciles with his wife at the end of *The Seduction of Joe Tynan*, it is less a case of regenerated love as pragmatic politics because he needs her for his run for the presidency. Tim Robbins' *Bob Roberts* schemes and tricks his way into the U.S. Senate, raising questions as to what nefarious ventures he plans for the Congress. Even Robert Redford's Bill McKay is a victorious, but imperfect senator, unsure of himself since in winning the election, he has lost his soul in the process. Warren Beatty's cartoonish Senator Bulworth raises some serious questions about class and race but tempers them with tongue-in-check comedy.

Recently, Hollywood has been bold enough to feature politicians as despicable characters, like the womanizing governor in *Primary Colors* and the rapist president in *Absolute Power*. Whenever the political figure is portrayed in a totally positive light, however, the film character is apt to be cast in the unlikely role of action-hero like Harrison Ford's (*Air Force One*) and Bill Pullman's (*Independence Day*) presidents. In an age when the average film budget exceeds fifty to sixty million dollars (minus marketing costs), the major studios are unlikely to take risks with multidimensional politicians and complex political issues. Simplification and dramatization are the buzzwords in the entertainment industry today, where human characteristics and people-oriented plots are replaced by special effects featuring the latest weapons of destruction. The trend is depressing but possibly inevitable. In studying feature films on the Congress, one scholar has concluded that Hollywood's need for simplification is irrevocably at odds with the complexities of life on Capitol Hill where cooperation and compromise are often necessary for the passage of legislation or the enactment of a balanced budget.[20]

It is because of Hollywood's inability or unwillingness to focus on the intricacies of the political process that the studios have turned to the more dramatic, and potentially more profitable, territory of scandals and corruption. Unfortunately, these negative views often are reinforced by other social institutions and by the news media. The end result has been a complete debunking of American politics, defined on screen as a corrupting process fit only for villains.[21] No wonder our students have rejected politics as a career choice. No wonder young people fail to vote more than any other age group.

The present mood depicted in Hollywood films is a disservice to the majority of decent, honest, hard-working people in government. The current climate recalls the time when, as a young man in Missouri, Harry Truman told his disapproving mother that he intended to run for political office. Her response was terse: "Politics cheapens a man." Recent Hollywood fare mimic her words.

Seven

Picturing Justice: Law and Lawyers in Hollywood Films

"The first thing we do, let's kill all the lawyers."
Shakespeare, *Henry VI, Part II*

"If there were no bad people, there would be no good lawyers."
Mark Twain

"The law is a ass, a idiot." —Dickens, *Oliver Twist*

"I am the law." —Frank Hague, Mayor of Jersey City, 1937

"I have three rules. I never believe what the prosecutor or the police say, I never believe what the media say and I never believe what my client says." —Alan Dershowitz

Law and Popular Culture

Lawyers, like politicians, make dramatic film subjects because their characters have the capacity for both good and evil and their actions affect the lives of others in significant ways. The good lawyer insures a client's personal freedom or economic well-being; the client who has a mediocre lawyer may end up in prison or the poorhouse. Furthermore, lawyers, judges, and the police are perceived by the citizenry to be representatives of the country's values as expressed through its legal system. That system is supposed to dispense justice in every case; failure to provide a right decision adversely affects its credibility. Therefore, images that represent the legal culture can reinforce its authority or undermine its popular support.

According to law professor Stewart Macaulay,[1] these representations are present in everyday life, from the schoolroom to the sports arena. Of particular importance to Macaulay is the contribution of the entertainment arts because, as he correctly suggests, the visual media are especially significant in the formulation of the popular image of the law and the legal profession. Why is the media's influence so compelling? The legal culture consists of statutes, case law, and scholarly essays on jurisprudence-all of which shape and affect ordinary life. Yet as Macaulay observes, relatively few Americans read the legal literature; even fewer are involved in litigation or see the inside of a courtroom. He cites the study by the Hearst Corporation[2] when it was discovered that only twenty percent of the survey population had ever been a party in a civil suit, that only sixteen percent had actually served on a jury, that fifteen percent had been witnesses in a personal injury suit, and that as few as ten percent had been victims. Therefore, where do Americans learn about the law? Macaulay's response is that they learn the law from the experiences of ordinary life—school, sports, and entertainment. He reasons that more Americans learn about the legal system from the visual arts, especially film and television, than from any firsthand experience.[3]

Macaulay's thesis has been expanded by another colleague, John Denvir,[4] who argues that films can serve as legal texts; visual opportunities for filmmakers to challenge the conventional wisdom and established doctrine on particular legal issues such as abortion and capital punishment. According to Denvir, films like *The Godfather* can serve as legal texts, supplementing material found in the law reports. In the legal culture, law is but one of the myths seeking popular acceptance. Hence, to investigate movies that serve primarily as legal texts is to actually study one aspect of the legal culture.

The Reel World of the Law

Macaulay's contention is that movies reflect the legal culture, contradictions and all.[5] On the one hand, there are the film texts that reinforce the legal principles which lend support to the ruling authority and foster compliance with the established law, while on the other hand, there are legal texts in film that challenge those in control and portray public officials and authority figures as dishonest and corrupt. However, as in the case of film texts on American politics, Hollywood movies often try to avoid direct attacks on the institutions of government, including the justice system, preferring instead to present the imperfections in a context that blames human weakness rather than a flawed legal system. This chapter examines movies as legal texts in Hollywood films in several contexts.

Frontier Justice

Historians describe the frontier as the demarcation line that divides civilization from the wilderness. In the American past, the frontier's edge moved westward from Pittsburgh until it met the Pacific. Historian Frederick Jackson Turner believed that the American character was shaped by those pioneers who settled the West.[6]

Whether Hollywood subscribed to the Turner thesis or not, the film industry exploited the dramatic potential in its visual exploration of the migration westward. Thus, it should not come as a surprise that the first narrative to come out of Hollywood, *The Great Train Robbery* (1903), had a western action plot. Thereafter, westerns became a staple of the film industry well into the 1960s. Hollywood's version of the western genre often reduced the plots to simplified morality tales in which the forces of evil are dispatched, usually violently, after the climactic barroom brawl or street shootout with the virtuous good guys. Frontier justice was normally achieved by brute strength and the quick draw rather than by persuasion or the appeal to reason.

But occasionally the western film served as a legal text.[7] Recall that James Stewart's lawyer character (Ransome Stoddard) in *The Man Who Shot Liberty Valance* eventually proved that in the new West, the law book would replace Tom Doniphon's (John Wayne's character) six-shooter. Wayne, of course, began his film career in the thirties by appearing in a series of short westerns for Republic Pictures. In one such film set in the 1870s, *King of the Pecos* (1936), Wayne plays John Clayborn, a young lawyer out to avenge his parents' murder at the hands of the local cattle baron, Alexander Stiles. Somehow the young Clayborn manages to escape unharmed from the shootout that killed his parents. Stiles's strategy is to claim most of the open range for himself, either through buying out deceived ranchers or killing those, like Clayborn's parents, who refuse to sell. Stiles, however, fails to file legal claim to the land, preferring instead to control the water rights. Unless ranchers sell their cattle to him at a low price, Stiles threatens to cut off their water supply. Ten years pass and the grown-up Clayborn returns to town as a lawyer and persuades the court to accept the waterholes as property held in the public domain. When the legal system rules against him, Stiles resorts to violence. Although Clayborn is committed to using the law to settle disputes, he comes to realize that his law books are no match for Stiles's guns. Reluctantly, Clayborn straps on his gunbelt and after a fierce battle, shoots Stiles and kills most of his gang in the climactic gunfight.

Afterwards, Clayborn throws away his guns, an act symbolic of his new commitment to the practice of law.

King of the Pecos relied on the legal system and the use of force to achieve justice. Sometimes, however, frontier justice on the big screen meant vigilantism and mob rule.[8] In *The Ox-Bow Incident* (1943), a pair of saddle tramps, Henry Fonda and Harry Morgan, reluctantly join a posse in search of cattle rustlers who have killed a local rancher. Disregarding the instructions of the sheriff, the posse, led by an ex-Confederate major, stumble onto three men, preside over a kangaroo trial, and then lynch them for the crime. Fonda and Morgan try to persuade the men to wait for the sheriff to arrive but they are overruled by the mob. On their way back to town, the posse meets the sheriff who informs them that the real culprits are in custody and that the rancher who was shot had not died. When the sheriff learns about the lynching, he promises to hold those involved accountable. Back in town, the major commits suicide while the rest of the posse gathers in the local saloon to drown their guilt. Fonda, however, reads aloud the letter one of the victims had written to his wife in which he refers to the law as the "conscience of humanity." In taking the lives of three innocent men, the posse had become judge and jury, losing its humanity and deteriorating into an uncivilized mob.

A variation on the mob vigilantism theme, but still within the western genre, is found in the film story of *The Life and Times of Judge Roy Bean* (1972). Paul Newman plays the title character, a drifter who declares himself "the law" in a small town west of the Pecos. There he dispenses his brand of justice, usually at the end of a rope. Based on a post-Civil War character, Bean comes into the frontier town of Vinegaroon, Texas, where there is neither law nor order. He proceeds to kill or drive out all the outlaws, and armed only with a copy of *The Revised Statutes of Texas*, proclaims himself "Judge of the territory." Converting the town brothel into a saloon/courthouse, he dispenses justice so harshly that he acquires a reputation as the "hanging judge." In this film, the law literally is what Bean says it is. When the statute book fails to conform to his predetermination, Bean rips the page out of the law book. When an outlaw is brought before Bean for killing a Chinese man, Bean's jurisdiction is challenged because "Chinks, Niggers, and Injuns" are excluded as "persons" in the statute books. But Judge Bean will not hear of it; regardless of the statute book, all persons are considered equal before him. Since Bean and the law share the same body, the outlaw is sentenced to hang. Part-history and part-legend,[9] the film constructs an idol out of an outlaw who tried and sentenced his victims arbitrarily, sometimes on the basis of personal whim. Roy Bean had to be the worst kind of judge to represent the legal system. His story

A kangaroo court's brand of frontier justice condemns three innocent ranchers in the western, *The Ox-Bow Incident*. (c. 1943 Twentieth Century Fox Film Corporation. All rights reserved.)

demonstrates, though, what can happen when a vacuum exists in territories where official authority has yet to be established.

While hangings, lynchings, and shootouts fit the mythology of the old West, such violence in the twentieth-century is more likely to arouse public wrath. Yet lynchings and mob brutality continued well into the thirties, especially in selected regions of the country. While lynchings occurred throughout the U.S., the act had become primarily a southern and racial phenomenon by the late nineteenth century. For example, studies indicate that almost 4,000 lynchings took place in the South between 1880 and 1930;[10] most of the victims were blacks lynched by white mobs. A correlation usually existed between economic conditions and the prevalence of lynching. When economic times were good lynchings decreased, but when farm prices paid to white farmers dropped, lynchings increased. Economically distressed whites found blacks to be convenient scapegoats and took out their aggression and frustration on them.

During the Depression era, Hollywood produced several social message films, including two on mob rule. Both German director Fritz Lang's *Fury* (1936) and Warner Brothers' *They Won't Forget* (1937) confronted the issue of mob violence directly. *Fury* starred Spencer Tracy as an innocent young man, mistakenly arrested for a fugitive kidnapper. Tracy is arrested on the basis of circumstantial evidence together with being an outsider unknown to the townsfolk. While he languishes in the local jail, a large angry mob develops outside. The sheriff asks for state assistance but the governor is up for re-election and reluctant to intervene. The self-appointed vigilantes, unable to break into the jail to lynch Tracy, set it on fire instead. Tracy is presumed dead but, unknown to the mob, has managed to escape. Meanwhile, the real kidnappers are captured and the local District Attorney brings murder charges against twenty-two identified members of the lynch mob. Embittered by the events, Tracy refuses to reveal himself, content to allow his persecutors to be tried for a murder they did not commit. After the defendants are found guilty, Tracy has a change of heart and decides to intervene. He walks into the courtroom in the final scene while the trial judge is handing out the sentences. Although Tracy's reappearance saved the defendants from certain death, nonetheless, he admits to the court that he has lost faith in the ability of the legal system to deliver justice. While Lang's film was a box office failure, it did help to establish his reputation in Hollywood.

Unlike *Fury*, *They Won't Forget* (1937) is a fictionalized account of the 1913 Leo Frank case. Set in a Southern town, *They Won't Forget* retells the story of a teenage secretarial student found murdered in her school building. The politically ambitious district attorney pounces on the case as a potential springboard into the U.S. Senate. But he needs to make an arrest and secure a conviction if the crime is to advance his career. The D.A. narrows his suspects to a young teacher, a Northerner and outsider, who was in the school building on the day the student was murdered. The teacher is quickly arrested and convicted, largely on the basis of circumstantial evidence. The governor, however, commutes his sentence from death to life imprisonment. On his way to prison, the teacher is taken off the train by a vicious mob and lynched. As was true in the actual case, the accumulation of circumstantial evidence supported by anti-Yankee prejudice, yellow journalism, and political ambition led to Leo Frank's conviction and eventual death because it was assumed that "we can lynch a nigger anytime but when do we get the chance to hang a Yankee Jew?"[11] Georgia Governor John Slaton commuted Frank's sentence; a brave act which destroyed his political career. Leo Frank was taken from the prison farm a few months later and lynched.[12] His killers were not prosecuted even though several were identified. Films like *Fury* and *They Won't Forget* serve as reminders that prejudice and violence did not end at the frontier.

Military Justice

Because the U.S. was designed as a federal system with powers shared by both the national and state governments, the country has fifty-one legal systems—one for the federal government and one for each of the fifty states. In addition, the federal court system is distinguished by two types of courts: constitutional and legislative. Constitutional courts are created under the language of Article III of the U.S. Constitution, which authorizes the Congress to establish courts inferior to the Supreme Court. Legislative courts, on the other hand, are created pursuant to a congressional legislative function. For example, under Article I, Congress has the power to organize, arm, and discipline the militia. Discipline is held so vital for military success that even the U.S. Supreme Court has ruled that an orthodox Jew cannot wear his Yarmulke instead of regulation headgear.[13] The Congress, therefore, has the power to establish military tribunals to discipline soldiers. One example of a legislative court is the U.S. Court of Military Appeals, which reviews the decisions of courts-martial. Its caseload consists primarily of military personnel discharged for bad conduct or sentenced to the stockade for violations of the Uniform Code of Military Justice. Offenses while in the military service, crimes committed on military bases, and other infractions which are "service connected" fall within the jurisdiction of the Uniform Code. While military personnel do not forfeit their constitutional rights while in the service, the application of the code differs from civilian life. For instance, while the Fourth Amendment protection against "unreasonable searches and seizures" applies to service personnel, routine inspections and shakedowns are not considered searches and are therefore permissible. Nor do military personnel accused of a crime have a right to post bail.

Hollywood has ignored military trials as screen material with several notable post-World War II exceptions. In *The Court Martial of Billy Mitchell* (1955), Gary Cooper plays the title role of the Brigadier General who commanded the American Expeditionary Air Force during the First World War and later, served as assistant chief of the Army Air Service. He differed with his superiors over the role of air power in future wars, including the military potential of strategic bombing, airborne forces, and polar air routes. His incessant and sharp criticism of military leaders led to his court-martial in 1925. The film recounts Mitchell's advocacy of a strong air force against military leaders in both the war and navy departments who were committed to naval power and the infantry. When one of Mitchell's friends dies in an air crash, he accuses the war and navy departments of incompetence and negligence. His accusations and insubordination lead to his court-martial under Article 134 of the Uniform Code which prohibits conduct that discredits the armed forces or is prejudicial to order and discipline. Mitchell's legal strategy is to use the courtroom as a public forum, a place where he can expound his ideas, including the vulnerability of Pearl Harbor to air attack. But, naturally, Mitchell is found guilty because, as a maverick, he dared to question the entrenched establishment. What the trial demonstrates is that the military chain of command requires blind obedience to orders regardless of the consequences. As punishment, Mitchell was suspended for five years, subsequently resigned from the army, but continued to lecture on the use of air power until his death. Unfortunately, his ideas were not accepted by the military until the advent of World War II.

Mutiny, rather than insubordination, is at the heart of the 1955 film, *The Caine Mutiny*. Article 184 of the Uniform Code defines mutiny as the refusal to obey orders from a proper authority in concert with others with the intention to override military authority. Mutiny, of course, is one of the most serious offenses under the Military Code and is punishable by death. The mutiny in the film occurs in World War II during a Pacific typhoon when a group of naval officers led by Lt. Maryk (Van Johnson) and Ensign Keith (Robert Francis) seize control of the *Caine* from its commanding officer, Captain Queeg (Humphrey Bogart). Queeg, a strict disciplinarian, had assumed command of the *Caine*, a battered minesweeper, from a lackadaisical officer. He manages to get the ship back in shape but has become increasingly paranoid as a result of excessive combat. He is too preoccupied with unimportant details like improper dress on board ship. His erratic behavior comes to a climax in his obsession with locating missing strawberries. Queeg orders a thorough investigation for the strawberries, even though it is obvious to the other officers that they had been eaten and were no longer available to be produced. But when Queeg freezes during the typhoon and hesitates to take action, Maryk and Keith assume command. Both are subsequently charged with mutiny. Their military lawyer, Barney Greenwald (Jose Ferrer) reluctantly defends them at the court-martial by attacking Queeg in an attempt to destroy his credibility. Under intense questioning, Queeg breaks down on the stand, rolling the steel balls in his hands more violently as the cross-examination intensifies. Greenwald's strategy works as Queeg cracks under pressure and Maryk and Keith are cleared of all charges. But at a post-victory celebration, Greenwald defends Queeg as a good officer who was worn down by the stress of command. In return for the cooperation of the U.S. Navy, film changes had to be made in the Herman Wouk novel to direct blame for the mutiny on the conduct of individuals rather than on the military establishment. Still, the film conveys both a sense of the importance of hierarchical decision-making for military effectiveness and a perception of fairness within the military justice system.

Severe hazing (Code Red) that leads to murder on a military base forms the basis for the film, *A Few Good Men* (1992). Loosely based on an incident at the marine base in Guantanamo Bay in the 1980s, *A Few Good Men* recounts the story of Pvt. Santiago, an unhappy marine scheduled to snitch to the authorities on two fellow marines for shooting on the fenceline in Cuba. To frighten him into silence, the two marines initiate Code Red when they stuff a rag down Santiago's throat and tape his mouth shut. As a consequence, Santiago dies and the two marines are charged with his murder. Their base commander, Col. Nathan Jessep (Jack Nicholson), a gung-ho marine who refused to transfer Santiago, tries to minimize the incident as an accident. The U.S. Navy also would like to whitewash the incident; it therefore appoints a young and brash, but untested trial lawyer, Lt. Daniel Kaffe (Tom Cruise) to head the court-martial defense team. Kaffe is willing to accept the prosecutor's plea bargain because he has never tried a case, but changes his mind after a meeting with Jessep and after the constant goading of his colleague, Lt. Cmdr. JoAnne Galloway (Demi Moore). Kaffe and Galloway believe their clients did not act on their own and to substantiate their suspicions, they subpoena Jessep. The strategy works as Jessep, under intense examination, admits the Code Red order. During the heated court-martial exchange, Jessep defends the hazing order because Santiago was a whiner, a weakling, and not a true marine. He berates Kaffe as well, arguing that when the U.S. goes to war it calls upon men like himself—real marines—instead of the soft, bookish lawyers in white dress like Kaffe, to do the dirty work. When the country is in crisis, discipline and strength, not weakness and self-indulgence, are required of the military services. As he is being led out of the courtroom by the Military Police, Jessep screams that men like Kaffe undermine the strength of the country. From one viewpoint, Kaffe's first trial is a success; his clients are acquitted of the murder charge. But since they are dishonorably discharged from the corps, the sentence raises the question of whether it is fair to punish lower echelon military personnel for carrying out a crime under orders from a superior officer? Yet the Nuremberg War Crimes Trial after World War II[14] established the principle that military personnel cannot rely on illegal orders, such as a Code Red, to absolve them of wrongdoing. However, for subordinates to disobey an order is a serious offense under military law. Within the context of the film, the two marines would have had to pass judgment on Jessep's order—which was not to kill Santiago but simply to toughen him up, frighten him into becoming a real marine. That is a no-win situation for lower echelon military personnel who apply the Uniform Code to preserve discipline and obedience rather than the attainment of just ends.

Trials and Tribulations: Lawyers on the Big Screen

In the American legal system it is the lawyer who is the pivotal character in the resolution of legal contests. Having an adversarial legal system places the lawyer center stage. Hollywood films about the law tend to portray the profession in three contexts: as larger-than-life heroes, as sleazy shysters available for hire, and as fallen idols seeking redemption through their clients.

Heroic Lawyers

A hero or heroine is usually characterized as a person who has committed an act of courage or bravery without regard for personal consequences. Heroes are admired and held in high esteem by the rest of society. Hollywood action-adventure films consistently feature characters that perform heroic deeds or overcome extreme obstacles to right a wrong. But such heroes cannot serve as role models because their escapades are often implausible and belong more to the realm of the imagination than to real life.

Courtroom movies, however, can utilize the trial as a paradigm for the confrontation between good and evil. Trial movies provide opportunities for lawyers to become heroic figures as their legal strategy saves the life of an innocent client or delivers just compensation to the plaintiff in a civil suit. The film industry has exploited the dramatic potential of the heroic lawyer in pursuit of truth and justice for more than half-a-century. What young person would not want to grow up to become Abe Lincoln (Henry Fonda), the advocate with a social conscience, in *Young Mr. Lincoln* (1939). Not only does the Springfield lawyer prove the innocence of two brothers accused of murder, but he saves them from a lynch mob and, in typical Perry Mason fashion, exposes the real killer in the final scene. Nor is attorney Lincoln reluctant to engage in courtroom tricks, including reliance on the *Farmers' Almanac* to identify the real killer.

Could there be a more heroic lawyer than Atticus Finch in *To Kill a Mockingbird*? Gregory Peck plays Atticus in the 1962 film adaptation of the Harper Lee novel about a small-town Southern lawyer who defends a black man accused of raping a white woman. Atticus, a widower and a respected lawyer, is struggling to raise his two children during the Depression years. When asked by the local judge to accept the rape case, Atticus never hesitates although his client's case appears hopeless. Atticus' acceptance is a lesson to audiences that even marginalized groups are entitled to the best defense possible under the American legal system. Like the young Lincoln, Atticus also faces down a lynch mob. But despite an impassioned closing argument in which he asks the all-white jury to lay aside their racial prejudices, the jury convicts his client. But in 1930s Alabama, a black man accused of raping a white woman had no chance whatsoever. Blacks were sent to prison just for "leering" at white women. While it is unlikely that any lawyer could have saved Atticus' client, his insistence on uncovering the truth despite the personal consequences represents the best tradition of defense lawyers.

Lincoln and Atticus Finch are noble characters, fighting for justice in the courtroom. They symbolize Hollywood's most ideal representation of lawyers on the big screen. They are flawless characters, a credit to the legal profession. Other screen lawyers who fit this mold include Humphrey Bogart in *Knock on Any Door* (1949), Glenn Ford in *Trial* (1955), and Matthew McConaughey in *A Time to Kill* (1996). McConaughey's liberal lawyer, Jake Brigance, has the formidable task of defending Carl Lee Hailey, the black Mississippi farmer accused of killing the two rednecks who raped and beat his ten-year-old daughter. All three film lawyers represent minority defendants in trials permeated with prejudice and hostility.

In *Knock on Any Door*, attorney Andrew Morton (Bogart) defends a young hoodlum, Nick Romano (John Derek), accused of murdering a policeman during a robbery. Morton takes the case despite a warning that his acceptance jeopardizes his chance for a full partnership. But Morton identifies with Romano because both were products of the urban slum; yet Morton became a respected attorney. He believes that Romano too, the son of immigrant parents, can still be rehabilitated. However, Romano is too weak to stay out of trouble, flaunting an attitude of "Live fast, die young and have a good looking corpse." Morton's defense strategy is to put society on trial, to have the jury believe that Romano is a decent kid who never had a chance to go straight. But when cross-examined on the stand, Romano is provoked by the D.A. into confessing to the crime. Morton, then, has no choice but to make an impassioned plea to the judge to save Romano's life, citing the arguments of the social determinists that environment is largely responsible for crime. If Romano is guilty, Morton argues, then so is society because it failed to provide him with a decent home and a good neighborhood. Despite his passionate defense, Romano is sentenced to death in the electric chair, thereby making his prophecy of dying young and having a good-looking corpse come true.

David Blake's (Glenn Ford) client, Angel Chavez, in *The Trial*, is a Mexican-American high school student accused of murdering his WASP girlfriend. Blake is a law professor on the verge of getting fired because he lacks trial experience. To save his job, Blake accepts an offer to spend the summer as an assistant to local attorney, Barney Castle (Arthur Kennedy). Castle convinces Chavez's mother to let him handle the case. But instead of doing the trial work himself, Castle assigns it to Blake on the pretense that he will be too busy raising the legal funds necessary for the defense. Unknown to Blake, Castle actively promotes the Chavez case, turning it into a cause celebre for the Communist Party. The party needs a martyr (Chavez), and an inexperienced trial lawyer like Blake is the perfect candidate to lose the case. Meanwhile, local bigots surround the courthouse, anxious to dispense with the trial altogether and lynch Chavez on the spot. But the National Guard is called out and the local sheriff dissuades the crowd from doing violence. Back in the courtroom, Blake is learning the law on the job, his mistakes corrected by the patient trial judge. At least Blake has enough sense not to put Chavez on the stand. He is overruled on this matter by Castle, who has the support of Chavez's mother. As expected, the vulnerable Chavez crumbles under cross-examination and the jury finds him guilty. Blake is devastated by the verdict but because he believes that somewhere in the law, "where there is a wrong, there is a remedy," he decides to try one last legal tactic.

During the sentencing hearing, Blake convinces the judge, with the consent of the prosecution, to send Chavez to reform school rather than the gas chamber. In order to save Chavez, however, Blake must confess to his incompetence and admit that he had been duped by Castle in an effort to aid the communist cause. The film concludes at this point, but the implication is that while Blake did the right thing, he should return to the classroom and avoid the courtroom at all cost. An interesting footnote to *Trial* is that while the film's action takes place in the year 1947, the film itself was released in 1955 after McCarthy's censure. Thus MGM, the film's distributor, could safely include the film's anti-communist message without fear of reprisal.

Al Pacino plays beleaguered Baltimore criminal defense attorney, Arthur Kirkland, in *And Justice For All* (1979). The opening scene finds Kirkland in jail for contempt after he takes a punch at his nemesis, Judge Fleming (John Forsythe). Kirkland represents the sensitive lawyer with a conscience. He is angry with Fleming for refusing to reopen the case of a wrongly convicted client. In addition to the jail time, Kirkland is under investigation by the judicial ethics committee to determine whether he continues to be fit to practice law. After his release from jail, Kirkland is asked by Fleming to defend him against a rape charge. Kirkland is put in a catch-22 situation; he despises the Judge, but if he refuses to take the case, he most likely will be disbarred. Laying aside his personal feelings, Kirkland accepts the case and provides an aggressive defense until he discovers that the Judge is guilty. In the final scene, Kirkland confesses his client's guilt to the stunned courtroom, an act which leads to his disbarment. While Kirkland is an improbable lawyer, *And Justice for All* is the rare Hollywood film that is willing to cast aspersions on the criminal justice system itself rather than on the individual participants, the film presents an unending parade of corrupt officials, scenes of judicial abuse of power, and questionable plea bargain deals. Although it tends towards exaggeration, the audience leaves the theater with a feeling that the urban legal system requires not justice, but compromise and expediency, in order to survive. Kirkland represents the idealistic and ethical lawyer trying to exist in an irrational system which overwhelms, and eventually, destroys him.

Michigan attorney Paul Biegler, Jimmy Stewart's character in *Anatomy of a Murder* (1959), would rather fish for trout and play jazz on the piano than practice law. Biegler is less the heroic lawyer than the duped attorney depicted in the Alan Dershowitz story of the lawyer who cables his client that "Justice has prevailed," to which the client responds: "Appeal immediately."[15] Biegler agrees to handle the case of an Army officer, Lt. Manion (Ben Gazzara), charged with killing the man who allegedly raped his wife. When Biegler interviews Manion at the local jail, he tells his client that there is no such thing in the law as an unwritten rule that acquits a husband who protects his wife's honor. In desperate need of a viable defense, Biegler skirts the code of ethics when he lays out the various excuses for such a crime and, after repeated questioning, gets Manion to admit that he "must have been crazy" when he shot and killed his wife's attacker. The lead allows Biegler to develop the "irresistible impulse" strategy, a defense permitted under Michigan law. Legal scholars contend that Biegler's coaching is just one of several legal improprieties evident in the film.[16] Biegler's legal tactics prove successful as Manion is acquitted. Afterwards, Biegler goes to the trailer court to collect his fee, only to learn that the Manions had an irresistible impulse to skip town. Like the client in the Dershowitz story, Manion was guilty as sin.

Occasionally, Hollywood will take a real lawyer or a famous case to dramatize on the big screen. Dershowitz, for instance, was portrayed by actor Ron Silver in *Reversal of Fortune* (1990), the film version of the Claus von Bulow case. Dershowitz and his Harvard law students were successful in convincing the Rhode Island Supreme Court to reverse von Bulow's attempted murder conviction.

Noted criminal lawyer Clarence Darrow is represented on screen in two of his famous cases. In the so-called "Monkey Trial," Darrow was retained by the American Civil Liberties Union (ACLU) to defend teacher John T. Scopes on trial for teaching the theory of evolution against state law. The film version of the Scopes trial, *Inherit the Wind* (1960), had Spencer Tracy playing Darrow. As in the actual trial, Darrow made William Jennings Bryant, his adversary, look foolish on the stand. But what is often not known about the real trial (and omitted from the film) is that the Scopes trial was what is known in the law as a "test case." The ACLU sought to challenge the Tennessee anti-evolution statute, but needed a teacher to volunteer to break the law. Scopes answered the ACLU advertisement. Moreover, unlike the rest of the fundamentalist Dayton, Tennessee, community, the town merchants actually believed that a national trial would be good for business.[17] In the other film, *Compulsion* (1959), Orson Welles played Darrow in a fictionalized account of the famous Leopold-Loeb murder case of the 1920s. The film story concerns two brilliant law students who want to commit the "perfect crime" and plot to kidnap and kill a small boy. Arrested for the crime, their families hire Darrow to defend them. While his bravado courtroom performance failed to win an acquittal, Darrow's two-day closing argument that the boys were mentally disturbed and unable to comprehend the enormity of their crime saved them from the death penalty. Darrow's summation, in which he asked the court to be more compassionate and kinder than his clients, still serves as a convincing argument today against capital punishment. These two cases secured Darrow's reputation as America's most outstanding criminal lawyer.

Shyster Lawyers

Hollywood films, where lawyers are portrayed as disreputable characters, are either silly comedies or crime and gangster movies. But there are exceptions. As early as the 1930s, Hollywood films characterized lawyers as "ambulance chasers," unscrupulous leeches who thrived on the misfortune of others. One film, *The Nuisance* (1933), featured a lawyer who works legal scams with the aid of a drunken doctor and a professional accident victim.[18]

More common were Hollywood comedies where the laughs were at the expense of an incompetent or unscrupulous lawyer. Take the case of the Joe Pesci character, Vincent Gambini, in the 1992 film, *My Cousin Vinny*. Vinny is a recent graduate from an unidentified law school who travels to the Deep South to defend his nephew against a wrongful murder charge. Armed with his fiancee, Mona Lisa Vito, and his cowboy boots, Vinny is the kind of relative most people would like to disown. He is brash, vulgar, dresses in black leather and chains, and has failed the bar exam six times. Nonetheless, he still manages to get his cousin acquitted in a silly, but harmless, film.

Funny, but not quite as harmless, is Willie Gingrich (Walter Matthau), the lawyer character Billy Wilder created for his film, *The Fortune Cookie* (1966). If you would not want Vinny Gambini as a cousin, you certainly would not want Willie Gingrich as a brother-in-law. Willie is an ambulance-chasing personal injury lawyer who richly deserves his nickname: "Whiplash Willie." When his brother-in-law, Harry Hinkle (Jack Lemmon), a CBS sportscaster, is run over by a Cleveland Browns football player and ends up in the hospital, Willie sees an opportunity for a megabuck insurance settlement. Harry, of course, is not seriously injured but Willie convinces him to accept the splints, neck braces, and wheelchair charade, at least until the insurance settlement. The insurance scam almost works until Harry's conscience upsets the fraudulent scheme. In Willie Gingrich, Wilder created one of the funniest lawyers in film history but also one of the sleaziest. Willie is an unprincipled opportunist whose philosophy is summed up in the phase, "life is a racket." Matthau's performance won him an Oscar because, in the opinion of one reviewer, it came close to the truth.[19]

The origin for "shyster"[20] remains unclear but the word found its way into Hollywood gangster movies in the thirties. The lawyers in these crime films worked for the mob and valued money and power over the legal code of ethics. As illustrations of the shyster lawyer, consider these two 1930s films, *The Mouthpiece* and *Lawyer Man.* As their titles suggest, these are portraits of charming rogues who either work for the underworld or for crooked politicians.[21] The attorney in *The Mouthpiece* (1932), for example, is an assistant D.A. who turns to drink when he discovers that the defendant he convicted, and later executed, was actually innocent of the crime. Unable to overcome his guilt, he becomes an attorney for hire, even to the criminal class. He receives his just deserts when he is shot down by mobsters at film's end. The fortunes of unscrupulous lawyers like *The Mouthpiece* were usually tied to the mobsters they defended.[22]

The importance of the lawyer to the criminal and to organized crime is best exemplified by *The Godfather* trilogy (1972, 1974, and 1990). The collaboration of writer Mario Puzo and director Francis Ford Coppola, *The Godfather* films are the saga of the "Corleones"—Vito and Michael—two generations of Mafia chieftains. A key figure in this intergenerational story of a Mafia family is the role of the "consigliore," the Corleones' adopted son and legal adviser. Played by actor Robert Duvall in Parts I & II and by actor George Hamilton in Part III, the consigliore acted similarly to the legal department in the modern corporation. As the Corleones' illegal business empire grows, the greater the need for the Don—"the Godfather"—to rely upon him for advice and counsel. It would be inconceivable that the consigliore later could deny knowledge of the organization's illegal activities. To make that point clear, the Puzo novel included a line, cut from the film version, where Don Corleone says: "A lawyer with his briefcase can steal more than a hundred men with guns."[23] To the Mafia leadership, lawyers were "hired guns"; yet they also were important players within the organizational structure. In every sense of the word, they were lawyers for the mob.

Fallen Idols

A common theme in the entertainment arts is the concept of redemption; narratives are built around a major character who falls from a position of prestige and high status into the lower depths, usually due to alcohol, drugs, or bad women (restricted to women since men dominated positions of power in the film industry). Hollywood has applied this traditional plot idea in its films to all sorts of occupations, including the legal profession.

As early as the thirties, the studios began to grind out films in which prominent lawyers succumb to the pleasures of the flesh. Occasionally, Hollywood produced a film where the lawyer's descent was not due to a "femme fatale" or to substance abuse but to a failure to live up to personal ideals. Two films, both involving Jewish lawyers, concern characters who have lost their souls to greed and the temptations of a lifestyle that only money can buy. Elmer Rice's stage play, *Counsellor-At-Law* was adapted for the screen in 1933 and starred John Barrymore as George Simon, a successful Jewish lawyer with an office in the Empire State Building. Simon has progressed from humble boyhood in the lower East Side ghetto to become a highly respected and successful attorney. From all outward appearances, Simon has a flourishing practice. But he has a troubled soul. His socialite wife and her two children from a previous marriage look down on him because of his humble background while his mother reprimands him for rejecting his heritage. For example, his mother embarrasses Simon into defending the son of a Jewish woman from the old neighborhood, a communist arrested for making speeches in Union Square. The young man is completely out of place in Simon's plush offices and during their consultation, he refuses to listen to Simon's advice that he refrain from making more speeches. The disparity between Simon's wealth and the young man's Marxist ideals are so obvious to Simon that all the attorney can do is shrug his shoulders. Simon's descent begins when a rival lawyer threatens to expose some wrongdoing in Simon's past; knowledge of a false alibi provided one of his former clients. To add even more misery to his possible disbarment, Simon discovers that his wife has been unfaithful. In a moment of utter despair, he considers jumping out his office window but is prevented by a loyal secretary who adores him. With new inspiration and true love, Simon decides to fight the disbarment charge rather than commit suicide.

John Garfield is another beleaguered Jewish lawyer, Joe Morse, who has climbed his way out of the New York slums and into a plush Wall Street office in *Force of Evil* (1949). Joe's decision to make lots of money by working for Tucker, a racketeer and mobster, has made him a successful lawyer, but one without scruples. In contrast, Joe's older brother, Leo (Thomas Gomez), sacrificed to put him through college and law school; a familiar scenario among lower class immigrant families. Without an education, Leo tries his hand at several businesses that fail. Eventually, he goes to work in the illegal numbers policy racket as an independent operator. When Joe's boss, Tucker, has a scheme to control the numbers racket, Joe tries to warn Leo, but his brother refuses his help. In a plot too complicated to detail here, Leo and his bookkeeper are kidnapped by Tucker's men. In the process, the bookkeeper is killed and Leo dies from a heart attack brought on by the shock. Joe learns of Leo's death and takes revenge on Tucker in a dramatic shootout. At film's end, Joe decides to turn himself in to the special prosecutor who has been appointed to investigate the numbers racket. Looking at Leo's body on the banks of the Hudson River, Joe's voice-over expresses his remorse and his hope for redemption:

> I found my brother's body at the bottom there, like an old dirty rag nobody wants. He was dead and I felt that I had killed him. I turned back to give myself up to Hall. Because if a man's life can be lived so long and come out this way, like rubbish, it's something that is horrible and has to be ended one way or another. And I decided to help.

Force of Evil is one of those multilayered films that operates on several levels. At its most obvious level of understanding, it is a gangster story. On a second level, it is a retelling of the story of Cain and Abel. At a third level, it is also a story of personal redemption. Finally, at its highest level of understanding, it can be construed as a critique of the capitalist system. The story of Joe Morse's rise from ghetto to Wall Street raises the moral question of whether it is possible to become financially successful within the capitalist system without becoming corrupted by it.[24] This is not an inappropriate interpretation of the film since it was the collaboration of Abraham Polonsky, who directed and did the screenplay, and actor John Garfield's short-lived independent company, Enterprise Productions. Both men would come under the scrutiny of HUAC during the Hollywood hearings. Polonsky would be blacklisted as one member of the Hollywood Ten while Garfield was subpoenaed but refused to appear and died shortly thereafter.

Counsellor-At-Law and *Force of Evil* were not typical Hollywood redemption films. More common within the industry are films where the major character's fall from grace is due to a personal flaw or addiction. For instance, alcoholism is the cause of the descent in films like *The People Against O'Hara* (1951) and *The Verdict* (1982). Spencer Tracy plays a noted criminal attorney in *The People Against O'Hara* forced to retire because of alcoholism. But he agrees to defend young O'Hara on a murder charge because the family is poor and can only afford to pay a fee of $325 for legal services; a situation rectified by the creation of the public defender system in the 1960s. However, due to inebriation, carelessness, and old age, Tracy loses the case. He still believes O'Hara is innocent, however, and launches his own investigation which leads him to the real killer. Although he secures sufficient evidence to free O'Hara, he is killed in the process, thus providing redemption through death.

Alcoholism proves the downfall, also, of Frank Gavin (Paul Newman) in *The Verdict*. Gavin is a shabby, alcoholic attorney who begins his day with a shot and a beer chaser. Understandably, he has not had a decent case in years and is reduced to ambulance-chasing and hustling up business at wakes. His career is at rock bottom, and he is one step from disbarment when he is given a medical malpractice suit by default. Since the suit is against a Catholic hospital, few lawyers in Boston are willing to take a case where the Catholic Church is the defendant. Gavin rejects an out-of-court settlement by the Boston Archdiocese after he visits the comatose victim in the hospital and decides to go to trial and seek a greater justice and a larger settlement. He sobers up and his pre-alcoholic lawyering skills return. Meanwhile, the Diocese has hired a high-priced legal team to defend its case. Gavin once again proves his competence as an attorney but he must contend with considerable opposition: the defense team has put a corporate spy (Charlotte Rampling) onto him, many of his witnesses are discredited, and the rulings of a prejudicial judge eliminate most of his evidence. His case is saved at the last minute by a surprise witness, a hospital nurse, whose testimony establishes the negligence Gavin requires for a victorious verdict. By film's end, Gavin is sober, has won his big case to restore his reputation, and his clients have received substantial personal injury damages. While it is true that almost half the lawyers who are disbarred or disciplined are alcoholics or drug addicts, the legal community was most unhappy with the film for its erroneous presentation of tort law, trial lawyering, and judicial behavior. The film's legal lapses led two law professors to complain that "If justice is blind, justice got lucky in *The Verdict*."[25]

Drugs, rather than alcohol, is the substance that brings down Eddie Dodd in *True Believer* (1989). Eddie (James Woods) is the former civil rights activist turned dope-sniffer and ambulance chaser. A fighter for liberal causes in the sixties, Eddie's law practice has been neglected by his addiction and his clients are mostly drug dealers and dope pushers. He has become so disillusioned by the legal system that he accepts the injustice of the system since "everybody's guilty of something, therefore, justice is an irrelevant commodity." Goaded by his young protege, Eddie is pressured to take one last "lost cause"—the kind of hopeless cause Jefferson Smith reminds Senator Paine of in *Mr. Smith Goes to Washington*—the case of Kim, an Asian-American inmate, accused of murdering another prisoner. Supported by his protege, who reminds Eddie of himself in his early years, and the legitimacy of his client's self-defense claim, Eddie's investigation reveals that his client is innocent of the crime that sent him to prison in the first place. In the final scene, Kim is met by his family as he leaves prison while Eddie looks on, his confidence renewed and his faith in the justice system restored.

A new twist on the redemption plot is found in *The Devil's Advocate* (1997). Keanu Reeves goes to work for a prestigious New York law firm headed by Satan (Al Pacino). Pacino recruits Reeves after the young lawyer has successfully defended a child molester he knew to be guilty of the crime. In fact, Reeves has a perfect record as prosecutor and defense counsel. It is his desire to win regardless of whether justice is done that makes him the perfect candidate for Pacino's firm. Thus, blind ambition and the lure of financial success seduces Reeves into the New York firm where he learns what it means to work for the devil. During the fiery climax, Reeves asks Pacino why he selected lawyers to do his bidding. Pacino's answer is similar to the reason Macaulay gave: the law touches everyone at some point in life.

Another overly ambitious personal injury lawyer (John Travolta) takes on the case of eight families in Woburn, Massachusetts, whose household members contract leukemia and die. Based on the Jonathan Harr best-selling book, *A Civil Action* (1998), the film identifies two large corporate giants, W. R. Grace and Beatrice Foods, as the industrial polluters who poison the town's water supply. Playing real-life Boston lawyer, Jan Schlichtmann, Travolta appears to be the "white knight" for these families. But his personal greed, legal mistakes, and oversized ego results in the bankruptcy of his law firm and no compensation to his clients. However, the real-life Schlichtmann has undergone a transformation of sorts as he specializes in legal suits against business America in an effort to recover damages due to corporate negligence or indifference.

Women Trial Lawyers

With the exception of the 1930s, women trial lawyers were not major characters in Hollywood films until the decade of the eighties. Contrary to popular belief, Hollywood churned out a dozen or more films in the thirties that featured women lawyers.[26] This is somewhat surprising since at the time women comprised twenty-four percent of the workforce but only three percent of the national bar.[27] Nonetheless, the film industry turned to female lawyers for screen plots in the thirties and forties. Some of these movies were "B" films like *Scarlet Pages* (1930) where actress Elsie Ferguson defends a murderess who turns out to be her illegitimate daughter. Others, however, featured established female stars like Fay Wray (*Ann Carver's Profession*, 1933), Jean Arthur (*The Defense Rests*, 1934) and Claire Trevor (*Career Woman*, 1936). The trend continued until World War II when Hollywood produced more than a dozen films that centered around women lawyers. But what distinguishes these films from the ones that will reappear in the 1980s is the pre-feminist message that women lawyers cannot have successful professional careers and happy personal lives. For instance, Fay Wray's character in *Ann Carver's Profession*, wins an important murder case but afterwards relinquishes her career to save her marriage.

Plots involving women lawyers largely disappeared from the screen over the next four decades, due largely to the industry's interest in war movies, westerns, and musicals. The one notable exception is Katharine Hepburn's character, Amanda Bonner, in the 1950 film, *Adam's Rib*, where she co-starred with Spencer Tracy. *Adam's Rib* is a romantic comedy where Hepburn and Tracy play a husband-and-wife attorney team, except Tracy (Adam Bonner) is an assistant D.A. When Amanda takes the case of a ditzy blonde (Judy Holliday) charged with the attempted murder of her unfaithful spouse, she does not know that Adam has been assigned to prosecute. Hence, the comedy comes from the complications caused by spouses representing different sides of the law. However, what gives the film substance is the fact that Amanda sees in the case an opportunity to criticize the socially acceptable double standard and preach the cause of legal equality. On the other hand, Adam insists that the facts, which are not in dispute, logically lead to an inevitable guilty verdict. But Amanda's defense is that if her client were a man, her actions would be excused under the "unwritten law" that married men have a right to protect their home and their honor. In her summation, Amanda tells the jury that equality is on trial, rather than her client, because she had just as much right to defend her family and home as her husband. The argument proves persuasive and Amanda wins the case. Although the trial has caused domestic problems, Adam and Amanda are reconciled at the end. It is not hyperbole to suggest that Amanda Bonner is an early feminist who would have made an excellent screen attorney for the nineties.[28]

The film industry did not produce movies featuring women trial lawyers again until the 1980s, a sign that feminism had its desired effect on Hollywood, and the studios, as usual, wanted to board the politically correct bandwagon. After all, Hollywood could hardly ignore the significant gains by women in law school acceptances, private sector practice, and judicial prominence. One notable statistical trend involved applications to law school. Women applicants went from three percent of the total law school enrollment in the late-1940s to thirty-four percent in the 1980s. The greatest surge occurred in the seventies where the number of women law students tripled. By the mid-nineties, women comprised forty-four percent of the law school population.[29] Meanwhile, the number of women practicing law moved from pre-World War II single digits to roughly one-quarter of the almost 900,000 practicing lawyers in the U.S. today, with seventy percent in private practice rather than in government employ as district attorneys or public defenders.[30] Additionally, women hold virtually every professional legal role, including U.S. Supreme Court Justice and U.S. Attorney-General.

Beginning in the mid-eighties, Hollywood recognized the change in the legal demographics by releasing more than half-a-dozen feature films with major actresses portraying women lawyers as central characters. Glenn Close, Barbara Hershey, and Jessica Lange played defense lawyers in *Jagged Edge* (1985), *Defenseless* (1991), and *The Music Box* (1989), Debra Winger and Kelly McGillis were district attorneys in *Legal Eagles* (1986) and *The Accused* (1988), Cher portrayed a public defender in *Suspect* (1987), and Mary Elizabeth Mastrantonio a corporate lawyer in *Class Action* (1991).

Hollywood is to be commended for producing films that provide starring roles that previously had been reserved exclusively for male actors. Even so the female-lawyer films cited above have raised serious questions within the legal establishment. The acceptance of women in professional roles is offset by the manner in which these women conduct their professional and personal lives. On a personal level, women lawyers in films are portrayed as either unmarried or divorced, lonely, and frequently without children. Their private lives are often out of synch, giving the appearance of unfulfillment. When children are present, the relationship with their mother is often estranged. Glenn Close's defense lawyer in *Jagged Edge*, for example, has a son who resents her working.[31]

As members of the legal profession, women trial lawyers are being depicted in stereotypical terms as incompetent and unethical attorneys who often exercise poor judgment. For instance, Glenn Close (*Jagged Edge*) sleeps with her client (Jeff Bridges) during his murder trial while Barbara Hershey (*Defenseless*) has an on-going affair with her married client. Both women breach professional ethics and contradict the conventional wisdom that a lawyer should never become involved with a client in order to retain objectivity. Jessica Lange violates a corollary of that principle in *The Music Box* when she decides (unwisely) to represent her father against charges that he had been a war criminal. Meanwhile, Mary Elizabeth Mastrantonio (*Class Action*) is carrying on an office affair with her law supervisor, which clouds her judgment in a civil suit where the plaintiff is represented by her father. Actress Cher (*Suspect*) allows a juror (Dennis Quaid) to provide her with clues in a murder case. Consorting with a juror, for whatever reason, is grounds for disbarment. In

Defenseless, Hershey defends a client in a murder case without informing her or the police that she is a material witness to the crime. Kelly McGillis's district attorney does a disservice to a crime victim (Jodie Foster) in *The Accused* when she plea-bargains away the gang rape charge in favor of going after the witnesses to the crime who encouraged and supported the rape. Worse yet, Mastrantonio conspires with her father in a civil case to destroy her own client.[32]

The examples of outright negative screen portrayals of women lawyers are too numerous to document here. A few examples will suffice. Take the film adaptation of Scott Turow's novel, *Presumed Innocent* (1990), where D.A. Harrison Ford is having an affair with one of the female assistants in his office. Apparently this woman has slept her way up the career ladder since she previously was the mistress of the district attorney. Christine Lahti's character in *And Justice For All* is having an affair with Al Pacino while she sits on the ethics panel that will decide whether he should be disbarred. Charlotte Rampling's ambitious lawyer, seeking to restart her career after a failed marriage, allows herself to be exploited by the legal team representing the Boston Archdiocese in *The Verdict*. She agrees to seduce the opposition lawyer, Frank Gavin (Paul Newman) and spy on him, feeding the collected information back to her boss. Rebecca DeMornay's criminal defense lawyer in *Guilty as Sin* (1993) plants evidence to implicate her own client (Don Johnson) once she realizes that he is guilty of the murder of his wife. Mary Elizabeth Mastrantonio commits several serious blunders in *Class Action*. For openers, she is sleeping with her immediate supervisor, a partner in a prestigious law firm who is in a position to control her career ladder. But she also is guilty of a conflict of interest since she defends a client that is being sued by her father's client. Finally, she knowingly permits her bedmate boss to perjure himself on the stand while she remains mute. Not only do these actions violate the ethical rules of the profession, but they are all likely to lead to disbarment. These are certainly not the kind of lawyers to recommend to your friends.

Doing Justice, Hollywood Style

Statistics reveal that there are more practicing lawyers in the U.S. than in any other country in the world. There is one lawyer for every 300 Americans, yet according to one legal filmography[33] there are just 120 sound films that feature lawyers as central characters or that have plots where the critical action takes place in a courtroom out of the hundred thousands that have been produced in the English language. If Hollywood were interested in filming subjects proportional to their ratio in the larger population, it would have had to produce more than five times the 120 movies that appear in the filmography.

One observation to be drawn from the evidence presented here is that Hollywood has slighted the legal profession to the same extent that it has ignored the politician as screen material. Another is that when the industry does treat the law and lawyers in its films, it generally gets everything wrong. For example, Hollywood has an aversion to presenting a balanced, objective view of the profession. Screen lawyers are more likely to be ready for sainthood (*Young Mr. Lincoln*, *To Kill a Mockingbird*) or candidates for prison (*True Believer*) and the unemployment line (*The Verdict*). Even if we grant dramatic license to the filmmaker, lawyers as a distinct class are no more likely to be one-dimensional characters than politicians or plumbers.

Second, screen lawyers behave as if they flunked law school, repeating the kind of mistakes that are usually corrected during moot court. The public reputation of lawyers (politicians too) as an honorable profession declined considerably after the Watergate scandal and their portrayal in recent Hollywood films has done little, if anything, to alter that perception. Film lawyers not only make stupid mistakes and behave badly, but worse yet, they commit serious offenses that in real life would most certainly lead to disbarment.

Hollywood has been especially unkind to women lawyers in this regard. Their depictions convey the impression that modern women who opt for legal careers are likely to end up unhappy and alone and sometimes indebted to a male colleague. Mary Elizabeth Mastrantonio's lawyer in *Class Action*, for example, defends an automaker in a personal injury suit whose car self-destructs on impact due to a faulty design. The plaintiff is represented by her father (Gene Hackman), a famous liberal-left attorney. The script discriminates against Mastrantonio's character because she works for a law firm that hides damaging evidence, steals documents, and generally lies to cover up its illegal activities. At the end, Mastrantonio has a change of heart and works with her father (against her client, the automaker) to achieve a settlement for the plaintiff. At a victory party in a local hangout, father and daughter dance and reconcile; daughter will join dad's law firm and work for the good guys. This sappy ending reinforced the film's message that "father still knows best."[34] Moreover, film depictions of women lawyers have had an influence on the real world expectations, particularly regarding appropriate dress, demeanor, and lifestyle. According to one source, what these screen portrayals have led to is the "androgynous female attorney" who wears pants suits and adopts other male characteristics in order to avoid appearing too feminine.[35]

But rather than view these characterizations as a conspiracy of the male power structure within the film industry,[36] a more plausible scenario has to do with box office receipts than political ideology. The discussion in this chapter indicates that male lawyers on screen are often just as flawed as their female counterparts. Spencer Tracy and Paul Newman portrayed alcoholic lawyers while James Woods's attorney was a drug addict. In addition, no female screen lawyer yet has even come close to Walter Matthau's unscrupulous sleazy lawyer, "Whiplash Willie," in Billy Wilder's *The Fortune Cookie*.

However, what is of greater concern for the legal profession than gender representation is the question of how justice is achieved in Hollywood films. Aristotle considers two kinds of justice in his *Nicomachean Ethics*: distributive and corrective. Distributive or social justice concerns how honor, prestige, and material goods are distributed throughout society. Hollywood virtually never constructs a film plot around the unequal share of the goods and rewards of society. *Force of Evil* is the rare exception that challenges the economics and the morality of the capitalist system. However, it was not a conventional film for its time since it was produced by an independent company owned by a Marxist writer-director and a leftist-liberal actor.

Aristotle's second kind of justice is corrective, where the law is used as an instrument to provide remedies for those wrongly victimized. Hence, Aristotle's concept of corrective justice requires both an injury and a wrongdoing. The party that has committed the wrong should be identified and punished for it and the law is much more interested in the wrongful injury than in the character of the parties involved. But in Hollywood films, justice is often achieved through unlawful procedures, a timely accident, or last-minute evidentiary discovery. This unrealistic depiction serves to remind us once again that Hollywood is not in the business of presenting reality but in marketing products that sell at the box office. In so doing, the film industry has done a disservice to the moral principles underlying the American legal system and to the men and women who serve as its practitioners.

Eight

Hollywood Goes to War: From the Great War to the Good War

"In war, truth is the first casualty." —Aeschylus

"War is hell." —General William Sherman, Civil War

"Wars may be fought with weapons, but they are won by men."
—General George S. Patton

"World War II? Isn't that the one they fought in black-and-white?"
—A student in Historian Stephen Ambrose's class

"It seems as if all my life I have been waiting for men to return from war:
In the 40s my uncle,
In the 50s my college friends. Some did not return.
In the 60s I waited for my husband to return from two tours in Vietnam." —Homefront woman

The film industry has a special interest in the combat/warfare film genre since the typical war movie is a variation on the standard action-adventure film which normally does well at the box office. The persistent popularity of war movies is evident by their production during peacetime; some like Steven Spielberg's *Saving Private Ryan* (1998) do remarkably well at the box office while others, like Terrence Malick's *The Thin Red Line* (1998), fail to attract a national audience.[1] Surprisingly, one source lists some 5000 war-related film titles distributed during Hollywood's first century.[2]

The appeal of the war movie to the film industry is understandable since the genre allows the studios to fulfill the audience's heroic fantasies while it celebrates national patriotism. The war movie permits the industry to rally round the flag while exploring the dualities of the human condition: individual decency and courage versus brutality of the enemy, individual loyalty and duty versus self-interest and survival and self-sacrifice versus the collective good. The genre also is vulnerable to jingoistic preaching and government enticement since often it is necessary to secure the assistance of the Pentagon or a government agency like the Department of Defense (DOD) to shoot a war film. John Wayne, for instance, could not have made his pro-Vietnam film, *The Green Berets*, without government support, both financial and material.[3] However, when the war film is produced at the direction of the state or under its control, it can easily serve as an instrument for government propaganda. It is highly unlikely that any government, democratic or totalitarian, would support films that question or raise doubts about the wisdom or necessity of the war it is conducting. A nation's power to wage war, Supreme Court Chief Justice Hughes wrote in the Minnesota Moratorium case,[4] is the power to wage it successfully.

Photographing battle scenes dates back to the Civil War and the work of Matthew Brady. By the late nineteenth-century, the French film pioneers, the Lumiere brothers, were taking pictures of training maneuvers. Other filmmakers, however, were not as adventurous, preferring to stay at home and recreate the Boxer Rebellion or the Russo-Japanese War in their backyards. Still others, seeking more realism, urged the military to do battle in daylight to facilitate the shooting. One such incident occurred during the Mexican Revolution when a film company paid Pancho Villa to engage in battle only if the filming conditions were right. Sometimes audiences were at a loss to decipher whether the film they were watching on the Boer War was shot in South Africa or New Jersey.[5] Real combat may be hell but making a war movie often posed no more threat to the participants than suffering from the vagaries of the local weather.

World War I: The Great War

The technology and economics of the motion picture business had advanced sufficiently by the time war broke out in Europe in 1914 that many of the countries involved—particularly Germany, France, and Britain—already had established film industries. Hollywood, however, was still preoccupied with the growing pains associated with the development of a new industry. Prior to 1917, when the U.S. entered the European war, the film industry imitated the "official" government neutrality policy by making films that would appease both isolationists and interventionists. Films like J. Stuart Blackton's *Battle Cry of Peace* (1915) and Thomas Ince's *Civilization* (1916) cancelled each other out, preaching warmongering and pacifism, respectively. Hollywood produced films which characterized the Germans as "Huns" and brutes, alternating these with anti-war movies which cautioned Americans against becoming cannon fodder in a predominately European conflict.

The situation changed dramatically after President Wilson's 1916 election to a second term. President Wilson appointed George Creel to head the Committee on Public Information (CPI) with authority to oversee all propaganda activities, including a special department "to sell the war to America," once the U.S. officially joined the Allied side. The Creel Committee was responsible for the distribution of official Army and Navy war footage and for the production of such films as *Pershing's Crusaders*, about the Army Expeditionary Forces, *America's Answer*, which dealt with mobilization efforts, and *Under Four Flags*, which promoted the role of the Allies in the war—all released in 1918. But since U.S. involvement in the war was relatively brief (around nineteen months) little documentary footage was shot of trench warfare involving American troops.[6] Hollywood neglected the European war until after 1917 when twenty-three feature films about the war were released, amounting to almost one-quarter of Hollywood's total film production for that year. With the arrival of the armistice in November 1918, however, Hollywood was left with a plethora of war movies that American audiences largely ignored.[7]

When the mood of the country turned towards isolationism under the presidencies of Harding and Coolidge, the film industry rejected narratives that portrayed war in idealistic images in favor of stories that depicted the futility of war and the virtues of pacifism. Consequently, for two decades Hollywood made films about the war that were skeptical, or at least, contradictory. Unlike previous patriotic World War I films, *The Big Parade* (1925), *What Price Glory?* (1926), and *Wings* (1928) presented ambivalent images of suffering as noble events while they questioned the validity of American anti-German propaganda. Disillusionment with the war is the theme of *The Big Parade* where silent screen star John Gilbert played a wounded veteran returning to an indifferent, and even callous, homefront. Then in *All Quiet on the Western Front* (1930), the classic anti-war film of trench combat presented from the German point of view, a young recruit is killed by a sniper's bullet as he reaches over the parapet for a butterfly in the closing days of the war. This scene epitomized the futility of war for almost all the participants. Nor can a moviegoer find a stronger anti-war sentiment than the one in *The Eagle and the Hawk* (1933), where a burnt-out pilot

(Fredric March) regrets the shooting down of German planes during air combat. In a scene filled with sarcasm and self-loathing, he raises his glass in a toast, saying: "I give you war," before he goes off and shoots himself.[8]

When war swept across Europe and Asia in the 1930s, Hollywood reacted cautiously. The industry continued to sell mostly entertainment to American audiences while the interventionist-isolationist scenario from the First World War replayed itself to another generation. But as fascism gained a stronghold in Europe and Japan waged an imperialist war in Asia, several film studios sought to reverse the demythologization of World War I as meaningless slaughter and wasted idealism in a series of films that warned the county against the threat of fascism and that justified war as a necessary means to protect democracy. Between 1939 and 1941, the studios turned out fourteen anti-Nazi films, six military preparedness movies, and two World War I films that glorified wartime heroics.[9]

Warner Brothers' *Confessions of a Nazi Spy* (1939) brought the threat of fascism close to home as it depicted the FBI crackdown on a Nazi spy ring in America. The film's message was clear: America was not immune against Nazi subversion. The following year, Alfred Hitchcock's *Foreign Correspondent* (1940) reiterated the warning to an indifferent America when the film's hero, an American correspondent based in London, broadcasts a message in terms reminiscent of Edward R. Murrow: "The lights have gone out in Europe! Hang on to your lights, America—they're the only lights still on in the world!" Meanwhile, MGM's *The Mortal Storm* (1940) portrayed the evils of Nazism in personal terms as a university professor is sent to a concentration camp for his anti-Nazi opposition and his daughter is killed trying to escape to Switzerland. In that same year, Charlie Chaplin used satire and comedy to poke fun at Hitler and Mussolini in *The Great Dictator*, but turned quite serious in the final scene where Hynkel, Chaplin's alter ego, asks the army to overthrow the dictators and restore power to the people. Even Bogart's character in *Casablanca*, the disillusioned owner of "Rick's Cafe," comes to realize that the threat of fascism must take precedence over his love for Ingrid Bergman. By giving his visa papers to Bergman and her husband, a leader of the Free French resistance, Bogart facilitates their escape from North Africa to continue the fight against fascism.

Additionally, Warner Brothers, the producers of *Casablanca*, also sought to restore enthusiasm for war by portraying combat death as a form of personal redemption. In both *The Fighting 69th* (1940) and *Sergeant York* (1941), the major characters are transformed by their war experiences. Both films sought to revive positive memories of the "Great

War" despite statistics that proved the First World War as the costliest war in human history up to that time. *The Fighting 69th* confined itself to recounting the adventures of a tough New York kid (James Cagney) assigned to an Irish regiment that acquitted itself nobly in battle. The story centers around the Cagney character as he goes from cowardice under fire to heroic death. The New York regiment suffered heavy casualties, but the film neglected the pain and suffering in favor of the value of wartime camaraderie. The actual war, however, was not quite as romantic since it was fought with the new technologies of its time: machine guns, air bombing, armored tanks, flame-throwers, and poison gas, resulting in enormous casualties on both sides. In the first five months of the war, for instance, the French suffered casualties that exceeded all the British losses in World War II. One campaign, the Battle of the Somme, was fought over a four month period for six miles of French soil at the cost of over 300,000 lives.[10] In yet another engagement, the 1916 Battle of Verdun, a staggering 700,000 French and German soldiers were killed.[11] For its nineteen month participation, American casualties, dead and wounded, exceeded 320,000.[12]

On the other hand, the major character in *Sergeant York* is a poor Tennessee country-boy who is transformed from Christian pacifist to combat hero while serving in the trenches. The film biography of Alvin York allowed Warner Brothers to glorify war and make it morally respectable when fought for honorable ends. In the film, York becomes a one-man army after he concludes that killing Germans would help to end the war and bring about peace. In this sense, *Sergeant York* represents an attempt to erase the memory of those anti-war films of the twenties and early thirties.

However, the Japanese attack on Pearl Harbor altered the course of world events and transformed Hollywood along with the rest of the country. President Roosevelt followed the lead of his predecessor, President Wilson, by creating an Office of War Information (OWI) as a successor to the Creel Committee. In 1942, the administration established a Bureau of Motion Pictures within the OWI to provide leadership and guidance on how the industry could best contribute to the war effort. Between Hitler's invasion of Poland in 1939 and the Japanese surrender in September 1945, Hollywood released a number of motion pictures that touched on the war, either directly through films of military training and combat or through stories that dealt with the hardships of life at home.

World War II: The Good War

If the First World War was dubbed the "Great War" because of the tremendous human cost in waging it, these losses pale in comparison to the millions[13] of lives lost in World War II. Considered by Americans to be a "good war" in the sense that it unified the nation to wage a successful war against an ideology that sought world domination while it stimulated a depressed economy at home, providing jobs and opportunities for women and minorities that could not be denied in the future. And these objectives were achieved without physical damage to the country. Yet describing World War II as the "good war" is an oxymoron to the rest of the world when the actual damage of the war is realized: more than 45 million dead, including 20 million Russians; whole cities like London and Dresden virtually leveled by systematic bombing; six million Jews and another five million gentiles, Jehovah's Witnesses, gypsies, and homosexuals victims of the European holocaust; the cities of Hiroshima and Nagasaki demolished by atomic bombs; and much of Europe and Asia left in ruins that would take decades to rebuild.[14]

The war proved advantageous for some Americans who traded in the black market or for corporations that enjoyed surplus profits from the war machine. Corporations and businesses that were converted to war production or engaged in the manufacture of war-related goods enjoyed soaring profits. The shift from civilian goods to war production created jobs in defense plants and war factories that were filled by women and minorities complemented by 4-F (nondraftable) men.

The film industry also profited from the war financially but not without paying a price. Some of its most established male stars—Edward Albert, Douglas Fairbanks, Jr., Henry Fonda, Clark Gable, Robert Montgomery, Tyrone Power, James Stewart, and Robert Taylor—entered the military, with most seeing combat duty.[15] But declaring oneself a conscientious objector (CO) like actor Lew Ayers could ruin your film career.[16] Several movie stars lost their lives during the war years. British actor Leslie Howard, one of the leads in *Gone With the Wind*, had his plane shot down by the Germans over Portugal while actress Carole Lombard died in a plane crash on her return home from a war bond drive. Many entertainers toured with the United Service Organization (USO) or worked in local service canteens. Other Hollywood stars were active in raising money for the war or in supporting rationing efforts. Gene Kelly, for example, came to Williamsport, a small town in northcentral Pennsylvania, to make a war bond film that featured local servicemen.

The film industry also profited as film attendance increased during the war. Going to the local movie theater became a weekly activity.

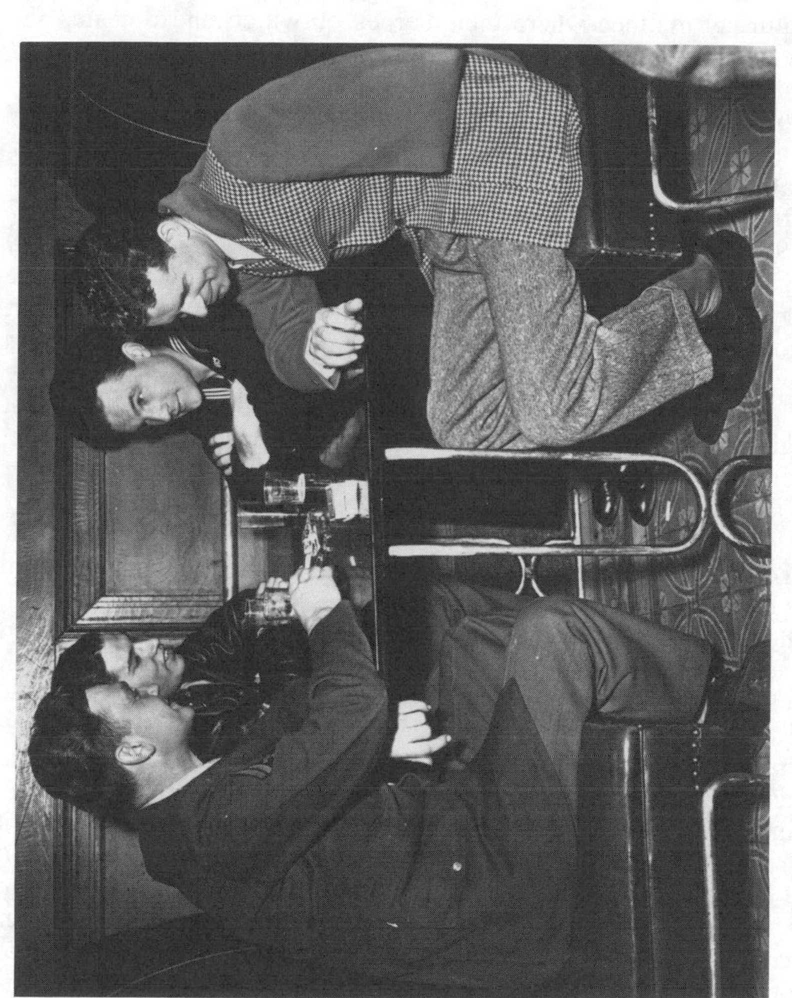

Actor Gene Kelly and local citizens relaxing in the Old Corner Hotel, Williamsport, Pa., during the shooting of a World War II bond film. (Courtesy: Charlotte Gordon.)

Movie attendance skyrocketed, resulting in the doubling of box-office receipts.[17] Defense plant workers, often working overtime shifts, looked forward to the weekly three hours of relaxation at the movies. Parents and spouses sought respite from the boredom and anxiety of waiting for their loved ones to return home. School-aged youngsters eagerly awaited the Saturday matinee where their heroes outwitted and defeated the enemy on a weekly basis. For these youngsters, the lessons of war were learned from films and newsreels.

Hollywood responded to the public demand for entertainment by grinding out almost 400 films a year to meet the needs of all age groups. While the film industry continued to churn out musicals, comedies, and westerns, around one-quarter of the 1,500 films released between 1942 and 1945 were movies with war-related themes.[18] These are broadly classified into combat films, including military training and pre-battle preparation and homefront movies about the domestic impact of the war. The government contributed to the mix with its own documentaries and propaganda films. All shared a common purpose, namely, to depict the world as divided into good and evil forces, slave and free states, and that the fighting of the war would regenerate the country and lead to national harmony and unity.

Combat Films

World War II movies fall into four categories: the pure combat film, the hybrid training-battle action film, the resistance of our Allies film, and the homefront film, when men were away in the service and women entered the workforce. Jeanine Basinger,[19] in her seminal work on movies of the Second World War, insists that Hollywood produced few combat films, particularly before 1943. According to Basinger, the industry produced many more films where combat was secondary to the military training or preparation for battle. These hybrid films—part-training, part-combat—were less expensive to shoot and often did not require government assistance. The formula was successful because it could be recycled, substituting one branch of the service for another. For example, *Crash Dive* (1943) depicts naval training before the crew goes into combat while *Sands of Iwo Jima* (1949) depicts a similar scenario for the Marines. Actually Hollywood made less than two dozen films where the action centers around combat fought on the ground, in the air, or on the sea and where the armed forces face death and destruction in reaching, or holding, a military objective. Basinger considers these films "special" because many included actual newsreel footage, which added to the realism of the action scenes, and because most required the support of the military and the Department of Defense to be made.

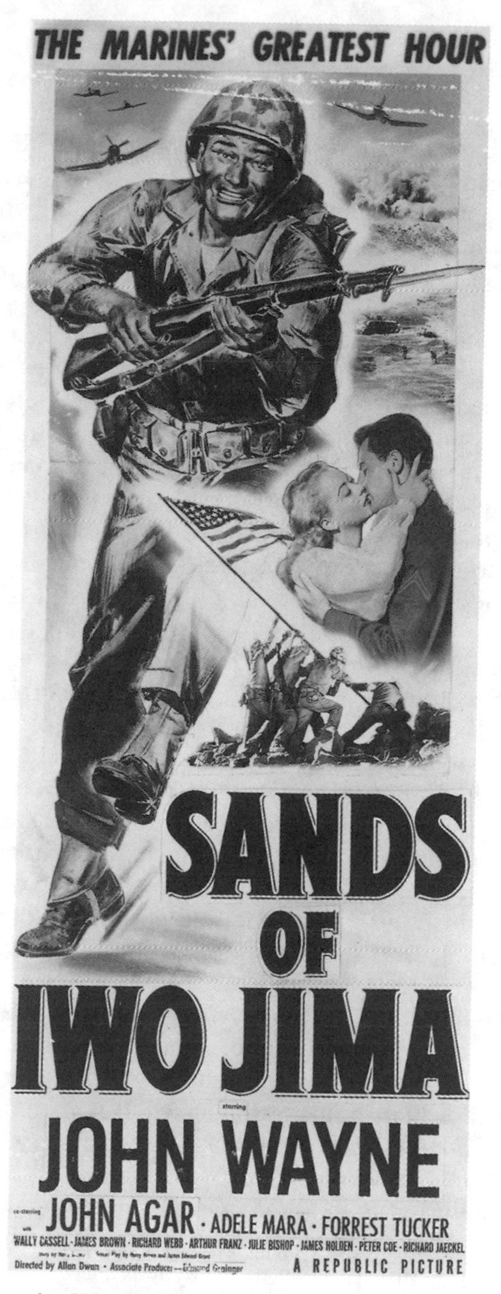

Theater poster for the World War II film, *Sands of Iwo Jima*, used by the Marine Corps as a recruitment device. (Courtesy: Republic Entertainment Inc.)

Wake Island (1942) was the first World War II combat film distributed to movie theaters. The film deposits the audience on a small Pacific island where a Marine detachment's job is to protect the island because it serves as a refueling base for flights from the West Coast to Asia. After the attack on Pearl Harbor, the Japanese fleet bombarded the island, softening it up for a land invasion. Although outnumbered, the Marines refuse to surrender, holding the enemy at bay for sixteen days. No American soldier is alive at film's end. Although U.S. forces suffered a military defeat at *Wake Island*, Hollywood, with the assistance of the OWI, could still turn the film into a positive propaganda piece by having the commanding officer send this final message to headquarters: "The enemy has landed; the issue is still in doubt." The Defense Department thought so highly of the film that it became an integral part of military training, providing a rationale for the value of the human sacrifice against what the film described as "the forces of destruction."

The pace picked up considerably in 1943 as thirteen combat films were released to theaters. Several, like *Bataan* and *Action in the North Atlantic*, depicted American defeats or unsuccessful forays against the enemy similar to *Wake Island*. But such films disappeared once the war turned in favor of the Allies; in the Pacific the U.S. victory in the Battle of Midway proved decisive while in Europe, the surrender of Italy not only took the Italians out of the war but also paved the way for the Normandy invasion. The American defeat suffered at Wake Island was reversed in *Guadalcanal Diary* which glorified the Marines' victory over the Japanese in several battles in the Solomon Islands. The film was based on an eyewitness account, but it contained stock characters that appeared in most war movies: the stereotypical group of tough sergeants, sensitive chaplains, and typical melting-pot GI platoon featuring rural Southerners, ethnic and racial minorities, and the always-present wise guy from Brooklyn. Fifty years later, Terrence Malick's *The Thin Red Line* revisits Guadalcanal for a new generation of moviegoers. In depicting the fierce battle between American and Japanese forces for control of this strategic island, Malick's film preaches that war transforms its participants into less than human characters. But it remains problematic whether *The Thin Red Line* could have been made while the U.S. was engaged in the Second World War.

Combat movies after *Guadalcanal Diary* featured established male stars like John Wayne in predictable plots that depicted successful combat missions against the enemy. Wayne was kept busy during the war years because he did not qualify for military duty and leading men were in demand. Wayne played a PT commander fighting the Japanese in John Ford's *They Were Expendable* (1945) and also portrayed an American officer working with the Filipino resistance movement in *Back to Bataan* (1945). By recreating MacArthur's return to the islands, the film sought to reverse the demoralizing effect of the infamous Bataan death march in which thousands of starving American and Filipino troops, captured by the Japanese in the early days of the war, died as a result of the forced march through the jungle. Made with the full cooperation of the U.S. government, *Back to Bataan* describes the almost three-year guerrilla war waged by the Filipino resistance against the Japanese invaders. Wayne again is cast as a heroic figure, leading his undermanned and poorly armed Filipino fighters against the superior Japanese forces. The two *Bataan* films depict the Japanese in particularly brutal terms, including scenes which detail the hanging of a school principal for refusing to take down the American flag, the beating of a young boy to extract information, and the shooting, stabbing, and inhumane treatment of the death marchers. There is one scene where Wayne tries to explain the war to a young Filipino boy by saying, "You're the guy we're fighting this for." It is a line that Wayne would reuse at the end of his Vietnam film, *The Green Berets*, thirty years later.

Meanwhile, another Hollywood leading man (Errol Flynn) portrayed a leader of an American paratroop battalion dropped behind enemy lines on a mission to disable a Japanese radio station in *Objective Burma* (1945). After completing their mission, however, Flynn and his men are cut off by Japanese forces and must fight their way back to Allied lines. The remainder of the film describes their escape from enemy forces.

On the European front, movies like *The Story of GI Joe* (1945), about war correspondent Ernie Pyle and *A Walk in the Sun* (1945), about an infantry platoon in Italy that achieves its mission despite the loss of its officers, extolled the virtues of the foot soldier. Pyle is the centerpiece of *The Story of GI Joe*, a modest war film that concentrates on the ordeal of the infantry soldiers—the soldiers that would be characterized as the "grunts" of the Vietnam war. Although the real Pyle was in his forties, he insisted on walking along with the Army infantry unit during the Italian campaign. It was said that his column was read by forty million Americans back home. Pyle served as technical advisor on the film, then returned to the front where he was killed by a sniper. He never did see the completed film. *A Walk in the Sun* also views war on a small scale as the film follows the adventures of one platoon in achieving its modest objective—the capture of a strategic farmhouse held by the Germans, but not without significant casualties. War is hell for the infantrymen in these two films.

Hybrid World War II films usually began in boot camp as the military trains and prepares its troops for battle. This preparedness sequence may take up to half of the film's running time. For example, in *Crash Dive* (1943), actors Tyrone Power and Dana Andrews play sub commanders who complete a successful raid against a Japanese installation. But as was common in these hybrid war films, the two men spend most of their time competing for the love of a woman back home. Meanwhile, in *Gung Ho!* (1943) Randolph Scott is placed in charge of a specially created Marine battalion, Carlson's Raiders, that destroys the Japanese installation at Makin Island, signalling the beginning of the American offensive in the Pacific.

Another favorite wartime movie subject had to do with the resistance of our Allies against the Axis powers. These films portrayed ordinary people as heroes, engaged in extraordinary and courageous feats against an invading enemy. The Russians were portrayed heroically in two 1943 films, *The North Star* and *Days of Glory*. Both films extolled the virtues of the Russian people and the love expressed for their homeland. *The North Star* was the work of a talented group: writer Lillian Hellman, composers Aaron Copland and Ira Gershwin, and director Lewis Milestone. The film focused on a battle of wits between the German commander and the village leader. *Days of Glory*, on the other hand, was a B-movie with a cast of unknowns. Dedicated to the bravery of the Russian people, especially the peasants, the film stars Gregory Peck (in his film debut) as the leader of a small group of guerrillas, all of whom are dead by film's end. *Days of Glory* is an obvious effort to drum up American support for its Russian allies, but Hollywood could not resist the temptation to romanticize the war. While the Russians suffered tremendous losses, the film failed to do justice to their cause. Although there are enough "comrade" greetings in the film to fill Red Square, Hollywood dealt in cliché characterizations (Germans as brutes, Russians as happy peace-loving people who sing, dance, and quote Pushkin) and fantasy images of the war on the Russian front. Ironically, some of the people involved in these sympathetic screen portrayals would later come under the scrutiny of HUAC, even though these pro-Russian films had received the approval of the OWI.

Meanwhile, the exploits of the Norwegians during World War II are described in two films: *The Commandos Strike at Dawn* (1942) and *Edge of Darkness* (1943). The question of Norwegian resistance, however, is equivocal. When war broke out in Europe, Norway proclaimed its neutrality and continued to trade iron ore to the Germans. It was in 1940 after Churchill ordered the Norwegian waters to be mined to prevent the Germans from reaching their iron ore supply that the Nazis responded by invading Norway. After the Norwegian government capitulated to the Germans, a growing guerrilla movement developed among the population; it is the resistance of ordinary people that is celebrated in these films. Made before Pearl Harbor, *The Commandos Strike at Dawn* was filmed with the cooperation of the Canadian and British governments and starred a contingent of American and British actors. On the other hand, *Edge of Darkness* was strictly Hollywood as Errol Flynn (an Australian by birth) played a local fisherman who leads the Norwegian underground against the Nazis. Meant as a tribute to the Norwegian resistance, the film was cast with stock actors from the Warner Brothers studio and it looked like it was filmed on the backlot. Still the film contains two scenes of German brutality, involving the beating and public humiliation of the town's intellectual and the rape of a resistance woman, which, under Production Code guidelines, had to be implied rather than depicted. Both crimes were revenged in typical Hollywood fashion.

While men saw combat duty, women joined the armed services as nurses and as noncombatant replacements for the men at the front. Almost 400,000 women, including nurses, saw military service during the war; some lost their lives in the performance of that duty. The Army Air Force, for example, commissioned over 1,000 women as pilots to fly ferry planes and to tow gunnery targets in an effort to release men for combat duty overseas. Although not officially recognized by the government as military personnel, thirty-eight women died in plane crashes in the course of flying sixty million miles until the unit was disbanded by Congress in December 1944.[20]

Regrettably, Hollywood chose to ignore these women and others like them. When women appeared in World War II films they usually were cast in the roles of USO entertainers, homefront workers, and sometimes, as spies. Mainly, however, Hollywood minimized their contribution by portraying them as romantic interests or as volunteers and workers in field hospitals. There were two notable exceptions to this generalization: *So Proudly We Hail* (1943) and *Cry Havoc* (1943). Both films concerned nurses serving under combat conditions. An estimated 50,000 nurses served in the military during the Second World War, receiving military as well as medical training. Nurses served in all military branches and in all the war zones; some became prisoners of war when Corregidor fell, others were killed when field hospitals were shelled by the enemy.[21] Ironically, both Paramount's *So Proudly We Hail* (1943) and MGM's *Cry Havoc* were released in the same year and paid tribute to Red Cross nurses. In *So Proudly We Hail* an all-star cast of actresses is trapped in the early days of the Pacific war. The film depicts their daily hardships, including several encounters with the enemy. In one such confrontation, a nurse sacrifices herself by becoming a human bomb, permitting the

Jacqueline Cochran, Director of Women Pilots, with Women Airforce Service Pilots (WASPs) at Camp Davis, N.C. during World War II. (Courtesy: The Woman's Collection, Texas Woman's University.)

other nurses to escape from the advancing Japanese. The story line requires virtually non-stop combat conditions, but Paramount, bowing to projected market demand, permitted a few romantic interludes. The film concludes with the fall of Bataan; despite that defeat the film remains more optimistic than is warranted by the actual status of the war at the time. Repeating the patriotism of the Marines in *Wake Island*, the nurses in *So Proudly We Hail* represent an American confidence that democracy will prevail over the forces of evil.

MGM's *Cry Havoc*, another token entry by a major Hollywood film studio regarding the role of women during World War II, also relates the plight of nurses caught behind enemy lines during the American retreat from Bataan, including one casualty when a nurse is machine-gunned to death while swimming. It remains a mystery why two film studios virtually made the identical movie on a similar subject and released them during the same year. Whether by accident or design, these films influenced the federal government to act to recognize the heroism of the women who served. Washington finally erected a Women's Memorial at the entrance to Arlington National Cemetery to commemorate the contribution of women to the country's military service, beginning with the American Revolution and continuing through the Persian Gulf War.[22]

Hollywood did not do right by women or minorities during World War II but the film studios certainly knew how to churn out hate propaganda against the enemy. No one expected Hollywood to present heroic images of the enemy, but the studios took every opportunity to inject propaganda into their screenplays. The war, of course, was being fought at home as well as at the front. The research of film scholars,[23] applying content analysis to World War II movies, reveals a strong film bias against the Japanese relative to the Germans and the Italians. The Japanese bias led to racist images on the screen. This was less true of war films involving the Germans because the war with Germany was being waged ideologically in wartime movies, that is, it was being waged against the German government—the Nazis—and not necessarily against the German people. As a matter of fact, even before *Schindler's List*, there were a few films where Germans befriend Allied soldiers or protect civilians from potential harm. Such an event occurs in *Desperate Journey* (1942) where Errol Flynn and his squadron are aided by some "good" Germans. Again, in *The Moon Is Down* (1943), a film about the Nazi occupation of Norway, one of the German officers is portrayed rather sympathetically. He is tired of the war and is homesick. His softness leads to his death, but not before his character has the opportunity to voice the sentiments of a sane Germany. This is definitely not the case for the Japanese, who fared so badly in these war movies as to suggest a more racist depiction rather than an ideological treatment. Take the 1942 B-movie, *Little Tokyo, U.S.A.*, for instance. In this story of domestic espionage in Southern California, the film implied that any person of Japanese ancestry was a spy or saboteur. All the Japanese characters were portrayed as treacherous and not to be trusted. The movie was considered so prejudicial that even the War Relocation Authority, the government agency that administered the internment camps, complained to the OWI about the film.[24] The following year, RKO Pictures released *Behind the Rising Sun* (1943), a piece of anti-Japanese propaganda that concerned the efforts of a Japanese father to persuade his Americanized son to join the Sino-Japanese war. In approximately ninety minutes of running time, the film contains scenes of Japanese raping women, bayoneting children, and torturing prisoners by placing needles under their fingernails, burning them with cigarettes, and hanging them by their wrists until dead.[25] While it is true that these were primarily low-budget B-films rushed into release after Pearl Harbor and could be excused on that account, the depictions of Japanese soldiers in feature films like *Wake Island* and *Guadalcanal Diary* also were overtly racist. Derogatory terms like "Nips," "monkeys," and "apes" were used to refer to the Japanese. Meanwhile, Japanese soldiers did not fight by the rules; in contrast, American GIs harbored little hatred toward their enemies and even tended to their wounds. On the screen, the Japanese had no redeeming qualities.[26] These negative depictions of the Japanese should be considered part of a continuous line of racial stereotypes of Asians historically traceable to the Philippine insurgency following the Spanish-American War and reinforced during the war in Vietnam.

Whatever misgivings film scholars and historians have regarding Hollywood war movies, there is no denying the staying power of the genre. The box office success of World War II films challenged the conventional wisdom in the film industry that the public would not go to war movies. To test the market, Hollywood released nine combat films in 1949 alone, including *Sands of Iwo Jima*, which grossed $25 million, a considerable figure at that time. The financial success of these war films a few years after the end of hostilities encouraged the industry to generate more movies in the same genre over the next four decades. Combat films included *The Longest Day* (1962), *Battle of the Bulge* (1965), and *Patton* (1970); prison camps were featured in *Stalag 17* (1953), *The Bridge on the River Kwai* (1957), and *The Great Escape* (1963).

In fact, between 1948 and 1970, Hollywood released at least one World War II combat film every year.[27] Even into the nineties, the studios continued to find the Second World War good box office with several major films such as *Saving Private Ryan* (1998)[28] critical and financial successes.

Homefront

World War II movies remained in the Hollywood repertory for a good forty years after the war's closure but many of these were action/combat films. Only a few Hollywood films had plots that revolved around life at home during the war, showing the housing shortage, scarcity of consumer goods, and food rationing. Hollywood produced just two major feature films about the homefront during the war, *Tender Comrade* (1943) and *Since You Went Away* (1944). In *Tender Comrade*, five women (girlfriends, wives, and mothers) live together while their men are in the service.[29] Ginger Rogers stars as a woman who decides to share a house with three other women who work with her in the same defense plant after her husband is drafted. The fifth member of the group is a German woman who, because she is not a citizen and cannot work in the defense plant, serves as cook and housemaid for the others. The women in *Tender Comrade* are depicted as independent characters and not mere extensions of their menfolk. The film was considered a "woman's" picture because the audience learns details about the war off-camera. *Tender Comrade* was written by Dalton Trumbo and directed by Edward Dmytryk, later to be identified as members of the Hollywood Ten. Their involvement with the film, coupled with the word "tender" in its title and its communal living arrangements ("Share and share alike"), led HUAC to label it "un-American" after the war.

In *Since You Went Away* (1944), Claudette Colbert's husband is called to military duty, leaving her to care for their two children. The film focuses on the plight of a middle-class family struggling to survive the war years. Money becomes a primary concern as the family is forced to take in a boarder. Similar to *Tender Comrade*, *Since You Went Away* features major female characters, (even Colbert's children are girls), with the studio's intention to appeal to women in the audience who could relate to the situation on the screen. Much like the World War II combat film, these homefront movies glorified individual sacrifice for the good of the country. Colbert's character is compelled to enter the workforce as a welder (aka Rosie the Riveter) in a defense plant.

However, the most honored film about the homefront turned out to be *The Best Years of Our Lives* (1946), based on an story published in 1944 about problems that veterans faced in adjusting to civilian life again. Production was delayed for two years and the film was not released until the war had ended. Using three different characters—Al Stephenson (Fredric March), a middle-aged banker turned army sergeant,

Three returning World War II veterans (Dana Andrews, Fredric March, and Harold Russell) must adjust to civilian life in *The Best Years of Our Lives*. cc1946. The Goldwyn Entertainment Company. (Courtesy MGM CLIP+STILL.)

Fred Derry (Dana Andrews), an Air Force hero and former drugstore clerk, and Homer Parrish (Harold Russell in his first film role) as a Navy vet who lost both hands in combat—as composites to represent war veterans, the film focused on issues that faced the discharged soldiers' return to civilian life, namely, employment, marriage, family, and social acceptance.[30] The film was a box office hit and proved to be an artistic success as it won seven Oscars, including best picture.

Documentaries

Possibly Hollywood could be excused for glamorizing the war film, exploiting the setting to depict acts of heroism and self-sacrifice and to show individual deeds of glory as the means to build character and test manhood. But the federal government cannot be absolved from treating the film medium as another weapon of war. The OWI, through its Bureau of Motion Pictures, had primary responsibility for oversight of Hollywood films produced during the war years. But the OWI also commissioned war movies of its own, some intended for the armed forces, others for general release. The U.S. government distributed 164 films between 1941 and 1945, with thirteen pre-Pearl Harbor films acting as promotionals for the USO and the Red Cross.[31] Commencing in 1942, however, the emphasis shifted to films that would directly aid the war effort through recruitment in the Coast Guard and through special pleadings to women to consider working in defense plants. For instance, government-made movies appealed to feelings of patriotism in soliciting war bonds sales, conserving resources, and planting victory gardens. On the other hand, some government films served as warnings against profiting from the war (black marketeering) and the dangers of loose lips and careless talk.

The government sought to offset the more romantic and fantasized images of the Hollywood film war by shooting its own combat footage. These films were commercially distributed through five newsreel companies, including MGM's News of the Day, Paramount News, RKO-Pathé News, 20th Century-Fox's Movietone News, and Universal Newsreel, and were shown as part of the weekly movie program in at least two-thirds of the nation's theaters.[32] These government-produced films, known as official reports, supposedly cost the government $50 million a year to produce and distribute. Many of these are still available in the National Archives. The government was fortunate to have the services of such prominent Hollywood directors as John Ford, Frank Capra, George Stevens, William Wyler, and John Huston at its disposal, either as civilians under contract or as military personnel assigned to a combat unit. Some of the more important documentaries made by these men included *The Memphis Belle* (1944), in which Wyler depicted the last mission of a B-52 bomber, part of the Eighth U.S. Air Force Command, from ground crew preparation to its return from a bombing mission over Germany. John Huston was commissioned by the War Department to make two films; one, *Report from the Aleutians* (1943) about a bombing raid and the second, *The Battle of San Pietro* (1945) about the Italian campaign. To capture the sense of combat, Huston accompanied a front-line unit and shot footage while the battle raged. But the Army disliked the film because it shattered the warrior myth. It gave the film a "secret" classification, insuring that it would be kept out of public circulation. Huston's documentary was not distributed to the public until almost one-third of its footage was cut from the original.[33] Another Hollywood director, John Ford, recreated the attack on Pearl Harbor in *December 7th: The Movie* (1943).[34] Previously, Lt. Commander Ford, on duty in the Pacific, shot film during the fierce naval and air war being waged at the time. Ford filmed as the battle raged and then edited and released the result as *The Battle of Midway* (1942). The Navy was so impressed with the film that it was used to stimulate war bond sales.[35] Films like *The Battle of Midway* and commercial newsreel containing actual footage depicted the war in terms that even Hollywood, with all its money, talent, and technical resources, failed to replicate. Although edited in some cases, these documentaries portrayed the Second World War in more realistic terms than the traditional Hollywood version, that is, until the first hour of *Saving Private Ryan*.[36]

Korea: The Forgotten War

There are many reasons why the Korean conflict (1950-53) (Congress did not declare war) has been dubbed "the forgotten war." One explanation is that the war was fought under the auspices of the United Nations (UN), even though the U.S. contributed a majority of the troops and supplies. In effect, the UN sanctioned the sending of troops as part of America's right to meet its treaty obligations since the North Koreans were the aggressors. Eventually other UN members contributed troops to what was referred to as an "international police action." Moreover, it was a war fought for limited objectives. From the UN viewpoint, the war was not about gaining territory or furthering political or military objectives. The sole purpose of the UN action was to drive the North Koreans back across the 38th parallel and restore the territorial status quo. Meanwhile, the fighting between North and South waged for three years and included Chinese and U.S. intervention. A year after the initial clash between

North and South Korean troops, cease-fire talks were initiated while sporadic fighting continued for two more years until an armistice was signed in 1953. Unlike Vietnam, however, Korea was not a television war. Instead, the networks continued to rely on government reports for their news rather than journalists in the field, a facsimile of the way news was collected during World War II. Therefore, the Korean war was not filmed as it happened.

Nor did the war affect the collective conscience of the nation as did its predecessor. A memorial to its veterans was not constructed in Washington until 1995, more than forty years after the armistice and thirteen years after the erection of the Vietnam Wall, despite the more than 54,000 casualties suffered in the Korean conflict. Finally, Hollywood did not seem terribly interested in the war; it failed to stir the emotions of the stars or serve as a resource for screen plots. Possibly because the war in Korea was one of attrition and stalemate rather than liberation and military victory, the film studios believed they could not duplicate the patriotism and idealism of the World War II movies.

A reliable indication of how Hollywood neglected Korea is found in the production statistics covering the years between 1950 and 1970 when the industry released four times as many World War II movies as films on the Korean War. The two most popular war movies during this period were films about the Second World War: *From Here to Eternity* (1953) and *The Bridge on the River Kwai*(1957). Also, no film on the Korean War has won an Oscar in any of the major categories in contrast to the number of awards presented to World War II and Vietnam War films.

But when Hollywood treated the subject, it usually did so in low budget B-movies without production values and minus strong marketing campaigns. Basinger reports that many of the Korean war films were replays of World War II combat films in terms of narrative development, characterizations, and symbolic events.[37] For example, the Korean war films continued to utilize the composite combat group, including ethnic diversity, as the basis for plot development. The film's hero was still the tough officer or sergeant and the central action was a "single mission" to knock out an enemy objective or to make a last stand against overwhelming enemy forces. To make the films more plausible, Hollywood updated its military hardware to match the requirements of the new conflict, hence, the carbine replaced the M1 rifle, the helicopter and jet plane replaced the B-52 bomber and fighter planes, and the Mobile Army Surgical Hospitals (MASH) replaced base hospitals.

Hollywood did exploit one new methodology used by the enemy—brainwashing. *The Manchurian Candidate* is not a Korean combat film but rather a study of communist brainwashing. The plot concerns an officer, captured in Korea, who is taken to China and programmed to carry out political assassinations. In *Prisoner of War* (1954), Ronald Reagan stars as an Army Intelligence officer who allows himself to be captured by the North Koreans. He avoids the torture and brainwashing administered to the other prisoners by pretending to cooperate with the communists. In this way, he is able to collect evidence on the mistreatment of American POWs. Brainwashing was a major concern during the Korean War and it proved a sticking point during the two years of peace talks because the North Koreans insisted on a return of all their prisoners while the U.S. and its UN allies wanted POWs to have freedom of choice. Although brainwashing as a device for political assassinations and terrorist attacks had dramatic potential, Hollywood, with one exception, assigned films on the subject only low priority.

Several films on the Korean War, however, deserve consideration. Two, *The Steel Helmet* and *Fixed Bayonets*, were made by the decorated World War II combat veteran, Samuel Fuller, and released in 1951 during the early stages of the war; a third, *Pork Chop Hill* (1959), was released on the eve of the growing American presence in Vietnam. Like most of Fuller's war movies, *Steel Helmet* and *Fixed Bayonets* were lean, tough films, shot in black and white with their focus on the foot soldier, reminiscent of World War II combat movies. In *Fixed Bayonets*, Fuller's drama centers around a platoon of forty-eight men left behind during a Korean winter to fight a rear guard action against the enemy in order to save the 15,000 members of the battalion. Made with the cooperation of the War Department, *Fixed Bayonets* has a formula familiar to World War II audiences that remembered *Bataan* and *Wake Island.* It included acts of courage and self-sacrifice and the major character, a noncommissioned officer who must lead his platoon back to its regiment, displays the kind of courage under fire that symbolize the coming of manhood in World War II movies.

The Steel Helmet was Fuller's first war film; a *tour de force* since Fuller wrote the screenplay and served as producer and director. The film was completed in ten days and dedicated to the U.S. infantry. Like many of Fuller's films, it has a straightforward plot but its strength lies in its characterizations. The simple story concerns a tough, experienced sergeant and his platoon who are ordered to capture and hold a Buddhist Temple, which will serve as an observation post for directing artillery fire. Most of the action takes place within the temple. The film ends with a fierce battle between the handful of American troops and hundreds of communist forces. But inside this B-movie, Fuller touches on racial issues; a subject considered taboo by the traditional film studios at that time. The racial issue is raised when the platoon discovers a North

Korean major hiding inside the temple. The major wants to know why the black medic and the Japanese-American (Nisei) soldier are fighting with white men against the oppressed peoples of color. The North Korean reminds the black medic that his platoon members are unlikely to eat with him in civilian life. Addressing the soldier, the major cannot understand why the Nisei would be fighting in Korea when his family had been interned in a relocation camp during the Second World War.[38] Although Fuller's characters provide unsatisfactory answers, raising the racial question in a film that was released three years before the desegregation decision in *Brown v. Board of Education* is a expression of his liberal sympathies toward the world's "underdogs," whether minorities mistreated by their homeland or infantry soldiers resigned to doing the dirty work of war.[39]

Pork Chop Hill had the sound and smell of combat; not surprising since it was directed by Lewis Milestone of *All Quiet on the Western Front* fame, based on essays written by a veteran, S.L.A. Marshall, and made with the cooperation of the U.S. Army. Lt. Clemons's (Gregory Peck) outfit is ordered to retake Chinese-held Pork Chop Hill and hold the position until reinforcements arrive. His men suffer tremendous casualties before reaching the top of a hill that has no military value. Outnumbered by overwhelming Chinese forces, Clemons asks headquarters for reinforcements or permission to withdraw. However, he is ordered to hold the hill at all costs. Later on he learns that his platoon was used as a bargaining chip at the negotiating table at Panmunjon. As one U.S. general at the peace talks puts it: "Are we as willing as the Chinese to spend lives for nothing?" The answer is a qualified "yes" as reinforcements finally arrive, but only after 80 percent of Peck's unit has been sacrificed as political pawns. Although there were rumors that the film had been edited, what remains clearly illustrates the futility of waging war for political ends. *Pork Chop Hill* serves to bridge the gap between the heroics of the World War II combat films and the disillusionment of American involvement in Vietnam.

Hollywood made few films about the impact of the Korean War at home. One notable exception was *I Want You* (1952), starring Dana Andrews, who had appeared in *The Best Years of Our Lives* and a number of other World War II movies. Andrews plays an ex-GI, married with a family and living in small town America. His father had served in the First World War while he had seen action in the Second. Andrews has a younger brother and when the Korean War begins, the key plot issue involves the draft and military service. Should Andrews write a letter to the local draft board asking for a deferment for his brother who works in the family architectural firm? Examining his conscience,

Andrews decides against asking for special privileges for his brother, which leads to his induction into the Army. The draft issue during the Korean conflict was not as dramatic or divisive as in the sixties with Vietnam; yet college-age males received automatic deferments until graduation. This special treatment of college students would reach a climax during the Vietnam era when males who sought refuge from the draft either bought time in college or skipped to Canada. In *I Want You*, complaints to draft boards about why a particular young man was not in the service came from the parents of those drafted into military duty while whispers and gossip around town questioned the fairness of the selective service system. The issue is conveniently resolved in the film as Andrews's brother is assigned to Germany rather than Korea; he therefore avoids combat duty. But when Andrews is asked by his former commanding officer to rejoin his old World War II outfit to help build airfields in Korea, Andrews chooses to reenter the military rather than seek an exemption. Their mother has the best line in the film when she declares to her family, "It seems all my life I've been saying goodbye to my sons."

Most Americans learned about the Korean War from *M*A*S*H*, the popular television series in the seventies that was based on the Robert Altman film. The television show about a mobile medical unit in Korea became one of the most popular shows on the air but its relationship to battlefield conditions in Korea existed only in the imagination of sitcom writers. Sadly, a whole generation of Americans viewed the Korean conflict through the antics of television characters like Hawkeye, Radar, Trapper John, and "Hotlips" Houlihan.

In his book, *Just and Unjust Wars*, Walzer categorizes Korea as a "just war" for three reasons.[40] First, U.S. involvement rested on assisting South Korea against a full-scale invasion by 60,000 North Korean troops. Second, the United Nations authorized the American participation. Third, the military objective underneath the intervention was to restore the *status quo ante bellum* and reestablish the 38th parallel as the demarcation line between North and South as defined by treaty. But the very nature of a "just war" precludes a nation from bragging over the war's events. In fighting "just wars" nations do not punish their enemies or celebrate military victories; two necessary dramatic effects in any combat war movie. After years of decisive World War II films in which the enemy was clearly defined and in which commitment to total victory was absolute, it was understandable that the ambiguity of the Korean "police action" discouraged the making of salutary films about the war. The Korean War was not so much forgotten as ignored by Hollywood and the

American people. However, the nation's inherent frustration with that unresolved war would explode soon thereafter in Southeast Asia.

Korean War veterans marching in Williamsport, Pa. to promote recognition of the "Forgotten War." (Courtesy: *Williamsport Sun-Gazette*.)

Marilyn Monroe performing in 1954 during the Korean War cease-fire as Hollywood continued the tradition of entertaining the troops during wartime.

Nine

Remembering Vietnam: The War on Film

"I love the smell of napalm in the morning."
—Col. Kilgore, *Apocalypse Now*

"The Oriental doesn't put the same high price on life as does the westerner." —General William Westmoreland

"We are here to help the Vietnamese, because inside every gook, there is an American trying to get out." —Marine Colonel, *Full Metal Jacket*

"Vietnam Was a War Not a Movie." —1990s Bumper Sticker

Unlike the Korean conflict, Vietnam was very much a television war, with the fighting and dying vividly displayed on the evening news. Bringing the war into the home was best expressed in a scene from the film *Summertree* (1971) when actor Michael Douglas drops out of college and is shipped to Vietnam. The poignant moment occurs in the final scene when his parents, watching the late night television news in their bedroom, click off the set just as their son's bodybag is being loaded onto a helicopter. This dramatic scene depicts the pervasiveness of the war, from the soldiers at the front to civilians in the comfort of their home. To avoid its presence would have required a life of isolation, a monk's existence without access to the daily newspaper or television set. In urban centers and on university campuses, the war often pre-empted academic studies as picketers waved their placards, demonstrators chanted their antiwar slogans, protesters blocked the entrances into campus buildings, and police clashed with students. In short, the spirit of the war permeated the country, its presence was felt even when its effects were not always visible.

The Vietnam War era was a time of affliction for the U.S., generating pain and suffering at home and abroad. The war cost the U.S. an estimated $165 billion. The number of American dead exceeded 58,000, with another 300,000 wounded. A considerable number of veterans returned home alive, but either physically disabled or mentally impaired. The number of suicides among Vietnam vets is proportionally higher than among other segments of the population. Often neglected in the human tragedy are the casualties suffered by the Vietnamese people; over one million South Vietnamese troops, North Vietnamese Army regulars, and Vietcong (VC) guerrillas were killed, together with an additional one million civilian casualties. The bombing and napalm destroyed more than 5.2 million acres of Vietnamese land.[1] These are tremendous losses for what correspondent Bernard Fall once characterized as "a small war."[2] Fall had placed Vietnam within the post-World War II era characterization of a period of modest revolutionary wars. But once the casualties from these forty-eight minor wars is computed, Fall acknowledged that they would equal losses suffered in either of the two world wars.

The setback in Vietnam was difficult for Americans to accept since the national character is preconditioned to military victories rather than defeats. The Korean conflict, conducted under UN authority, was accepted by the country, albeit reluctantly, as a bona fide stalemate. At least after the Panmunjon negotiations, Korea remained a divided country with the communists in control of the northern half. But in Vietnam, the entire country was lost to the communists once the U.S. withdrew its armed forces as part of the Paris Accords; the fall of Saigon in 1975 marked the official end of South Vietnam. But the conclusion of this divisive war left thousands of loyal South Vietnamese to the mercy of the enemy; this decision by the U.S. was considered by many a shameful act of betrayal.

Furthermore, outside of the internal strife that accompanied the civil war in Vietnam, the Americanization of the war divided generations, families, races, and socioeconomic classes. Fathers who served in the "Good War" clashed with their sons over the merits of the war just as Michael Douglas did with his father in *Summertree*. Laborers and the working-class generally supported the war while intellectuals, academics, and college students opposed it. Civil rights leaders argued that young black men were being sent to Vietnam to fight against another minority while the smart, rich white boys retreated to the security of a college or university campus and then proceeded to protest the war from within their safe haven. Police entered college campuses to quell student demonstrations. Students, in turn, boycotted classes, harassed prowar professors, and locked administrators in their offices. Antiwar students literally shut down colleges and universities; at Villanova, for example, a rally by Tom Hayden and the Students for a Democratic Society (SDS) led the university to suspend operations for five days. It seemed in the sixties that America was a fractured society, one part at war against a foreign foe, another segment at odds against the government in particular, and authority in general.

Vietnam was not a war that could be ignored. Neutrality was virtually an impossible position to defend, politically or philosophically; one was either for the war or against it. Also, unlike World War II soldiers, the Vietnam veterans did not receive a warm homecoming; there were no parades or marching bands to greet them. Instead, Vietnam veterans returned to America in silence; they were either ignored or scorned by their country. There were no heroes in this war.

The national feeling of ambivalence toward Vietnam was reflected in the films of the era. While the war movie genre continued to do well at the box office, the film studios doubted that there was much commercial value in Vietnam during the early stages of the conflict. Eventually, Hollywood would release four times the number of films on Vietnam than it did on Korea, but the studios proceeded cautiously. One early B-movie entry, *To the Shores of Hell* (1965), proved a commercial failure. It recounted the story of an American marine who attempts to rescue his brother from the Vietcong. Perhaps its failure was predictable given its low-budget production and largely unknown cast.

The film's poor reception, however, did not deter John Wayne, who with the assistance of the U.S. military, produced, directed, and starred in *The Green Berets* (1968); the only American film to unequivocally support U.S. involvement in the war. The major film studios were reluctant to fund such a project but Wayne was willing to risk his money and his considerable reputation. Supposedly, Wayne wrote to President Johnson that it was "extremely important that not only the people of the U.S. but those all over the world should know why it is necessary for us to be there [Vietnam]" and that furthermore, the "most effective way to accomplish this is through the motion picture medium." Wayne told LBJ that the film "would inspire a patriotic attitude on the part of fellow Americans."[3] Jack Valenti, LBJ's aide, was receptive to Wayne's plea for government support and persuaded the president to grant the actor the military assistance required to complete the project. The aid provided included arms and equipment as well as advisors and permission to shoot the film at Fort Benning, Georgia. *The Green Berets* turned out to be a commercial for the special forces and a polemic propaganda piece for the Johnson administration. The film's rhetoric flaunted a Cold War mentality since its message was that Vietnam was one small part of the worldwide communist conspiracy; therefore, the American presence was necessary. Similar to many of the World War II combat movies, *The Green Berets* is a hybrid part-training part-battle film. Using a skeptical journalist (David Janssen) as a convenient plot device, Wayne took every script opportunity to articulate the government's position that Vietnam was not a civil war since the North received aid from the Chinese and the Russians. America is in Vietnam, Wayne's film insisted, because the U.S. had to protect the Vietnamese people from the vicious Vietcong. For the film's finale, Wayne would repeat almost verbatim the line he used in *Back to Bataan* two decades before, but this time to a Vietnamese orphan, explaining that the U.S. was fighting the war for children like him. The use of force for humanitarian reasons was echoed thirty years later by President Clinton to justify a bombing campaign in Kosovo. *The Green Berets* turned a profit despite poor reviews, antiwar protests, and an ill-timed theatrical release during the year of the Tet offensive and the MyLai massacre. Its box office success was testimony to Wayne's star power, but the film was recognized as an attempt by Wayne to structure the film as if it were a formulaic western or World War II movie. Hence, *The Green Berets* proved to be nothing more than the standard action yarn about good guys (cowboys, U.S. cavalry, U.S. military) versus bad guys (Indians, North Vietnamese Army, Vietcong).[4] Its poor reception by critics and public alike ensured that it would have no imitators.

Both *To the Shores of Hell* and *The Green Berets* were aberrations as Hollywood ignored the Vietnam war movie in the turbulent sixties. When the film industry decided to utilize the war as screen material, it did so with a vengeance. In the late seventies, the studios renewed their interest in the war after the Tet offensive and the fall of Saigon. By 1975, the literature on the war was extensive and scholars from several fields, among them history, politics, and film studies, wrote scripts and directed visual images of the Vietnam war from their respective disciplines. Their scholarship, although overlapping in analysis, is best understood as two contrasting perspectives on Hollywood's version of the war; either outlook reflects the methodology of their particular discipline merged with their personal attitude towards the war.

The Wave Theory

Several scholars have advanced a "wave theory" analysis of Vietnam films characterized by saturation marketing where Hollywood releases a batch of war films within a concentrated time span.[5] According to this theory, the film industry dealt with the war in clusters, releasing films about the war in two distinct waves; the first group released to theaters occurred between 1978 and 1979, the second appeared between 1985 and 1989.

The first wave of Vietnam war movies includes two combat (in country) films, *Go Tell the Spartans* (1978) and *Apocalypse Now* (1979), one hybrid training-combat film, *The Boys in Company C* (1978), one hybrid combat-returning veteran film, *The Deer Hunter* (1978), and one film, *Coming Home* (1978), that concerns the reassimilation of the returning veteran.

Contrary to the World War II movies, the Vietnam combat films differ considerably from their predecessors in two respects: they refuse to reconstruct a false image of American unity and military competence in Vietnam, and they avoid the unequivocal acts of courage by individual soldiers. In fact these "grunts" commit acts of cowardice and participate in unspeakable crimes. In *Go Tell the Spartans*, a film that represents the early years of the war when the American military served primarily as advisers to the South Vietnamese government, the major characters explicitly criticize the strategy of the high command in fighting the war. When a veteran U.S. major (Burt Lancaster) is ordered to move his troops to defend an isolated outpost, he reluctantly obeys because the new position is vulnerable to attack and holds no strategic importance. True to his prediction, Lancaster's troops, composed of raw recruits and South Vietnamese militia, are overrun and killed by the Vietcong. Only one soldier, an idealistic volunteer, survives to relate the tragedy to headquarters. But his idealism has been destroyed together with his fallen comrades. To add insult to injury, the Vietcong strip the bodies, leaving the naked soldiers as a symbol that the Americans will be unable to accomplish what the French had failed to achieve in over a century of administrative rule.

The other combat film, *Apocalypse Now*, could belong in a category of its own because it contains both positive (prowar) and negative (antiwar) images of fighting an insurgency war where the enemy is dressed as soldier, farmer, or civilian. Drawing from Joseph Conrad's early twentieth-century novella, *Heart of Darkness*,[6] the film relates the CIA-directed mission of Captain Willard (Martin Sheen) to locate the renegade ex-Special Forces Colonel Kurtz (Marlon Brando) and terminate him "with extreme prejudice." The renegade Kurtz has taken his army of Montagnards into Cambodia and established a camp from which his forces engaged in indiscriminate killing. Willard's journey up river into Cambodia, where he locates Kurtz, is meant to represent America's intervention in Vietnam and the film's commercial and artistic failure proved to be a perfect metaphor for the war itself. At some point in time, Kurtz realized that the war could not be fought by conventional means, nor could it be won by civilized methods. The imposition of brutality, however, led to even greater horror until the excesses of war changed the humanity of man. Whether meant as a metaphor for the end of civilization or a depiction of America's descent into hell, Coppola's *Apocalypse Now* would never be mistaken for a World War II film where the forces of good and evil are explicitly delineated.

On the other hand, *The Boys in Company C*, is the type of hybrid combat film that was familiar to World War II audiences. The film traces the fortunes of five recruits from marine boot camp in San Diego to combat in Vietnam. The contrast between the competence and efficiency of their drill sergeant (portrayed by a real marine DI) and the incompetence of their field commanders is not coincidental. Field officers put the troops at risk when, in order to deliver booze and other supplies for the commanding general's birthday, they lead their convoy into an ambush. Constant bickering between the company's officers over strategy needlessly cost the lives of their men. As further evidence of military corruption, the American forces are ordered to "lose" a soccer match with the South Vietnamese, an action the team rejects, even though it would guarantee their remaining days in Vietnam be spent in the relative safety of base headquarters rather than on jungle patrol. Hence, the soccer match becomes a metaphor for the senselessness of the war itself.

Both Michael Cimino's *The Deer Hunter* and Hal Ashby's *Coming Home* confront the physical and psychological problems that faced the Vietnam veteran on his return home. Cimino's film focuses on three working-class men, Michael (Robert DeNiro), Nick (Christopher Walken), and Steven (John Savage), living in a small Pennsylvania steel town that believes in God and country. They enlist and are sent to Vietnam where they are captured by the Vietcong. During their imprisonment, they are subject to the torture of playing Russian roulette for the enjoyment of their captors. Eventually, the three friends engineer a daring escape from the prison camp but their experience in Vietnam has permanently altered their lives. Steven is wounded in the escape and returns home a paraplegic who prefers to remain in the VA hospital rather than go home to his wife. Nick remains in Vietnam, becoming a drug addict with such low self-esteem that he gambles and loses his life playing Russian roulette. Michael is the sole survivor who returns home physically whole but psychologically damaged. This bleak portrait of the harm done to those who served in Vietnam is offset by the final scene at Nick's wake where, despite their personal suffering, the mourners still are able to sing God Bless America. In contrast, at the heart of the film *Coming Home* are the veterans who regret their Vietnam experience and are transformed into antiwar activists. Different though these films may be from each other, what they share in common is an ambivalence toward the war and America's involvement in it.

The films of the second wave (1985-89) are more explicitly critical of the war and symbolize greater cynicism about American involvement. Films such as Oliver Stone's *Platoon* (1986), Stanley Kubrick's *Full Metal Jacket* (1987), John Irvin's *Hamburger Hill* (1987), and Brian DePalma's *Casualties of War* (1989) express dismay, if not disgust, at American militarism. The soldiers in these films would not qualify for good conduct medals; rather they are presented as cowards, murderers, and rapists. These films are revisionist exercises that indict the U.S. for its wrongful intervention in the war. One hybrid training-combat film, Stone's *Born on the Fourth of July* (1989), follows real-life Vietnam veteran, Ron Kovic, from gung-ho marine to pro-war activist. Kovic returns home, physically and emotionally scarred. He is consumed with guilt for atrocities over which he had little, if any, control. When his platoon invades a village and riddles it with gunfire, the company inadvertently kills women and children. Kovic and several of his buddies try to assist the wounded but are ordered to withdraw as an artillery strike is planned against the village.

These Vietnam combat films were flawed in two significant respects. First, the Vietnam war movies focused on the grunts, the infantry soldiers, who fought the ground war in villages and jungle terrain. These films led audiences to believe that the foot soldier was the heroic figure in Vietnam when most of damage, in lives and property, resulted from air and artillery strikes rather than the firepower of combat soldiers. Second, the films presented an American perspective on the war. The Vietnamese are either portrayed as Vietcong or spectators to the war.[7] The second-wave films are symbolic of the Americanization of the war.

Films that also would fit within the timeframe of the second wave include the first two Rambo (Sylvester Stallone) films, *First Blood* (1982) and *Rambo: First Blood 2* (1985), and the Braddock (Chuck Norris) trilogy *Missing in Action* (1984), *Missing in Action 2: The Beginning* (1985), and *Braddock: Missing in Action III* (1988) as well. These films present a view of the war that places the blame for the failure squarely on politicians and civilian bureaucrats at home.[8] When ex-green beret John Rambo is asked by his former commanding officer, Colonel Trautman, in *Rambo: First Blood, Part 2* (1985) to return to Vietnam to rescue American POWs, Rambo replies: "Do we get to win this time?"[9] The question is rhetorical but the film answers it anyway. The Sylvester Stallone character had an immediate impact on the public as visitors at the Vietnam Memorial Wall search for the name "Arthur John Rambo" to make rubbings to take home as souvenirs.[10]

The Phase Analysis

On the other hand, social historian William Palmer[11] considers the Vietnam films as progressive stages in the filmic representation of the war as a visual text, evolving from an epic phase (1976-79) to two overlapping stages in the 1980s—the comic book and the symbolic nihilist. Palmer's theory is that the Vietnam films are best understood as a series of evolving texts related to political and social developments. In the epic phase (1976-79) such films as *The Deer Hunter*, *Apocalypse Now*, and *Coming Home* renewed America's interest in the war as each film, in its own way, served as consciousness-raising stimuli in the mass culture. Palmer views these films as "the publicists of a Vietnam War consciousness that was abroad in the country yet dormant for various reasons (bitterness, shame, depression, decompression, inarticulateness)."[12] He considers these films to be traditional narratives that are related to previous literary texts (like Stephen Crane's *Red Badge of Courage*) and World War II movies like *Sergeant York* and *Sands of Iwo Jima.*

The second phase of the Vietnam war films, the comic book stage, occurred, not surprisingly, during the chauvinistic policies of the Reagan administration. Films like the Rambo series and the Braddock trilogy supported the president's belief that America did not lose the war in Vietnam. Moreover, the Reagan administration implied that similar "small wars" could be refought and rewon in places like Grenada, the Middle East, and Central America. Palmer notes the similarities between the popular comic book figure at the time, Sergeant Rock, and the Rambo film character. As Rambo's picture appeared on magazines and in newspapers throughout the country, he became the icon for the restoration of American military power in the world. Stallone even was invited to dine with the Reagans at the White House and was treated as if he were a Congressional Medal of Honor recipient.[13]

The third phase, identified as the symbolic nihilist phase between 1987 and 1988, includes films like *Platoon* (1986), *Full Metal Jacket* (1987), and *Hamburger Hill* (1987); visual attempts to capture the disorder, chaos, and futility of the war. Within a sixteen-month timeframe, Hollywood released six major features on the war, all except one set in Vietnam. Two films, *Platoon* and *Hamburger Hill*, were inspired by Vietnam veterans who saw combat in the war and who centered the action in their productions around foot soldiers—the grunts—who come to view the war as senseless. If Vietnam is commonly identified with the swish, swish, swish of the helicopter and the sound of artillery fire and aerial bombing, its "dirty war" was fought on the ground. In *Hamburger Hill*, for example, the 101st Airborne unit's objective is to take a hill away from the enemy. After a fierce ten-day firefight in which the outfit suffered 70 percent casualties, the Americans secured the hill, but then casually abandoned it as the fighting moved forward. Much like the hill in the Korean war film, *Pork Chop Hill*, the territory fought over in the *Hamburger Hill* movie was of psychological rather than strategic importance.

The second half of Kubrick's *Full Metal Jacket* takes place in Vietnam during the 1968 Tet offensive where a squad of marines is picked off one by one by a Vietcong sniper. The marines have been so thoroughly indoctrinated with the "born to kill" mentality that they become as brutal as the enemy. At the end only one marine has survived and he has been dehumanized by the war. Similarly, the Everyman character in Stone's *Platoon*, Chris Taylor (Charlie Sheen), arrives in Vietnam a naive recruit and leaves three months later alive but with a damaged soul. The film is as much a rite of passage story as a war movie in which Taylor loses his innocence but becomes a man. During his short tour of duty, Taylor not only experiences the anguish of trying to survive in a war where the enemy lacks an identifiable face, but in the process he becomes transformed into a murderer when he revenges the death of Sergeant Elias by shooting his killer, Sergeant Barnes. After the burning of a local village and the gang rape of a young Vietnamese girl, Taylor writes home that "I don't know right from wrong anymore." If Taylor represents Everyman, then America lost its soul in Vietnam.

The Political Expediency Factor

These interpretations of Vietnam war films may be valid explanations for how the war was presented to the American public, but there is a third perspective that also is worth consideration. Historically, the film industry is bifurcated politically; selected executives and movie stars are liberals while the traditional studios are still run by conservatives who view movies predominately as a business. Hollywood neglected the Vietnam war movie because there was no consensus in the country on the war. That would also explain why the major studios avoided treating Vietnam as source material until it was relatively safe to tackle the subject once American troops left Saigon. That would explain why Wayne's chauvinistic *Green Berets* was not duplicated by any other studio. Those few films made about Vietnam before the 1970s were low-budget action pictures, not million dollar projects. However after the fall of Saigon, the film industry was willing to take a minimal risk and treat the war and its aftermath on film.

But an examination of those late seventies' films reveal the traditional Hollywood practice of hedging its bets. What is *The Deer Hunter* save an affirmation of the attitude, "my country right or wrong!" Although the lives of the three major characters have been irrevocably altered by Vietnam (Nick is brought home dead, Steven is disabled, and Michael has lost his appetite for hunting and the kill), they and their townsfolk can still pay homage to flag and country in the final scene.

Apocalypse Now, on the other hand, is more ambiguous since it lends support for both pro and antiwar interpretations.[14] The battle at Charlie's Point, for instance, where the mad Colonel Kilgore (Robert Duvall) destroys a Vietnamese village, demonstrates the superiority of American firepower. But Kilgore's helicopter assault, intended to provide a place for soldiers to surf while the loudspeakers blast Wagner's "Ride of the Valkyries," also reveals the madness, the total insanity of the war long before Willard locates Kurtz. Even the returning veteran film, *Coming Home*, is most believable as a love story between a marine officer's wife (Jane Fonda) and a wounded veteran turned anti-war activist (Jon Voight) than as an anti-war polemic. The film conveniently neglected several important issues associated with the Vietnam veteran, namely, the government's denial of the effect of Agent Orange on troops and civilians alike, the difficulty of dealing with the veterans' administration bureaucracy, and the problem of post-traumatic stress disorder (PTSD) and the survivor guilt syndrome. However, one issue that Hollywood exploited for screen material was the returning veteran as a "walking timebomb"—sick, angry, and even psychotic.[15] The Travis Bickle (Robert DeNiro) character in *Taxi Driver* (1976) is an unstable veteran whose outbursts of violence against urban immorality escalates into murder and assassination plots. The following year, *Rolling Thunder* (1977) reached the screen with a plot that had a Vietnam POW return home to an unloving wife and unfriendly son. When some thieves rob his prized coin collection, disfigure him, and kill his family, the Vietnam veteran extracts his own brand of revenge. Revenge is the motive, also, in a number of B-movies about returning Vietnam veterans. For example, in *Angels from Hell* (1968), a Vietnam veteran returns home to organize his own motorcycle gang and tangles with both rival bikers and the police while in *Chrome and Hot Leather* (1971), an ex-green beret seeks his own brand of justice from bikers who are responsible for his fiancee's death. Contrary to the World War II veterans in *The Best Years of Our Lives*, these Vietnam veterans are often portrayed as a menace to the community and a danger to society. The only comforting news about these B-films is that most Americans never saw them.

With President Reagan's election in 1980, the film studios acknowledged a change in government attitude and in the national mood and sought to take advantage of the transformation. What has been described as the comic book phase in representations of the war, also were political tracts and propaganda pieces that tried to blame misguided bureaucrats and impotent politicians, rather than the American military, for what happened in Vietnam. The "winning the war" syndrome films focused on the exploits of the individual superhero—Rambo and Braddock—who single-handedly rescue MIAs and POWs and do considerable damage to the life and property of the enemy. Similarly, in *Uncommon Valor* (1983) the heroics are supplied by a commando team of experts and specialists put together by a former Vietnam officer (Gene Hackman) and supported with funds from the private sector. Their objective is to return to Vietnam/Laos to find POWs, including Hackman's son, despite objections from the CIA and Congress. Hackman tells his group of six that there are 2500 soldiers still missing and that the U.S. government either refuses or is unable to bring them home. Thus, this rogue band of misfits (most of the six recruits cannot adjust to civilian life), with the help of local guides, penetrate into Laos, locate the prison camp, and rescue a handful of prisoners. But Hackman's son is not among the group, having died in the camp. The venture, however, cost the lives of two guides and two Americans, hardly a cost-effective undertaking. Yet the film preaches that the U.S. remains a commanding military power to be reckoned with despite the fact that the film is about private armies rather than sanctioned military forces. The film's rather alarming lesson is that private armies can complete successful missions by force rather than wait for such policy decisions to be negotiated through diplomacy. It is a lesson not lost on the paramilitary groups scattered across the U.S. today.

Admittedly, the period from 1985 to 1989 also saw the release of films like *Platoon* and *Hamburger Hill*, but these came from independent filmmakers. Furthermore, these films, as well as *Casualties of War* (1989), also can be legitimately viewed as personal statements since Stone, *Hamburger Hill*'s Jim Carabatsos, and *Casualties of War*'s David Rabe were Vietnam veterans whose scripts were memory plays. These films, together with *Full Metal Jacket*, share important similarities with the war-is-hell combat movies of the Second World War. The difference, of course, is that the World War II soldier was always cast as the hero.

The Vietnam war films, therefore, can be viewed as reflecting the political expediency factor in Hollywood that requires that a film never alienate its audience, especially by challenging the dominant political ideology. But while these interpretations may claim some modicum of validity, there is one criticism of the Vietnam war film that all share, namely, Hollywood focused on the American presence rather than on the Vietnamese people who endured and suffered through the war. Regardless of political ideology, there is no denying that the war was fought in their country—on their land, villages, and rice paddies. What is largely missing from Hollywood's versions of the war are the Vietnamese, as if they were spectators to the event. No Vietnam film that came out of Hollywood doubted, or even raised, the fundamental question of who was morally responsible for all the human suffering and property damage?[16] Even independent filmmakers like Stone avoided the issue of American involvement in the war, preferring instead to dramatize the plight of the ordinary soldier.

Post-Vietnam Skirmishes

The U.S. engaged in two minor wars and one major engagement after Vietnam. In October 1983, the Reagan administration responded to a request from the Organization of Eastern Caribbean States to invade the tiny island of Grenada to insure the safety of American citizens. Within a few days, the combined strength of U.S. Marines and Army Rangers, joined by a token force from six Caribbean nations, overwhelmed the local militia and their "Cuban advisers," evacuated American citizens, and deposed the Marxist government. Politically, the Grenada invasion was to President Reagan what the Falkland Islands war was to Mrs. Thatcher—an opportunity to reassert military superiority at the expense of an unworthy foe.

Possibly that mismatch of military might cautioned Hollywood against churning out war movies that demonstrated that America had not lost its will after Vietnam. Perhaps the struggle was too brief to sustain enough dramatic interest. Whatever the reason, the film industry ignored Grenada except for director-producer, actor Clint Eastwood. An admirer of Sam Fuller's work, Eastwood decided to emulate him by making *Heartbreak Ridge* (1986), a cliche-ridden hybrid-World War II movie about the Grenada invasion.[17] Eastwood hired Jim Carabatsos, the Vietnam veteran and writer of *Hamburger Hill*, to do the screenplay. Eastwood stars in the film as the tough, but anti-establishment, drill sergeant who has seen action in Korea and Vietnam and who has problems adjusting to the largely civilian volunteer army. Unfortunately, Eastwood devotes two-thirds of the film to the preparation of his green recruits; a formula familiar to World War II movies. As a consequence,

Heartbreak Ridge, like many of its predecessors, failed to meet the criteria for a combat film and did poorly at the box office.

The second minor war—really a limited "police action"—occurred in December 1989 when President Bush sent 24,000 U.S. troops into Panama to drive General Manuel Noriega from power because he had engaged in international drug smuggling. The brief military action led to Noriega's capture and deportation to the U.S. to stand trial, where he was convicted and sent to prison. The U.S. action was criticized in Latin America and other parts of the world, but Hollywood preferred to turn the other cheek and ignore the entire episode altogether.

The Middle East was the scene of the third, and most costly, war that the U.S. has fought since Vietnam. That war began rather suddenly in August 1990 when the Iraqi forces of Saddam Hussein invaded Kuwait. President Bush acted quickly to organize American military forces to protect Saudi Arabia as part of Operation Desert Shield. By the end of January 1991, the defensive objective of the initial operation was replaced by the offensive firepower of Desert Storm with the intention of toppling Hussein and initiating a "New World Order" in the area. The Persian Gulf War, the president assured the nation, would not be another Vietnam. That promise was kept as the war was over within months after Iraq's infrastructure was reduced to the "preindustrial age," but Hussein remained in power and the new world order was more slogan than reality. President Bush was delighted with the victory, exclaiming, "By God, we've kicked the Vietnam syndrome once and for all."[18] In the flush of the military victory, the president could be forgiven for engaging in a bit of hyperbole but the war did serve to ease, if not erase, the burden of the defeat in Vietnam.

As was true for Vietnam, the Persian Gulf War lent itself to television as CNN filed nightly reports directly from the front. It was also a war that proved attractive to the video market and made celebrities out of Generals Schwarzkopf and Powell. At least a dozen videos were produced on various aspects of the war. Additionally, several documentaries were released about the war, having such titles as *Desert Storm: Eagles Over the Gulf* (1991) and *Sandstorm in the Gulf: Digging Out* (1991). One documentary video, *Desert Storm Cockpit Videos of Bomb Runs* (1992) places the viewer in the pilot's seat on bombing missions. The video comes with a warning that it would never appear on national television because of the offensive language. TV journalists also secured a piece of the action as Dan Rather narrated the war from beginning to end in the three-volume set, *Desert Triumph*, while Diane Sawyer and Barbara Walters conducted interviews and provided commentary in a four-volume series, entitled *Persian Gulf: The Images of a Conflict*.

Once again, however, Hollywood did not join in the national hoopla by flooding the theater screens with films about the war. Except for a couple of quickie B-films released in 1991, *The Finest Hour* and *Heroes of Desert Storm*, the major studios ignored the war. By the mid-nineties, Hollywood had released only one feature film, *Courage Under Fire* (1996) that concerned the conduct of the war. In this film, Denzel Washington stars as an officer assigned the task of investigating the merits of awarding the Congressional Medal of Honor to helicopter pilot Meg Ryan, the first woman in U.S. history to be so designated. Ryan is in charge of a flight rescue mission when her helicopter is shot down over Kuwait. The crew manages to hold off the Iraqis until another chopper arrives and most return to base safely, except for Ryan who is killed and her body left behind. After interviewing the crew survivors and receiving conflicting versions of what happened in the field under fire, the question for Washington is to uncover the truth, that is, was Ryan a hero or a coward? Although the film contains occasional combat scenes, the action could have taken place in any war. In this sense, *Courage Under Fire* is more a mystery about the discovery of truth than a conventional combat film. But as one reviewer[19] observed, film is the worst possible medium to discuss truth honestly since it is edited, cut, and reshot so as to construct a logical story that an audience will accept. War, on the other hand, is neither sensible nor logical.

Just Wars, Real Wars

On rare occasions, Hollywood has produced political films but hardly ever has the industry used the medium to deliver ideological messages except for war movies. While these are popular with audiences, Hollywood, nonetheless, treats the genre with political sensitivity. When Europe was at war in 1914, the official American policy of neutrality was observed by the film studios. One preparedness or interventionist film was offset by another preaching peace and pacifism. But once the U.S. entered the war, Hollywood condemned the enemy just as strongly as the government. In the period between the two world wars, the film industry was careful not to offend foreign governments. When Germany and Italy prohibited the importation of American films, Hollywood decided to be more adventurous and treat the subject of fascism on the screen. During the Second World War, the industry wholeheartedly devoted its resources to the war effort. However, when the wars are indecisive like Korea or unpopular like Vietnam, then the pragmatism of the industry tests the audience market before plunging into film production. The studios avoided Vietnam until the remaining American troops were home. When Hollywood eventually plotted stories around the war, it omitted any consideration of the validity of the American involvement in Vietnam. But according to Michael Walzer,[20] the answer to that fundamental question was pivotal to whether Vietnam was a just or unjust war. No Hollywood film on Vietnam, whether produced by the studios or by independents such as Stone, ever questioned directly the legality or morality of the American presence. The war may have been divisive and unpopular at home but political expediency dictated that Hollywood stick to tradition and play it safe.

Even though Vietnam combat films like *Platoon* and *Hamburger Hill* were praised for their gritty realism, they remain representations and creative inventions of that war rather than the war itself.[21] While these films come close to letting the audience "experience Vietnam," they remain works of fiction. Films about the grunts (the dog soldiers) did not spare the realism of fighting a guerrilla war in the jungle, where the foot soldiers were subject to leeches, snakes, and heavy rains while slogging through mud and rice paddies to search for an enemy without an identifiable face. No audience would ever understand the disappointment, which intensified into anger and hatred, when the endurance of these conditions failed to secure loyalty and gratitude. Imagine the shock in this scene from *Go Tell the Spartans* when an idealistic soldier discovers he has been betrayed by the Vietnamese family he befriended. Or take the disk jockey character Robin Williams portrays in *Good Morning, Vietnam* (1987) who comes to realize that the brother of the Vietnamese woman he loves is a Vietcong terrorist.

Despite their attempts at authenticity, these Hollywood film wars remain fantasies, unsuccessful imitations of the realities of actual combat where, for example, air strikes are errant and artillery fire often goes astray, killing friend and foe alike. Helicopters, which appear on cue in the movies, do not always appear on time to pick up the wounded. Armies and troops are not always where they are supposed to be and, especially in a place like Vietnam, battles with the enemy are often characterized by confusion, disorder, and chaos. Except for *Saving Private Ryan*, what other war film would have the courage to depict a sense of fear before battle so strong that soldiers vomit and soil their pants? As one veteran in a VA hospital put it in the documentary, *Dear America: Letters Home from Vietnam* (1987), "Heroes are for the late show." When World War II veteran Samuel Fuller was asked about the honesty in his combat films, *The Steel Helmet* (Korean) and *The Big Red One* (1980, Second World War), he supposedly replied that the only way to get at the truth in a war film was to put a machine gun behind the camera and gun down the audience.[22] No doubt Fuller's reply was not meant to be taken literally but it reminded moviegoers that viewing "war in the dark" is a far different experience from being there.

Ten

Hollywood Confronts the Nuclear Holocaust

"The seventeenth century was the century of mathematics, the eighteenth that of the physical sciences and the nineteenth that of biology. Our twentieth century is the century of fear." —Albert Camus

"I survived Three Mile Island." —1979 T-shirt

An exchange of dialogue between a California couple awakened from a sound sleep:

"What's that?"

"Oh, go back to sleep. It's only an atomic bomb test."

"All right. I was afraid one of the kids had fallen out of bed."

—1952 issue of the *Reader's Digest*

In accepting the Nobel Prize for Literature in 1957, French philosopher and author, Albert Camus, proclaimed: "Probably every generation sees itself as charged with remaking the world. Mine, however, knows it will not remake the world. But its task is perhaps even greater, for it consists in keeping the world from destroying itself."[1] Camus, of course, was referring to the atom bomb. August 6, 1945, is often cited as the beginning of the nuclear age when "Little Boy," the code name for the uranium bomb, was dropped on Hiroshima. Three days later, "Fat Man," the plutonium bomb, leveled Nagasaki and persuaded the Japanese to surrender, thus bringing the Second World War to an end. The atomic era actually began years before when President Roosevelt gave approval to the Manhattan Project, the code name for the secret development of the atom bomb. The project united a number of European emigres and American scientists to produce the bomb. It was a cold December day in 1942 at the University of Chicago when Enrico Fermi and his team of scientists achieved the first sustained nuclear reaction; this experiment changed the course of human history. The initial atomic pile contained 385 tons of graphite and 50 tons of uranium and caused a chain reaction for only a few minutes. But the demonstration showed enough promise to warrant the movement of the Manhattan Project to Los Alamos, New Mexico, and placed under the leadership of General Leslie Groves, who recruited J. Robert Oppenheimer to head the scientific team. Under Groves' command, the U.S. Army appropriated over 54,000 acres, relocated the residents, and build an entire self-contained community and military compound on the land. Eventually 7,000 people would come to live and work at the Los Alamos base. The actual testing ground, code name "Trinity," was set sixty miles south at the White Sands Missile Range near Alamogordo. A successful nuclear bomb was detonated on July 16, 1945, in the New Mexico desert as a prelude to Hiroshima.

As Paul Boyer observes in his book, *By the Bomb's Early Light*, once news of the bomb became public, people knew that life would never be the same again.[2] H. V. Kaltenborn, the noted radio commentator, expressed this sentiment for mankind when he said: "We have created a Frankenstein!"[3] The bomb's devastation far exceeded the scientific estimates; Oppenheimer, for example, thought the death toll would be under 20,000. The actual figures proved to be much higher; 80,000 people were killed immediately at Hiroshima with another 60,000 deaths caused by radiation and other illnesses attributed to the fallout. At Nagasaki, 35,000 died immediately and another 35,000 died from the effects of the blast.[4]

While these statistics are tragic, still the fatalities from the atomic bombs rank ninth among the worst accidents and disasters in human history, far below the seventy-five million deaths attributed to the bubonic plague (Black Death) in fourteenth-century EurAsia, the thirty-five million Chinese slaughtered during the Mongol genocide in the same century, and the twenty-one million deaths attributed to the 1918 worldwide influenza epidemic.

Statistics alone do not define the aftermath of the atomic blasts. Boyer cites the dropping of the atom bombs as a benchmark for the twentieth century, setting off what came to be identified in the popular culture as the "nuclear age"; an era marked by public apprehension and indifference. Once the Soviets acquired the bomb, fear of a nuclear war between the two Superpowers led to a renewed interest in civilian defense. Americans built over 100,000 bomb shelters during the fifties. Many families located these shelters in their backyards, stuffing them with canned goods, candles, blankets, and other amenities thought necessary to survive life after a nuclear attack. For those who could not afford a private bomb shelter, their old Fords and Chevys would do nicely.

Buried in hugh holes in the ground and stocked with provisions, these old cars were thought to be an adequate substitute. The civilian population was not the only naive participant in these survival strategies; the U.S. government's postal service printed emergency change of address cards to insure that the daily mail would continue to be delivered after a nuclear attack despite weather conditions, mad dogs, and radioactivity. The federal government apparently considered the delivery of the Sears catalog a high priority item while the country struggled with death, disease, contamination, and even anarchy. City governments also did their part in the preparedness drive; New York City installed over 700 sirens within the city limits and tested these every month until the mid-sixties. Meanwhile, the nation's public schools included bomb drills as part of the normal curriculum. One popular civilian defense film shown to schoolchildren featured a cartoon character named Burt the Turtle, who instructed the youngsters that in case of a nuclear explosion they should "duck and cover."[5] Such misleading instructions severely underestimated the physical and psychological damage from an atomic attack. However, filmmakers Frank and Eleanor Perry were much more realistic than the government or the local school district. Their 1963 film, *Ladybug, Ladybug*, was based on an actual incident that documented the reaction of rural schoolchildren to a civil defense warning, signifying an impending nuclear attack. Although the warning turns out to be a false alarm, several children suffered harm under the stress of the expected attack. Unfortunately, *Ladybug, Ladybug* remains an ignored and forgotten film despite its more accurate scenario.

Public concern also took the form of cooperative efforts by citizen groups to protest extensive government testing as part of the Cold War competition with the Soviet Union. American testing in the Pacific atoll during the fifties scattered radioactive dust over 7000 square miles, causing death and illness within an eighty-mile radius. Closer to home, reports of radioactive rain falling on Chicago, together with the discovery of deadly strontium 90 in the milk supply, extended public fear of nuclear war to anxiety over the effects of fallout from nuclear testing.[6]

Serious concerns over nuclear war and the effects of nuclear testing on humans and the environment also had its lighter side as demonstrated by the story of the California couple reported in a 1952 issue of the *Reader's Digest* who mistakenly thought an atomic bomb test was a child falling out of bed! The commercial sector seized an opportunity to profit from the new technology. Boyer reports jewelry manufacturers marketing atomic earrings and pins, producers of breakfast foods stuffing atomic rings and other nuclear-related prizes in their cereal boxes, and the shameless commercialization even extended to a French designer

LOOKING BACK

THE DIABETIC AND THE ATOMIC BOMB

Read the Government's small pamphlet called SURVIVAL UNDER ATOMIC ATTACK. Get it from your Civil Defense organization. READ IT!

Carry your identification (diabetic) card with you at all times, if you have one. If not, Civil Defense may supply one.

WHERE TO GO

In the event of an atomic bomb attack on your city, the chance of you and your home escaping injury is very good. If, however, you are within the destruction range of the bomb, you could either be injured or uninjured, but your home would probably be partially or entirely destroyed. If you are injured, you will be cared for, and your diabetic condition will have attention—rest assured of that. If you are homeless and you have friends who will care for you, you need not worry.

PREPARE TO TAKE CARE OF YOURSELF completely, if you are uninjured. Your family and friends should be taught enough about diabetes to take care of you in an emergency.

EVERY DIABETIC should know how to take insulin. There is plenty of insulin.

INSULIN

EVERY DIABETIC TAKING INSULIN should have his usual ONE extra bottle in addition to current needs, and one EXTRA insulin syringe with two needles. This is because insulin is your best friend and with it you have the best insurance there is. ALWAYS USE YOUR OLDEST BOTTLE FIRST. Regular insulin is superior to the other forms for emergency purposes. Carry a little case with your insulin syringe, if you have one. If an emergency arises and you must change from long-acting insulin (protamine zinc insulin, globin insulin, or NPH insulin) to regular insulin, take 2 doses of the regular—the morning dose equalling 3/5 of the number of units of your usual dose of the long-acting insulin, and the evening dose, 2/5 of the units. If you have no food, reduce your dose to 1/2 or 1/3 of these amounts to avoid reactions. TEST YOUR URINE. KEEP TO YOUR DIET AS NEARLY AS POSSIBLE IN ALL CIRCUMSTANCES. It is better to eat too little than too much. Here is a simple emergency diet one can get under most any circumstances:

EMERGENCY DIET

BREAKFAST	NOON & NIGHT
Bread, 2 or 3 slices Butter or margarine Coffee and canned milk, or in place of bread, a cereal and a can of milk	Meat or cheese sandwich, or bread and butter, 3 slices, or meat and potatoes, with such vegetables as are available.

You can get along on this simple fare for several days, if necessary.

5

From *Diabetes Forecast*, January 1952, page 5

(Published for use with the U.S. government's civilian defense pamphlet "Survival Under Atomic Attack.")

Diabetes Forecast November 1998 91

A 1950s Cold War instruction pamphlet for diabetics in case of an atomic bomb attack. Reprinted with permission from *Diabetes Forecast*, a publication of the American Diabetes Association. Originally published January 1952.

who named his brief two-piece swimwear a "bikini" after the Pacific tests because it would grab the attention of men.[7] Television as well sought to cash in on the latest interest with the development of new science-fiction shows like the *Twilight Zone* and the *Outer Limits*.

Naturally, the film industry was not to be denied. For example, the plot of the 1946 film, *The House on 92nd Street*, concerned Nazi spies but was revised by the studio prior to distribution to include a foreword that explained to the audience that what the Nazi agents were really after was the formula for the atomic bomb.[8] Fears that the atom bomb would be used against the U.S. in another world war,[9] were offset by surveys taken between 1954 and 1963 that revealed public ignorance about the bomb, indifference to the larger problem of nuclear weapons, and apathy to the dangers of radioactive fallout.[10] But if the American public had equivocal feelings about the nuclear age, Hollywood perceived the subject as a potentially rich source for film plots.

Films of the Nuclear Age

Hollywood was quick to cash in on the nuclear technology. Besides updating *The House on 92nd Street*, the film studios moved promptly to incorporate the bomb into forthcoming screen projects. Within eighteen months after "Little Boy" was dropped on Hiroshima, MGM studios released *The Beginning or the End*, a docudrama on the making and deployment of the first atom bomb.[11] The 1947 film was an artistic disaster and a box office failure. The entire project was plagued from the beginning by internal and external squabbles within the scientific community, the military establishment, and the MGM studio. As a consequence, the film was revised several times, and the final version reflected the various compromises—a mixture of fact and fiction but with entertainment values predominate over historical accuracy. What began as an enlightened cooperative venture between the film industry and the liberal wing of the scientific community turned out to be a disappointing experience. It proved a bitter lesson for MGM and it may have encouraged other studios to avoid the subject altogether, particularly if the participants were still alive.

These reservations notwithstanding, Hollywood tackled the subject again in 1952 with another A-bomb film, *Above and Beyond*. However, the film focused on Colonel Paul Tibbets, the pilot of the Enola Gay, the plane that dropped the bomb on Hiroshima.[12] Thus, *Above and Beyond* became a personal story about Tibbets, his family, and the events leading up to the August 6th bombing. Hollywood did not produce another film on the subject until the 1980s when it released *Manhattan Project* and *Fat Man and Little Boy*. Neither film made much of an impact, even though the latter's political message doubted the wisdom of using the bomb. Actor Paul Newman accepted the role of General Groves with some trepidation since he was a committed anti-nuclear activist who had served as a delegate to the 1978 United Nations Special Session on Disarmament. But his apprehension was misplaced since the film directed most of the blame for the bomb on the military rather than the scientific community. While the film accurately depicts the team of scientists working to develop the bomb, it was Groves who manipulated Oppenheimer to remain on the project and bring it to a successful conclusion. The film, however, conveniently neglects to mention that both Klaus Fuchs and David Greenglass (Julius Rosenberg's brother-in-law) were Los Alamos employees who passed details of the bomb to the Soviets. Yet when Oppenheimer lost his security clearance during the anti-communist hysteria of the 1950s because of his past communist associations, General Groves's loyalty was never questioned, even though he was responsible for security at the Los Alamos facility. *Fat Man and Little Boy* conveniently places the blame for the bomb on the military when, in fact, it was the scientists who urged Roosevelt to support the project lest the Germans develop the weapon before the U.S. The urgency felt by the scientists, some of whom were émigrés from fascism, made the Manhattan Project a moral as well as a scientific challenge.[13] Still the fact that these films were commercial failures reinforces the conventional wisdom that the public goes to the movies to be entertained, not enlightened. But it also could have signaled that the American public had lost interest in the topic. Certainly by the mid-eighties liberals in the film industry, whose political activities either influence or reflect what is fashionable in the general culture, had deserted the nuclear disarmament/nuclear freeze campaign in favor of AIDS research and environmental causes.[14]

Rather than avoid the subject, the film industry embraced nuclear technology. The post-World War II film formula transformed the Nazis and Japanese into the new Cold War enemies—the Soviets and communist agents—and the scripts converted weapon blueprints and war plans into spies and atomic secrets. One filmography on nuclear movies listed some 874 films released in thirty-six countries (with almost two-thirds produced in the U.S.), whose themes involved nuclear war, nuclear accident, or the after-effects of an atomic blast, including the battle against radioactive fallout.[15] Not surprisingly, most of these films were distributed after the end of World War II, with more than one-third released in the 1980s. Included in the filmography are a dozen Godzilla movies and various clones of the "atomic monster" variety in films that dealt with annihilation and world destruction and at least a dozen of the James Bond films that employed scenarios of nuclear technology, conflict over possession of nuclear weapons, and efforts to secure the materials to manufacture nuclear armaments.[16]

The new technology also proved a script bonanza for the weekly serials, which continued to be a staple of the Saturday afternoon matinee well into the 1950s. At least a dozen serials, some with the exotic titles of *Zombies of the Stratosphere* and *Radar Men from the Moon*, included the atom bomb or nuclear weaponry in their narratives. Naturally, popular Saturday serial favorites like Superman did not ignore the potential scripts that could be culled from the new scientific discoveries. For instance, in 1950, Columbia Pictures produced fifteen episodes of the serial *Atom Man versus Superman* in which our hero saves Metropolis from an arsenal of atomic weapons and other gadgets of the space age such as thermal guns, flying saucers, and stratospheric vehicles. Previously, Universal-International had released a serial entitled, *Lost City of the Jungle* (1946), in which, for thirteen weeks, the hero, federal agent Rod Stanton, battled against a villain who had discovered a metal in the lost city with the capability to defend against atomic bombs and who planned to sell the discovery to the highest bidder. Some of the serial villains speak with a German accent, an obvious reference to Nazi war criminals not prosecuted at Nuremberg and other war crimes trials while the crude "special effects" would not fool any contemporary youngster with access to a computer. Still, nuclear technology provided Hollywood writers with an opportunity to replay the old formulas by merely substituting the A-bomb for previous weapons of destruction.

When the Saturday matinee serials vanished from theater screens, displaced by television cartoons, feature films about the atomic age remained into the eighties. Rather than lose interest in the subject, Hollywood instead continued to mine it as if the industry had struck gold. Admittedly, films of the nuclear age could qualify as a separate "genre" and be organized into various categories since the breadth of the topic provides for overlap and identification with other more established genres. For example, should the genre include those dozen James Bond movies as well as films along the order of *The Fourth Protocol* (1987) and *The Package* (1989)? Or are these films really Cold War action thrillers where the new technology serves as a plot gimmick to advance the narrative?

Regardless, the hundreds of movies that comprise the genre can be topically subdivided into four distinct categories:

- science-fiction/horror films where nuclear power has released an assortment of beasts on the civilized world
- nuclear war/attack films where warring governments unleash disaster on the world
- nuclear accident or disaster films where human or mechanical error has caused a threat to life and the environment
- nuclear survival films where the world has been destroyed and those unharmed after the blast or those who have survived the radioactive fallout struggle to remain alive.

Nuclear Age Science Fiction Films

The fifties have been characterized as a decade of paranoia and mass hysteria brought on by the creation of the atom bomb and the subsequent arms race competition between East and West that typified the Cold War. The science-fiction films of this era reflected the national mood at the time since Hollywood had made few such films before 1950.[17] Most of these science-fiction films are best characterized as low-budget B-flicks; "monster" movies where atomic testing or radioactivity produces mutations—giant grasshoppers, huge ants, overgrown spiders—or awakens long buried beasts—that proceed to create havoc and destruction on the human population.[18] What these films share in common is a warning of what is possible when science and technology transcend the boundaries of humanity by manufacturing weapons of mass destruction. One of the earliest of this type was the 1951 film, *The Thing,* featuring actor James Arness, who played a carrot-like creature defrosted as a result of nuclear testing. In order to survive, the creature needs blood. During the course of the film, *The Thing* creates carnage and mayhem on an Arctic military base as it searches for human victims. When it is finally destroyed by fire at the end of the film, a survivor says to the audience: "Tell the world. Watch the skies— everywhere—watch the skies!"

Hollywood, however, did not follow its own advice. While it is true that a few films like *Invasion of the Body Snatchers* did involve creatures from outer space or aliens from another planet, more often than not the evil forces came from below the earth or from under the sea in films with titles like *Them*, *Tarantula*, *The Deadly Mantis*, and *It Came from Beneath the Sea*. For example, in *Them* (1954), the creatures are twelve foot mutant ants, resulting from the radioactivity deposited by the nuclear tests at Alamogordo. In *It Came from Beneath the Sea* (1955), the monster is a radioactive octopus that is transformed into a carnivorous giant intent on devouring San Francisco. Meanwhile, in *The Beast from 20,000 Fathoms* (1953), atomic testing in the Arctic dislodges a 100 million year old dinosaur, which proceeds to eat its way southward until destroyed by a combined force of police and military personnel at Coney Island Park in the Big Apple. Still, in another film, *The Terror from the Year 5000* (1958), scientists experimenting in their private laboratory somewhere in central Florida create a mutant creature, a highly radioactive woman who looks like a deformed cat dressed in a sequin gown and speaks with a foreign accent. She proceeds to kill a few people before she is forced into a large oven-type apparatus that resembles an old washing machine and is melted down.

Although it is unlikely that adults took these films seriously, nonetheless, Hollywood added a disclaimer that warned that experimentation with the new technology was dangerous. In fact, a few science-fiction films of this period such as *The Day the Earth Stood Still* (1951) and *It Came from Outer Space* (1953) feature aliens that are kind and loving creatures in contrast to the harmful pods that take over human bodies in Don Siegel's 1956 film, *Invasion of the Body Snatchers*. For example, Klaatu (Michael Rennie), the alien leader in *The Day the Earth Stood Still*, has a powerful weapon of destruction (aka: atom bomb) but comes to earth to further interplanetary peace rather than war. He is met, however, by government mistrust, public fear, and accusations of being a communist agent.[19] Shot by the police, Klaatu warns Earth that unless it ceases its nuclear arms race, his planet will destroy the world. Such serious science-fiction films, however, were atypical of the period.

Nuclear War Films

A few films delivered apocalyptic visions of a nuclear holocaust brought on by scheming politicians, deranged military commanders, or public officials who misplaced their reliance on, or were unable to control, modern technology. What these films express is a view of the bomb as a catastrophic force with the capability to destroy the entire world. In this sense, these films present the same kind of negative "end of civilization" scenario of the bomb found in the earlier science-fiction films.

An initial entry in this category was Stanley Kramer's 1959 film, *On the Beach*, based on the Nevil Shute novel. The film opens with the war a *fait accompli*, resulting in the destruction of much of the world except for Australia, where the survivors await the inevitable sickness and death brought on by radioactive dust ("Black Rain") carried by the winds to the South Pacific. Kramer's film featured an all-star cast and was a major production unlike the low budget B-science fiction films. But with the exception of one scene where the scientists and military blame each other for what has happened, the film presents a sanitized version of extinction. While Kramer's film may have been intended as a warning to the nuclear powers that the next war would be the last for mankind, it never does assign responsibility for the bomb or its deployment, nor does it visualize the end of civilization in a horrific manner. Essentially, *On the Beach* is an old-fashioned romance, a love story between married Gregory Peck, the American submarine commander, and Ava Gardner, the single woman he meets and falls in love with. *On the Beach* is no nuclear horror show because it lacks even one scene of death or destruction. While Kramer's ending message is for mankind to reform before it is too late, the punch line of the final scene as the characters wait for the nuclear fallout to reach them loses its impact because of the romanticized perspective that dominates the film. Here is a film about the nuclear holocaust without pain or suffering. In light of the film's romanticism, why the Pentagon refused to provide Kramer with assistance on the film remains a mystery.[20]

To demonstrate just how romantic Kramer's film is, it should be contrasted with Peter Watkins's short 1965 film, *The War Game*, made for the British Broadcasting Corporation (BBC). In the film's fictional narrative, the war begins when the U.S. threatens to use atomic weapons against the Chinese who have invaded South Vietnam. The Soviet Union enters the picture when it warns the U.S. to desist or it will take over West Berlin. When NATO forces are overwhelmed by superior Russian military might, the West resorts to tactical nuclear weapons. The Soviets respond with missiles of their own but several that were designed for military installations in Britain fall short of their targets and hit the civilian population of Kent. Given the military alliances of NATO and the Warsaw Pact during the Cold War, Watkins's launching of the war presented a plausible scenario. *The War Game* depicts the effects of a nuclear attack on the city of Kent in southeast England. Integrating newsreel footage and simulated events, the film visualizes the immediate effects suffered by the population after the bomb explodes. *The War Game* fills the screen with images of unending horrors—mass hysteria, panic, firestorms, suffocation due to a lack of oxygen, and even mercy killing of the sick and wounded. It proved to be too graphic for the BBC to televise. Although the film won an Academy Award as Best Feature Documentary and was eventually released to theaters, it has yet to be shown on British television.[21] *The War Game* proved too realistic for its own good.

Sidney Lumet's 1964 film, *Fail Safe*, concerns a limited nuclear war between the U.S. and the Soviets caused by a mechanical malfunction. The film could easily fit into the category of a nuclear accident except that its focus is on the decision-making process by which political leaders control the damage inflicted by the nuclear technology when the bomb's deployment is unintended. The plot has the U.S. president, played by Henry Fonda, offering the Soviet premier an opportunity to bomb New York City as a way to avoid World War III after an American plane breaks through the "fail-safe" security system and mistakenly drops a nuclear bomb on Moscow—a kind of tit for tat arrangement. Lumet's film is a well-crafted exercise in presidential decision-making. Purposely confining the action of the film to three interior sets, Lumet wants the audience to concentrate on the president's dilemma, that is, risk total nuclear war or offer the Soviets an opportunity to drop a bomb (unannounced) on a major American city. This may have been the only film during the Cold War where the audience was encouraged to cheer when the U.S. military shot down its own planes.

Like *Fail Safe*, Stanley Kubrick's *Dr. Strangelove or: How I Learned to Stop Worrying and Love the Bomb*, is also about the inadequacies of mechanical safeguards, military control, and communication devices to prevent unauthorized preemptive nuclear strikes against a political enemy. Only Kubrick's 1964 film is a satirical comedy populated with exaggerated characters like the lunatic general (Jack D. Ripper) who is convinced the communists are destroying his "precious bodily fluids" through fluoridation of the country's water supply and orders an unauthorized nuclear strike against the Soviets; a right-wing cold war "nuke'em dead" chief of staff (General Buck Turgidson) who acts more like an ape than a human being; a presidential advisor (Dr. Strangelove) whose bionic arm cannot stop giving the Nazi salute; and a cowboy Air Force pilot (Major Kong) who straddles a nuclear bomb like a bronco as it descends on the Soviet Union while the lyrics on the sound track sing: "We'll meet again, don't know where, don't know when."

Kubrick took a serious suspense story, *Red Alert*, and turned it into a black comedy about the nuclear apocalypse. He was denied assistance from the U.S. Air Force and shot the film in England where he thought he would have more artistic freedom. The result is a believable, yet devastatingly funny, film fantasy on how the world could end. There are many hilarious scenes in the film but one in particular stands out. It takes place in the American war room as the world teeters on the brink of atomic annihilation and the U.S. president tries to reach his Soviet counterpart on the red phone:

> Hello, Dmitri? Listen, can't hear too well. Do you suppose you could turn the music down just a little? Oh, that's much better. Yes, fine. I can hear you now, Dmitri, clear and plain and coming through fine. I'm coming through fine too, eh? Good, then. Well, then, as you say, we're both coming through fine. Good. Well, it's good that you're fine and I'm fine. I agree with you. It's great to be fine. Now then, Dmitri, you know how we've always talked about the possibility of something going wrong with the bomb? The *bomb*, Dmitri. The

> *hydrogen bomb*. Well, now what happened, is, um, one of our base commanders, he had a sort of . . . well, he went a little funny in the head. You know,just a little *funny*, and he went and did a silly thing. Well, I'll tell you what he did: He ordered his planes to attack your country. Well, let me finish, Dmitri. Let me finish, Dmitri. Well, listen, how do you think I feel about it? Can you imagine how I feel about it, Dmitri? Why do you think I'm calling you? Just to say hello? Of course, I like to speak to you. Of course, I like to say hello. Not now but anytime, Dmitri. I'm just calling up to tell you something terrible has happened. It's a friendly call, of course, it's a friendly call. Listen, if it wasn't friendly, you probably wouldn't have even got it.

If the film's scenario seemed far-fetched in the sixties, it must strike viewers today as dated after the end of the Cold War and the dissolution of the old Soviet Union. Hollywood's latest film enemies are more likely to be aliens (*Independence Day*, *Mars Attacks*)—creatures from another planet—who threaten the country's security. But the assumption that the world is safe from nuclear annihilation is incorrect because the nuclear threat is greater today due to the proliferation of nuclear weapons and the addition of Third World powers to the nuclear arms race. The knowledge that India and Pakistan have the bomb, that Israel possesses the capability, and that Iran and Iraq have the desire to produce nuclear weapons increases, rather than diminishes, the prospects of a nuclear holocaust. If anything, Kubrick's film is more relevant today than when it was originally released more than thirty years ago.

At least five nuclear war scenarios are plausible;[22] with one or two more likely than the rest. One possibility is that a nuclear war will be touched off by terrorists; another potential cause is mechanical failure. Human error could lead to the catastrophe in a third scenario. A fourth likelihood would revolve around a misunderstanding or miscommunication among nuclear club members such as the confrontation between the U.S. and the Soviets during the 1963 Cuban Missile Crisis. Finally, computer error could lead to a false alert which subsequently could trigger a real nuclear reaction. Hollywood explored this scenario in *War Games* (1983). Based on the premise that machines are not infallible, the film's scenario envisions a foul-up in the attack-alert warning system which mistakenly indicates that the country is under attack, thereby precipitating the retaliatory strike. The film would have the audience believe that a young computer hacker (Matthew Broderick) could bring the country to the brink of thermonuclear war through accidental access into the command room of NORAD, the North American Radar Air Defense. Although the premise may have seemed implausible in the eighties, the subsequent revelation that a British teenager was able to break into U.S. government files from his home computer makes *War Games* less entertaining and more frightening. At film's end, the computer is asked to imagine the outcome of a nuclear war and determine a "game winner"; the computer flashes out the words: "There is no winner."

The plot of *War Games* and similar films is predicated on the possibility of nuclear war. But is nuclear war a likelihood today or just a screenwriter's fantasy? If you dare to think the unthinkable, remember that during the Cold War the U.S. Government prepared for just such an eventuality in its secret Outpost Mission project which trained and prepared an elite corps of helicopter pilots to rescue the president from the White House in the event of a nuclear attack. Other so-called "doomsday" operations included saving important historical documents such as the Declaration of Independence and priceless works of art from the National Gallery in Washington. The Outpost Mission operation consumed twenty years of government preparation for the unthinkable—a nuclear strike against the United States.[23]

Nuclear Accidents

Ironically, Hollywood has made only two serious films about nuclear accidents, although a significant number of incidents and mishaps have actually occurred.[24] With the release of *The China Syndrome* and *Silkwood*, an ecological dimension was added to the nuclear war-doomsday threat. *The China Syndrome* (1979) explored the issue of death at the hands of an invisible force—radiation. This perceptive film details an attempted cover-up of a nuclear accident at a California power plant. Plant manager (Jack Lemmon) realizes that the radiation leak could trigger a core meltdown—the "China Syndrome" of the film title—and tries to prevent the facility from reopening. He manages to take over the control room and the nuclear power company calls in the authorities to take care of Lemmon, described as an emotionally disturbed employee. Lemmon's plea falls on deaf ears; instead the S.W.A.T. team breaks into the control room and shoots him. What Lemmon was trying to do was to prevent the possibility of a core meltdown where many more people would be killed from the radiation leak than from any bomb blast. The film could not have been more timely since it was released to theaters two weeks before the leak at the Three Mile Island nuclear plant near Harrisburg, Pennsylvania. In this case, life imitated art.

The film was more prescient than first suspected. The situation in *The China Syndrome* was virtually duplicated in real-life seven years later at the Chernobyl nuclear plant in the Ukraine. The explosion at Chernobyl was due to a combination of faulty design and human error which resulted in an estimated 6000 deaths, numerous cases of thyroid cancer, birth deformities, and the contamination of some 16,000 square miles of fertile land. It should also be noted that almost nine million people in the Ukraine, Byelorussia, and the Russian Federation were affected by the explosion. Chernobyl remains the worst nuclear accident in global history.[25]

At the other end of the nuclear holocaust spectrum, a comparatively minor incident is at the heart of Mike Nichols's 1983 film, *Silkwood*, based on a true story. Nichols's film is a reenactment of the real case of Karen Silkwood, a blue-collar worker in a plutonium plant, who died under mysterious circumstances while on her way to deliver documentary evidence to a *New York Times* reporter. Supposedly, the documents would verify the poor safety conditions at the Kerr-McGee factory where plutonium rods for nuclear weapons were being manufactured. However, Karen never made the interview as she died when her car went off the road. Nichols's film is multidimensional because at one level it is a mystery story that concerns itself with the strange death of Karen Silkwood. Did the corporate leaders at Kerr–McGee have Karen eliminated because she blew the whistle on the dangerous working conditions at their plant? Or was it merely a coincidence and a legitimate driving accident that led to her death? On another level, however, *Silkwood* serves as a reminder that not only are nuclear age weapons unlike conventional weapons and require greater care but the people who work with nuclear materials also require the highest levels of protection and concern for their personal safety. One Chernobyl incident in a lifetime is enough.

Nuclear Survival Films

The last category of nuclear age films include those that primarily concern themselves with survival after an atomic explosion, blast, or attack. These films focus on individuals or families that must adjust to an entirely different, and often hostile, environment and face new challenges successfully in order to stay alive. In some ways, the origin of such films is traceable to stories featuring the settlement of the frontier or the taming of the wilderness, except that in the westerns individuals had a chance against a human enemy or a wild beast. But in the nuclear films, death from the bomb explosion or the radiation exposure is inescapable.

The nuclear survival film and its derivations proved to be a popular subject with the film studios, quite possibly because of their similarity to science-fiction movies. Thus, while the topic itself is morbid and hardly a source for entertainment, the plot variations are endless. Three such films, *Five*, *Panic in Year Zero*, and *The World, the Flesh, and the Devil*, had optimistic endings. Two films, the made-for television, *The Day After*, and the film, *Testament*, were both more pessimistic and provided little comfort to viewers. Meanwhile, Roger Corman's B-film, *The Last*

Woman on Earth, promised more intrigue and excitement in its title than it delivered on the screen.

The plots of *Five* and the *World, the Flesh, and the Devil (WFD)* are similar. Arch Obler's 1951 film, *Five*, the first survivor film of the nuclear age, and the 1959 *WFD* both take place in limited worlds—contained environments—where the survivors, groups of five and three persons, respectively, each contain one woman. This fact is crucial to plot development because both films see hope through the reproductive organs of the surviving female. Both flirt with the issue of sexuality and race but are too timid to pursue that subject with any conviction. Also, the two films present fairly romanticized versions of a post-holocaust world without horror, pain, or human suffering.

The location for Roger Corman's film, *The Last Woman on Earth* (1960), is Puerto Rico and while the viewer is shown dead bodies lying in streets, cars, and jungle terrain, they are posed so peacefully as to suggest an afternoon siesta rather than nuclear death. Here the plot revolves around a married couple and the husband's lawyer (male) who survive the nuclear holocaust when deep-sea diving. Once it is established that they are the sole survivors on the island, the film sinks to a formulaic romantic love triangle and is unintentionally funny. For example, in a scene after the trio has learned of their rather desperate situation, they return to their hotel rooms and very carefully pack all their nice suits and dresses in suitcases as if preparing for a holiday rather than certain death.

Panic in Year Zero (1962) is another variation on the nuclear survival film. Actor-director Ray Milland focuses on the struggle for survival of a single family fleeing Los Angeles after a nuclear attack. But in *Panic* there are plenty of other survivors, and it is these people who pose more of a threat to this family than any nuclear bomb or radioactive matter. This is a conventional middle-class family that comes to adopt Herbert Spencer's principle of survival of the fittest. In order to protect his family, the father (Milland) takes guns and ammunition from a hardware store and gasoline from a service station. When the father is assaulted by three young thugs, the son comes to his rescue by wounding one of the hoodlums. Later, when his daughter is raped by this same trio, the father and son track them down and kill two of them in cold blood. The film is filled with mixed messages. On the one hand, it supports individualism over cooperation in a crisis and promotes the idea that the ends justify the means. On the other hand, the film occasionally stops to allow the family members (primarily the mother) to engage in moralistic speeches and to have the family commit one or two acts of kindness. At the end, when the unnamed warring powers have agreed to a truce and the family is headed home, Milland comes to realize that he has changed and that a future incident may force him to resort to similar behavior in order to survive. But this film is less about the horror of nuclear war than fear of human behavior under stress. An earthquake or tornado might have produced similar results as those presented in the film.

Two 1983 films, *The Day After* and *Testament*, treat the subject of nuclear attack quite differently. Both personalize the experience, focusing on the impact of the attack on one family (*Testament*) and on several major characters (*The Day After*). The ABC network turned *The Day After* into a media event as it promoted the film's showing as an educational opportunity when it encouraged teachers, students, and their schools, churches and congregations, and families to share the film experience together.[26] Before the film's showing, the network announced that while the film was based on scientific fact, it still was a work of fiction. After the screening, the network presented a discussion panel of experts to review the film. But while the story of ordinary people caught up in an unexpected nuclear attack contained many of the expected images: dead bodies, radiation sickness, virulent epidemics, scarce supply of uncontaminated food and water, and outbreaks of violence and lawlessness, the film seems to want to shock its audience through special effects and gruesome makeup more than enlighten it. There was something artificial about the firing squad and the looters, so that at the end all that remained for the viewer was a feeling that nuclear war is terrible.

Testament, on the other hand, was a small, under two-hour film about the effect of a nuclear attack on one California middle-class family. The opening scene finds the father away on business, leaving the mother and children to face the nuclear holocaust alone. After the initial blast, the film moves quickly to show the community covered by radioactive dust as a result of World War III. The remainder describes how the family and the community cope with the aftermath of such a catastrophe. There are no special effects or expensive makeup requirements in *Testament*. The emphasis here is on the personal drama. For instance, in the final scene, when the mother, her son, and his friend await certain death, it is clear that the end of the family is a metaphor for the end of civilization. But as T. S. Elliot wrote, that end is likely to come "not with a bang but with a whimper."

While the flashier *The Day After* drew a viewing audience of 100 million, *Testament* virtually disappeared from sight. The film had a strange history. Originally produced for Paramount Pictures and first screened at the New York Film Festival, the film starred Jane Alexander as the mother; a role that brought her an Academy Award nomination. But the film had a limited theatrical release and eventually was shown on

PBS as part of its American Playhouse television series. Unlike *The Day After*, the rather unemotional, but more realistic, ending of life as depicted in *Testament* failed to capture the public's imagination and the film went virtually unnoticed.

A derivation of the nuclear survival genre can be found in films like *A Boy and His Dog* (1975) and the *Mad Max* trilogy of films starring Mel Gibson, which take place in a post-apocalyptic world—an arid wasteland—inhabited by a population whose major preoccupation is with survival. While the situations in these films are caused by nuclear war, their narratives concern a more distant time, lending themselves closer to futuristic thrillers like *Terminator* than to a film like *Testament* where the characters confront the immediate aftermath of nuclear destruction.

Disaster scenarios work well visually, especially on the big screen, in case the reader was among the handful who failed to see *Twister*, *Dante's Peak*, or *Independence Day*. In a sense, films with nuclear themes are disaster movies of a particular type. While tornados and volcanic eruptions are natural phenomena and alien invaders are hypothetical scenarios, nuclear war is manmade and therefore, avoidable. The fundamental question, then, is this: Are there lessons to be learned from exposure to nuclear films? Unfortunately, social scientists have yet to provide a definitive answer. However, limited experiments conducted on school-age children offer a clue. Studies conducted in North Carolina among high school students and college freshmen in 1982 and again in 1984 after the televising of *The Day After* reveal that young people are more affected by visual images than what is described on the printed page.[27] But while the sample population in these surveys underwent an attitude change regarding nuclear weapons that uncovered a better understanding of their destructive capabilities, there was no corresponding change in political knowledge after seeing *The Day After*, reading Jonathan Schell's *The Fate of the Earth*, and being made aware of the Reagan Administration's deployment of cruise and Pershing II missiles in Europe. The students, therefore, continued to divorce the horrors of a nuclear holocaust from the glamour of the administration's "star wars" project.

The Nuclear Age Today

The atomic era began in 1942 on a squash court at the University of Chicago where the first nuclear reaction took place. During the past half-century, the energy released by the atom has been harnessed more for destruction than for peaceful purposes. It no longer matters who is responsible for this turn of events because all of those involved should be held accountable: the scientists laid the foundation by splitting the atom; the military seized the opportunity to use that advantage by developing weapons of tremendous destruction; and the politicians made the decisions as to when, how, and under what circumstances these weapons would be utilized. Later, scientists like Oppenheimer regretted what they had done, but by then it was too late. Had the Second World War continued longer, the Germans might have developed the bomb and used it against the Allies. Would the Japanese not have done so too had they had the capability? No matter. Scientific progress cannot be contained, only delayed. The real problem with atomic energy lies not in its discovery, but in its utilization. As Einstein remarked after the dropping of the A-bombs on Hiroshima and Nagasaki, "The release of atom power has changed everything except our way of thinking."[28]

Einstein proved to be prescient. Revisionist historians now claim that Truman used the A-bomb primarily as a future bargaining chip in negotiations with the Soviet Union rather than as a calculated means to save lives (American and Japanese) by bringing World War II to an end. Eisenhower, Truman's successor in the White House, also saw the bomb as a political rather than a purely military weapon; a means to regain the Cold War initiative from the Soviets. Reportedly, Eisenhower moved atomic warheads to Okinawa to impress the Chinese and later, during the Formosa Straits confrontation, ordered the military to be in a state of nuclear readiness. At one point in his administration, Eisenhower reportedly said: "I see no reason why they [nuclear weapons] shouldn't be used just exactly as you would use a bullet or anything else."[29] As Einstein predicted, Eisenhower the president failed to distinguish conventional armaments from nuclear weapons.

Some cooperation has occurred since the 1963 Partial Test Ban Treaty banned atmospheric nuclear testing. The five admitted nuclear powers (U.S., Soviet Union, China, France, and the United Kingdom) have sought to prohibit above-ground testing and to limit underground tests. The 1968 Non-Proliferation Treaty, however, failed to restrict the spread of nuclear weapons as the recent bomb tests in India and Pakistan demonstrate. Since 1945, more than 2000 atmospheric and underground nuclear tests have been conducted worldwide.[30] An effort to ban all nuclear explosions has been supported in the United Nations General Assembly by 158 members, but India refuses to sign the Comprehensive Test Ban Treaty as it now stands. In addition to these universal steps, both the U.S. and the Soviet Union (now Russia) agreed in the 1991 Start Treaties to reduce their nuclear stockpile by two-thirds by the year 2003. Still, each country would be left with over 3000 strategic nuclear weapons—land-based, air, and submarine-launched nuclear warheads at their disposal—enough firepower to cause a nuclear Armageddon.

On the nonmilitary front, atomic energy has been utilized in the U.S. as a source of electric power since 1951. By the mid-nineties, there were over 100 nuclear power plants from Maine to California generating almost one-quarter of the nation's energy. However, two problems have plagued the nuclear power industry. One is safety, the other is cost. Most Americans can recall the partial meltdown incident at the Three Mile Island plant and a good deal of the world is unlikely to forget the Chernobyl disaster. But there have been other so-called "near misses" which raise serious concerns about plant safety. These "disasters-in-waiting" include complaints about shoddy workmanship, safety lapses, faulty equipment, and drug and alcohol usage by plant workers. The most serious incident so far occurred at the New England Haddam Neck plant where a seal failure in 1984 almost caused a complete meltdown.[31] The other problem involves costs. A number of planned nuclear power plants, such as the one at Shoreham, Long Island, remain unfinished and others like the Connecticut Yankee plant in New England have been forced to close. Still, 107 nuclear plants were in operation during the summer of 1998.[32] As the nuclear power plants age, the U.S. will have to make some tough decisions concerning future power sources.

One thing is certain, however. Nuclear technology, whether designed to produce domestic energy or weapons of war, is a permanent fixture of modern life. The challenge facing political decision-makers is daunting: how to harness nuclear energy to improve the quality of life rather than destroy it. Maybe the United Nations should schedule a showing of *On the Beach*, make it required viewing, and focus particularly on the film's final scene where the radioactive dust has extinguished all life and a draped banner reads: "There is still time, brother." Get the message?

Eleven

Political Film in the Next Century

Hollywood and Washington have shared a marriage of convenience for almost a century. The connection between film and politics is demonstrated in the world of practical politics, where money buys access and influence, and on the big screen, where the industry controls the content of a medium with the capability to deliver explicit and covert political messages. Additionally, during the last three decades, members of the Hollywood community have sought to capitalize on their film experience as a springboard into national politics.

It is becoming increasingly clear that the road to national office, especially for Democrats, passes through Hollywood. Candidates for national office test the political waters at lavish fundraising events while lobbyists seek financial support for political causes that range from returning the Dalai Lama to Tibet to preservation of abortion rights. Monetary support is especially crucial today given the excessive costs of political campaigns. When the Democratic Party sought to raise money for its 1998 congressional campaign, it was the president who raised almost one million dollars during a weekend in the Hamptons (Long Island), hobnobbing with entertainment celebrities.[1] Such staged fundraising occurrences are crucial events to a candidate seeking funding or political parties that seek to replenish party coffers.[2] But Hollywood "fat cats" no longer are satisfied with a handshake and a photo session. For their donations, these contributors seek to influence public policy. What consequences this latest development in campaign finances will have on national politics is still speculation, but it could further strengthen the voice of the rich and the powerful in national affairs.

The Hollywood–Washington relationship survived a rocky beginning. Congress and state legislatures initially sought to control film content until the industry decided to police itself. This strategy eventually paid off, aided considerably by the Supreme Court's breakthrough decision in the *Burstyn v. Wilson* case that brought movies under the protection of the First Amendment. For all practical purposes, this ruling virtually eliminated the prospect of government control over screen content, except for legally obscene material. Since the major film studios neither make obscene nor pornographic movies, Hollywood has enjoyed considerable freedom in the selection and treatment of screen subjects for almost half a century. Moreover, since the sixties, state and local governments have accepted the process of self-regulation, whereby the industry determines the suitability of its films for particular age groups dependent on content and treatment. The rating system has become so widely accepted in the American value system that President Clinton relied upon the film industry experience to support a similar system for television programming.

From Hollywood's perspective, the fruits of this relationship have largely freed the film industry from the imposition of governmental controls and regulations regarding screen content. The industry is much more interested today in global markets for its films since even major film productions rely on foreign sales for half of their gross. In financial terms this means that many Hollywood productions would be unable to show a profit if their films relied on domestic distribution alone. This financial fact of life helps to explain why the industry seeks to avoid giving offense, particularly if the overseas market for Hollywood films shows significant potential. It is not surprising, then, that studios took steps to reassure the Chinese government on the screen treatment regarding the two 1997 films on the Dalai Lama, *Seven Years in Tibet* and *Kundun*, particularly since China represents an additional five billion dollars in movie tickets sales despite their less than ideal cinema locations.[3] Hollywood envisions the day when American films fill all those theater seats.

Film Content: Entertainment or Ideology?

The film industry is a business that depends on public acceptance and support. Hollywood sells movies just as Ford sells cars. Even though the film industry is a for-profit business, it also delivers political messages in films since *Birth of a Nation* was released in 1915. This D. W. Griffith film romanticized life in the Old South while it supported the institution of slavery and the policy of racial segregation. Eight decades later, Oliver Stone's *JFK* sought to persuade audiences that President Kennedy was the victim of an elaborate conspiracy. Both Griffith and Stone designed their political messages to change public attitudes, even alter behavior, but stayed within the boundary of commercial entertainment. Operating within the shadowy world between fantasy and reality, Hollywood often is able to have its cake and eat it too.

Another important aspect of the Hollywood–Washington relationship is the utilization of film as a politicizing agent. Although social scientists have yet to establish a positive correlation between film content and political consequences, the medium has the capacity to influence attitudes and beliefs through the rearrangement of realities that either reinforce or reject current political values.[4] Some commercial features are not works of complete fiction; films like *Amistad* (1997), *Do the Right Thing* (1989), and *Mississippi Burning* (1988) have narratives firmly embedded in historical events. If the mass media seek only to entertain, then why would dictators, past and present, want to control the means of communication? Similarly, why would democratic governments rely heavily on media support during wars and periods of national emergencies? Why would the W. K. Kellogg Foundation, for instance, provide substantial funding to business schools that encourage their students to analyze films for clues as to leadership ability?[5] The non-empirical but common sense answer is that film is a powerful tool with the potential to do great harm or good, particularly when it is employed to establish and sustain mass movements.

It is true that Hollywood makes few films that are political in the sense that their intention is to promote a political idea or cause, disclose government corruption and bureaucratic inefficiency, or expose human rights violations. But even the most innocuous Hollywood movie designed for entertainment is still capable of delivering political messages even while audiences laugh, cry, or shriek with fear. These messages are likely to be less overtly racist than those presented in *Birth of a Nation*, which depicted the newly freed slave as a threat to white civilization. Still, such films are harmful to the body politic if they reinforce stereotypical images, promote racist and sexist values, lend credibility to selfish or corrupt social and economic institutions, support governmental policies detrimental to public health and welfare, and champion foreign policy initiatives that result in disastrous consequences. In this sense, the vast majority of Hollywood films are political simply because they accept, and therefore promote, the status quo.

In reconstructing reality, Hollywood films are instrumental in shaping popular images. Politics is one subject field where the industry has misrepresented the workings of government, preferring instead to perpetuate stereotypes or to disguise the political drama within an action thriller or romantic comedy. On those infrequent occasions when the film studios explore serious political issues, the risk is minimized since the emphasis falls on the individual rather than the institutions of government. Thus, a crooked Senator Paine (*Mr. Smith Goes to Washington*) or a devious, unscrupulous right-winger like the titled character (*Bob Roberts*) are presented as politicians with personal flaws rather than products of an imperfect political system.

Law and lawyers are another subject area frequently misrepresented in Hollywood films. Similar to their political colleagues, lawyers who are substance abusers (Frank Gavin in *The Verdict* and Eddie Dodds in *True Believer*) are depicted as personal weaknesses rather than reflections of a competitive, cut-throat legal system where the mentality of "winning is everything" dominates the judicial proceedings. To add insult to injury, Hollywood is guilty of perpetuating the male power structure within the legal community when it portrays female lawyers as incapable of managing career and family successfully or as prone to exercising poor judgment in the courtroom and the bedroom. What potential client would consider a female attorney after seeing Glenn Close (*Jagged Edge*) and Mary Elizabeth Mastrantonio (*Class Action*) at work? At best, these film characterizations fail to instill confidence in women as professional attorneys; at worst, they endorse the traditional homemaker role of women within the nation's social structure.

Rather it is the exceptional Hollywood political film that deviates from recycled plots and formulaic solutions. Instead the industry places blame for the country's political problems on corrupt politicians and greedy businessmen representing special interests. Rarely does Hollywood provide a substantial analysis of a political problem such as the corruption of public officials.

These simplistic exposes are superficial, ignoring what Lincoln Steffens defined in *The Shame of the Cities* as corruption inherent in a political system which provides public officials with patronage rewards to distribute to cronies and financial backers.[6] His expose of urban corruption questioned whether capitalistic democracy is compatible with the public good. Political machines, Steffens observed, were nourished off the exchange of votes for personal favors such as jobs and lucrative city contracts. But rather than examine the source of local corruption, which Steffens identified as the "apple" in the biblical story of Adam and Eve, Hollywood continues to blame "temptation" residing in the form of the devil (*City Hall*, *The Devil's Advocate*) or in the failings of dishonorable men (*All the King's Men, The Great McGinty*, *The Glass Key*). Hollywood is unlikely to present the Frank Skeffingtons (*The Last Hurrah*) and the Willie Starks (*All the King's Men*) as decent men corrupted by a political system that rewards self-interest and political ambition over the public interest.

Similarly, when Hollywood portrays the justice system it often fails to acknowledge that many plea bargains are struck mainly for convenience; a way to unclog crowded courtroom dockets. Yet these negotiated pleas in criminal cases often fail to provide justice to defendants or community alike. When defense lawyer Al Pacino (*And Justice for All*) explodes against a corrupt and inefficient legal system, his lawyering days are over in a film that never questions the selection process of judges or the legitimacy of the justice system itself. When Hollywood decided in the 1980s to be politically correct and portray women in career roles, their depiction was flawed and even damaging. The women lawyers in *Defenseless*, *Jagged Edge*, and *Suspect* engage in improper, even stupid, conduct. These films do not advance the cause of professional women.

Moreover, the industry has shown little interest in becoming proactive by making movies that lobby for specific political outcomes like election campaign reform, a more equable economic distribution system, or the expansion of economic rights for minorities. Warren Beatty tried to deal with such important policy issues as campaign finance reform and the pervasive influence of special interests in *Bulworth*, but he encased these legitimate concerns inside a farcical plot without offering any remedies. Instead, *Bulworth* is content to deliver a grocery-list of current social wrongs to the tune of rap music, preferring to entertain rather than enlighten.

In truth, except during wartime, Hollywood has failed to exhibit much courage. Rather than take a moral stand in the 1950s, the industry contributed to the Cold War communist hysteria in two ways. First, the major studios deserted their employees—actors, directors, screenwriters—during the HUAC hearings with little regard for individual culpability. Second, the studios reinstated the blacklist against the Hollywood Ten and the other unfriendly HUAC witnesses; a punishment previously reserved for labor organizers. With its capitulation to HUAC, the industry deprived itself of a talented pool of writers, directors, and actors. With very few exceptions, Hollywood either ignored or refused to respond to HUAC's accusations. Moreover, the industry remained silent rather than attack the committee for violating fundamental American rights and liberties. Instead, Hollywood knuckled under and contributed to the red scare through motion pictures like *Big Jim McLain*, *My Son John*, and *The Red Menace*, which lent credence to the mass hysteria of an imminent communist conspiracy to takeover the world.

Nor was Hollywood's reluctance to stand up to political pressure in the fifties an isolated phenomenon. Even when the industry was churning out the "social messages" films of the 1930s and 1940s in films like *I Am a Fugitive from a Chain Gang* (1932), *Black Legion* (1936), *Dead End* (1937), *They Won't Forget* (1937), *Crossfire* (1947), *Gentleman's Agreement* (1947), and *Intruder in the Dust* (1949), it rarely questioned the capitalist economic system or blamed racial and ethnic bigotry for the social problems exposed in these films. Thus these social message films led audiences to believe that anti-Semitism, racism, prejudice, and intolerance were personal defects of the film characters rather than symbolic flaws within the American character. Throughout the history of the industry, the prevailing concern has been for profits rather than for social causes. As an industry, Hollywood religiously adhered to the popular maxim that you never bite the hand that feeds you.

What Future for Political Film?

Hollywood has come to believe its own rhetoric; that movies are harmless diversions not intended to be taken seriously. While this generalization is accurate for the most part, it is incomplete because it ignores a minority of films with unmistakable political content. But whenever Hollywood is challenged to defend its own mythology, however, the industry responds that audiences are not persuaded or influenced by the visual images shown on theater screens. Although the film medium may lack the capability to treat complex ideas as thoroughly and analytically as print, nonetheless, film remains a powerful instrument to visualize ideas embedded in strong narratives that have the capacity to overwhelm audiences. Such images can remain with the viewer far longer than the film itself. For example, the opening scenes of the Normandy invasion in *Saving Private Ryan*, photographed so as to depict the chaos, horror, and futility of war, remain fixed in memory long after the viewer has left the theater. In short, the historical record contradicts Hollywood's projected image as merely the handmaiden of its viewing audience.

But given Hollywood's commitment to entertainment and the profit motive, what future exists for political films? On the surface, the prospects are not encouraging. Hollywood's history excludes making innovative films, especially ones that challenge the status quo. The Hollywood that the public closely identifies with is still represented by the big studios of the past—MGM, Paramount, Twentieth-Century Fox, and Warner Brothers—film studios that turned out commercial features almost exclusively and that remain market driven. A financially successful film is virtually certain to be imitated. If anything, the Hollywood represented by the major studios is more reinvention than creation.

To be fair to Hollywood, however, the economics of the film industry render moviemaking a high-risk business venture. Special effects and star salaries reaching $20 million per film have driven up the average cost to produce, distribute, and market a Hollywood film to somewhere between $50 and $75 million. Although Hollywood sells billions of tickets at American theaters every year, escalating costs actually have depressed profits at home and many more films must rely on foreign receipts to turn a profit.[7] Even children's films, once considered a fairly safe investment, are risky ventures in today's market. Take the case of the 1995 film, *A Little Princess*. Made for $15 million, the film failed to earn enough to break even.[8]

Several examples of audience indifference to American films with political themes (*Wag the Dog*, *Primary Colors*, and *Bulworth*) confirms their high risk despite fortuitous timing that exploited current political events in Washington. *Wag the Dog,* for instance, describes the efforts of spin doctors to salvage the political career of a sexually charged president while the real life drama was unfolding in the Clinton Administration. Despite the fortunate timing, release of the film was still a box office disappointment. Also *Primary Colors*, which recounts the exploits of a philandering Southern governor (designed to resemble Bill Clinton) who seeks the presidency. Although released while the Paula Jones and Monica Lewinsky affairs were front-page news, audiences refused to flock to the theaters. Finally, *Bulworth*, a satiric look at campaign politics, disappeared from first-run theaters after five weeks despite some good reviews. Apparently, audiences were indifferent to a storyline where a depressed, white-liberal politician, on the verge of suicide, finds love and truth while imitating a black rapper. These poor showings bode ill for political films made by the Hollywood establishment.

Nor is it likely that these films will benefit much from foreign audiences since they too have a preference for the Hollywood blockbuster. But even the expensive, spectacular film can fail to guarantee audience popularity. For every successful *Forrest Gump*, there is a costly disaster like *The Postman* (1997). Production costs of blockbuster films are exceeding $100 million, without the additional marketing and distribution expenses.[9] The latest Hollywood version of the *Titanic*,[10] which cost $200 million, has set a new standard for industry blockbusters. Since the average Hollywood film should earn at least twice its cost to break even or realize a small profit, consider what a blockbuster must gross to recoup costs of $200 million? No wonder the major Hollywood studios remain timid as usual. Unfortunately, only a severe economic depression or the development of a more discriminating audience is likely to reverse the current spending trend, given the present mindset in Hollywood.

The likelihood is that business will be conducted as usual in Hollywood. Yet this rather bleak landscape offers a small ray of hope for political films in the twenty-first century. Whatever future exists for the political film genre rests on the shoulders of auteurs like Oliver Stone and on the continued growth of independent filmmakers whose movies are characterized by modest budgets, unknown casts, and subjects often ignored by the mainstream studios.

The Indies

The so-called "indies" provide the best hope for political films. While no one definition accurately represents independent filmmaking in the U.S. today, a consensus exits that four characteristics are usually present in such films: first, the films are produced outside the traditional studio system; second, they have modest budgets and are financed with funds from non-conventional sources; third, they are distributed outside the normal theater chains; and lastly, they are made by young directors at the beginning of their careers or by established "auteurs" who are in a position to freelance.

The essence of the independent film, however, is greater than its origin or distribution. Its most defining characteristics include imagery and ideas counter to commercial cinema, film projects that reflect the personal statement of their creators or express an idiosyncratic vision.[11] In sum, the narrative of the independent film is constructed in a universe outside the conventional Hollywood plot that relies heavily on the requisite sex, explicit violence, expensive special effects, mindless auto-chases, spectacular explosions, and hi-tech gadgetry to attract audiences into theaters.

Historically, independent filmmakers survived on the margins of the film industry. Ironically, their emergence as a viable alternative to the traditional Hollywood screen fare began in the 1970s in response to the tremendous financial success of blockbuster films like *Jaws* (1975) and *Star Wars* (1977); both grossed more than $100 million in their initial first-run distribution.[12] Their success led the major studios to believe that one blockbuster picture could carry a studio for an entire year. As the major studios pursued the $100 million blockbuster, independent filmmakers like the Coen brothers, Wayne Wang, Jim Jarmusch, Quentin Tarantino, Carl Franklin, and Allison Anders made small budgeted films that caught the attention of critics and audiences alike. By the mid-eighties, film audiences came to appreciate their work, and the major studios began to finance their film projects through subsidiary companies. The increasing popularity of their work is demonstrated by their production schedule: approximately fifty indies were produced in 1986 while ten years later, that number had multiplied twenty times. Furthermore, their commercial success caught the attention of the major studios; twenty-five features received a significant enough theatrical release to gross at least one million.[13] By the mid-nineties, virtually one-quarter of the 400 films produced by the Hollywood studios are independents released through subsidiaries such as Miramax, New Line Cinema, Samuel Goldwyn, October, and Fox Searchlight. But what really caught the attention of the major studios was the realization that four of the five films nominated for Academy Awards as "Best Picture of 1996" were independent productions.[14]

The division that has developed within the film industry is best described as a bifurcation, resulting in the emergence of two Hollywoods[15]; one that turns out blockbusters with high-priced stars for the global market and the other that produces small films with modest budgets that emphasize plot and characterization. If political films have any future in Hollywood, their brightest prospects appear to be with the independent filmmakers who can challenge entrenched institutions and the underlying values of a consumer culture. A small market exists in American popular culture for such works because their reasonable costs are attractive to the major studios. If this idea seems farfetched, remember that in the early days of film history, the American Federation of Labor (AFL) and other labor organizations financed and produced some of their own films. Similar models exist in Hollywood history; recall that the Abraham Polonsky/John Garfield film, *Force of Evil* (1948), was independently produced and still made a profit. Imagine if environmental groups and public interest organizations joined labor unions in producing films, not necessarily documentaries, that would have some popular appeal? Admittedly such endeavors could lead to biased productions and propaganda tracts but viewers at least would benefit from alternative choices in the film marketplace. For that competition to occur, however, requires a degree of assurance that the films have a venue for their exhibition. During 1996, for instance, less than three percent of the indies were picked up by national distributors.[16] Just as labor struggled to find a theater for its films in the early part of the twentieth-century, political films of the future may have to rely on universities, public libraries, and other community-based venues for their exhibition. Several alternative outlets presently exist for indies, namely cable and video. The new version of *Lolita* (1998) is a prime example of a film that initially was shown on cable because it could not find a distributor. *Lolita* was eventually released to theaters several months later.

The growth of independent film festivals throughout the U.S. and Canada is a good omen for the future of alternative films. The most popular venue for independent films in the U.S. is Robert Redford's Sundance Institute in Utah. Founded in 1980, Redford's Institute sponsors a January film festival that serves as a national showcase for young talent. The festival is highly competitive; in 1998 the judges selected 110 works to be shown out of a pool of 1500 submitted features, documentaries, short subjects, and animated films.[17] Each year, a new group of festival winners are discovered by national distributors based on their Sundance reception. Sundance already is credited for launching the careers of minority and disenfranchised filmmakers, spotlighting films that are iconoclastic, and others that express marginal viewpoints. It was at Sundance that American audiences were introduced to the work of directors Steven Soderbergh (*Sex, Lies and Videotape*, 1989), Quentin Tarantino (*Reservoir Dogs*, 1992), Kevin Smith (*Clerks*, 1994), Edward Burns (*The Brothers MacMullen*, 1995) and Brad Anderson (*Next Stop Wonderland*, 1998). While these pictures are not necessarily political, Sundance still provides an opportunity to filmmakers to exercise more creative freedom than under the traditional studio system. In such an environment, filmmakers can deliver political messages in works that at least have the potential to reach a national audience. A perfect example of the contribution being done by the private sector is the financial support Sundance provided to Tony Bui's film, *Three Seasons* (1999), the first feature shot in Vietnam since the end of the war.

Increasing enthusiasm in the private sector for independent films should encourage the more than 2700 independent theaters[18] in the U.S. to include films that have been critically acclaimed at Sundance and at other film festivals, including the annual Robert Flaherty Film Seminar held at various sites throughout the country. The growing popularity of indies is best illustrated by a New York City filmmaker who initiated an annual film festival in the seventies. Two decades later, her Independent Feature Film Market brings together young filmmakers, studio executives, and national distributors to a week-long festival where some 400 films are viewed and analyzed. It was the Independent Feature Film Market that provided a showcase for *Roger and Me* in the eighties.[19]

Two further developments offer hope for the indies and the cultivation of an audience. One recent initiative is the work of financiers who establish film companies for investment purposes instead of funneling their monies into the stock market and mutual funds. Several such companies already exist; Lions Gate Entertainment funds movie projects with budgets between $3 and $10 million while the Stratosphere Entertainment Group prefers to invest in film projects with $6 to $8 million budgets.[20] These investors dream of financing films that cost several million dollars but return one hundred times their cost. Political films might be of interest to such modest-risk takers.

The second initiative, undertaken by actor Robert Redford, is a joint venture with inner-city universities that could prove mutually beneficial. Redford, in fact, has taken the first step in that direction with plans to open a chain of Sundance Cinemas, in conjunction with the University of Pennsylvania, that would provide an outlet for documentaries and independent films and that would revitalize the neighborhood surrounding the Philadelphia campus. If the experiment is successful, other Sundance Cinema centers are planned for Boston, Chicago, and Portland, Oregon.[21]

The further expansion of venues for independent films and the progress of entertainment investment groups represents the more likely scenario for developing a market for American political films in the twenty-first century. Together with the growing acceptance of independent films by better educated audiences, these two recent developments offer the best hope for politically conscious filmmakers to exhibit their work and discover an audience. The future for political film never looked brighter.

Notes

One

Hollywood and Washington: The Marriage of Film and Politics

1. See Neal Gabler, *Life The Movie: How Entertainment Conquered Reality* (New York: Alfred A. Knopf, 1998).
2. Neal Gabler, *An Empire of Their Own: How the Jews Invented Hollywood* (New York: Crown, 1988).
3. The material on the Hollywood-Washington relationship comes from Ronald Brownstein, *The Power and the Glitter* (New York: Pantheon, 1990).
4. Gabler, An Empire of Their Own, 291.
5. See ibid., 245, 311.
6. Leslie Wayne, "A Hollywood Production: Political Money," *New York Times*, Sept. 12, 1996, 1.
7. Reported in the *New York Times*, December 1, 1998, A24.
8. R. W. Apple Jr., "On Washington," *New York Times Magazine*, Nov. 15, 1998, sec. 6, 42.
9. Reported in the *Williamsport Sun-Gazette*, Nov. 9, 1995, 13.
10. Brownstein, *The Power & the Glitter*, 3–6.
11. Ibid., 225–74. Brownstein reports that actor Paul Newman was active in the anti-nuclear campaign and Robert Redford in environmental problems in the state of Utah, where he had purchased a home and created the Sundance Film Institute. Also actor Marlon Brando had been a long-time supporter of better treatment for Native Americans. But probably the most famous (or infamous) activist was Jane Fonda for her anti-Vietnam activities. In addition, it was Hollywood money that helped to fund the liberal lobby group, People for the American Way, and the liberal political campaign group, Network.
12. Ibid. Brownstein develops this theme in Part II of his book.
13. Harvey B. Feigenbaum, "The Culture of Production and the Production of Culture" (paper presented at the annual meeting of the American Political Science Association, Chicago, August 31–Sept. 3, 1995), 24.
14. *Variety*, June 22–28, 1998, 8.
15. The economic domination of Hollywood movies is demonstrated in David Puttnam, with Neil Watson, *Movies and Money* (New York: Knopf, 1997).
16. Richard Maltby and Dan Craven, *Hollywood Cinema* (Cambridge: Blackwell Publishers, 1995). The authors support the view that political movies are high box office risk, citing at least six pre-World War II political films, including Abe Lincoln in Illinois, that either lost money or were financial disappointments to their studios.

17. Quoted in Maltby and Craven, 363.
18. Gary Crowdus, ed., *The Political Companion to American Film* (Chicago: Lake View Press, 1994), x.
19. See reports and reviews of the film in the *New York Times*, Dec. 17, 1995, sec. 2, 1 and Dec. 20, 1996, sec. C, 11.
20. See Charles Maland, "Politics and Auteurs: From Chaplin to Wajda," in James Combs, ed., *Movies and Politics* (New York: Garland Publishing, 1993), 239–69.
21. Walter Benjamin, "The Work of Art in the Age of Mechanical Reproduction," in Illuminations, edited with an introduction by Hannah Arendt (New York: Schocken Books, 1968).
22. The quote by Cassavetes is in Michael Genovese, *Politics and the Cinema* (Lexington, MA: Ginn Press, 1986), 67. Certainly, Neal Gabler agreed with that assessment in his book, *An Empire of Their Own*, detailing how the Jewish immigrants who founded Hollywood portrayed an idealized version of their new homeland in their films.
23. Dan Nimmo, "Political Propaganda in the Movies: A Typology," in Movies and Politics, 271–94.
24. Ibid., 283–84.
25. Quoted in John E. O'Connor and Maring A. Jackson, eds., *American History/American Film*, with a Foreword by Arthur Schlesinger, Jr. (New York: Frederick Unger, 1979), xv. The film was the first motion picture shown at the White House.
26. See Mark C. Carnes, ed., *Past Imperfect* (New York: Henry Holt, 1995). Carnes takes the position that Hollywood filmmakers generally have distorted the facts.
27. Stephen Vaughn, *Ronald Reagan in Hollywood* (New York: Cambridge University Press, 1994).
28. See Ernest Giglio, "The Decade of 'The Miracle' 1952–1962: A Study in the Censorship of the American Motion Picture" (Ph.D. diss., Syracuse University, 1964) and I. C. Jarvie (editor) et al., *Children and the Movies*: Media Influences and the Payne Fund Controversy (New York: Cambridge University Press, 1996).
29. See comments in the *New York Times*, June 2, 1995, 24, and June 4, 1995, 20.
30. After the initial outcry had quieted, it was discovered that a number of firebombings had occurred in the New York subway system in the 1980s. Because of these incidents, the city's Transit Authority, while cooperating with Columbia Pictures, refused permission to film that scene in the subway. Actually, a Burt Reynolds police drama, *Fuzz*, released in the 1970s, contained a scene where a man is doused with a flammable liquor and set on fire. Public criticism was raised after a copycat crime occurred shortly after the film's theatrical release. But the furor declined as the crime became accepted as an isolated incident.
31. William R. Elliott and William J. Schenck-Hamlin, "Film, Politics and the Press: The Influence of "All the President's Men," *Journalism Quarterly* 56, no. 3 (1979): 546–53.
32. Thomas S. Bateman, Tomoaki Sakano, and Mokoto Fujita, "Roger, Me, and My Attitude: Film Propaganda and Cynicism toward Corporate Leadership," *Journal of Applied Psychology* 77, no. 5, (1992): 768–71.

Two

Defining the Political Film: From Riefenstahl to the *Three Stooges*

1. Clifford Geertz, *The Interpretation of Cultures* (New York: Basic Books, 1973), 196.
2. See, e.g., Terry Christensen, *Reel Politics* (New York: Blackwell, 1987); Gary Crowdus, ed., *The Political Companion to American Film* (Chicago: Lake View Press, 1994) and Mark Litwak, *Reel Power* (London: Sedgwick & Jackson, 1987) as scholars, critics, and writers who fit into this group.
3. Peter Rainer, "Politicization of Films: A Mirror of Our Time," *Los Angeles Herald*, Dec. 16, 1984, 1, 14, analyzes the films of the eighties.
4. Herbert J. Gans, "Hollywood Entertainment: Commerce or Ideology?" *Social Science Quarterly* 74, no. 1 (1993): 150–53.
5. The figures are from *Variety*, June 22–28, 1998, 8 and the *New York Times*, July 10, 1998, B18.
6. John Simon, *Movies Into Film* (New York: Dell Publishing Co., 1970), 66.
7. Ibid.
8. See, Michael Genovese, *Politics and the Cinema* (Lexington, MA: Ginn Press, 1986), Don Georgakas and Lenny Rubenstein, eds., *The Cineaste Interviews* (Chicago: Lake View Press, 1983), Michael Ryan and Douglas Kellner, *Camera Politica: The Politics and Ideology of Contemporary Hollywood Film* (Bloomington: Indiana University Press, 1988) and Sidney Wise, "Politicians: A Film Perspective," *News for Teachers of Political Science*, 32 (winter 1982): 1.
9. Georgakas and Rubenstein in *The Cineaste Interviews* do include a few American filmmakers such as John Sayles and Paul Schrader among their political directors as well as screenwriters like Budd Schulberg and John Howard Lawson. But their exclusive list of political filmmakers is dominated by Europeans and non-Americans.
10. Genovese, *Politics and the Cinema*, 2–3.
11. Cass Sunstein, "Free Speech Now," *University of Chicago Law Review* 59 (1992): 304.
12. On this point, see Nimmo, "Political Propaganda in the Movies: A Typology," in *Movies and Politics*, 277. For the view that the film was about Hollywood, see Crowdus, *A Political Companion to American Film*, 153–54 and Christensen, *Reel Power*, 93.
13. Christine Noll Brinckmann, "The Politics of Force of Evil: An Analysis of Abraham Polonsky's Preblacklisted Film," *Prospects* 6 (1981): 369.
14. Peter Biskind, *Seeing Is Believing: How Hollywood Taught Us to Stop Worrying and Love the Fifties* (New York: Pantheon Books, 1983), 5.
15. Crowdus, *A Political Companion to American Film*, 235–36, maintains that Kramer's social message pictures were commercial successes because he provided simple-minded solutions to complex problems. For example, in *Guess Who's Coming to Dinner?* the film suggests that racism can be resolved at the personal level of two families having a friendly discussion over a cup of coffee. Furthermore, Crowdus questions Kramer's political liberalism since off-screen he deserted friends during the time of McCarthyism and the blacklist.
16. See Charles Chaplin, *My Autobiography* (New York: Simon and Schuster, 1964 and David Robinson, *Chaplin: His Life and Art* (New York: McGraw-Hill, 1985).

17. Don B. Morlan, "A Pie in the Face: The *Three Stooges* Anti-Aristocracy Theme in Depression-Era American Film" (paper presented at the annual meeting of the Popular Culture Association, Chicago, April 1994), "Slapstick Contributions to World War II Propaganda: The *Three Stooges* and *Abbott & Costello*, *Studies in Popular Culture* 17 (Oct. 1994): 29–43, and "Pre-World War II Propaganda: Film as Controversy" (paper presented at the annual meeting of the American Political Science Association, Chicago, September 1995).
18. Leonard Maltin, *The Great Movie Shorts* (New York: Crown Publishers, 1972) identifies the Stooges as "low comedians" who recycled one basic plot formula in all their films, namely, where would they be most out of place? All story lines developed from that one premise. Maltin admits that the Stooges made one political film, *Three Dark Horses*, a satire about a crooked presidential campaign. But the public embraced the shorts and ignored the film.

Three

Nonfiction Film: Investigating the Real

1. Bill Nichols, *Blurred Boundaries* (Bloomington: Indiana University Press, 1994), 47–48.
2. See Jill Godmilow, "How Real Is the Reality in Documentary Film?" *History and Theory* 36, no. 4 (December 1997), 80–81.
3. Richard M. Barsam, "From Nonfiction Film: A Critical History," in Gerald Mast and Marshall Cohen, eds, *Film Theory and Criticism*, 3rd ed. (New York: Oxford University Press, 1985), 583–85.
4. Guido Convents,"Documentaries and Propaganda Before 1914," *Framework*, no. 35 (1988): 107–08.
5. The Library of Congress, "The Motion Picture Camera Goes to War." Online. Internet. February 19, 1998
6. See Steven J. Ross, "Struggles for the Screen: Workers, Radicals, and the Political Uses of Silent Film," *American Historical Review* 96, no. 2 (April 1991): 333–67.
7. Richard M. Barsam, *Non-Fiction Film*, rev. ed. (Bloomington: Indiana University Press, 1992), 32–38.
8. Brian Winston, *Claiming the Real: The Documentary Film Revisited* (London: British Film Institute, 1995), 69–70.
9. Ross, "Struggles for the Screen," 349–61.
10. See Barsam, *Non-Fiction Film*, chapter 10, for a discussion of American films made during World War II.
11. Kopple's recent documentary, *Wild Man Blues* (1998), is about Woody Allen's jazz band.
12. See Barry Keith Grant, *Voyages of Discovery: The Cinema of Frederick Wiseman* (Urbana: University of Illinois Press, 1992) where the author describes Wiseman's films as "voyages of discovery" in which both the filmmaker and the viewer rediscover themselves.
13. Ibid., 27–34.
14. Ibid., 9.
15. See Raymond Fielding, *The March of Time, 1945–51* (New York: Oxford University Press, 1978), chapter 8, 187–201. Fielding claims that the newsreel took

footage originally filmed in Germany and reshot most of it around Hoboken, New Jersey, using anti-Nazi German-Americans.

16. According to Matthew Bernstein, "Documentaphobia and Mixed Modes," in Barry Keith Grant and Jeannette Sloniowski, eds, *Documenting the Documentary* (Detroit: Wayne State University Press, 1998), 397, Moore admitted to the fact in an interview.
17. See the reviews and commentary by Richard Corliss in *Time*, February 12, 1990, 58, Pauline Kael in *The New Yorker*, January 8, 1990, 90–92 and John Simon in *National Review*, June 11, 1990, 54. Michael Moore's second endeavor, *Canadian Bacon*, a feature film with Hollywood actors, did not fare well at the box office or with critics.
18. Richard Bernstein, "'Roger and Me': Documentary? Satire? or Both?" *New York Times*, February 1, 1990, C20.
19. See Miles Orwell, "Documentary and the Power of Interrogation: American Dream and Roger & me," *Film Quarterly*, 48 (winter 1994/95): 10–18.
20. Reported in Winston, *Claiming the Real*, 239.
21. Quoted in David Culbert, "Our Awkward Ally: Mission to Moscow," in O'Connor and Jackson, eds, *American History/American Film*, 145, ft.# 62.
22. For a history of the term, see Garth S. Jowett, "Propaganda and Communication: The Re-emergence of a Research Tradition," *Journal of Communication* 37, no. 1, (winter 1987), 113–14.
23. Barsam, *Nonfiction Film*, 200–205. For a detailed account of the German film industry under Goebbels, see DavidWelch, *Propaganda and the German Cinema, 1933–1945* (New York: Oxford University Press, 1983).
24. Ibid., 123–25.
25. See Winston, *Claiming the Reel*, 74–78 and 108–9, David Hackett, film review of "The Wonderful, Horrible Life of Leni Riefenstahl," *American Historical Review* 100, no. 4, (Oct. 1995), 1227–28, and Frank P. Tomasulo, "The Mass Psychology of Fascist Cinema," in Grant and Sloniowski, eds *Documenting the Documentary*, 99–118. Tomasulo argues that Riefenstahl's film created a spectacle rather than documented one because of the presence of sixteen cameramen, 135 technicians, and several high-ranking Nazi officers—all for the purpose of constructing a mythic representation of Hitler and the nation as one entity, with Hitler in the role of the strong father-figure destined to lead a confused Germany in restoring its rightful place as a world power.
26. Don B. Morlan, "Pre-WW II Propaganda: Film as Controversy," (paper presented at the annual meeting of the American Political Science Association, Chicago, Sept. 1995).
27. John Canemaker, "World War II Animated Propaganda Cartoons," in Crowdus, *A Political Companion to American Film*, 496–500. The cartoon won an Oscar for Best Animated Short.
28. See Melvin Small, "Buffoons and BraveHearts: Hollywood Portrays the Russians, 1939–1944," *California Historical Society* 52, (winter 1973), 326–37.
29. See Culbert in O'Connor and Jackson, *American History/American Film*, 121–45. Culbert insists that Stalin, acting as the Soviet censor, only permitted some two dozen American films, including *Mission to Moscow*, to be shown in the Soviet Union between 1939 and 1945. The film remains a source of embarrassment to Warner Brothers, its distributor, since the studio denied the author permission to use a photo still from the film.
30. For an eyewitness, but subjective account of the filming, consult blacklisted director Herbert Biberman's book, *Salt of the Earth* (Boston: Beacon Press, 1965).

31. See James E. Combs and Sara T. Combs, *Film Propaganda and American Politics* (New York: Garland Publishing Co., 1994), 3–13.
32. Nichols, *Blurred Boundaries*, 122–26.
33. Dan Nimmo, "Political Propaganda in the Movies: A Typology," in Combs ed., *Movies and Politics*, 271–94.
34. See Leon F. Litwack, "The Birth of a Nation," in Carnes, *Past Imperfect: History According to the Movies*, 136–41. While it is true that similar stereotypes appeared in Margaret Mitchell's 1936 novel, *Gone With the Wind*, much of the racially offensive material was omitted from the movie version.

Four

Flesh and Blood: Regulating Sex and Violence on Screen

1. Quoted in the *New York Times*, Sept. 19, 1996, B10.
2. *The Catholic Light*, July 6, 1995, 2.
3. For a discussion of early film censorship, see Ernest Giglio, "The Decade of 'The Miracle' 1952–1962: A Study in the Censorship of the American Motion Picture" (Ph.D. diss., Syracuse University, 1964).
4. 343 U.S. 495 (1952).
5. See Charles Lyons, *The New Censors: Movies and the Culture Wars* (Philadelphia: Temple University Press, 1997).
6. Ibid., 14.
7. See Marybeth Hamilton, *When I'm Bad, I'm Better: Mae West, Sex, and American Entertainment* (Berkeley: University of California Press, 1997).
8. Gregory D. Black, *Hollywood Censored: Morality Codes, Catholics, and the Movies* (Cambridge, UK: Cambridge University Press, 1994).
9. Ibid., see chapter 6, 149–97, for details on the activities of the Legion during the 1930s.
10. For a detailed account of the battle between Selznick and the Breen Office, see Leonard J. Leff and Jerold L. Simmons, *The Dame in the Kimono: Hollywood, Censorship, and the Production Code from the 1920s to the 1960s* (New York: Grove Weidenfeld, 1990), chapter 5.
11. For the story behind the establishment of the rating system, see Jack Valenti, *The Voluntary Movie Rating System* (Washington, DC: Motion Picture Association of America, 1996).
12. Ibid., 3.
13. Stories of the film cuts were reported in the *New York Times*, January 30, 1992, C15 and March 15, 1992, H17 and the *Westchester Dispatch*, February 16, 1992, F1. The R-rated version contained scenes of sexual bondage, one rough sex scene that bordered on rape, and several brutal killings. Rumor had it that the cuts involved a shot of Michael Douglas's penis in a turgid state and an oral sex scene. Supposedly these scenes were included in the film version released in Europe. In the U.S., however, an NC-17 version appeared on laser disc, while an unrated director's cut was made available on video in addition to the edited R-rated version.

14. All the statistical data was provided by CARA, Motion Picture Association of America, September 25, 1996.
15. Lyons, *The New Censors*, 183–92.
16. See Lyons, chapter 5, for a case study on the religious opposition to the film.
17. Hortense Powdermaker, *Hollywood the Dream Factory* (Boston: Little, Brown, 1950).
18. Frank Rich, "From Here to Zapruda," *New York Times*, July 4, 1998, A25. Echoing Powdermaker, Rich argues that Hollywood movies tend to substitute reel solutions to genuine social and economic problems rather than confront these in the real ghettos of South Bronx (New York) and Watts (Los Angeles).
19. Peter Keough, ed., *Flesh and Blood* (San Francisco: Mercury House, 1995), Introduction.
20. Valenti, *The Voluntary Movie Rating System*, 9.
21. Ibid., 11.
22. Trip Gabriel, "The Rating Game at the Cineplex," *New York Times*, Feb. 18, 1996, sec. 2, 1.
23. Before the 1952 *Burstyn* decision, consult:
    Gitlow v. New York, 268 U.S. 652 (1925)
    Whitney v. California, 274 U.S. 357 (1927)
    Near v. Minnesota, 283 U.S. 697 (1931)
    Thornhill v. Alabama, 310 U.S. 88 (1940)
    West Virginia State Board v. Barnette, 319 U.S. 624 (1943)
    After 1952, consult:
    Roth v. U.S., 354 U.S. 476 (1957)
    New York Times Co. v. Sullivan, 376 U.S. 255 (1964)
    Brandenburg v. Ohio, 395 U.S. 444 (1969)
    New York Times v. U.S., 403 U.S. 713
24. For the story, see Caryn James, "A Movie America Can't See," *New York Times*, March 15, 1998, sec. 2, 1, 213. It should be noted that this second version of Vladimir Nabokov's novel was shown in several European cities before Lyne sold his film to cable television. Afterwards, the film had a limited run in select theaters.
25. Michael Medved, *Hollywood v. America* (New York: HarperCollins, 1992).
26. British Board of Film Classification, *Annual Report for 1995–96* (London: BBFC, July 1996), 5–7.

Five

HUAC and the Blacklist: The Red Scare Comes to Hollywood

1. The first film on the subject, *The Front* (1976), included a number of blacklisted participants. The second, *Fellow Traveler* (1989), had an American-British cast and was made for cable television.
2. See Greg Mitchell, *Tricky Dick and the Pink Lady: Richard Nixon vs. Helen Gahagan Douglas-Sexual Politics and the Red Scare* (New York: Random House, 1950).

3. Victor Navasky, "Has *Guilty by Suspicion* Missed the Point?" *New York Times*, March 31, 1991, H9.
4. Richard Fried, *Nightmare in Red* (New York: Oxford University Press, 1990), 42.
5. See, e.g., David M. Oshinsky, *A Conspiracy So Immense* (New York: Free Press, 1983); Richard Rovere, *Senator Joe McCarthy* (New York: Harcourt, Brace, 1959) Thomas C. Reeves, *The Life and Times of Senator Joe McCarthy* (New York: Stein and Day, 1982) and Albert Fried, *McCarthyism: The Great American Red Scare* (New York: Oxford University Press, 1997).
6. Quoted in David Halberstam, *The Fifties* (New York: Villard Books, 1993), 55.
7. *American Heritage* 3d ed (New York: Houghton Mifflin, 1992), 1114. But according to Richard Rovere, *Senator Joe McCarthy*, 7, the term was first used by cartoonist Herbert Block in the *Washington Post*.
8. Albert Fried, *McCarthyism: The Great American Red Scare*, introduction, 1–9.
9. See stories by Bernard Weinraub in the *New York Times*, Oct. 1, 1997, B3 and Oct. 5, 1997, sec. 4, 5.
10. Fried, *Nightmare in Red*, 88.
11. John Patrick Diggins, *The Proud Decades* (New York: Norton, 1989), 175–76.
12. Mike Nielsen and Gene Mailes, *Hollywood's Other Blacklist* (London: British Film Institute, 1995).
13. Nielsen and Mailes book has the advantage of being part scholarship, part oral history. Other valuable sources include: Richard and Louis Perry, *A History of the Los Angeles Labor Movement* (Berkeley: University of California Press, 1963); Hugh Lovell and Tasile Carter, *Collective Bargaining in the Motion Picture Industry* (Berkeley: University of California Press, 1955); Murray Ross, *Stars and Strikes* (New York: Columbia University Press, 1941) and U.S. House of Representatives, Committee on Education and Labor, *Jurisdictional Disputes in the Motion Picture Industry* (Washington: Government Printing Office, 1948).
14. Quoted in Nielsen and Mailes, *Hollywood's Other Blacklist*, 130.
15. The episode is described in Nielsen and Mailes, 155.
16. These episodes are recounted in Nielsen and Mailes, chapters 5 and 8.
17. See Robbie Lieberman, "Communism, Peace Activism, and Civil Liberties: From the Waldorf Conference to the Peekskill Riot," *Journal of Popular Culture* 18, no. 3 (fall 1995): 59–65.
18. See U.S. Congress, House Committee on Un-American Activities, *Hearings Regarding the Communist Infiltration of the Motion Picture Industry*, 80th Congress, 1st. sess., 1947.
19. Larry Ceplair and Steven Englund, *The Inquisition in Hollywood* (Garden City: Anchor Press/Doubleday, 1980), 371–73. Of the fifty-eight informers, the authors identify thirty-one or slightly more than half, as important Hollywood artists. The "naming of names" varied from one informer to another. For example, writer Martin Berkeley gave up 155 names to the committee while at the other extreme, writer Gertrude Purcell identified only one colleague as a communist. See Appendix 7, 447–48.
20. The high estimate of 250 Hollywood workers who lost jobs and were placed on the blacklist comes from the American Movie Classics 1995 documentary, *Blacklist: Hollywood on Trial* while the lesser figure of 200 is cited by Brian Neve in his *Film and Politics in America* (London: Routledge, 1992), 271. Ceplair and Englund, *The Inquisition in Hollywood*, 387 puts the number blacklisted at 212. However, Dalton Trumbo, in a 1957 TV program, identified 235 writers alone who were blacklisted and could not work under their real names. If Trumbo was

correct, the blacklist would have had to exceed 250 names. See Dalton Trumbo papers, State Historical Society of Wisconsin (hereafter cited as SHSW).

21. Dan Georgakas, "Hollywood Blacklist" in *Encyclopedia of the American Left* (New York: Garland, 1990), 327–28.
22. Some of the organizations included The Civil Rights Congress, National Federation for Constitutional Liberties, The Actors Laboratory, the Screenwriters Guild, and the Hollywood Writers Mobilization.
23. Herbert Biberman papers, SHSW. When called to testify, Ferrer swore under oath that he was not a communist.
24. Victor S. Navasky, *Naming Names* (New York: Penguin Books, 1981), 236. In his defense, Edward Dmytryk in his memoir, *Odd Man Out: A Memoir of the Hollywood Ten* (Carbondale: Southern Illinois University Press, 1996) reasons that he did not want to be punished further for a cause he no longer believed in; his flirtation with the CPUSA rested on anti-fascist grounds rather than ideological principle.
25. Dalton Trumbo papers, SHSW.
26. Neve, *Film and Politics in America*, 176–80.
27. Communist Party Headquarters in New York refused to provide any membership data to the author, thereby continuing the speculation as to its actual strength as opposed to government figures and academic estimates. Edward Schapsmeier and Frederick Schapsmeier in their book, *Political Parties and Civic Action Groups* (Westport, CT: Greenwood Press, 1981), 110–112 present the votes garnered by Communist Party candidates in the presidential elections as follows: in 1932, 102,785 votes out of 40 million cast; in 1936, the number totaled 80,159; and in 1940, the votes for the Party dropped to 46,251. Of course, these votes do not imply actual membership in the Party. Another scholar, L. Sandy Maisel, in her book, *Political Parties and Elections in the United States* (New York: Garland Publishing, 1991), 177–78 puts Communist Party membership at 75,000 based upon registration at the party's 1938 convention. Since party membership was on the decline after peaking in 1932, it is conceivable that membership had dropped to 40,000–50,000 by World War II.
28. Georgakas, *Encyclopedia of the American Left*, 328.
29. See Joyce Milton, *Tramp: The Life of Charlie Chaplin* (New York: HarperCollins, 1996), a new biography that focuses on Chaplin's political life. Also consult Charles Chaplin, *My Autobiography* (New York: Simon and Schuster, 1964).
30. Nixon, of course, would make his political mark later during the Hiss-Chambers spy hearings. Of the other eight HUAC members, J. Parnell Thomas, committee chair, would end up in prison for defrauding the government, Karl Mundt would be elected to the U.S. Senate, and the remaining members would fade from the political scene.
31. Richard A. Schwartz, "How the Hollywood Blacklist Worked," (paper presented at the annual meeting of the American Culture Association/Popular Culture Association [ACA/PCA], Orlando, April 1998), claims that the studios relied on a list of 300 names of alleged communists furnished by the American Legion. That list was converted into a *de facto* blacklist.
32. Pamphlet found in the Albert Bessie papers, SHSW. The pamphlet listed some of the biggest stars in Hollywood at the time, including Humphrey Bogart, Lauren Bacall, Charlie Chaplin, Melvyn Douglas, Gene Kelly, Frank Sinatra, Orson Welles, Danny Kaye, Katherine Hepburn, Gregory Peck, and Burt Lancaster, the majority of whom were never cited or named as communists or fellow travelers by any other source. True, nothing came of the mobilization efforts but the fact that

this unsubstantiated pamphlet was taken seriously by HUAC says plenty about the committee and the red scare hysteria.

33. Larry Ceplair, "Hollywood Left," in *Encyclopedia of the American Left*, 330–32.
34. See Ceplair and Englund, *The Inquisition in Hollywood*, 66–79.
35. Dorothy B. Jones, "Communism and the Movies: A Study of Film Content," in John Cogley, *Report on Blacklisting I: Movies* (New York: The Fund for the Republic, 1956), 197.
36. Dalton Trumbo papers, SHSW. The film scripts offered as evidence to the committee included *A Guy Named Joe*, *Thirty Seconds Over Tokyo*, *Our Vines Have Tender Grapes*, and *Kitty Foyle*. Trumbo also had letters of praise from the military and juvenile court judges for several of his films. As a general rule, HUAC would not permit the reading of statements or the introduction of evidence during the hearings.
37. See Dorothy B. Jones, "Communism and the Movies: A Study in Film Content," Table 8, 272. The list includes only 150 films because nine were described as unclassified.
38. Quoted in Ring Lardner, Jr., papers, SHSW. Friendly HUAC witness, writer Ayn Rand, testified that the film was communist because it showed the Russian people in a better socioeconomic position than was actually true. Similarly, Lela Rogers testified that the film, *None but the Lonely Heart*, was communist propaganda because it was critical of the free enterprise system. See the Biberman-Sondegaard papers, SHSW. She also complained about *Tender Comrade* on grounds that five women sharing a house during wartime was socialism.
39. Georgakas, *Encyclopedia of the American Left*, 326–29.
40. Quoted in the Ned Young papers, SHSW.
41. Larry Parks papers, SHSW. Parks made one film in England after the hearings, but Columbia Pictures refused to pick up his option after his HUAC testimony, an act which basically ended his film career.
42. Abraham Polonsky papers, SHSW. Polonsky also wrote screenplays; however, he went seventeen years before he received screen credit for his work.
43. Albert Maltz papers, SHSW. Maltz surmised that the Army pressured the government to deny assistance in the film's production. Maltz attributes other rejections directly to the HUAC hearings and the blacklist. His novel, *The Journey of Simon McKeever*, was purchased by Twentieth-Century Fox, but the screenplay was shelved due to pressure from the Motion Picture Alliance.
44. Ceplair and Englund, *The Inquisition in Hollywood*, 425.
45. The project was the collaborative effort of Shirley Clarke and Conrad Bromberg. The interviews produced eleven hours of tape. The staff at the University of Wisconsin Film Archives believe that the tapes have not been shown to the public.
46. Andy Mersler, "How Blacklisting Hurt Hollywood Children," *New York Times*, August 31, 1995, C13.
47. See Emma Horcombe, "Attitudes to Informing and the Informer" (Master's Degree, University of Nottingham, UK), 1994).
48. According to Fried, *McCarthyism: The Great American Red Scare*, 135–37, Kazan took out a one-page ad in the *New York Times* in the form of an open letter to the American people to explain his decision to cooperate with HUAC. His reasoning for informing on friends and colleagues came down to his disenchantment with the Communist Party because it had become authoritarian and manipulative. Of course, this is specious reasoning since Kazan could have preserved his honor, if not his career, by accepting the Miller-Hellman position of restricting his testimony to himself.

49. Was it coincidental that forty years had to pass before Miller's play reached the screen? When the film version of *The Crucible* opened in 1996, the critics found its story of witchcraft in seventeenth-century Salem powerful drama. But historians disputed its accuracy.
50. Kazan became a victim of Hollywood's unofficial blacklist since the film industry had refused to honor him for his lifetime achievement. The industry, however, had a change of heart and awarded Kazan an honorary Oscar at the 1999 Academy Awards. For more on this issue, see Editorial, *New York Times*, January 19, 1997, 14 and the *New York Times*, January 13, 1999, B3.
51. Neve, *Film and Politics in America*, 171–210.
52. See Lynne Arany, Tom Dyja and Gary Goldsmith, *The Reel List* (New York: Dell Publishing, 1995), 283.
53. See Tom C. Williams, "The Day the Earth Stood Still: Cold War Parable or Messianic Metaphor?" (paper presented at the annual meeting of the American Culture Association/Popular Culture Association (ACA/PCA), Las Vegas, March 1996).
54. See Stuart Samuels, "The Age of Conspiracy and Conformity: Invasion of the Body Snatches (1956)," in John O'Connor and Martin A. Jackson, *American History/American Film* (New York: Frederick Unger, 1979), 203–17.
55. See Arany, Dyja and Goldsmith, *The Reel List*, 284.
56. Ceplair and Englund, *The Inquisition in Hollywood*, 335–36.
57. In his latest book, Peter Biskind, *Easy Riders, Raging Bulls: How the Sex-Drugs-and-Rock n' Roll Generation Saved Hollywood* (New York: Simon & Schuster, 1998) advances the thesis that the success of *Easy Rider* (1969) heralded a decade of rebellious young filmmakers whose films challenged (and saved the industry from) the old studio system.

Six

Reel Politics: American Politicians on Screen

1. For the perspective on Nixon, see Irv Letofsky, "All the Presidents' Movies (And Not All PG)," *New York Times*, April 13, 1997, sec. 2, 29; for the view on Reagan, see Elizabeth Traube, *Dreaming Identities: Class, Gender and Generation in 1980s Hollywood Movies* (Boulder: Westview Press, 1992), 48.
2. See Sidney Wise, "Politicians: A Film Perspective," *News for Teachers of Political Science*, no. 32 (winter 1982): 1–3 and Robert Thompson, "American Politics on Film," *Journal of Popular Culture* 20 (summer 1986): 27–47.
3. See Richard Maltby and Jan Craven, *Hollywood Cinema* (Oxford: Blackwell Publishers, 1995), 361–411.
4. Ibid., 380–81.
5. See William L. Riordon, *Plunkitt of Tammany Hall* (New York: E. P. Dutton & Co., 1963).
6. *All the King's Men* was a critical success as it was nominated for eight Academy Awards, winning three Oscars for Best Picture, Actor, and Supporting Actress. When, forty years later, Hollywood decided to make a film about Huey's brother, Earl, three-time governor of Louisiana, the results were less gratifying. The film, *Blaze* (1989) proved a disappointment despite the casting of Paul Newman in the

title role. Quite possibly the film's problem lay in the script since it was based on the memoirs of Earl's lover, stripper Blaze Starr. In this case, the combination of politics and sex failed to mesh.

7. In real life, Meade Esposito, Kings County political boss, was convicted of influence peddling and bribery while Donald Manes, his Queens counterpart, committed suicide just as Aiello does in the film. But not all deals end in prison or death. While the film crew was permitted to shoot inside most of City Hall, Mayor Giuliani put the Mayor's Office and the ceremonial Blue Room off limits. All was not lost, however. The studio struck a deal with the City Council Speaker. In return for the use of his large office to reconstruct a set to resemble the Mayor's Office and Blue Room, the Speaker had his office painted, carpeted and redecorated for free. No taxpayers objected to the deal, although rumor had it that some Council colleagues were envious.
8. Recall a similarity with the real life situation in the Democratic Party when Governor Mario Cuomo was picked to make the presidential nominating speech at the 1984 convention. Cuomo's stirring speech placed him high among Democratic presidential contenders for 1988, although he declined to be a candidate. Also, Franklin Roosevelt's nomination of Al Smith at the 1924 convention failed to win the nomination for Smith, but it did raise Roosevelt's stock among Democratic Party delegates and voters.
9. Historian Ron Briley notes in "Hollywood and the American Presidency: A Nation Seeks to Define Itself" (paper presented at the annual meeting of the American Political Science Association, Washington, Aug. 1977), that the film was criticized because President Hammond used authoritarian methods to achieve his goals.It was not a coincidence that the film was produced by William Randolph Hearst in conjunction with Metro-Goldwyn-Mayer, and that it opened in the early days of Roosevelt's New Deal administration.
10. Reportedly, however, Presidents Bush and Clinton had Secret Service agents who closely resembled them in appearance. See Maureen Dowd, "Film View: Of Hems and Haws: The Insider's Guide to *Dave*," *New York Times*, May 16, 1993, sec. 2, 17.
11. George McGovern, "Nixon and Historical Memory: Two Reviews," *Perspectives, AHA Newsletter* 34, no. 3 (March 1996): 3. A view of the Watergate scandal, rather than of Nixon himself, is presented in *All the President's Men* (1976), based on the story by Carl Bernstein and Bob Woodward, the two young reporters on the *Washington Post* whose investigations exposed the political corruption. *All the President's Men* became the top grossing film in 1976.
12. Similarly, *The Manchurian Candidate* was withdrawn from theatrical circulation for twenty-five years after the Kennedy assassination.
13. Why is Barbara Jean, rather than Walker, assassinated? Political scientist G. Alan Tarr's review in *Notes for Teachers of Political Science*, no.22 (Summer 1979): 21, believes that Altman's choice reflects his view that Americans are indifferent to politics, preferring instead the private lives of celebrities such as a country-western singer. Symbolically therefore, her death is much more significant than the assassination of any political candidate.
14. Robert S. Robins and Jerrold M. Post, *Political Paranoia: The Psychopolitics of Hatred* (New Haven: Yale University Press, 1997).
15. Actually Robbins and Post, 240, counted eight different conspiracy loci in the film, e.g., the CIA, military, Dallas police, weapons manufacturers, establishment press, renegade anti-Castro Cubans, the White House, and the Mafia. Take your pick!

16. See Gerald Posner, "Garrison Guilty: Another Case Closed," *New York Times Magazine*, sec. 6, August 6, 1995, 40–41. Historian Stanley Karnow agrees with Posner and other Stone critics on the unsubstantiated notion that Kennedy intended to withdraw from Vietnam, one reason for his death. See his "JFK" in Mark C. Carnes, *Past Imperfect: History According to the Movies* (New York: Henry Holt & Co., 1995), 270–73.
17. See the advertisement for the *JFK* opening in the *New York Times*, Dec. 15, 1991, sec. 2, 10 with a large photo of Kevin Costner portraying D. A. Garrison in the film, with the blurb: "He's a District Attorney. He will risk his life, the lives of his family, everything he holds dear for the one thing he holds sacred . . . the truth. Also see the ad for *JFK* in the *New York Times*, April 2, 1992, C17, where the text includes this dedication: "The truth is the most important value we have."
18. Michael Barkun, "Conspiracy Thinking in Contemporary America," *Maxwell Perspective* (Syracuse University) 8, no. 1 (fall 1997): 23.
19. In a recent article, Allen Rostron, "Mr. Carter Goes to Washington," *Journal of Popular Film & Television* 25, no. 2 (summer 1997): 57–67, contends that Jimmy Carter came to Washington much like Jefferson Smith—an innocent outsider from a small town who wanted to restore decency and morality to government. Why Carter failed in Washington where Smith succeeded, Rostron argues, has more to do with external factors like the backlash from Vietnam and Watergate, than to any personal flaws.
20. Michael Canning, "The Hill on Film: Hollywood's Take on the U.S. Congress and Its Members" (paper presented at the annual meeting of the American Political Science Association, Washington, August 1997).
21. William M. Jones, "Monumental Disasters: From *Mr. Smith Goes to Washington* to *Independence Day*" (paper presented at the annual meeting of the American Political Science Association, Washington, August 1997), concludes that the present trend in Hollywood to find national monuments and revered public buildings expendable and, therefore, subject to destruction, reflects the current cynicism on the part of American filmmakers. This attitude deviates considerably from Frank Capra's *Mr. Smith Goes to Washington* where the monuments are treated as national shrines.

Seven

Picturing Justice: Law and Lawyers in Hollywood Films

1. Stewart Macaulay, "Images of Law in Everyday Life: The Lesson of School, Entertainment, and Spectator Sports," *Law & Society Review* 21, 2 (1987): 185–218.
2. Hearst Corporation, *The American Public, the Media and the Judicial System* (New York: Hearst Corporation, 1983).
3. Macaulay, 192–97.
4. John Denvir, ed., *Legal Reelism: Movies as Legal Texts* (Urbana: University of Illinois Press, 1996), introduction.
5. Macaulay, 208.

6. "The Significance of the Frontier in American History," first presented to the American Historical Association in 1893 and later republished in his essays, *The Frontier in American History* (New York: Henry Holt & Co., 1920).
7. For a detailed discussion of 1930s westerns, see Francis M. Nevins, "Through the Great Depression on Horseback" in John Denvir, ed., *Legal Reelism*, 44–69.
8. For a discussion of film vigilantism, see Frankie Y. Bailey, "Getting Justice: Real Life Vigilantism and Vigilantism in Popular Films," (paper presented at the annual meeting of the Criminal Justice Sciences Association, Pittsburgh, March 1992).
9. Bruce Watson, "Hang'em first, try'em later," *Smithsonian* 29, 8 (June 1998): 96–107. Watson claims that the real Judge Bean was a paunchy fellow with a gray beard, hardly resembling actor Paul Newman. It is also dubious whether Bean actually hanged anybody. Nor did Bean die in a climactic shootout; rather his death took place in a bar after a drinking binge.
10. For data on Southern lynching, see W. Fitzhugh Brundage, *Lynching in the New South* (Urbana: University of Illinois Press, 1993) and Stewart E. Tolenay and E. M. Beck, *A Festival of Violence: An Analysis of Southern Lynching, 1882–1930* (Urbana: University of Illinois Press, 1995).
11. Quoted in Paul Bergmann and Michael Asimow, *Reel Justice: The Courtroom Goes to the Movies* (Kansas City: Andrews and McMeel, 1996), 226. The authors note that there were sixty-six lynchings in the early years of the Depression, 1933–35. Moreover, it was rare for lynch mob participants to be apprehended and punished.
12. For a case study, see Leonard Dinnerstein, *The Leo Frank Case* (New York: Columbia University Press, 1968). Dinnerstein came to the conclusion that Frank was innocent but convicted of the murder of Mary Phagan, the thirteen-year-old girl who worked in his Atlanta, Georgia, factory, on the basis of circumstantial evidence, the damaging testimony of the Negro janitor which tarnished Frank's reputation, and the pervasive climate of anti-Semitism in the South. When Governor Slaton commuted Frank's sentence, Jewish businesses were told by vigilantes to close or suffer the consequences. Meanwhile, Christians were warned to avoid patronizing Jewish merchants.
13. *Goldman v. Weinberger*, 475 U.S. 503 (1985). The military regulation was reversed by the Congress two years later.
14. Bergmann and Asimow, *Reel Justice*, 76.
15. Alan M. Dershowitz, *The Best Defense* (New York: Vintage Books, 1983), xvi.
16. See Bergmann and Asimow, *Reel Justice*, 232–38.
17. Ibid., 14–20.
18. For a discussion of such films, see Roger Dooley, *From Scarface to Scarlett: American Films in the 1930s* (New York: Harcourt Brace Jovanovich, 1979), 310–18.
19. Leonard Maltin, *1997 Movie & Video Guide* (New York: Penguin Books, 1996).
20. According to Gerald Leonard Cohen, *Origin of the Term "Shyster"* (Frankfurt: Peter Lang, 1982), 1, lexicographers agree that the term originated in the 1840s in New York City newspapers to describe unscrupulous lawyers of that era. The word later was applied to other professions. There is some support, however, for the view that the term comes from the Shylock character in Shakespeare's *The Merchant of Venice*.
21. See Andrew Bergman, *We're in the Money* (New York: New York University Press, 1971), 18–29.
22. For a discussion of gangster films in the 1930s, see Dooley, *From Scarface to Scarlett: American Films in the 1930s*, 289–300.

23. Quoted in David Ray Papke, "Myth and Meaning: Francis Ford Coppola and Popular Response to the Godfather Trilogy," in John Denvir, ed., *Legal Reelism*, 3.
24. For the development of this argument, see Christine Noll Brinckmann, "The Politics of Force of Evil: An Analysis of Abraham Polonsky's Preblacklisted Film," *Prospects* 6 (1981): 357–86.
25. Bergmann and Asimow, *Reel Justice*, 306. The legal errors and unethical conduct depicted in the film include the following: (1) Gavin breaks into a mailbox to intercept a letter—a federal offense, (2) Gavin turns down a settlement without consulting his clients, (either act would get him disbarred), and (3) the trial judge conspires with the defense to protect the Boston Archdiocese.
26. For a discussion of these films, see Dooley, *From Scarface to Scarlett*, 317–18 and Ric Sheffield, "On Film: A Social History of Women Lawyers in Popular Culture 1930 to 1990," 14 *Loyola of Los Angeles Entertainment Law Journal* (1993): 73–114.
27. Sheffield, "On Film: A Social History of Women Lawyers in Popular Culture 1930 to 1990," 79.
28. For a contrary view that these early female lawyer films ultimately allowed the patriarchal power structure to win and dominate the action, see Cynthia Lucia, "Women on Trial; The Female Lawyer in the Hollywood Courtroom," *Cineaste* 19 (1993): 32–37.
29. "First Year Enrollment in ABA Approved Law Schools 1947–1996" [database online] (Chicago: American Bar Association) [cited 7 November 1997].
30. "Women in Law" [online] (Williamsburg, VA: National Center for State Courts) [cited 18 Nov. 1997] and "Goal IX Update" [online] (Chicago: American Bar Association) [cited 9 Feb. 1999].
31. See Lucia, "Women on Trial," 35.
32. See Bergman and Asimow, *Reel Justice*, 90–93.
33. Paul J. Mastrangelo, "Lawyers and the Law: A Filmography," *Legal Reference Services Quarterly* 3 (winter 1983): 31–72. Included among the 120 cited were twenty films that were produced outside the U.S., primarily in the UK.
34. See Mark Tushnet, "Class Action: One View of Gender and Law in Popular Culture," in Denvir, ed., *Legal Reelism*, 244–60.
35. Sheffield, "On Film: A Social History of Women Lawyers in Popular Culture 1930 to 1990," 109–111.
36. See Lucia, "Women on Trial," 37.

Eight

Hollywood Goes to War: From the Great War to the Good War

1. While *Saving Private Ryan* has grossed more than $200 million in North America, *The Thin Red Line* struggled to recoup its costs, despite seven Academy Award nominations.
2. *Corel All-Movie Guide 2*, 1996.
3. Leo Cawley, "The War about the War: Vietnam Films and American Myth," 74 in Linda Dittmar and Gene Michaud, eds., *From Hanoi to Hollywood: The Vietnam War in American Film* (New Brunswick, NJ: Rutgers University Press, 1990),

reports that the film cost the Pentagon over one million dollars for supplies, facilities, etc., but that it billed Wayne only $18,623 for the assistance provided on the film.

4. *Home Building and Loan Association v. Blaisdell*, 290 U.S. 398 (1934).
5. John Whiteclay Chambers II and David Culbert, eds. *World War II, Film, and History* (New York: Oxford University Press, 1996), Foreword.
6. According to Peter Rollins and John O'Connor, eds., *Hollywood's WWI: Motion Picture Images* (Bowling Green, OH: Popular Press, 1997), there is little footage of the First World War that is real. Much of the material was either censored or staged. The warring nations, for example, would not permit filming on the front lines or in the trenches.
7. Thomas Doherty, *Projections of War: Hollywood, American Culture and World War II* (New York: Columbia University Press, 1993), 88–91.
8. Ibid., 97.
9. Bernard F. Dick, *The Star-Spangled Screen: The American World War II Film*, rev. ed. (Lexington: University of Kentucky Press, 1996), 93–94.
10. Tom Wicker, "World War I," in Mark C. Carnes, ed., *Past Imperfect* (New York: Henry Holt & Co., 1995), 187.
11. Rudolph Chelminski, "The Maginot Line," *Smithsonian* 28, no. 3 (June 1997): 91.
12. U.S. Dept. of Commerce, Bureau of the Census, *Historical Statistics of the United States* (Washington, DC: Government Printing Office, 1975), 1140. Other estimates put the number of American soldiers dead and wounded at 350,000 to 400,000.
13. Estimates of losses vary and depend on sources and the timeframe utilized. But taking only the period from 1939 to 1945—from the invasion of Poland to the Japanese surrender—the total number of deaths due to the war has been estimated to be at least 30 million and as high as 60 million. American casualties, dead and wounded, is placed around one million, with 400,000 killed.
14. See Israel Gutman, editor in chief, *Encyclopedia of the Holocaust*, vol. 4 (New York: Macmillan Publishing Co., 1990); Richard C. Lukas, *The Forgotten Holocaust: The Poles Under German Occupation* (Lexington: University of Kentucky Press, 1986); and Betty Alt and Silvia Falts, *Weeping Violins: The Gypsy Tragedy in Europe* (Kirksville, MO: Thomas Jefferson University Press, 1996).
15. See James E. Wise, Jr. and Anne Collier Rehill, *Stars in Blue: Movie Actors in America's Sea Services* (Annapolis: Naval Institute Press, 1997).
16. By 1942 Lew Ayres was an established Hollywood star, best remembered as Dr. Kildare. But when the war came, Ayres refused combat duty on religious grounds and served instead as a medic and chaplain's aide. He was shunned by the film studios until 1948. The plight of conscientious objectors (COs) has yet to be fully detailed, although their numbers are considerable. In World War I, 60,000 were classified as COs but only 4,000 served in that capacity. In World War II, 12,000 COs served in the Civilian Service Program (CSP) with another 6,000 imprisoned. About 5,000 men served as COs during the Korean conflict. The war in Vietnam saw over 171,000 eligible men declare themselves COs and war resistors and fled to Canada to avoid the draft. Philip Borkholder, Executive Director, National Interreligious Service Board for Conscientious Objectors [email: July 9, 1997]. For the story of the CSP, see Albert N. Keim, *The CPS Story: An Illustrated History of Civilian Public Service* (Intercourse, PA: Good Books, 1990). For mistreatment of COs during the Vietnam period, see Stephen M. Kohn, *Jailed for Peace* (Westport, CT: Greenwood Press, 1986).

17. See William M. Tuttle, Jr., *Daddy's Gone to War* (New York: Oxford University Press, 1993), 148–54.
18. Clayton R. Koppes and Gregory D. Black, *Hollywood Goes to War* (Berkeley: University of California Press, 1987), 325. Recent research by Thomas Schatz, "World War II and the Hollywood War Film," in Nick Browne, ed., *Refiguring Genres* (Berkeley: University of California Press, 1998), 103–4 places the figure of World War II-related Hollywood features closer to 20% of the 1,636 films made between Pearl Harbor and the end of the war. Of these 340 war-related films, Schatz found that the most popular type were the combat films, followed by espionage and homefront movies.
19. Jeanine Basinger, *The World War II Combat Film* (New York: Columbia University Press, 1986).
20. See Ann Dorr, "The Women Who Flew-but Kept Silent," *New York Times Magazine*, May 7, 1995, sec. 6, 70–71. These women were buried without military honors and those who survived received no benefits.
21. Sally E. Parry, "How Proudly Did We Serve?: Popular Culture Images of Army Nurses in World War II" (paper presented at the Popular Culture Association meeting, Philadelphia, April 1995).
22. The $21 million Women's Memorial was dedicated in October, 1997.
23. See Basinger, *The World War II Combat Film*, 28 and Koppes and Black, *Hollywood Goes to War*, 248–77. In his unpublished paper, Ralph R. Donald, "Savages, Swine and Buffoons: Hollywood's Selected Stereotypical Characterizations of the Japanese, Germans and Italians in Films Produced During World War II" (paper presented at the Popular Culture Association meeting, Orlando, April 1998), advances the thesis that a descending order of brutality existed in Hollywood World War II movies. He maintains that the Italians received the most neutral characterization, usually portrayed as buffoons and hapless soldiers. The Nazis were despised and often depicted as military gangsters, but Hollywood distanced them from the German people. Donald argues that the most vicious attacks were saved for the Japanese, resulting in negative images "unmatched in American film propaganda," 7.
24. The entire episode is described in Koppes and Black, *Hollywood Goes to War*, 72–77.
25. Recent research by Iris Chang, *The Rape of Nanking: The Forgotten Holocaust of WWII* (New York: Basic Books, 1997), describes Japanese atrocities in the Chinese city of Nanking in 1937 where 200,000 to 350,000 civilians were slaughtered, almost half of the population. Yet American feeling towards the Japanese probably was influenced more by the "sneak attack" on Pearl Harbor.
26. Hollywood tried to redeem itself after the war when MGM released *Go for Broke* (1951), a film about the exploits of the 442nd Regimental Combat Team composed mainly of Japanese-American (Nisei) volunteers. The Nisei fought in seven major European campaigns and suffered 9,486 casualties. Their bravery and courage under fire earned them over 18,000 individual decorations and seven presidential citations. Two facts are interesting about the film version. First, that Hollywood wisely focused on the Nisei rather than Van Johnson, the male star. Second, the film became a blatant piece of postwar propaganda. After the credits, the film displays President Roosevelt's message of support for the establishment of Nisei units, commenting that being American is a matter of heart and not race or ancestry. But it was Roosevelt who issued Executive Order 9066 which began the evacuation and internment of over 115,000 Japanese-Americans (three-quarters of whom were U.S. citizens) from the West Coast.

27. Kathryn Kane, "The World War II Combat Film, 1942–45," in Wes D. Gehring, ed., *Handbook of American Film Genres* (Westport, CT: Greenwood Press, 1988), 85–86.
28. On the other hand, not every World War II film is a commercial success. Terrence Malick's version of the James Jones novel, *The Thin Red Line* (1998), flopped at the box office.
29. For an analysis of the film, see Sally E. Parry, "So Proudly They Serve: American Women in World War II Films" (paper presented at the annual meeting of the American Political Science Association, San Francisco, August/Sept. 1996).
30. The Harold Russell character (Homer) represented the more than 670,000 Americans who suffered war wounds, with 83,000 receiving treatment at VA hospitals. See Tuttle, *Daddy's Gone to War*, 216.
31. See Doherty, *Projections of War*, Appendix, 304–8.
32. Ibid., 229.
33. Bruce Shapiro, "Lugging the guts into the next room," [database online] (Salon Media Circus) [cited 30 July 1998].
34. Basinger, *The World War II Combat Film*, 125–31. Ford's film, *December 7th*, has an interesting history. This government funded film of the Japanese attack on Pearl Harbor alienated the U.S. Navy because it implied naval complacency before the assault. As a consequence, the government confiscated the film's negative and instead released an edited version of the film, which, nonetheless, won an Academy Award. The complete uncensored version was withheld from public view until the 1990s.
35. See Doherty, *Projections of War*, 237.
36. For a contrary view of the film by a military historian, see Roger J. Spiller, "War in the Dark," *American Heritage*, 50, no. 1 (February/March 1999), 41–51.
37. Basinger, *The World War II Combat Film*, 176–79.
38. More than 115,000 Japanese-Americans were interned during World War II on the basis of an executive order by President Roosevelt despite the fact that three-fourths were American citizens. In a series of cases, the U.S. Supreme Court upheld the internment order on national security grounds. Less known to the public is the treatment accorded Italian-Americans, mostly aliens, who were interned during the war in military camps in Montana, Minnesota, and Ellis Island and were forced to leave their homes on the West Coast, and branded "enemy aliens" by the U.S. government. The introduction of the Wartime Violation of Italian American Civil Liberties Act in 1997 was an attempt by Congress to force the Justice Department to document government mistreatment of Italian-Americans during the Second World War.
39. 374 U.S. 483 (1954).
40. Michael Walzer, *Just and Unjust Wars* 2d ed. (New York: Basic Books, 1992), 117–24.

Nine

Remembering Vietnam: The War on Film

1. Charles Molir, "History and Hindsight: Lessons from Vietnam," *New York Times*, April 30, 1985, 6.
2. Transcript of lecture delivered at the Naval War College, December 10, 1964.
3. Quoted in Andrew Martin, *Receptions of War: Vietnam in American Culture* (Norman: University of Oklahoma Press, 1993), 107.
4. Michael Coyne, *The Crowded Prairie* (London: I. B. Tauris Publishers, 1997), 145 characterizes *The Green Berets* as "a John Wayne western set in Vietnam."
5. See Thomas Doherty, *Projections of War: Hollywood, American Culture, and World War II* (New York: Columbia University Press, 1993), 282–98 and Richard T. Jamesson, ed., *They Went Thataway: Redefining Film Genres* (San Francisco: Mercury House, 1994), 263–79.
6. Joseph Conrad, *Heart of Darkness*, ed. Robert Kimbrough, 2d ed. (New York: W. W. Norton & Company, 1971). According to Kimbrough, *Heart of Darkness* appeared in three different versions: a magazine version in 1899, a book edition in 1902, and a revised edition in 1921 considered by scholars to be Conrad's final text.
7. See Mark C. Carnes, *Past Imperfect: History According to the Movies* (New York: Henry Holt & Co., 1995).
8. According to Arnold R. Isaacs, *The War, Its Ghosts, and Its Legacy* (Baltimore: Johns Hopkins University Press, 1998), the idea that politicians, along with a hostile media and subversive demonstrators, prevented victory in Vietnam is a myth. Instead, Isaacs' thesis is that the country turned against the war when the military failed to win in the field.
9. Michael Rogin, *Ronald Reagan, the Movie* (Berkeley: University of California Press, 1988), 7, reports that after the American hostages in Lebanon, taken as part of the 1985 TWA skyjacking, were released, the president watched *First Blood, Part 2* and supposedly told aides, "Boy, I saw *Rambo* last night. Now I know what to do the next time this happens."
10. Marita Sturken, "Reenactment, Fantasy, and the Paranoia of History: Oliver Stone's Docudramas," *History and Theory* 36, no. 4 (December 1997), 66.
11. William J. Palmer, *The Films of the Eighties* (Carbondale: Southern Illinois University Press, 1993), 16–60.
12. Ibid., 18.
13. Ibid., 21.
14. See Frank P. Tomosulo, "The Politics of Ambivalence: Apocalypse Now as Prowar and Antiwar Film," in Linda Dittmar and Gene Michaud, eds., *From Hanoi to Hollywood* (New Brunswick: Rutgers University Press, 1990), 145–58.
15. See Palmer, *The Films of the Eighties*, 61–113.
16. See Leonard Quart, "The Deer Hunter: The Superman in Vietnam," in Dittmar and Michaud, *From Hanoi to Hollywood*, 159–68.
17. For an analysis that suggests more significance than normally accorded the film, see Pat Aufderheide, "Vietnam: Good Soldiers" in Mark Crispin Miller, ed., *Seeing Through Movies* (New York: Pantheon Books, 1990), 81–111.
18. Quoted in Maureen Dowd, "A Different Bush Conforms to a Nation's Mood," *New York Times*, March 2, 1991, A7.

19. Michael Norman, "Carnage and Glory, Legends and Lies," *New York Times*, sec. 2, July 7, 1996, 19.
20. In *Just and Unjust Wars*, 97–101, Walzer concludes that the war was unjust because the U.S. could not justify its intervention for two reasons. First, the South Vietnamese government could not survive on its own. Therefore it lacked public support despite American aid. Second, when the U.S. intervened militarily, it did so to pursue its own policies. The war, then, became an American war fought in another country. In contrast, Korea was a just war because the North Korean aggression was undisputed and because the goal of counter-intervention was to restore the status quo rather than win a military victory. Michael Ryan and Douglas Kellner, *Camera Politica* (Bloomington: Indiana University Press, 1990), 194–216 agree with Walzer that Vietnam was an unjust war but for a different reason. For Ryan and Kellner, the U.S. involvement was unjust because it lent support to a corrupt and undemocratic regime.
21. See Michael Anderegg, ed., *Inventing Vietnam: The War in Film and Television* (Philadelphia: Temple University Press, 1991) where he argues that, even though Vietnam was given life through film, the visual images remain subjective creations of the filmmakers.
22. Reported in Norman, "Carnage and Glory, Legends and Lies," 19.

Ten

Hollywood Confronts the Nuclear Holocaust

1. Charles Rolo, "Camus at Stockholm," *The Atlantic Monthly* 201 (May 1958): 33–34.
2. Paul Boyer, *By the Bomb's Early Light* (Chapel Hill: University of North Carolina Press, 1994).
3. Quoted in Boyer, *By the Bomb's Early Light*, 5.
4. "ShockWave," *Time* July 31, 1995, 50. These are conservative figures because countless other deaths were likely caused by radioactivity. *The Catholic Light*, August 3, 1995, 2, put the Hiroshima deaths alone attributed to the atomic blast at 200,000 with another 39,000 dead in the Nagasaki blast. By any count, the numbers are considerable. However, estimates of the damage from the March 1945 air raids on Tokyo range from 100,000 to 200,000 deaths while the total number of Japanese dead from conventional bombs and fire bombs was put at 500,000. On the other hand, estimates of the number of American casualties, had President Truman opted for an invasion of the Japanese islands, vary from 100,000 to 200,000. These figures are disputed by revisionist historian, Gar Alperovitz, in his book, *The Decision to Use the Atomic Bomb* (New York: Alfred A. Knopf, 1995). Moreover, Alperovitz maintains that the number of American casualties was not the deciding factor in Truman's decision. Instead, he argues that Truman used the atom bomb as part of his post-war diplomacy to send a message to the Soviets to stay out of Asia.
5. James Barron, "Nuclear Winter of the Psyche Fading Away," *New York Times*, October 13, 1991, E3.
6. Boyer, *By the Bomb's Early Light*, 352. Similarly, the number of significant Americans who received amounts of radiation from atmospheric testing in New

Mexico between 1951 and 1962 and who later developed cancer as a result remains unknown but the guess is that the number affected could be in the tens of thousands.

7. Ibid., 10–11.
8. Garth S. Jowett, "Hollywood, Propaganda and the Bomb: Nuclear Images in Post World War II Film," *Film and History* 18, no. 2 (May 1988): 27.
9. Boyer, *By the Bomb's Early Light*, 23.
10. Michael J. Strada, "Kaleidoscopic Nuclear Images of the Fifties," *Journal of Popular Culture* 20, no. 3 (1986): 191.
11. For a case study on the film, consult Nathan Reingold, "A Footnote to History: MGM Meets the Atomic Bomb," in Philip S. Cook, Douglas Goney, and Lawrence W. Lichty, *American Media* (Washington, DC: The Wilson Center Press, 1989). According to Jack Shaheen, ed., *Nuclear War Films* (Carbondale: Southern Illinois University Press, 1978), 8, the film was cut and reedited several times. One scene between an officer and a crew member that was mercifully left on the cutting room floor involved this verbal exchange: Crew Member: "Is it true that if you fool around with this stuff [atomic equipment] long enough, you don't like girls anymore?" To which the officer replied: "I hadn't noticed it."
12. History repeated itself when the Smithsonian Museum in Washington, DC, ran into controversy when it planned to mark the 50th anniversary of the dropping of the A-bombs to end World War II. Originally, the museum intended a big exhibition to include material on the decision to use the bomb, the horror caused by the bomb, and the subsequent arms race that followed the Cold War—all centered around the fuselage of the Enola Gay. But criticism from veterans groups and members of Congress that the planned exhibition exaggerated Japanese suffering and minimized Japanese aggression forced the museum to cut back. When the exhibition officially opened what remained was the plane, a video, and a plaque. For the story, see the *New York Times*, February 5, 1995, E5.
13. See Michael Walzer, *Just and Unjust Wars* 2d ed. (New York: Basic Books, 1992).
14. See "How Hollywood Learned to Start Worrying and Hate the Bomb," *American Film* 8, no. 1 (October 1982): 57–63. Other film stars who were active in the antinuke campaign besides Newman included Ellen Burstyn, Jill Clayburgh, Sally Field, Meryl Streep, and Joanne Woodward.
15. See Mick Broderick, *Nuclear Movies* (Jefferson, NC: McFarland & Co., 1991), Filmography, 55–191.
16. The original *Godzilla* (1954) movie was a low-budget Japanese film that reflected the horrors of Hiroshima and Nagasaki. The film was edited and released in the U.S. in 1956 as *Godzilla, King of the Monsters*. The American film identified Godzilla as a radioactive monster that terrorizes Japan.
17. See Nora Sayre, *Running Time: Films of the Cold War* (New York: The Dial Press, 1982) chapter VII for a Cold War analysis of science-fiction films of the fifties.
18. Jane Caputi has tried to establish a relationship between certain horror films such as *Night of the Living Dead* and the nuclear age. Her thesis is that although such films make no explicit references to nuclear technology, the ghouls are byproducts of nuclear contamination. See her "Films of the Nuclear Age," *Journal of Popular Film and Television* 16, no. 3 (fall 1988): 100–07.
19. See Cyndy Hendershot, "The Atomic Scientist, Science Fiction Films, and Paranoia," *Journal of American Culture* 20, no. 1 (spring 1997): 31–41.
20. Reported in Lawrence Suid, "The Pentagon and Hollywood: Dr. Strangelove," in John O'Connor and Martin Jackson, eds, *American History/American Film*, 224.

The same lack of cooperation was accorded the Stanley Kubrick film, *Dr. Strangelove*.

21. As an epilogue to *The War Game*, Watkins went into self-exile in Sweden. In the 1980s, one of Britain's two private television channels commissioned Watkins to begin work on another nuclear war film. This time Watkins intended to trace the effect of a nuclear strike on one family that would include a look at the government's measures before the strike and its response after the strike. But the project was canceled amidst charges of overspending by the television station and censorship by Watkins. For his comments on the television ban, see Peter Watkins, "The Fear of Commitment," *Literature/Film Quarterly* 11, no. 4 (1983): 221–33. For other articles on the subject, see *ibid*, 234–48. Also see James Welsh, "Banned in Britain," *American Film* 8, no. 1 (October 1982): 64, 69–71.
22. See Bonnie Szumski, ed., *Nuclear War: Opposing Viewpoints* (St. Paul: Greenhaven Press, 1985), 15–42.
23. Ted Guy, "The Doomsday Blueprints," *Time* August 10, 1992, 32–34.
24. A number of incidents and mishaps have occurred in the UK involving American nuclear planes, dating as far back as the 1950s. But since the UK has an Official Secrets Act which allows the government of the day to operate in secret, information about such matters must be secured through utilization of the Freedom of Information Act in the U.S. Finally, in 1996, the Ministry of Defense, after prodding by the Campaign for Freedom of Information in the UK, admitted to twenty nuclear incidents since 1960 but assured the public that none involved the release of radioactive material. Whether one should trust the credibility of a government that operates largely behind closed doors or believe journalist I. F. Stone's maxim that "All governments are run by liars" is left to the reader.
25. Holly Stratts, "Chernobyl: Aftermath of a Catastrophe," *Villanova Magazine* 11, no. 4 (fall 1996): 26. Also see the book by Grigori Medvedev, the chief engineer at Chernobyl at the time of the explosion, *The Truth About Chernobyl* (New York: Basic Books, 1991) where Medvedev not only provides an insider's description and analysis of what happened, but also claims that there had been eleven accidents in the Soviet Union and twelve in the U.S. involving nuclear reactors that provided data that could have predicted the disaster at Chernobyl.
26. See Gregory A. Waller, "Re-placing the Day After," *Cinema Journal* 26, no. 3 (spring 1987): 3–20.
27. See Richard L. Zweigenhaft, "Students Surveyed About Nuclear War," *Bulletin of the Atomic Scientists* (February 1985): 26–27.
28. Quoted in Broderick, *Nuclear Movies*, 1.
29. Quoted in Strada, "Kaleidoscopic Nuclear Images of the Fifties," 182.
30. *New York Times*, September 11, 1996, A5.
31. Eric Pooley, "Nuclear War," *Time*, March 4, 1996, 47–54.
32. For information on the state of American nuclear power plants, see stories in the *New York Times*, December 5, 1996, 1; January 3, 1997, D1 and July 12, 1998, 14.

Eleven

Political Film in the Next Century

1. According to press reports, (*Williamsport Sun-Gazette*, August 2, 1998, 3), the president collected the one million at one cocktail party and two dinners during a long weekend.
2. See Joan Goodman, "How Hollywood Whispers in the President's Ear," *New York Times Magazine*, March 23, 1997, sec. 6, 21. Goodman reports that President Clinton collected four million dollars from Hollywood fundraising events to help pay off campaign debts left from the 1996 election.
3. Seth Faison, "A Chinese Wall Shows Cracks," *New York Times*, November 21, 1995, D1. An estimated 5 billion movie tickets were sold in China in 1995. In contrast, Americans spent $6.4 billion in 1997 on movie tickets. While Americans view films in relative luxury, the Chinese look at films in 3000 urban cinemas and 180,000 factories and outdoor theaters.
4. Richard Maltby and Ian Craven, *Hollywood Cinema* (Cambridge: Blackwell Publishers, 1995), 365, maintain that the lynching of blacks increased after the release of Griffith's *Birth of a Nation*. But whether the increase was due to the film per se or to other variables is uncertain.
5. *New York Times*, Nov. 5, 1995, 7.
6. Lincoln Steffens, *The Shame of the Cities* (New York: Peter Smith, 1948). The book was a compilation of Steffens' muckraking articles on individual American cities from St. Louis to Philadelphia.
7. Neal Gabler, "The End of the Middle," *New York Times Magazine*, sec. 6, November 16, 1997, 78. In 1980, the average cost of a Hollywood film was under $30 million, with 5 billion tickets sold at the box office. Contrast these figures with 1996 statistics where an average film doubled in cost to $60 million. Although Hollywood domestic receipts almost reached $7 billion in 1998, the profit margin was offset by the increasing costs. See the *New York Times*, December 23, 1997, Bl and the *Williamsport Sun-Gazette*, December 31, 1998, 18.
8. *New York Times*, November 17, 1997, D9.
9. *Premiere*, 11, no. 3 (November 1997): 79. One 1997 film, *Batman & Robin*, cost a staggering $160 million to produce. Two 1998 blockbusters, *Armageddon* and *Godzilla* cost $200 million to make and market.
10. Bernard Weinraub, "Making a Trailer Pull the Movie," *New York Times*, December 14, 1997, sec. 4, 2. After fifteen weeks in its North American release, *Titanic* grossed over $500 million, exceeding the box office receipts for *Star Wars* (1977). The global receipts have surpassed $2 billion.
11. Geoff Gilmore, "The State of Independent Film," *National Forum* 77, no. 4 (fall 1997): 10.
12. *Information Please Almanac 1978* (New York: The Viking Press, 1977), 636 reports that *Jaws* took in $118 million while *Information Please Almanac 1980* (New York: Simon & Schuster, 1979), 831 reports that *Star Wars* grossed $164 million during its first run.
13. Gilmore, "The State of Independent Film," 11.
14. In 1997, another independently produced film, *The Full Monty*, was nominated in the "best picture" category. The term "independent film," however, is in the process of redefining itself in the 1990s as the major studios have created subsidiary divisions to produce specialized films that would otherwise qualify as

indies. For example, Disney has established Miramax, Time-Warner/New Line, MGM/Samuel Goldwyn, Fox/Searchlight, and Universal/October. These subsidiaries enjoy the advantages of major media coverage and fairly extensive distribution, but their budgets are usually restricted.

15. See the special issue, "The Two Hollywoods," *New York Times Magazine*, November 16, 1997, sec. 6, 75.
16. Gilmore, "The State of Independent Film," 11.
17. *New York Times*, January 26, 1998, B3.
18. Barry Monash, *International Motion Picture Almanac* (New York: Quigley Publishing Co., 1996), 647–66. No reliable source exists for the actual number of operating independent theaters in the U.S. A more accurate figure is the 2500 screens in the U.S. that exclude drive-ins and that are not part of a national theater chain. Therefore, the reference to independent theaters is more likely to describe ownership than the kind of films being exhibited.
19. Reported in the *New York Times*, September 23, 1998, B4.
20. *New York Times*, December 21, 1998, C7.
21. *New York Times*, January 3, 1999, sec. 4A, 10.

Select Bibliography

Books

Alperovitz, Gar. *The Decision to Use the Atomic Bomb*. New York: Alfred A. Knopf, 1995.
Alt, Betty, and Silvia Falts. *Weeping Violins: The Gypsy Tragedy in Europe*. Kirksville, MO: Thomas Jefferson University Press, 1996.
Anderegg, Michael, ed. *Inventing Vietnam: The War in Film and Television*. Philadelphia: Temple University Press, 1991.
Arany, Lynne, Tom Dyja, and Gary Goldsmith. *The Reel List*. New York: Dell Publishing Co., 1995.
Barsam, Richard M. *Non-Fiction Film*. Rev. ed. Bloomington: Indiana University Press, 1992.
Basinger, Jeanine. *The World War II Combat Film*. New York: Columbia University Press, 1986.
Benjamin, Walter. *Illuminations*. Edited with an introduction by Hannah Arendt. New York: Schocken Books, 1968.
Bergman, Andrew. *We're in the Money*. New York: New York University Press, 1971.
Bergmann, Paul, and Michael Asimow. *Reel Justice: The Courtroom Goes to the Movies*. Kansas City: Andrews and McMeel, 1996.
Biberman, Herbert. *Salt of the Earth*. Boston: Beacon Press, 1965.
Biskind, Peter. *Easy Riders, Raging Bulls*. New York: Simon & Schuster, 1998.
_____. *Seeing Is Believing*. New York: Pantheon Books, 1983.
Black, Gregory D. *Hollywood Censored: Morality Codes, Catholics, and the Movies*. Cambridge, UK: Cambridge University Press, 1994.
Boyer, Paul. *By the Bomb's Early Light*. Chapel Hill: University of North Carolina Press, 1994.
British Board of Film Classification. *Annual Report for 1995-96*. London: BBFC, 1996.
Broderick, Mick. *Nuclear Movies*. Jefferson, NC: McFarland & Co., 1991.
Browne, Nick, ed. *Refiguring Genres*. Berkeley: University of California Press, 1998.
Brownstein, Ronald. *The Power and the Glitter*. New York: Pantheon Books, 1990.
Brundage, W. Fitzhugh. *Lynching in the New South*. Urbana: University of Illinois Press, 1993.
Carnes, Mark C., ed. *Past Imperfect*. New York: Henry Holt, 1995.
Ceplair, Larry, and Steven Englund. *The Inquisition in Hollywood*. Garden City, NY: Anchor Press/Doubleday, 1980.
Chambers, II, John Whiteclay, and David Culbert, eds. *World War II, Film, and History*. New York: Oxford University Press, 1996.
Chang, Iris. *The Rape of Nanking*. New York: Basic Books, 1997.
Chaplin, Charles. *My Autobiography*. New York: Simon and Schuster, 1964.

Christensen, Terry. *Reel Politics*. New York: Blackwell Publishers, 1987.

Cogley, John. *Report on Blacklisting I: Movies*. New York: Fund for the Republic, 1956.

Combs, James, ed. *Movies and Politics*. New York: Garland Publishing Co., 1993.

Combs, James E., and Sara T. Combs. *Film Propaganda and American Politics*. New York: Garland Publishing Co., 1994.

Conrad, Joseph. *Heart of Darkness*. Edited by Robert Kimbrough, 2d ed. New York: W. W. Norton & Company, 1971.

Cook, Philip S., Douglas Goney, and Lawrence W. Lichty. *American Media*. Washington, DC: The Wilson Center Press, 1989.

Michael Coyne. *The Crowded Prairie*. London: I.B. Tauris Publishers, 1997.

Crowdus, Gary, ed. *The Political Companion to American Film*. Chicago: Lake View Press, 1994.

Denvir, John, ed. *Legal Reelism: Movies as Legal Texts*. Urbania: University of Illinois Press, 1996.

Dershowitz, Alan M. *The Best Defense*. New York: Vintage Books, 1983.

Dick, Bernard F. *The Star-Spangled Screen: The American World War II Film*. Lexington: University Press of Kentucky, 1996.

Diggins, John Patrick. *The Proud Decades*. New York: Norton, 1989.

Dinnerstein, Leonard. *The Leo Frank Case*. New York: Columbia University Press, 1968.

Dittmar, Linda, and Gene Michaud, eds. *From Hanoi to Hollywood: The Vietnam War in American Film*. New Brunswick, NJ: Rutgers University Press, 1990.

Dmytryk, Edward. *Odd Man Out: A Memoir of the Hollywood Ten*. Carbondale: Southern Illinois University Press, 1996.

Doherty, Thomas. *Projections of War: Hollywood, American Culture and World War II*. New York: Columbia University Press, 1993.

Dooley, Roger. *From Scarface to Scarlett: American Films in the 1930s*. New York: Harcourt Brace Jovanovich, 1979.

Fielding, Raymond. *The March of Time, 1945-51*. New York: Oxford University Press, 1978.

Fried, Albert. *McCarthyism: The Great American Red Scare*. New York: Oxford University Press, 1997.

Fried, Richard. *Nightmare in Red*. New York: Oxford University Press, 1990.

Gabler, Neal. *An Empire of Their Own*. New York: Crown Publishers, 1988.

______. *Life the Movie: How Entertainment Conquered Reality*. New York: Alfred A. Knopf, 1998.

Geertz, Clifford. *The Interpretation of Cultures*. New York: Basic Books, 1973.

Gehring, Wes, ed. *Handbook of American Film Genres*. Westport, CT: Greenwood Press, 1988.

Genovese, Michael. *Politics and the Cinema*. Lexington, MA: Ginn Press, 1986.

Georgakas, Dan. *Encyclopedia of the American Left*. New York: Garland Publishing Co., 1990.

Georgakas, Dan, and Lenny Rubenstein, eds. *The Cineaste Interviews*. Chicago: Lake View Press, 1983.

Grant, Barry Keith. *Voyages of Discovery: The Cinema of Frederick Wiseman*. Urbana: University of Illinois Press, 1992.

______, and Jeannette Sloniowski, eds. *Documenting the Documentary*. Detroit: Wayne State University Press, 1998.

Gutman, Israel, ed. *Encyclopedia of the Holocaust*. Vol. 4. New York: Macmillan Publishing Co., 1990.

Halberstam, David. *The Fifties*. New York: Villard Books, 1993.

Hamilton, Marybeth. *When I'm Bad, I'm Better: Mae West, Sex, and American Entertainment*. Berkeley: University of California Press, 1997.

Hearst Corporation. *The American Public, the Media and the Judicial System*. New York: Hearst Corporation, 1983.

Isaacs, Arnold R. *The War, Its Ghosts, and Its Legacy*. Baltimore: Johns Hopkins University Press, 1998.

Jamesson, Richard T., ed. *They Went Thataway: Redefining Film Genres*. San Francisco: Mercury House, 1994.

Jarvie, I.C., et al., eds. *Children and the Movies: Media Influences and the Payne Fund Controversy*. New York: Cambridge University Press, 1996.

Keim, Albert N. *The CPS Story: An Illustrated History of Civilian Public Service*. Intercourse, PA: Good Books, 1990.

Keough, Peter, ed. *Flesh and Blood*. San Francisco: Mercury House, 1995.

Kohn, Stephen M. *Jailed for Peace*. Westport, CT: Greenwood Press, 1986.

Koppes, Clayton R., and Gregory D. Black. *Hollywood Goes to War*. Berkeley: University of California Press, 1993.

Leff, Leonard J., and Jerold L. Simmons. *The Dame in the Kimono: Hollywood, Censorship, and the Production Code from the 1920s to the 1960s*. New York: Grove Weidenfeld, 1990.

Lovell, Hugh, and Tasile Carter. *Collective Bargaining in the Motion Picture Industry*. Berkeley: University of California Press, 1955.

Lukas, Richard C. *The Forgotten Holocaust: The Poles Under German Occupation*. Lexington: University of Kentucky Press, 1986.

Lyons, Charles. *The New Censors*. Philadelphia: Temple University Press, 1997.

Maisel, Sandy L. *Political Parties and Elections in the United States*. New York: Garland Publishing, 1991.

Maltby, Richard, and Ian Craven. *Hollywood Cinema*. Cambridge: Blackwell Publishers, 1995.

Maltin, Leonard. *The Great Movie Shorts*. New York: Crown Publishers, 1972.

Martin, Andrew. *Receptions of War: Vietnam in American Culture*. Norman: University of Oklahoma Press, 1993.

Mast, Gerald, and Marshall Cohen, eds. *Film Theory and Criticism*. 3rd ed. New York: Oxford University Press, 1985.

Medved, Michael. *Hollywood v. America*. New York: HarperCollins, 1992.

Medvedev, Grigori. *The Truth About Chernobyl*. New York: Basic Books, 1991.

Miller, Mark Crispin, ed. *Seeing Through Movies*. New York: Pantheon Books, 1990.

Milton, Joyce. *Tramp: The Life of Charlie Chaplin*. New York: HarperCollins, 1996.

Mitchell, Greg. *Tricky Dick and the Pink Lady: Richard Nixon vs. Helen Gahagan Douglas-Sexual Politics and the Red Scare*. New York: Random House, 1950.

Navasky, Victor S. *Naming Names*. New York: Penguin Books, 1981.

Neve, Brian. *Film and Politics in America*. London: Routledge, 1992.

Nichols, Bill. *Blurred Boundaries*. Bloomington: Indiana University Press, 1994.

Nielsen, Mike, and Gene Mailes. *Hollywood's Other Blacklist*. London: British Film Institute, 1995.

O'Connor, John, and Martin A. Jackson, eds. *American History/American Film*. Foreword by Arthur Schlesinger, Jr. New York: Frederick Unger, 1979.

Oshinsky, David M. *A Conspiracy So Immense*. New York: Free Press, 1983.

Palmer, William J. *The Films of the Eighties*. Carbondale: Southern Illinois University Press, 1993.

Perry, Richard, and Louis Perry. *A History of the Los Angeles Labor Movement*. Berkeley: University of California Press, 1963.

Powdermaker, Hortense. *Hollywood the Dream Factory: An Anthropologist Looks at the Movie-makers*. Boston: Little, Brown & Company, 1950.
Puttman, David, with Neil Watson. *Movies and Money*. New York: Alfred A. Knopf, 1997.
Reeves, Thomas C. *The Life and Times of Senator Joe McCarthy*. New York: Stein and Day, 1982.
Riordon, William L. *Plunkitt of Tammany Hall*. New York: E.P. Dutton & Co., 1963.
Robins, Robert S., and Jerold M. Post. *Political Paranoia: The Psychopolitics of Hatred*. New Haven: Yale University Press, 1997.
Rogin, Michael. *Ronald Reagan, the Movie*. Berkeley: University of California Press, 1988.
Rollins, Peter C., and John E. O'Connor. *Hollywood's World War I: Motion Picture Images*. Bowling Green: Popular Press, 1997.
Ross, Murray. *Stars and Strikes*. New York: Columbia University Press, 1941.
Ross, Steven J. *Working Class Hollywood: Silent Film and the Shaping of Class in America*. Princeton: Princeton University Press, 1998.
Rovere, Richard. *Senator Joe McCarthy*. New York: Harcourt, Brace, 1959.
Ryan, Michael, and Douglas Kellner. *Camera Politica: The Politics and Ideology of Contemporary Hollywood Film*. Bloomington: Indiana University Press, 1988.
Sayre, Nora. *Running Time: Films of the Cold War*. New York: The Dial Press, 1982.
Schapsmeier, Edward, and Frederick Schapsmeier. *Political Parties and Civic Action Groups*. Westport: Greenwood Press, 1981.
Shaheen, Jack, ed. *Nuclear War Films*. Carbondale: Southern Illinois University Press, 1978.
Simon, John. *Movies Into Film*. New York: Dell Publishing Co., 1970.
Steffens, Lincoln. *The Shame of the Cities*. New York: Peter Smith, 1948.
Szumski, Bonnie, ed. *Nuclear War: Opposing Viewpoints*. St. Paul: Greenhaven Press, 1985.
Tolenay, Stewart E., and E.M. Beck. *A Festival of Violence: An Analysis of Southern Lynching, 1882-1930*. Urbana: University of Illinois Press, 1995.
Traube, Elizabeth. *Dreaming Identities: Class, Gender and Generation in 1980s Hollywood Movies*. Boulder: Westview Press, 1992.
Turner, Frederick Jackson. "The Significance of the Frontier in American History." In *The Frontier in American History*. New York: Henry Holt & Co., 1920. First published in the *Annual Report of the American Historical Association for the Year 1883*. Washington, DC, 1894.
Tuttle, William M., Jr. *Daddy's Gone to War*. New York: Oxford University Press, 1993.
Valenti, Jack. *The Voluntary Movie Rating System*. Washington, DC: Motion Picture Association of America, 1996.
Vaughn, Stephen. *Ronald Reagan in Hollywood*. New York: Cambridge University Press, 1994.
Walzer, Michael. *Just and Unjust Wars*. 2d. ed. New York: Basic Books, 1992.
Welch, David. *Propaganda and the German Cinema*. New York: Oxford University Press, 1983.
Winston, Brian. *Claiming the Real: The Documentary Film Revisited*. London: British Film Institute, 1995.
Wise, James E. Jr., and Anne Collier Rehill. *Stars in Blue: Movie Actors in America's Sea Services*. Annapolis: Naval Institute Press, 1997.

Articles

Barkun, Michael. "Conspiracy Thinking in Contemporary America." *Maxwell Perspective* (Syracuse University) 8, no. 1 (fall 1997): 23.

Bateman, Thomas S., Tomoaki Sakano, and Mokoto Fujita. "Roger, Me, and My Attitude: Film Propaganda and Cynicism toward Corporate Leadership." *Journal of Applied Psychology* 77, no. 5 (1992): 768-71.

Brinckmann, Christine Noll. "The Politics of Force of Evil: An Analysis of Abraham Polonsky's Preblacklisted Film." *Prospects* 6 (1981): 357-86.

Caputi, Jane. "Films of the Nuclear Age." *Journal of Popular Film & Television*. 16, no. 3 (fall 1988): 100-7.

Chelminski, Ralph. "The Maginot Line." *Smithsonian* 28, no. 3 (June 1997): 90-100.

Convents, Guido. "Documentaries and Propaganda Before 1914." *Framework*, no. 35 (1988): 107-8.

Elliott, William R., and William J. Schenck-Hamlin. "Film, Politics and the Press: The Influence of *All the President's Men*." *Journalism Quarterly* 56, no. 3 (1979): 546-53.

Gans, Herbert J. "Hollywood Entertainment: Commerce or Ideology?" *Social Science Quarterly* 74, no. 1 (1993): 150-53.

Gilmore, Geoff. "The State of Independent Film." *National Forum* 77, no. 4 (fall 1997): 10.

Godmilow, Jill. "How Real Is the Reality in Documentary Film?" *History and Theory* 36, no. 4 (December 1997): 80-101.

Hackett, David. "The Wonderful, Horrible Life of Leni Riefenstahl." *American Historical Review* 100, no. 4 (October 1995): 1227-28.

Hendershot, Cyndy. "The Atomic Scientists, Science Fiction Films, and Paranoia." *Journal of American Culture* 20, no. 1 (spring 1997): 31-41.

Jowett, Garth S. "Propaganda and Communication: The Re-emergence of a Research Tradition." *Journal of Communication* 37, no. 1 (winter 1987): 113-14.

_____. "Hollywood, Propaganda and the Bomb: Nuclear Images in Post World War II Film." *Film and History* 18, no. 2 (May 1988): 26-38.

Lieberman, Robbie. "Communism, Peace Activism, and Civil Liberties: From the Waldorf Conference to the Peekskill Riot." *Journal of Popular Culture* 18, no. 3 (fall 1995): 59-65.

Lucia, Cynthia. "Women on Trial: The Female Lawyer in the Hollywood Courtroom." *Cineaste* 19 (1993): 32-37.

Macaulay, Stewart. "Images of Law in Everyday Life: The Lesson of School, Entertainment, and Spectator Sports." *Law & Society Review* 21, no. 2 (1987): 185-218.

Mastrangelo, Paul. "Lawyers and the Law: A Filmography." *Legal Reference Services Quarterly* 3 (winter 1983): 31-72.

McGovern, George. "Nixon and Historical Memory: Two Reviews." *Perspectives* (AHA Newsletter) 34, no. 3 (March 1996): 3.

Morlan, Don. "Slapstick Contributions to WWII Propaganda: The Three Stooges and Abbott & Costello." *Studies in Popular Culture* 17 (October 1994): 29-43.

Orwell, Miles. "Documentary and the Power of Interrogation: American Dream and Roger & Me." *Film Quarterly* 48 (winter 94/95): 10-18.

Rolo, Charles. "Camus at Stockholm." *The Atlantic Monthly* 201 (May 1958): 33-34.

Ross, Steven J. "Struggles for the Screen: Workers, Radicals, and the Political Uses of Silent Film." *American Historical Review* 96, no. 2 (April 1991): 333-67.

Rostron, Allen. "Mr. Carter Goes to Washington." *Journal of Popular Film & Television* 25, no. 2 (summer 1997): 57-67.

Sheffield, Ric. "On Film: A Social History of Women Lawyers in Popular Culture 1930 to 1990." *Loyola of Los Angeles Entertainment Law Journal* 14 (1993): 73-114.

Small, Melvin. "Buffoons and BraveHearts: Hollywood Portrays the Russians, 1939-1944." *California Historical Society* 52 (winter 1973): 326-37.

Spiller, Roger J. "War in the Dark." *American Heritage* 50, no. 1 (February/March 1999): 41-51.

Strada, Michael J. "Kaleidoscopic Nuclear Images of the Fifties." *Journal of Popular Culture* 20, no. 3 (1986): 179-98.

Stratts, Holly. "Chernobyl: Aftermath of a Catastrophe." *Villanova Magazine* 11, no. 4 (fall 1996): 26.

Sturken, Marita. "Reenactment, Fantasy, and the Paranoia of History: Oliver Stone's Docudramas." *History and Theory* 36, no.4 (December 1997): 66.

Sunstein, Cass. "Free Speech Now." *University of Chicago Law Review* 59 (1992): 255-316.

Tarr, Alan. Review of "Nashville." *Notes for Teachers of Political Science*, no. 22 (summer 1979): 21.

Thompson, Robert. "American Politics on Film." *Journal of Popular Culture* 20 (summer 1986): 27-47.

Waller, Gregory A. "Re-placing the Day After." *Cinema Journal* 26, no. 3 (spring 1987): 3-20.

Watkins, Peter. "The Fear of Commitment." *Literature/Film Quarterly* 11, no. 4 (1983): 221-33.

Watson, Bruce. "Hang'em first, try'em later." *Smithsonian* 29, no.8 (June 1998): 96-107.

Welsh, James. "Banned in Britain." *American Film* 8, no. 1 (October 1982): 64ff.

Wise, Sidney. "Politicians: A Film Perspective." *News for Teachers of Political Science* 32 (winter 1982): 1.

Zweigenhaft, Richard L. "Students surveyed about nuclear war." *Bulletin of the Atomic Scientists* (February 1985): 26-27.

Cases

Brandenburg v. Ohio, 395 U.S. 444 (1969)
Brown v. Board of Education, 374 U.S. 483 (1954)
Burstyn v. Wilson, 343 U.S. 495 (1952)
Gitlow v. New York, 268 U.S. 652 (1925)
Goldman v. Weinberger, 475 U.S. 503 (1985)
Home Building and Loan Association v. Blaisdell, 290 U.S. 398 (1934)
Near v. Minnesota, 283 U.S. 697 (1931)
New York Times v. U.S., 403 U.S. 713 (1971)
New York Times Co. v. Sullivan, 376 U.S. 255 (1964)
Roth v. U.S., 354 U.S. 476 (1957)
Thornhill v. Alabama, 310 U.S. 88 (1940)
West Virginia State Board v. Barnette, 319 U.S. 624 (1943)
Whitney v. California, 274 U.S. 357 (1927)

Filmography

Features

Abe Lincoln in Illinois. Director: John Cromwell. Screenplay: Robert Sherwood. Cast: Raymond Massey, Gene Lockhart, Ruth Gordon. 110 mins. RKO. USA, 1940.(*)

Above and Beyond. Directors: Melvin Frank, Norman Panama. Screenplay: Norman Panama, Beirne Lay Jr., Frank Panama. Cast: Robert Taylor, Eleanor Parker, James Whitmore. 122 mins. MGM. USA, 1952.(*)

Absolute Power. Director: Clint Eastwood. Screenplay: William Goldman. Cast: Clint Eastwood, Gene Hackman, Ed Harris. 121 mins. Columbia. USA, 1996.(*)

The Accused. Director: Jonathan Kaplan. Screenplay: Tom Topor. Cast: Jodie Foster, Kelly McGillis. 101 mins. Paramount. USA, 1988.(*)

Action in the North Atlantic. Director: Lloyd Bacon. Screenplay: John Howard Lawson. Cast: Humphrey Bogart, Raymond Massey, Alan Hale, Julie Bishop. 126 mins. Warner Bros. USA, 1944.(*)

Adam's Rib. Director: George Cukor. Screenplay: Garson Kanin. Cast: Spencer Tracy, Katharine Hepburn, Judy Holliday, Tom Ewell. 101 mins. MGM. USA, 1950.(*)

Advise and Consent. Director: Otto Preminger. Screenplay: Wendell Mayes. Cast: Don Murray, Charles Laughton, Henry Fonda, Walter Pidgeon, Lew Ayres. 139 mins. Columbia. USA, 1962.(*)

Air Force One. Director: Wolfgang Peterson. Screenplay: Andrew W. Marlowe. Cast: Harrison Ford, Glenn Close, Gary Oldman. 124 mins. Columbia. USA, 1997.(*)

Alamo Bay. Director: Louis Malle. Screenplay: Alice Arlan. Cast: Ed Harris, Ho Nguyen, Amy Madigan. 99 mins. Tri-Star. USA, 1985.(*)

All Quiet on the Western Front. Director: Lewis Milestone. Screenplay: Lewis Milestone, Maxwell Anderson, Del Andrews, George Abbott. Cast: Louis Wolheim, Lew Ayres. 140 mins. Universal. USA, 1930.(*)

All the King's Men. Director: Robert Rossen. Screenplay: Robert Rossen. Cast: Broderick Crawford, John Ireland, Mercedes McCambridge, Joanne Dru. 109 mins. Columbia. USA, 1949.(*)

All the President's Men. Director: Alan J. Pakula. Screenplay: William Goldman. Cast: Robert Redford, Dustin Hoffman, Jason Robards Jr. 135 mins. Warner Bros. USA, 1976.(*)

The American President. Director: Rob Reiner. Screenplay: Aaron Sorkin. Cast: Michael Douglas, Annette Bening, Martin Sheen, Michael J. Fox. 115 mins. Columbia. USA, 1995.(*)

Amistad. Director: Steven Spielberg. Screenplay: David H. Franzoni. Cast: Anthony Hopkins, Matthew McConaughey, Djimon Hounsou. 150 min. Dreamworks. USA, 1997.(*)

Anatomy of Murder. Director: Otto Preminger. Screenplay: Wendell Mayes. Cast: James Stewart, George C. Scott, Lee Remick, Arthur O'Connell. 161 mins. Columbia. USA, 1959.(*)

And Justice for All. Director: Norman Jewison. Screenplay: Barry Levinson, Valerie Curtin. Cast: Al Pacino, Jack Warden, Christine Lahti. 120 mins. Columbia. USA, 1979.(*)

Angels From Hell. Director: Bruce Kessler. Screenplay: Jerome Wish. Cast: Tom Stern, Arlene Martel, Ted Markland. 86 mins. American International. USA, 1968.(*)

Angels With Dirty Faces. Director: Michael Curtiz. Screenplay: John Wexley, Warren Duff. Cast: James Cagney, Pat O'Brien, Humphrey Bogart, Ann Sheridan. 97 mins. Warner Bros. USA, 1938.(*)

Ann Carver's Profession. Director: Edward Buzzell. Screenplay: Robert Riskin. Cast: Fay Wray, Gene Raymond. 68 mins. Columbia. USA, 1933.

Apocalypse Now. Director: Francis Ford Coppola. Screenplay: Francis Ford Coppola, John Milius. Cast: Marlon Brando, Martin Sheen, Robert Duvall. 153 mins. Zoetrope Studios. USA, 1979.(*)

Armageddon. Director: Michael Bay. Screenplay: Jonathan Hensleigh. Cast: Bruce Willis, Billy Bob Thornton, Ben Affleck. 144 mins. Touchstone. USA, 1998.(*)

Baby Doll. Director: Elia Kazan. Screenplay: Tennessee Williams. Cast: Eli Wallach, Carroll Baker, Karl Malden. 115 mins. Warner Bros. USA, 1956.(*)

Back to Bataan. Director: Edward Dmytryk. Screenplay: Ben Barzman, Richard Landau. Cast: John Wayne, Anthony Quinn. 95 mins. RKO. USA, 1945.(*)

Bad Lieutenant. Director: Abel Ferrara. Screenplay: Zoe Tamerlaine Lund, Abel Ferrara. Cast: Harvey Keitel. 98 mins. Aries Films. USA, 1992.(*)

Basic Instinct. Director: Paul Verhoeven. Screenplay: Joe Eszterhas. Cast: Michael Douglas, Sharon Stone, George Dzundza, Jeanne Tripplehorn. 123 mins. Tri-Star. USA, 1992.(*)

Bataan. Director: Tay Garnett. Screenplay: Robert D. Andrews. Cast: Robert Taylor, George Murphy, Thomas Mitchell. 115 mins. MGM. USA, 1943.(*)

Battle Cry of Peace. Directors: J. Stuart Blackton, Wilfred North. Screenplay: J. Stuart Blackton. Cast: Charles Richman, Norma Talmadge. Nine reels. Vitagraph. USA, 1915.

Battle of the Bulge. Director: Ken Annakin. Screenplay: Philip Yordan, Milton Sperling, John Melson. Cast: Henry Fonda, Robert Shaw, Robert Ryan, Dana Andrews. 167 mins. Warner Bros. USA, 1965.(*)

The Beast from 20,000 Fathoms. Director: Eugene Lourie. Cast: Paul Christian, Paula Raymond, Cecil Kellaway, Kenneth Tobey. 80 mins. Warner Bros. USA, 1953.(*)

The Beginning or the End. Director: Norman Taurog. Screenplay: Robert Considine. Cast: Brian Donlevy, Robert Walker, Tom Drake, Beverly Tyler. 112 mins. MGM. USA, 1947.

Behind the Rising Sun. Director: Edward Dmytryk. Screenplay: Emmet Lavery. Cast: Tom Neal, J. Carrol Naish. 88 mins. RKO. USA, 1943.(*)

The Best Man. Director: Franklin J. Schaffner. Screenplay: Gore Vidal. Cast: Henry Fonda, Cliff Robertson, Lee Tracy, Margaret Leighton. 104 mins. United Artists. USA, 1964.(*)

The Best Years of Our Lives. Director: Willian Wyler. Screenplay: Robert Sherwood. Cast: Frederic March, Myrna Loy, Dana Andrews, Harold Russell, Teresa Wright. 170 mins. RKO. USA, 1946.(*)

Big Jim McLain. Director: Edward Ludwig. Screenplay: James Edward Grant, Richard English, Eric Taylor. Cast: John Wayne, Nancy Olson, James Arness. 90 mins. Warner Bros. USA, 1952.(*)

The Big Parade. Director: King Vidor. Screenplay: Lawrence Stallings, Harry Behn. Cast: John Gilbert, Renee Adoree, Hobart Bosworth. 126 mins. MGM. USA, 1925.(*)

The Big Red One. Director: Samuel Fuller. Screenplay: Samuel Fuller. Cast: Lee Marvin, Robert Carradine, Mark Hamill. 113 mins. United Artists. USA, 1980.(*)

Birth of a Nation. Director: D. W. Griffith. Screenplay: D. W. Griffith, Frank Woods. Cast: Henry B. Walthall, Mae Marsh, Miriam Cooper, Lillian Gish. 175 mins. Epoch Films. USA, 1915.(*)

Black Legion. Director: Archie Mayo. Screenplay: Robert Lord, Abem Finkel, William Wister Haines. Cast: Humphrey Bogart, Erin O'Brien Moore, Dick Foran, Ann Sheridan. 83 mins. Warner Bros. USA, 1937.(*)

Blockade. Director: William Dierterle. Screenplay: John Howard Wilson. Cast: Madeleine Carroll, Henry Fonda, Leo Carrillo, John Halliday. 85 mins. Warner Bros. USA, 1938.(*)

Blow-Up. Director: Michelangelo Antonioni. Screenplay: Tonino Guerra, Michelangelo Antonioni. Cast: David Hemmings, Vanessa Redgrave, Sarah Miles. 111 mins. MGM. UK/Italy, 1966.(*)

Bob Roberts. Director: Tim Robbins. Screenplay: Tim Robbins. Cast: Tim Robbins, Giancarlo Esposito, Alan Rickman. 105 mins. Paramount. USA, 1992.(*)

Bolshevism on Trial. Director: Harley Knoles. Screenplay: Thomas Dixon, Harry Chandler. Cast: Robert Frazer, Leslie Stowe. 85 mins. USA, 1919.

Born on the Fourth of July. Director: Oliver Stone. Screenplay: Oliver Stone, Ron Kovic. Cast: Tom Cruise, William Dafoe, Tom Berenger. 144 mins. Universal. USA, 1989.(*)

Bound. Directors: Andy and Larry Wachowski. Screenplay: Andy and Larry Wachowski. Cast: Jennifer Tilly, Gina Gershon. 107 mins. Gramercy. USA, 1996.(*)

A Boy and His Dog. Director: L.Q. Jones. Screenplay: Harlan Ellison, L.Q. Jones. Cast: Don Johnson, Suzanne Benton, Jason Robards Jr., Charles McGraw. 87 mins. Pacific Film Enterprises. USA, 1975.(*)

The Boys in Company C. Director: Sidney J. Furie. Screenplay: Sidney J. Furie. Cast: Stan Shaw, Andrew Stevens, James Canning. R. Lee Ermey. 127 mins. Columbia. USA, 1977.(*)

Braddock: Missing in Action III. Director: Aaron Norris. Screenplay: James Bruner, Chuck Norris, Steve Bing. Cast: Chuck Norris. 101 mins. Cannon. USA, 1988.(*)

The Bridge on the River Kwai. Director: David Lean. Screenplay: Michael Wilson, Carl Foreman. Cast: William Holden, Alec Guinness, Jack Hawkins, Sessue Hayakawa. 161 mins. Columbia. UK/USA, 1957.(*)

The Brothers MacMullen. Director: Edward Burns. Screenplay: Edward Burns. Cast: Edward Burns, Mike McGlone, Jack Mulcahy. 98 mins. 20th Century Fox. USA, 1995.(*)

Bulworth. Director: Warren Beatty. Screenplay: Warren Beatty, Jeremy Pikser. Cast: Warren Beatty, Halle Berry. 108 mins. 20th Century Fox. USA, 1998.(*)

The Caine Mutiny. Director: Edward Dmytryk. Screenplay: Stanley Roberts. Cast: Humphrey Bogart, Jose Ferrer, Van Johnson, Fred MacMurray. 125 mins. Columbia. USA, 1954.(*)

Canadian Bacon. Director: Michael Moore. Screenplay: Michael Moore. Cast: Alan Alda, Kevin Pollak, John Candy, Rhea Perlman. 91 mins. MGM/UA. USA, 1994.(*)

The Candidate. Director: Michael Ritchie. Screenplay: Jeremy Larner. Cast: Robert Redford, Peter Boyle, Don Porter, Allan Garfield. 105 mins. Warner Bros. USA, 1972.(*)

Career Woman. Director: Lewis Seiler. Screenplay: Lamar Trotti. Cast: Claire Trevor, Erville Alderson, Edward S. Brophy. 75 mins. 20th Century Fox. USA, 1936.

Casablanca. Director: Michael Curtiz. Screenplay: Julius J. Epstein, Philip C. Epstein, Howard Koch. Cast: Humphrey Bogart, Ingrid Bergman, Paul Henreid, Claude Rains. 102 mins. Warner Bros. USA, 1942.(*)

Casino. Director: Martin Scorsese. Screenplay: Nicholas Pileggi, Martin Scorsese. Cast: Robert DeNiro, Sharon Stone, Joe Pesci, James Woods. 182 mins. Universal. USA, 1995.(*)

Casualties of War. Director: Brian DePalma. Screenplay: David Rabe. Cast: Sean Penn, Michael J. Fox, Thuy Thu Le. 120 mins. Columbia. USA, 1989.(*)

The China Syndrome. Director: James Bridges. Screenplay: Mike Gray, T. S. Cook, James Bridges. Cast: Jane Fonda, Jack Lemmon, Michael Douglas. 123 mins. Columbia. USA, 1979.(*)

Chrome and Hot Leather. Director: Lee Frost. Screenplay: Michael Haynes, David Neibel, Don Tait. Cast: William Smith, Tony Young, Michael Haynes, Peter Brown. 91 mins. American International. USA, 1971.(*)

City Hall. Director: Harold Becker. Screenplay: Bo Goldman, Paul Schrader, Nicholas Pileggi, Ken Lipper. Cast: Al Pacino, John Cusack, Bridget Fonda, Danny Aiello. 111 mins. Columbia. USA, 1996.(*)

A Civil Action. Director: Steven Zaillian. Screenplay: Steven Zaillian. Cast: John Travolta, Robert Duvall. 113 mins. Touchstone. USA, 1998.(*)

Civilization. Director: Thomas Ince. Screenplay: C. Gardner Sullivan. Cast: Howard Hickman, Enid Markey, Lola May, Herschel Mayall. 80 mins. Blackhawk Films. USA, 1916.(*)

Class Action. Director: Michael Apted. Screenplay: Samantha Shad. Cast: Mary Elizabeth Mastrantonio, Gene Hackman, Larry Fishburne, Donald Moffat. 110 mins. 20th Century Fox. USA, 1991.(*)

Clerks. Director: Kevin Smith. Screenplay: Kevin Smith. Cast: Brian O'Halloran, Darryl Anderson. 92 mins. Miramax. USA, 1994.(*)

Clockers. Director: Spike Lee. Screenplay: Richard Price, Spike Lee. Cast: Harvey Keitel, John Turturro, Delroy Lindo, Mekhi Phifer. 129 mins. Universal. USA, 1996.(*)

A Clockwork Orange. Director: Stanley Kubrick. Screenplay: Stanley Kubrick. Cast: Malcolm McDowell, Patrick Magee. 137 mins. Warner Bros. UK, 1971.(*)

Coming Home. Director: Hal Ashby. Screenplay: Robert C. Jones, Waldo Salt. Cast: Jane Fonda, Jon Voight, Bruce Dern. 130 mins. United Artists. USA, 1978.(*)

Commandos Strike at Dawn. Director: John Farrow. Screenplay: Irwin Shaw. Cast: Paul Muni, Lillian Gish, Cedric Hardwick, Anna Lee. 100 mins. Columbia. USA, 1943.(*)

Compulsion. Director: Richard Fleischer. Screenplay: Richard Murphy. Cast: Orson Welles, Diane Varsi, Dean Stockwell, Bradford Dillman. 103 mins. 20th Century Fox. USA, 1959.(*)

Comrade X. Director: King Vidor. Screenplay: Ben Hecht, Charles Lederer. Cast: Clark Gable, Hedy Lamarr, Oscar Homolka. 87 mins. MGM. USA, 1940.(*)

Confession of a Nazi Spy. Director: Anatole Litvak. Screenplay: Milton Krims, John Wexley. Cast: Edward G. Robinson, Paul Lukas, George Sanders. 110 mins. Warner Bros. USA, 1939.

Conspiracy Theory. Director: Richard Donner. Screenplay: Brian Hegeland. Cast: Mel Gibson, Julia Roberts. 135 mins. Warner Bros. USA, 1996.(*)

Counsellor-At-Law. Director: William Wyler. Screenplay: Elmer Rice. Cast: John Barrymore, Beebe Daniels, Melvyn Douglas, Doris Kenton. 78 mins. Universal. USA, 1933.(*)

Country. Director: Richard Pearce. Screenplay: Bill Wittliff. Cast: Jessica Lange, Sam Shepard, Wilford Brimley. 109 mins. Touchstone. USA, 1984.(*)

Courage of the Commonplace. Director: Ben Turbett. Five reels. USA, 1917.

Courage Under Fire. Director: Edward Zwick. Screenplay: Patrick Sheane Duncan. Cast: Denzel Washington, Meg Ryan. 115 mins. 20th Century Fox. USA, 1996.(*)

The Court Martial of Billy Mitchell. Director: Otto Preminger. Screenplay: Emmet Lavery, Milton Sperling, (uncredited: Ben Hecht, Dalton Trumbo, Michael Wilson). Cast: Gary Cooper, Charles Bickford, Ralph Bellamy, Rod Steiger. 100 mins. Warner Bros. USA, 1955.(*)

Crash Dive. Director: Archie Mayo. Screenplay: Jo Swerling. Cast: Tyrone Power, Ann Baxter, Dana Andrews. 105 mins. 20th Century Fox. USA, 1943.(*)

Crime School. Director: Lewis Seiler. Screenplay: Vincent Sherman, Crane Wilbur. Cast: Humphrey Bogart, Dead End Kids. 85 mins. Warner Bros. USA, 1938.(*)

Crossfire. Director: Edward Dmytryk. Screenplay: John Paxton. Cast: Robert Young, Robert Mitchum, Robert Ryan. 86 mins. RKO. USA, 1947.(*)

The Crucible. Director: Nicholas Hytner. Screenplay: Arthur Miller. Cast: Daniel Day-Lewis, Winona Ryder, Paul Scofield. 123 mins. 20th Century Fox. USA, 1996.(*)

Cry Havoc. Director: Richard Thorpe. Screenplay: Paul Osborn. Cast: Margaret Sullivan, Ann Sothern, Joan Blondell. 97 mins. MGM. USA, 1944.(*)

Damage. Director: Louis Malle. Screenplay: David Hare. Cast: Jeremy Irons, Juliette Binoche, Rupert Graves, Miranda Richardson. 111 mins. New Line Cinema. France/UK/USA, 1992.(*)

Dances with Wolves. Director: Kevin Costner. Screenplay: Michael Blake. Cast: Kevin Costner, Mary McDonnell, Graham Greene. 181 mins. Tig Productions. USA, 1990.(*)

Dangerous Hours. Director: Fred Niblo. Screenplay: C. Gardner Sullivan. Cast: Lloyd Hughes. 88 mins. Blackhawk Films. USA, 1919.(*)

Dante's Peak. Director: Roger Donaldson. Screenplay: Leslie Bohem. Cast: Pierce Brosnan, Linda Hamilton. 109 mins. Universal. USA, 1997.(*)

The Dark Horse. Director: Will Jason. Screenwriter: Charles Marion, Leo Solomon. Cast: Jane Darwell, Ann Savage, Donald MacBride, Phillip Terry. 59 min. Universal. USA, 1946.(*)

Dave. Director: Ivan Reitman. Screenplay: Gary Ross. Cast: Kevin Kline, Sigourney Weaver, Frank Langella. 110 mins. Warner Bros. USA, 1993.(*)

The Day After. Director: Nicholas Meyer. Screenplay: Edward Hume. Cast: Jason Robards Jr., JoBeth Williams, John Lithgow, Steve Guttenberg. 126 mins. ABC Circle Films. USA, 1983.(*)

The Day the Earth Stood Still. Director: Robert Wise. Screenplay: Edmund North. Cast: Michael Rennie, Patricia Neal, Hugh Marlowe, Sam Jaffe. 92 mins. 20th Century Fox. USA, 1951.(*)

Days of Glory. Director: Jacques Tourneur. Screenplay: Casey Robinson, Melchior Lengyel. Cast: Tamara Toumanova, Gregory Peck, Alan Reed, Maria Palmer. 86 mins. RKO. USA, 1943.(*)

Dead End. Director: William Wyler. Screenplay: Lillian Hellman. Cast: Sylvia Sydney, Joel McCrea, Humphrey Bogart. 92 mins. United Artists. USA, 1937.(*)

The Deadly Mantis. Director: Nathan Juran. Screenplay: Martin Berkeley. Cast: Craig Stevens, William Hopper, Pat Conway. 79 mins. Universal. USA, 1957.(*)

Death Wish. Director: Michael Winner. Screenplay: Wendell Mayes. Cast: Charles Bronson, Vincent Gardenia, William Redfield, Hope Lange. 93 mins. Paramount. USA, 1974.(*)

The Deer Hunter. Director: Michael Cimino. Screenplay: Deric Washburn, Michael Cimino. Cast: Robert DeNiro, Christopher Walken, Meryl Streep, John Savage. 183 mins. Universal. USA, 1978.(*)

The Defense Rests. Director: Lambert Hillyer. Screenplay: Jo Swerling. Cast: Jack Holt, Jean Arthur. 70 mins. Columbia. USA, 1934.(*)

Defenseless. Director: Martin Campbell. Screenplay: James Cresson, Jeff Burkhart. Cast: Barbara Hershey, Sam Shepard, Mary Beth Hurt, J. T. Walsh. 106 mins. New Line Cinema. USA, 1991.(*)

Desperate Journey. Director: Raoul Walsh. Screenplay: Arthur T. Horman. Cast: Errol Flynn, Ronald Reagan, Raymond Massey, Nancy Coleman. 108 mins. Warner Bros. USA, 1942.(*)

Destination Tokyo. Director: Delmer Daves. Screenplay: Delmar Daves, Albert Maltz, Steve Fisher. Cast: Cary Grant, John Garfield, Alan Hale, Dane Clark. 135 mins. Warner Bros.(*)

The Devil's Advocate. Director: Taylor Hackford. Screenplay: Jonathan Lemkin, Tony Gilroy. Cast: Al Pacino, Keanu Reeves. 144 mins. Warner Bros. USA, 1997.(*)

Dive Bomber. Director: Michael Curtiz. Screenplay: Frank Wead, Robert Buckner. Cast: Errol Flynn, Fred MacMurray, Ralph Bellamy, Alexis Smith. 130 mins. Warner Bros. USA, 1941.(*)

Do the Right Thing. Director: Spike Lee. Screenplay: Spike Lee. Cast: Danny Aiello, Spike Lee, John Turturro. 120 mins. Universal. USA, 1989.(*)

Dr. Strangelove, or: How I Learned to Stop Worrying and Love the Bomb. Director: Stanley Kubrick. Screenplay: Terry Southern, Peter George, Stanley Kubrick. Cast: Peter Sellers, George C. Scott, Sterling Hayden, Slim Pickens. 93 mins. Columbia. UK, 1964.(*)

The Eagle and the Hawk. Director: Stuart Walker. Screenplay: Seton I. Miller, Bogart Rogers, John Monk Saunders. Cast: Fredric March, Cary Grant, Dennis O'Keefe. 68 mins. Paramount. USA, 1933.(*)

Easy Rider. Director: Dennis Hopper. Screenplay: Dennis Hopper, Peter Fonda, Terry Southern. Cast: Peter Fonda, Dennis Hopper, Jack Nicholson. 94 mins. Columbia. USA, 1969.(*)

Edge of Darkness. Director: Lewis Milestone. Screenplay: Robert Rossen. Cast: Errol Flynn, Ann Sheridan, Walter Huston, Nancy Coleman. 120 mins. Warner Bros. USA, 1943.(*)

The Execution of Private Eddie Slovak. Director: Lamont Johnson. Screenplay: Richard Levinson, William Link. Cast: Martin Sheen, Ned Beatty, Gary Busey. 122 mins. Universal TV. USA, 1974.(*)

Executive Action. Director: David Miller. Screenplay: Dalton Trumbo. Cast: Burt Lancaster, Robert Ryan, Will Geer. 91 mins. National General Pictures. USA, 1973.(*)

Fail Safe. Director: Sidney Lumet. Screenplay: Walter Bernstein. Cast: Henry Fonda, Dan O'Herlihy, Walter Matthau, Larry Hagman. 111 mins. Columbia. USA, 1964.(*)

The Farmer's Daughter. Director: H.C. Potter. Screenplay: Alan Rivkin, Laura Kerr. Cast: Loretta Young, Joseph Cotten, Ethel Barrymore. 97 mins. RKO. USA, 1947.(*)

Fat Man and Little Boy. Director: Roland Joffe. Screenplay: Bruce Robinson, Tony Garnett, Roland Joffe. Cast: Paul Newman, Dwight Schultz, Bonnie Bedelia, John Cusack. 127 mins. Paramount. USA, 1989.(*)

Fellow Traveler. Director: Philip Savile. Screenplay: Michael Eaton. Cast: Ron Silver, Imogen Stubbs, Hart Bochner, Daniel J. Travanti. 97 mins. BFI/BBC Films. UK, 1989(*)

A Few Good Men. Director: Rob Reiner. Screenplay: Aaron Sorkin. Cast: Tom Cruise, Jack Nicholson, Demi Moore, Kevin Bacon. 138 mins. Columbia. USA, 1992.(*)

The Fighting Seabees. Director: Edward Ludwig. Screenplay: Bordon Chase, Aeneas MacKenzie. Cast: John Wayne, Susan Hayward, Dennis O'Keefe. 100 mins. Republic. USA, 1944.(*)

The Fighting 69th. Director: William Keighley. Screenplay: Fred Niblo, Norman Reilly Raine, Dean Franklin. Cast: James Cagney, Pat O'Brien, George Brent. 90 mins. Warner Bros. USA, 1940.(*)

The Finest Hour. Director: Shimon Dotan. Screenplay: Shimon Dotan. Cast: Rob Lowe, Gale Hansen, Tracy Griffith. 105 mins. 21st Century Films. USA, 1991.(*)

First Blood. Director: Ted Kotcheff. Screenplay: Sylvester Stallone. Cast: Sylvester Stallone, Richard Crenna, Brian Dennehy. 96 mins. Carolco Pictures. USA, 1982.(*)

Five. Director: Arch Oboler. Screenplay: Arch Oboler. Cast: Susan Douglas, William Phipps. 93 mins. Columbia. USA, 1951.(*)

Fixed Bayonets. Director: Samuel Fuller. Screenplay: Samuel Fuller. Cast: Richard Basehart, Gene Evans. 92 mins. 20th Century Fox. USA, 1951.(*)

Flight Command. Director: Frank Borzage. Screenplay: Wells Root. Cast: Robert Taylor, Ruth Hussey, Walter Pidgeon. 110 mins. MGM. USA, 1940.(*)

Flying Tigers. Director: David Miller. Screenplay: Kenneth Gamet, Barry Trivers. Cast: John Wayne, Paul Kelly, John Carroll, Anna Lee. 101 mins. Republic. USA, 1942.(*)

For Whom the Bell Tolls. Director: Sam Wood. Screenplay: Dudley Nichols. Cast: Gary Cooper, Ingrid Bergman, Akim Tamiroff. 168 mins. Paramount. USA, 1943.(*)

Force of Evil. Director: Abraham Polonsky. Screenplay: Abraham Polonsky. Cast: John Garfield, Thomas Gomez, Marie Windsor, Sheldon Leonard. 78 mins. MGM. USA, 1948.(*)

Foreign Correspondent. Director: Alfred Hitchcock. Screenplay: Robert Benchley, Charles Bennett, Joan Harrison, James Hilton. Cast: Joel McCrea, Laraine Day, Herbert Marshall, George Sanders. 120 mins. United Artists. USA, 1940.(*)

Forrest Gump. Director: Robert Zemeckis. Screenplay: Eric Roth. Cast: Tom Hanks, Robin Wright, Sally Field, Gary Sinise. 142 mins. Paramount. USA, 1994.(*)

The Fortune Cookie. Director: Billy Wilder. Screenplay: Billy Wilder, I. A. L. Diamond. Cast: Jack Lemmon, Walter Matthau. 125 mins. United Artists. USA, 1966.(*)

The Fourth Protocol. Director: John MacKenzie. Screenplay: Frederick Forsythe, Richard Burridge, George Axelrod. Cast: Michael Caine, Pierce Brosnan, Ned Beatty, Joanna Cassidy. 119 mins. Rank Films. UK, 1987.(*)

From Dusk to Dawn. Director: Frank E. Wolfe. Screenplay: Frank E. Wolfe. Cast: Clarence Darrow. Five reels. USA, 1913.

From Here to Eternity. Director: Fred Zinnemann. Screenplay: Daniel Taradash. Cast: Burt Lancaster, Montgomery Clift, Frank Sinatra, Deborah Kerr. 118 mins. Columbia. USA, 1953.(*)

The Front. Director: Martin Ritt. Screenplay: Walter Bernstein. Cast: Woody Allen, Zero Mostel, Herschel Bernardi, Michael Murphy. 95 mins. Columbia. USA, 1976.(*)

Full Metal Jacket. Director: Stanley Kubrick. Screenplay: Michael Herr, Gustav Hasford, Stanley Kubrick. Cast: Matthew Modine, R. Lee Ermey, Vincent D'Onofrio, Adam Baldwin. 116 mins. Warner Bros. UK/USA, 1987.(*)

The Full Monty. Director: Peter Cattaneo. Screenplay: Simon Beaufoy. Cast: Robert Carlyle, Tom Wilkinson. 91 mins. 20th Century Fox. UK, 1997.(*)

Fury. Director: Fritz Lang. Screenplay: Fritz Lang, Bartlett Cormack. Cast: Spencer Tracy, Sylvia Sidney, Walter Abel. 96 mins. MGM. USA, 1936.(*)

Gabriel Over the White House. Director: Gregory LaVaca. Screenplay: Carey Wilson, Bertram Bloch. Cast: Walter Huston, Karen Morley, Franchot Tone. 87 mins. MGM. USA, 1933.(*)

Gandhi. Director: Richard Attenborough. Screenplay: John Briley. Cast: Ben Kingsley, Candice Bergen, Edward Fox. 188 mins. Columbia. UK, 1982.(*)

Gentleman's Agreement. Director: Elia Kazan. Screenplay: Moss Hart. Cast: Gregory Peck, Dorothy McGuire, John Garfield. 118 mins. 20th Century Fox. USA, 1947.(*)

The Glass Key. Director: Stuart Heisler. Screenplay: Jonathan Latimer. Cast: Alan Ladd, Veronica Lake, Brian Donlevy, William Bendix. 85 mins. Paramount. USA, 1942.(*)

Go For Broke. Director: Robert Pirosh. Screenplay: Robert Pirosh. Cast: Van Johnson. 92 mins. MGM. USA, 1951.(*)

Go Tell the Spartans. Director: Ted Post. Screenplay: Wendell Mayes. Cast: Burt Lancaster, Craig Wasson. 114 mins. Spartan Film Partners. USA, 1978.(*)

The Godfather. Director: Francis Ford Coppola. Screenplay: Mario Puzo, Francis Ford Coppola. Cast: Marlon Brando, Al Pacino, Robert Duvall, James Caan. 171 mins. Paramount. USA, 1972.(*)

The Godfather, Part 2. Director: Francis Ford Coppola. Screenplay: Mario Puzo, Francis Ford Coppola. Cast: Al Pacino, Robert DeNiro, Diane Keaton, Robert Duvall. 200 mins. Paramount. USA, 1974.(*)

The Godfather, Part 3. Director: Francis Ford Coppola. Screenplay: Mario Puzo, Francis Ford Coppola. Cast: Al Pacino, Diane Keaton, Andy Garcia, Joe Mantegna. 170 mins. Paramount. USA, 1990.(*)

Godzilla. Director: Roland Emmerich. Screenplay: Dean Devlin, Roland Emmerich. Cast: Matthew Broderick, Jean Reno. 140 mins. Tri-Star. USA, 1998.(*)

Gone With the Wind. Director: Victor Fleming. Screenplay: Sidney Howard. Cast: Clark Gable, Vivien Leigh, Olivia de Havilland, Leslie Howard. 231 mins. MGM. USA, 1939.(*)

Good Morning, Vietnam. Director: Barry Levinson. Screenplay: Mitch Markowitz. Cast: Robin Williams, Forest Whitaker, Bruno Kirby, Richard Edson. 121 mins. Touchstone. USA, 1987.(*)

The Grapes of Wrath. Director: John Ford. Screenplay: Nunnally Johnson. Cast: Henry Fonda, Jane Darwell, John Carradine, Charley Grapewin. 129 mins. 20th Century Fox. USA, 1940.(*)

The Great Dictator. Director: Charles Chaplin. Screenplay: Charles Chaplin. Cast: Charles Chaplin, Paulette Goddard, Jack Oakie. 127 mins. United Artists. USA, 1940.(*)

The Great Escape. Director: John Sturges. Screenplay: James Clavell, W. R. Burnett. Cast: Steve McQueen, James Garner, Richard Attenborough. 168 mins. United Artists. USA, 1963.(*)

The Great McGinty. Director: Preston Sturges. Screenplay: Preston Sturges. Cast: Brian Donlevy, Akim Tamiroff. 82 mins. Paramount. USA, 1940.(*)

The Great Train Robbery. Director: Edwin S. Porter. Screenplay: Edwin S. Porter. Cast: Marie Murray, Broncho Billy Anderson, George Barnes. 10 mins. Edison. USA, 1903.(*)

The Green Berets. Directors: John Wayne, Ray Kellogg. Screenplay: James Lee Barrett. Cast: John Wayne, David Janssen, Jim Hutton. 141 mins. Warner Bros. USA, 1968.(*)

Guadalcanal Diary. Director: Lewis Seiler. Screenplay: Jerome Cady, Richard Tregaskis, Lamar Trotti. Cast: Preston Foster, Lloyd Nolan, William Bendix, Richard Conte. 93 mins. 20th Century Fox. USA, 1943.(*)

Guess Who's Coming to Dinner. Director: Stanley Kramer. Screenplay: William Rose. Cast: Katherine Hepburn, Spencer Tracy, Sidney Poitier, Katherine Houghton. 108 mins. Columbia. USA, 1967.(*)

Guilty as Sin. Director: Sidney Lumet. Screenplay: Larry Cohen. Cast: Don Johnson, Rebecca DeMornay, Jack Warden, Stephen Lang. 120 mins. Buena Vista/Hollywood Films. USA, 1993.(*)

Guilty by Suspicion. Director: Irwin Winkler. Screenplay: Irwin Winkler. Cast: Robert DeNiro, Annette Bening. 105 mins. Warner Bros. USA, 1991.(*)

Gung Ho! Director: Ray Enright. Screenplay: Joseph Hoffman, Lucien Hubbard, W.S. LeFrancois. Cast: Robert Mitchum, Randolph Scott, Noah Beery Jr., Alan Curtis. 88 mins. Universal. USA, 1943.(*)

Hamburger Hill. Director: John Irvin. Screenplay: Jim Carabatsos. Cast: Michael Dolan, Daniel O'Shea, Dylan McDermott, Tommy Swerdlow. 104 mins. Paramount. USA, 1987.(*)

Heartbreak Ridge. Director: Clint Eastwood. Screenplay: Jim Carabatsos. Cast: Clint Eastwood, Marsha Mason. 130 mins. Warner Bros. USA, 1986.(*)

Hell's Kitchen. Directors: Lewis Seiler, E.A. Dupont. Screenplay: Fred Niblo Jr., Crane Wilbur. Cast: Ronald Reagan, Stanley Fields, Margaret Lindsay, Dead End Kids. 81 mins. Warner Bros. USA, 1963.(*)

Henry and June. Director: Philip Kaufman. Screenplay: Philip Kaufman. Cast: Fred Ward, Uma Thurman, Kevin Spacey, Richard E. Grant. 136 mins. Universal. USA, 1990.(*)

The Heroes of Desert Storm. Director: Don Ohlmeyer. Screenplay: Lionel Chetwynd. Cast: Daniel Baldwin, Angela Bassett. 93 mins. Prism Entertainment. USA, 1991.(*)

High Noon. Director: Fred Zinnemann. Screenplay: Carl Foreman. Cast: Gary Cooper, Grace Kelly, Lloyd Bridges, Lon Chaney Jr. 85 mins. United Artists. USA, 1952.(*)

Home of the Brave. Director: Mark Robson. Screenplay: Carl Foreman. Cast: Lloyd Bridges, James Edwards, Frank Lovejoy. 86 mins. United Artists. USA, 1949.(*)

The House on 92nd Street. Director: Henry Hathaway. Screenplay: Charles G. Booth. Cast: Lloyd Nolan, Signe Hasso. 89 mins. 20th Century Fox. USA, 1945.(*)

I Am a Fugitive from a Chain Gang. Director: Mervyn LeRoy. Screenplay: Howard J. Green. Cast: Paul Muni, Glenda Farrell, Preston Foster. 93 mins. Warner Bros. USA, 1932.(*)

I'm No Angel. Director: Wesley Ruggles. Screenplay: Mae West. Cast: Mae West, Cary Grant, Edward Arnold. 88 mins. Paramount. USA, 1933.(*)

I Married a Communist (aka: *Woman on Pier 13*). Director: Robert Stevenson. Screenplay: Charles Grayson, Robert Hardy Andrews. Cast: Laraine Day, Robert Ryan, Thomas Gomez. 73 mins. RKO. USA, 1950.

I Want You. Director: Mark Robson. Screenplay: Irwin Shaw. Cast: Dana Andrews, Dorothy McQuire, Farley Granger. 101 mins. Samuel Goldwyn. USA, 1951.(*)

I Was a Communist for the FBI. Director: Gordon Douglas. Screenplay: Crane Wilbur, Matt Cvetic. Cast: Frank Lovejoy, Dorothy Hart, Phil Carey. 83 mins. Warner Bros. USA, 1951.

Independence Day. Director: Roland Emmerich. Screenplay: Dean Devlin, Roland Emmerich. Cast: Will Smith, Bill Pullman, Jeff Goldblum. 145 mins. 20th Century Fox. USA, 1996.(*)

Inherit the Wind. Director: Stanley Kramer. Screenplay: Nathan E. Douglas (aka: Ned Young), Harold Jacob Smith. Cast: Spencer Tracy, Fredric March, Gene Kelly. 128 mins. United Artists. USA, 1960.(*)

Intruder in the Dust. Director: Clarence Brown. Screenplay: Ben Maddow. Cast: David Brian, Claude Jarmen Jr., Juano Hernandez. 87 mins. MGM. USA, 1949.(*)

Invasion of the Body Snatchers. Director: Don Siegel. Screenplay: Daniel Mainwaring. Cast: Kevin McCarthy, Dana Wynter, Larry Gates, King Donovan. 80 mins. Allied Artists. USA, 1956.(*)

It Came from Beneath the Sea. Director: Robert Gordon. Screenplay: Hal Smith, George Worthing Yates. Cast: Kenneth Tobey, Faith Domergue, Ian Keith, Donald Curtis. 80 mins. Columbia. USA, 1955.(*)

It Came from Outer Space. Director: Jack Arnold. Screenplay: Ray Bradbury, Harry Essex. Cast: Richard Carlson, Barbara Rush, Charles Drake. 81 mins. Universal. USA, 1953.(*)

It Can't Happen Here (MGM, unproduced)

Jagged Edge. Director: Richard Marquand. Screenplay: Joe Eszterhas. Cast: Jeff Bridges, Glenn Close, Robert Loggia. 108 mins. Columbia. USA, 1985.(*)

Jaws. Director: Steven Spielberg. Screenplay: Peter Benchley, Carl Gottlieb. Cast: Richard Dreyfuss, Roy Scheider, Robert Shaw. 124 mins. Universal. USA, 1975.(*)

JFK. Director: Oliver Stone. Screenplay: Oliver Stone, Zachary Sklar. Cast: Kevin Costner, Sissy Spacek, Kevin Bacon, Tommy Lee Jones. 189 mins. Warner Bros. USA, 1991.(*)

Johnny Guitar. Director: Nicholas Ray. Screenplay: Philip Yordan. Cast: Joan Crawford, Ernest Borgnine, Sterling Hayden, Mercedes McCambridge. 110 mins. Republic. USA, 1953.(*)

Judge Priest. Director: John Ford. Screenplay: Dudley Nichols, Lamar Trotti. Cast: Will Rogers, Stepin Fetchit, Anita Louise, Henry B. Walthall. 80 mins. 20th Century Fox. USA, 1934.(*)

Jungle Fever. Director: Spike Lee. Screenplay: Spike Lee. Cast: Anabella Sciorra, Wesley Snipes. 131 mins. Universal. USA, 1991.(*)

A King in New York. Director: Charlie Chaplin. Screenplay: Charles Chaplin. Cast: Charlie Chaplin, Dawn Addams, Michael Chaplin. 105 mins. Attica. UK, 1957.(*)

King of the Pecos. Director: Joseph Kane. Screenplay: Bernard McConville, Dorrell McGowan, Stuart McGowan. Cast: John Wayne, Muriel Evans, Cy Kendall, Jack Clifford. 54 mins. Republic. USA, 1936.(*)

Knock on Any Door. Director: Nicholas Ray. Screenplay: Daniel Taradash, John Monks Jr. Cast: Humphrey Bogart, John Derek, George Macready. 100 mins. Columbia. USA, 1949.(*)

Kundun. Director: Martin Scorsese. Screenplay: Melissa Mathison. Cast: Tenzin Thuthob Tsarong, Gyrurme Tethog, Robert Lin. 135 mins. Touchstone. USA, 1997.(*)

Ladybug, Ladybug. Director: Frank Perry. Screenplay: Eleanor Perry. Cast: Estelle Parsons, Jane Connell. 81 mins. United Artists. USA, 1963.

The Last Hurrah. Director: John Ford. Screenplay: Frank Nugent. Cast: Spencer Tracy, Jeffrey Hunter, Diane Foster, Pat O'Brien. 121 mins. Columbia. USA, 1958.(*)

The Last Temptation of Christ. Director: Martin Scorsese. Screenplay: Paul Schrader. Cast: Willem Dafoe, Harvey Keitel, Barbara Hershey, Harry Dean Stanton. 164 mins. Universal. USA, 1988.(*)

The Last Woman on Earth. Director: Roger Corman. Screenplay: Robert Towne. Cast: Antony Carbone, Edward Wain, Betsy Jones-Moreland. 71 mins. Filmgroup. USA, 1961.(*)

Lawyer Man. Director: William Dieterle. Screenplay: Rian James, James Seymour. Cast: William Powell, Joan Blondell. 70 mins. Warner Bros. USA, 1932.(*)

Legal Eagles. Director: Ivan Reitman. Screenplay: Jim Cash, Jack Epps Jr. Cast: Robert Redford, Debra Winger, Daryl Hannah, Brian Dennehy. 116 mins. Universal. USA, 1986.(*)

The Life and Times of Judge Roy Bean. Director: John Huston. Screenplay: John Milius. Cast: Paul Newman, Stacy Keach, Ava Gardner, Jacqueline Bisset. 124 mins. National General. USA, 1972.(*)

A Lion Is in the Streets. Director: Raoul Walsh. Screenplay: Luther Davis. Cast: James Cagney, Barbara Hale, Anne Francis. 88 mins. Warner Bros. USA, 1953.(*)

Little Caesar. Director: Mervyn LeRoy. Screenplay: Francis Faragoh, Robert E. Lee. Cast: Edward G. Robinson, Glenda Farrell, Sidney Blackmer, Douglas Fairbanks Jr. 80 mins. Warner Bros. USA, 1930.(*)

A Little Princess. Director: Alfonso Cuaron. Screenplay: Richard LaGravenese. Cast: Eleanor Bron, Liesel Matthews. 97 mins. Warner Bros. USA, 1995.(*)

Little Tokyo, U.S.A. Director: Otto Brower. Screenplay: George Bricker. Cast: Preston Foster, Brenda Joyce. 64 mins. 20th Century Fox. USA, 1942.

Lolita. Director: Adrian Lyne. Screenplay: Stephen Schiff. Cast: Jeremy Irons, Dominique Swain, Melanie Griffith, Frank Langella. 137 mins. Samuel Goldwyn. USA, 1997.(*)

Lone Star. Director: John Sayles. Screenplay: John Sayles. Cast: Chris Cooper, Kris Kristofferson, Matthew McConaughey. 135 mins. Castle Rock Entertainment. USA, 1996.(*)

The Longest Day. Director: Ken Annakin. Screenplay: Bernhard Wicki. Cast: John Wayne, Richard Burton, Robert Ryan, Robert Mitchum. 179 mins. 20th Century Fox. USA, 1962.(*)

Lost Boundaries. Director: Alfred L. Werker. Screenplay: Eugene Ling, Charles Palmer, Virginia Shaler. Cast: Mel Ferrer, Susan Douglas, Beatrice Pearson, Canada Lee. 99 mins. Film Classics. USA, 1949.(*)

Mad Max. Director: George Miller. Screenplay: George Miller. Cast: Mel Gibson, Joanne Samuel. 93 mins. American International. Australia, 1980.(*)

Mad Max: Beyond Thunderdome. Directors: George Miller, George Ogilvie. Screenplay: George Miller, Terry Hayes. Cast: Mel Gibson, Tina Turner. 107 mins. Warner Bros. Australia, 1985.(*)

Malcolm X. Director: Spike Lee. Screenplay: Spike Lee, Arnold Perl, James Baldwin. Cast: Denzel Washington, Angela Bassett, Albert Hall, Al Freeman Jr. 201 mins. Warner Bros. USA, 1992.(*)

The Man in the Gray Flannel Suit. Director: Nunnally Johnson. Screenplay: Nunnally Johnson. Cast: Gregory Peck, Frederic March, Jennifer Jones, Ann Harding. 152 mins. 20th Century Fox. USA, 1956.(*)

The Man Who Shot Liberty Valance. Director: John Ford. Screenplay: Willis Goldbeck, James Warner Bellah. Cast: James Stewart, John Wayne, Vera Miles, Lee Marvin. 123 mins. Paramount. USA, 1962.(*)

The Manchurian Candidate. Director: John Frankenheimer. Screenplay: George Axelrod, John Frankenheimer. Cast: Frank Sinatra, Laurence Harvey, Janet Leigh, James Gregory, Angela Lansbury. 126 mins. United Artists. USA, 1962.(*)

Manhattan Project. Director: Marshall Brickman. Screenplay: Marshall Brickman. Cast: John Lithgow, Christopher Collet, Cynthia Nixon, Jill Eikenberry. 112 mins. 20th Century Fox. USA, 1986.(*)

Man Hunt. Director: Fritz Lang. Screenplay: Dudley Nichols. Cast: Walter Pidgeon, Joan Bennett, George Sanders. 105 mins. 20th Century Fox. USA, 1941.(*)

Mars Attacks. Director: Tim Burton. Screenplay: Jonathan Gems. Cast: Jack Nicholson, Glenn Close, Annette Bening, Pierce Brosnan. 106 mins. Warner Bros. USA, 1996.(*)

A Martyr to His Cause. Produced by the AFL's McNamara Legal Defense Committee. Two reels. USA, 1911.

*M*A*S*H*. Director: Robert Altman. Screenplay: Ring Lardner, Jr. Cast: Donald Sutherland, Elliott Gould, Robert Duvall. 116 mins. 20th Century Fox. USA, 1970.(*)

Matewan. Director: John Sayles. Screenplay: John Sayles. Cast: Chris Cooper, James Earl Jones, Mary McDonnell, William Oldham. 130 mins. Cinecom Pictures. USA, 1987.(*)

Meet John Doe. Director: Frank Capra. Screenplay: Robert Riskin, Richard Connell, Robert Presnell. Cast: Gary Cooper, Barbara Stanwyck, Edward Arnold. 135 mins. Warner Bros. USA, 1941.(*)

Men in Black. Director: Barry Sonnenfeld. Screenplay: Lowell Cunningham, Ed Solomon. Cast: Tommy Lee Jones, Will Smith. 98 mins. Columbia. USA, 1997.(*)

Michael Collins. Director: Neil Jordan. Screenplay: Neil Jordan. Cast: Liam Neeson, Aidan Quinn, Stephen Rea, Alan Rickman, Julia Roberts. 133 mins. Geffen Pictures. UK/Ireland/USA, 1996.(*)

Missing. Director: Costa-Gavras. Screenplay: Costa-Gavras, Donald Stewart. Cast: Jack Lemmon, Sissy Spacek, John Shea. 122 mins. Universal. USA, 1982.(*)

Missing in Action. Director: Joseph Zito. Screenplay: James Bruner. Cast: Chuck Norris, M. Emmet Walsh. 101 mins. Cannon. USA, 1984.(*)

Missing in Action 2: The Beginning. Director: Lance Hool. Screenplay: Steve Bing. Cast: Chuck Norris, Soon-Teck Oh. 96 mins. Cannon. USA, 1985.(*)

Mission to Moscow. Director: Michael Curtiz. Screenplay: Howard Koch. Cast: Walter Huston, Ann Harding, Oscar Homolka. 123 mins. Warner Bros. USA, 1943.

Mississippi Burning. Director: Alan Parker. Screenplay: Chris Gerolmo. Cast: Gene Hackman, Willem Dafoe, Frances McDormand, Brad Dourif. 127 mins. Rank/Orion. USA, 1988.(*)

Modern Times. Director: Charles Chaplin. Screenplay: Charles Chaplin. Cast: Charles Chaplin, Paulette Goddard. 85 mins. Chaplin Studio. USA, 1936.(*)

Money Train. Director: Joseph Ruben. Screenplay: David Richardson, David Loughery. Cast: Wesley Snipes, Woody Harrelson, Jennifer Lopez, Robert Blake. 110 mins. Columbia. USA, 1995.(*)

The Moon Is Down. Director: Irving Pichel. Screenplay: Nunnally Johnson. Cast: Cedric Hardwicke, Henry Travers, Lee J. Cobb. 90 mins. 20th Century Fox. USA, 1943.

The Mortal Storm. Director: Frank Borzage. Screenplay: Claudine West, George Froeschel, Anderson Ellis. Cast: Margaret Sullavan, James Stewart, Robert Young. 100 mins. MGM. USA, 1940.(*)

The Mouthpiece. Directors: Elliott Nugent, James Flood. Screenplay: Joseph Jackson, Earl Baldwin. Cast: Warren William, Sidney Fox, Mae Madison, Aline MacMahon. 90 mins. Warner Bros. USA, 1932.

Mr. Smith Goes to Washington. Director: Frank Capra. Screenplay: Sidney Buchman. Cast: James Stewart, Jean Arthur, Edward Arnold, Claude Rains. 130 mins. Columbia. USA, 1939.(*)

Music Box. Director: Costa-Gavras. Screenplay: Joe Eszterhas. Cast: Jessica Lange, Frederic Forrest, Lukas Haas, Armin Mueller-Stahl. 126 mins. Tri-Star. USA, 1989.(*)

Mutiny on the Bounty. Director: Frank Lloyd. Screenplay: Talbot Jennings, Jules Furthman, Carey Wilson. Cast: Charles Laughton, Clark Gable, Franchot Tone. 132 mins. MGM. USA, 1935.(*)

My Cousin Vinny. Director: Jonathan Lynn. Screenplay: Dale Launer. Cast: Joe Pesci, Ralph Macchio, Marisa Tomei. 120 mins. 20th Century Fox. USA, 1992.(*)

My Fellow Americans. Director: Peter Segal. Screenplay: Jack Kaplan, Richard Chapman, Peter Tolan. Cast: Jack Lemmon, James Garner, Dan Aykroyd. 101 mins. Warner Bros. USA, 1996.(*)

My Son John. Director: Leo McCarey. Screenplay: Myles Connolly, Leo McCarey, John Mahin. Cast: Helen Hayes, Robert Walker, Dean Jagger, Van Heflin. 122 mins. Paramount. USA, 1952.

Nashville. Director: Robert Altman. Screenplay: Joan Tewkesbury. Cast: Keith Carradine, Lily Tomlin, Henry Gibson, Ronee Blakely, Barbara Harris. 159 mins. Paramount. USA, 1975.(*)

Natural Born Killers. Director: Oliver Stone. Screenplay: Quentin Tarantino, Oliver Stone. Cast: Woody Harrelson, Juliette Lewis, Robert Downey, Jr., Tommy Lee Jones. 119 mins. Warner Bros. USA, 1994.(*)

Next Stop Wonderland. Director: Brad Anderson. Screenplay: Brad Anderson, Lyn Vaus. Cast: Hope Davis, Alan Gelfant. 104 mins. Miramax. USA, 1998.(*)

Ninotchka. Director: Ernst Lubitsch. Screenplay: Billy Wilder. Cast: Greta Garbo, Melvyn Douglas. 110 mins. MGM. USA, 1939.(*)

Nixon. Director: Oliver Stone. Screenplay: Oliver Stone, Stephen J. Rivele, Christopher Wilkinson. Cast: Anthony Hopkins, Joan Allen, Powers Boothe, Ed Harris. 190 mins. Entertainment/Illusion/Cinergi. USA, 1995.(*)

No Way Out. Director: Roger Donaldson. Screenplay: Robert Garland. Cast: Kevin Costner, Sean Young, Gene Hackman, Will Patton. 114 mins. Orion. USA, 1987.(*)

Norma Rae. Director: Martin Ritt. Screenplay: Harriet Frank Jr., Irving Ravetch. Cast: Sally Field, Ron Leibman, Beau Bridges, Pat Hingle. 114 mins. 20th Century Fox. USA, 1979.(*)

The North Star. Director: Lewis Milestone. Screenplay: Lillian Hellman. Cast: Anne Baxter, Dana Andrews, Walter Huston, Farley Granger. 105 mins. RKO. USA, 1943.(*)

The Nuisance. Director: Jack Conway. Screenplay: Bella Cohen, Bella and Samuel Spevack. Cast: Lee Tracy, Madge Evans, Charles Butterworth. 80 mins. MGM. USA, 1933.

Objective, Burma! Director: Raoul Walsh. Screenplay: Ranald MacDougall, Lester Cole. Cast: Errol Flynn, James Brown, William Prince, George Tobias. 142 mins. Warner Bros. USA, 1945.(*)

On the Beach. Director: Stanley Kramer. Screenplay: John Paxon, James Lee Barrett. Cast: Gregory Peck, Ava Gardner, Fred Astaire, Anthony Perkins. 133 mins. United Artists. USA, 1959.(*)

On the Waterfront. Director: Elia Kazan. Screenplay: Budd Schulberg. Cast: Marlon Brando, Rod Steiger, Eva Marie Saint, Lee J. Cobb. 108 mins. Columbia. USA, 1954.(*)

The Ox-Bow Incident. Director: William A. Wellman. Screenplay: Lamar Trotti. Cast: Henry Fonda, Harry Morgan, Dana Andrews, Anthony Quinn. 75 mins. 20th Century Fox. USA, 1943.(*)

The Package. Director: Andrew Davis. Screenplay: John Bishop. Cast: Gene Hackman, Tommy Lee Jones, Joanna Cassidy, Dennis Franz. 108 mins. Rank/Orion. USA, 1989.(*)

Panic in Year Zero! Director: Ray Milland. Screenplay: John Morton (II), Jay Simms. Cast: Ray Milland, Jean Hagen, Frankie Avalon, Mary Mitchell. 92 mins. American International. USA, 1962.(*)

The Parallax View. Director: Alan J. Pakula. Screenplay: David Giler, Lorenzo Semple Jr., Loren Singer. Cast: Warren Beatty, Hume Cronyn, William Daniels, Paula Prentiss. 102 mins. Paramount. USA, 1974.(*)

Patton. Director: Franklin J. Schaffner. Screenplay: Francis Ford Coppola, Edmund H. North. Cast: George C. Scott, Karl Malden. 171 mins. 20th Century Fox. USA, 1970.(*)

The People Against O'Hara. Director: John Sturges. Screenplay: John Monk Jr. Cast: Spencer Tracy, Diana Lynn, Pat O'Brien. 102 mins. MGM. USA, 1951.

Pinky. Director: Elia Kazan. Screenplay: Philip Dunne, Dudley Nichols. Cast: Jeanne Crain, Ethel Waters, Ethel Barrymore. 102 mins. 20th Century Fox. USA, 1949.(*)

Platoon. Director: Oliver Stone. Screenplay: Oliver Stone, Richard Boyle. Cast: Charlie Sheen, William Dafoe, Tom Berenger. 113 mins. Hemdale Films. USA, 1986.(*)

Pork Chop Hill. Director: Lewis Milestone. Screenplay: James R. Webb. Cast: Gregory Peck, Harry Guardino, Rip Torn, George Peppard. 97 mins. United Artists. USA, 1959.(*)

The Postman. Director: Kevin Costner. Screenplay: Eric Roth, Brian Helgeland. Cast: Kevin Costner, Will Patton, Olivia Williams. 177 mins. Tig Production. USA, 1997.(*)

Presumed Innocent. Director: Alan J. Pakula. Screenplay: Frank Pierson, Alan J. Pakula. Cast: Harrison Ford, Brian Dennehy, Bonnie Bedelia, Greta Scacchi. 127 mins. Warner Bros. USA, 1990.(*)

Primary Colors. Director: Mike Nichols. Screenplay: Elaine May. Cast: John Travolta, Emma Thompson, Kathy Bates. 140 mins. Universal. USA, 1998.(*)

Prisoner of War. Director: Andrew Marton. Screenplay: Alan Rivkin. Cast: Ronald Reagan, Steve Forrest. 80 mins. MGM. USA, 1954.

The Public Enemy. Director: William Wellman. Screenplay: Kubec Glasmon, John Bright. Cast: James Cagney, Edward Woods, Jean Harlow, Jean Blondell. 83 mins. Warner Bros. USA, 1931.(*)

Pulp Fiction. Director: Quentin Tarantino. Screenplay: Quentin Tarantino, Roger Avary. Cast: John Travolta, Samuel L. Jackson, Uma Thurman, Harvey Keitel, Bruce Willis. 153 mins. Miramax. USA, 1994.(*)

The Racket. Director: Lewis Milestone. Screenplay: Del Andrews, Harry Behn. Cast: Helen Hayes, Louis Wolheim. 60 mins. Caddo/Paramount. USA, 1928.

Rambo: First Blood Part II. Director: George Pan Cosmatos. Screenplay: James Cameron, Kevin Jarre, Michael Kozoll, Phil Alden Robinson, Sylvester Stallone. Cast: Sylvester Stallone, Richard Crenna. 93 mins. Tri-Star. USA, 1985.(*)

Red Corner. Director: Jon Avnet. Screenplay: Robert King. Cast: Richard Gere, Bai Ling. 119 mins. MGM. USA, 1997.(*)

Red Dawn. Director: John Milius. Screenplay: Kevin Reynolds, John Milius. Cast: Powers Boothe, Ron O'Neal, Patrick Swayze. 114 mins. MGM/UA. USA, 1984.(*)

The Red Menace. Director: R. G. Springsteen. Screenplay: Albert Demond, Gerald Geraghty. Cast: Robert Rockwell, Hanna Axman. 81 mins. Republic. USA, 1944.(*)

Red Nightmare. Director: George Waggner. Produced for the Department of Defense. Cast: Peter Brown, Jeanne Cooper, Jack Kelly. 30 mins. Warner Bros. USA, 1962.(*)

Red River. Director: Howard Hawks. Screenplay: Borden Chase, Charles Schnee. Cast: John Wayne, Montgomery Clift, Walter Brennen, John Ireland, Joanna Dru. 133 mins. United Artists. USA, 1948.(*)

Reservoir Dogs. Director: Quentin Tarantino. Screenplay: Quentin Tarantino. Cast: Harvey Keitel, Tim Roth, Michael Madsen, Steve Buscemi. 100 mins. Miramax. USA, 1992.(*)

Reversal of Fortune. Director: Barbet Schroeder. Screenplay: Nicholas Kazan. Cast: Jeremy Irons, Glenn Close, Ron Silver, Annabella Sciorra. 112 mins. Warner Bros. USA, 1990.(*)

The Road Warrior (Mad Max 2). Director: George Miller. Screenplay: George Miller. Cast: Mel Gibson, Bruce Spence, Emil Minty. 95 mins. Warner Bros. Australia, 1982.(*)

Rolling Thunder. Director: John Flynn. Screenplay: Paul Schrader. Cast: William Devane, Tommy Lee Jones. 99 mins. American International. USA, 1977.(*)

Romero. Director: John Duigan. Screenplay: John Sacret Young. Cast: Raul Julia, Richard Jordan, Ana Alicia. 102 mins. Warner Bros. USA, 1989.(*)

Salt of the Earth. Director: Herbert Biberman. Screenplay: Michael Wilson. Cast: Rosaura Revueltas, Juan Chacon, Will Geer. 94 mins. Independent Film Company. USA, 1954.(*)

Salvador. Director: Oliver Stone. Screenplay: Oliver Stone, Richard Boyle. Cast: James Woods, James Belushi, John Savage, Michael Murphy. 123 mins. Hemdale Films. USA, 1986.(*)

Sands of Iwo Jima. Director: Allan Dwan. Screenplay: Harry Brown, James Edward Grant. Cast: John Wayne, Forrest Tucker, John Agar, Richard Jaeckel. 109 mins. Republic. USA, 1949.(*)

Saving Private Ryan. Director: Steven Spielberg. Screenplay: Robert Rodat. Cast: Tom Hanks, Edward Burns, Matt Damon, Tom Sizemore. 170 mins. Dreamworks. USA, 1998.(*)

Scarface. Director: Howard Hawks. Screenplay: Ben Hecht, W. R. Burnett. Cast: Paul Muni, Ann Dvorak, Karen Morley. 93 mins. United Artists. USA, 1931.(*)

Scarlet Pages. Director: Ray Enright. Screenplay: Walter Anthony, Maude Fulton. Cast: Elsie Ferguson, John Halliday. 65 mins. First National. USA, 1930.

Schindler's List. Director: Steven Spielberg. Screenplay: Steven Zaillian. Cast: Liam Neeson, Ben Kingsley, Ralph Fiennes. 195 mins. Universal. USA, 1993.(*)

Secret Honor. Director: Robert Altman. Screenplay: Donald Freed, Arnold Stone. Cast: Philip Baker Hall. 90 mins. Cinecom. USA, 1985.(*)

The Seduction of Joe Tynan. Director: Jerry Schatzberg. Screenplay: Alan Alda. Cast: Alan Alda, Barbara Harris, Meryl Streep, Melvyn Douglas. 107 mins. Universal. USA, 1979.(*)

The Senator. Director: Joseph Golden. Screenplay: Sydney Rosenfeld. Cast: Joseph Burke, Ben Graham, Phillip Hahn, Charles J. Ross. Five reels. Triumph-EQ. USA, 1915.

Sergeant York. Director: Howard Hawks. Screenplay: Abe Finkel, Harry Chandler, Howard Koch, John Huston. Cast: Gary Cooper, Joan Leslie, Walter Brennan. 134 mins. Warner Bros. USA, 1941.(*)

Seven Days in May. Director: John Frankenheimer. Screenplay: Rod Sterling. Cast: Burt Lancaster, Kirk Douglas, Edmond O'Brien, Fredric March. 117 mins. Paramount. USA, 1964.(*)

Seven Years in Tibet. Director: Jean-Jacques Annaud. Screenplay: Becky Johnston. Cast: Brad Pitt, David Thewlis, B. D. Wong. 139 mins. Tri-Star. USA, 1997.(*)

Sex, Lies, and Videotape. Director: Steven Soderberg. Screenplay: Steven Soderberg. Cast: James Spader, Andie MacDowell, Peter Gallagher. 101 mins. Miramax. USA, 1989.(*)

She Done Him Wrong. Director: Lowell Sherman. Screenplay: Harvey Theu, John Bright. Cast: Mae West, Cary Grant. 65 mins. Paramount. USA, 1933.(*)

Showgirls. Director: Paul Verhoeven. Screenplay: Joe Eszterhas. Cast: Elizabeth Berkley, Kyle MacLachlan, Gina Gershon. 131 mins. MGM/UA. USA, 1995.(*)

Silkwood. Director: Mike Nichols. Screenplay: Nora Ephron, Alice Arlen. Cast: Meryl Streep, Kurt Russell, Cher. 131 mins. 20th Century Fox. USA, 1983.(*)

Since You Went Away. Director: John Cromwell. Screenplay: David O. Selznick. Cast: Claudette Colbert, Jennifer Jones, Shirley Temple, Joseph Cotton. 172 mins. United Artists. USA, 1944.(*)

So Proudly We Hail. Director: Mark Sandrich. Screenplay: Alan Scott. Cast: Claudette Colbert, Paulette Goddard, Veronica Lake. 126 min. Paramount. USA, 1943.(*)

Song of Russia. Director: Gregory Ratoff. Screenplay: Paul Jarrico, Richard Collins. Cast: Robert Taylor, Susan Peters. 107 mins. MGM. USA, 1943.

Speechless. Director: Ron Underwood. Screenplay: Robert King. Cast: Michael Keaton, Geena Davis, Christopher Reeve. 98 mins. MGM. USA, 1994.(*)

Stalag 17. Director: Billy Wilder. Screenplay: Billy Wilder, Edwin Blum. Cast: William Holden, Don Taylor, Otto Preminger. 120 mins. Paramount. USA, 1953.(*)

Star Wars. Director: George Lukas. Screenplay: George Lukas. Cast: Mark Hamill, Carrie Fisher, Harrison Ford, Alec Guinness. 121 mins. 20th Century Fox. USA, 1977.(*)

State of the Union. Director: Frank Capra. Screenplay: Myles Connolly, Anthony Veiller. Cast: Spencer Tracy, Katherine Hepburn, Angela Lansbury, Van Johnson. 124 mins. MGM. USA, 1948.(*)

The Steel Helmet. Director: Samuel Fuller. Screenplay: Samuel Fuller. Cast: Gene Evans, Robert Hutton, Richard Loo. 84 mins. Lippert Studio. USA, 1951.(*)

The Story of GI Joe. Director: William A. Wellman. Screenplay: Leopold Atlas, Guy Endore, Philip Stevenson. Cast: Burgess Meredith, Robert Mitchum, Fred Steele. 108 mins. United Artists. USA, 1945.

Sudden Death. Director: Peter Hyams. Screenplay: Gene Quintano, Karen Baldwin. Cast: Jean-Claude Van Damme, Powers Boothe. 110 mins. Universal. USA, 1995.(*)

Suddenly. Director: Lewis Allen. Screenplay: Richard Sale. Cast: Frank Sinatra, Sterling Hayden, James Gleason, Nancy Gates. 75 mins. United Artists. USA, 1954.(*)

Summertree. Director: Anthony Newley. Screenplay: Edward Hume, Stephen Yafa. Cast: Michael Douglas, Brenda Vaccaro, Jack Warden. 89 mins. Columbia. USA, 1971.(*)

Sunrise at Campobello. Director: Vincent J. Donehue. Screenplay: Dore Schary. Cast: Ralph Bellamy, Greer Garson, Hume Cronyn, Jean Hagen. 143 mins. Warner Bros. USA, 1960.(*)

Suspect. Director: Peter Yates. Screenplay: Eric Roth. Cast: Dennis Quaid, Cher, Liam Neeson. 101 mins. Tri-Star. USA, 1987.(*)

Tanner '88. Director: Robert Altman. Screenplay: Gary Trudeau. Cast: Michael Murphy, Pamela Reed, Cynthia Nixon. 120 mins. HBO Video. USA, 1988.(*)

Tarantula. Director: Jack Arnold. Screenplay: Robert M. Fresco, Martin Berkeley. Cast: Leo G. Carroll, John Agar, Mara Corday. 81 mins. Universal. USA, 1955.(*)

Taxi Driver. Director: Martin Scorsese. Screenplay: Paul Schrader. Cast: Robert DeNiro, Jodie Foster, Harvey Keitel. 112 mins. Columbia. USA, 1976.(*)

Tender Comrade. Director: Edward Dmytryk. Screenplay: Dalton Trumbo. Cast: Ginger Rogers, Robert Ryan, Ruth Hussey, Kim Hunter. 101 mins. RKO. USA, 1943.(*)

The Terminator. Director: James Cameron. Screenplay: James Cameron, Gale Anne Hurd. Cast: Arnold Schwarzenegger, Michael Biehn, Linda Hamilton, Paul Winfield. 108 mins. Orion/Hemdale/Pacific Western. USA, 1984.(*)

The Terror from the Year 5000. Director: Robert J. Gurney Jr. Screenplay: Robert J. Gurney Jr. Cast: Joyce Holden, Ward Costello. 74 mins. American International. USA, 1958.(*)

Testament. Director: Lynne Littman. Screenplay: John Sacret Young, Carol Amen. Cast: Jane Alexander, William Devane, Lukas Haas, Roxana Zal. 90 mins. Paramount. USA, 1983.(*)

Them! Director: Gordon Douglas. Screenplay: Ted Sherdeman, Russell Hughes. Cast: James Whitmore. Edmund Gwenn, Joan Weldon, James Arness. 93 mins. Warner Bros. USA, 1954.(*)

They Were Expendable. Directors: John Ford, Robert Montgomery (uncredited). Screenplay: Frank W. Wead. Cast: John Wayne, Robert Montgomery, Donna Reed. 135 mins. MGM. USA, 1945.(*)

They Won't Forget. Director: Mervyn LeRoy. Screenplay: Robert Rossen, Aben Kandel. Cast: Claude Rains, Otto Kruger, Lana Turner, Alan Joslyn, Edward Norris. 95 mins. Warner Bros. USA, 1937.(*)

The Thin Red Line. Director: Terrence Malick. Screenplay: Terrence Malick. Cast: Sean Penn, Nick Nolte, John Cusack, Woody Harrelson, George Clooney. 166 mins. 20th Century Fox. USA, 1998.(*)

The Thing. Director: Christian Nyby. Screenplay: Charles Lederer, Ben Hecht. Cast: Kenneth Tobey, James Arness, Margaret Sheridan. 87 mins. RKO. USA, 1951.(*)

Three Seasons. Director: Tony Bui. Screenplay: Tony Bui, Timothy Linh. Cast: Harvey Keitel. 113 mins. October Films. USA/Vietnam, 1999.

A Time to Kill. Director: Joel Schumacher. Screenplay: Akiva Goldsman. Cast: Matthew McConaughey, Sandra Bullock, Samuel L. Jackson. 149 mins. Warner Bros. USA, 1996.(*)

Titanic. Director: James Cameron. Screenplay: James Cameron. Cast: Leonardo DiCaprio, Kate Winslet, Billy Zane, Kathy Bates. 195 mins. Paramount. USA, 1997.(*)

To Kill a Mockingbird. Director: Robert Mulligan. Screenplay: Horton Foote. Cast: Gregory Peck, Brock Peters, Robert Duvall, Philip Alford, Mary Badham. 129 mins. Universal. USA, 1962.(*)

To the Shores of Hell. Director: Will Zens. Screenplay: Will Zens, Robert McFadden. Cast: Marshall Thompson, Kiva Lawrence. 82 mins. Robert Patrick Productions. USA, 1965.(*)

Trial. Director: Mark Robson. Screenplay: Don Mankiewicz. Cast: Glenn Ford, Dorothy McGuire, Arthur Kennedy. 105 mins. MGM. USA, 1955.

True Believer. Director: Joseph Ruben. Screenplay: Wesley Strick. Cast: James Woods, Robert Downey Jr. 103 mins. Columbia. USA, 1989.(*)

True Colors. Director: Herbert Ross. Screenplay: Kevin Wade. Cast: John Cusack, James Spader, Imogen Stubbs, Mandy Patinkin. 111 mins. Paramount. USA, 1991.(*)

Truman. Director: Frank Pierson. Screenplay: Tom Rickman. Cast: Gary Sinise, Diana Scarwid, Richard Dysart. 135 mins. HBO Video. USA, 1995.(*)

Twelve Monkeys. Director: Terry Gilliam. Screenplay: Chris Marker, David Peoples, Janet Peoples. Cast: Bruce Willis, Madeleine Stowe, Brad Pitt, Christopher Plummer. 131 mins. Universal. USA, 1995.(*)

Twister. Director: Jan De Bont. Screenplay: Michael Crichton, Anne-Marie Martin. Cast: Helen Hunt, Bill Paxton. 113 mins. Universal. USA, 1996.(*)

Uncommon Valor. Director: Ted Kotcheff. Screenplay: Joe Gayton. Cast: Gene Hackman, Fred Ward, Patrick Swayze, Randall Cobb. 105 mins. Paramount. USA, 1983.(*)

The Verdict. Director: Sidney Lumet. Screenplay: David Mamet. Cast: Paul Newman, James Mason, Charlotte Rampling, Jack Warden. 122 mins. 20th Century Fox. USA, 1982.(*)

A View from the Bridge. Director: Sidney Lumet. Screenplay: Norman Rosten. Cast: Raf Vallone, Maureen Stapleton, Jean Sorel, Carol Lawrence. 110 mins. Allied Artists. France/Italy, 1962.

Wag the Dog. Director: Barry Levinson. Screenplay: David Mamet, Hilary Henkin. Cast: Dustin Hoffman, Robert DeNiro. 120 mins. New Line Cinema. USA, 1997.(*)

Wake Island. Director: John Farrow. Screenplay: W. R. Burnett, Frank Butler. Cast: Robert Preston, Brian Donlevy, William Bendix, MacDonald Carey. 88 mins. Paramount. USA, 1942.(*)

A Walk in the Sun. Director: Lewis Milestone. Screenplay: Robert Rossen. Cast: Dana Andrews, Richard Conte, John Ireland, Lloyd Bridges. 117 mins. 20th Century Fox. USA, 1946.(*)

War Games. Director: John Badham. Screenplay: Lawrence Lasker, Walter Parkes. Cast: Matthew Broderick, Dabney Coleman, John Wood, Ally Sheedy. 113 mins. MGM/UA. USA, 1983.(*)

Welcome to Sarajevo. Director: Michael Winterbottom. Screenplay: Frank Cottrell Boyce. Cast: Woody Harrelson, Marisa Tomei, Stephen Dillane. 102 mins. Miramax/Channel Four Films. UK/USA, 1997.(*)

What Price Glory? Director: Raoul Walsh. Screenplay: James T. O'Donohoe. Cast: Edmund Lowe, Victor McLaglen. 120 mins. 20th Century Fox. USA, 1926.(*)

Who's Afraid of Virginia Woolf. Director: Mike Nicholas. Screenplay: Ernest Lehman. Cast: Richard Burton, Elizabeth Taylor, George Segal, Sandy Dennis. 127 mins. Warner Bros. USA, 1966.(*)

Wilson. Director: Henry King. Screenplay: Lamar Trotti. Cast: Alexander Knox, Charles Coburn, Geraldine Fiztgerald, Thomas Mitchell. 154 mins. 20th Century Fox. USA, 1944.(*)

Wings. Director: William Wellman. Screenplay: Hope Loring, Louis D. Lighton. Cast: Charles (Buddy) Rogers, Clara Bow, Richard Arlen. 139 mins. Paramount. USA, 1927.(*)

Winter Kills. Director: William Richert. Screenplay: William Richert. Cast: Jeff Bridges, John Huston, Anthony Perkins, Richard Boone. 97 mins. Winter Gold Production. USA, 1979.(*)

The Wizard of Oz. Director: Victor Fleming. Screenplay: Noel Langley. Cast: Judy Garland, Margaret Hamilton, Ray Bolger, Jack Haley, Bert Lahr. 101 mins. MGM. USA, 1939.(*)

A Woman Under the Influence. Director: John Cassavetes. Screenplay: John Cassavetes. Cast: Peter Falk, Gena Rowlands. 155 mins. Faces International Films. USA, 1974.(*)

The World, the Flesh, and the Devil. Director: Ranald MacDougall. Screenplay: Ferdinand Reyher, Ranald MacDougall. Cast: Harry Belefonte, Inger Stevens, Mel Ferrer. 95 mins. MGM. USA, 1959.(*)

A Yank in the R.A.F. Director: Henry King. Screenplay: Karl Tunberg, Darrell Ware, Darryl F. Zanuck. Cast: Tyrone Power, Betty Grable, John Sutton. 98 mins. 20th Century Fox. USA, 1941.(*)

Young Mr. Lincoln. Director: John Ford. Screenplay: Lamar Trotti. Cast: Henry Fonda, Alice Brady, Marjorie Weaver, Arleen Whelan. 100 mins. 20th Century Fox. USA, 1939.(*)

Documentaries

America's Answer. Produced by the U.S. Signal Corps and the Committee on Public Information. USA, 1918.
American Dream. Director: Barbara Kopple. 100 mins. USA, 1989.(*)
Baptism of Fire. Director: Fritz Hippler. 50 mins. Germany, 1940.
The Battle of San Pietro. Director: John Huston. 43 mins. USA, 1944.(*)
The Battle of Midway. Director: John Ford. 28 mins. USA, 1942.
The Big One. Director: Michael Moore. 96 mins. USA, 1998.(*)
Britain Prepared. Produced by the British War Propaganda Bureau. UK, 1915.
Dear America: Letters Home from Vietnam. Director: Bill Couturie. 85 mins. USA, 1988.(*)
December 7th: The Movie. Director: John Ford. Narrators: Walter Huston, Harry Davenport, Dana Andrews, Paul Hurst. 82 mins. USA, 1943.(*)
The External/Wandering Jew. Director: Fritz Hippler. Germany, 1940.
Harlan County, U.S.A. Director: Barbara Kopple. 103 mins. USA, 1976.(*)
High School. Director: Frederick Wiseman. 75 mins. USA, 1968.
Hospital. Director: Frederick Wiseman. 84 mins. USA, 1970.
Juvenile Court. Director: Frederick Wiseman. 144 mins. USA, 1973.
Law and Order. Director: Frederick Wiseman. 81 mins. USA, 1969.
Meat. Director: Frederick Wiseman. 113 mins. USA, 1976.
The Memphis Belle. Director: William Wyler. 45 mins. USA, 1943.(*)
Nanook of the North. Director: Robert Flaherty. 55 mins. USA, 1922.
A Perfect Candidate. Directors: R.J. Cutler, David Van Taylor. 105 mins. USA, 1996.(*)
Pershing's Crusaders. Produced by the Committee on Public Information. USA, 1918.
The Plow That Broke the Plains. Director: Pare Lorentz. 49 mins. USA, 1934.(*)
Public Housing. Director: Frederick Wiseman. 200 mins. USA, 1997.
The Ramparts We Watch. Director: Louis de Rochemont. Screenplay: Robert L. Richards, Cedric R. Worth. Cast: Non-professional actors. 90 mins. USA, 1940.
Report from the Aleutions. Director: John Huston. U.S. Signal Corps. 47 mins. USA, 1943.
The River. Director: Pare Lorentz. Produced by the Farm Security Administration. 31 min. USA, 1937.(*)
Roger and Me. Director: Michael Moore. 91 mins. Warner Bros. USA, 1989.(*)
Rush to Judgment. Director: Emile de Antonio. 122 mins. USA, 1967.(*)
The Store. Director: Frederick Wiseman. 89 mins. USA, 1983.
Titicut Follies. Director: Frederick Wiseman. 89 mins. USA, 1967.
Triumph of the Will. Director: Leni Riefenstahl. 115 mins. Germany, 1934.(*)
Under Four Flags. Director: S. L. Rothafel. Produced by the U.S. Army Signal Corp. USA, 1918.
The War Game. Director: Peter Watkins. 47 mins. UK, 1967.(*)
The War Room. Director: Chris Hegedus, D.A. Pennebaker. 93 mins. USA, 1993.(*)
Who Killed Vincent Chin? Director: Christine Choy. 83 mins. USA, 1988.(*)
Why We Fight. Director: Frank Capra. A series of seven films produced by the U.S. War Department. USA, 1943-45.(*)
(*) denotes film is available on video

Index

('i' indicates an illustration)

C